AF479299

PICASSO

An exhibition organized with the exceptional
support of the Musée national Picasso-Paris
as part of the project
"Picasso-Méditerranée"

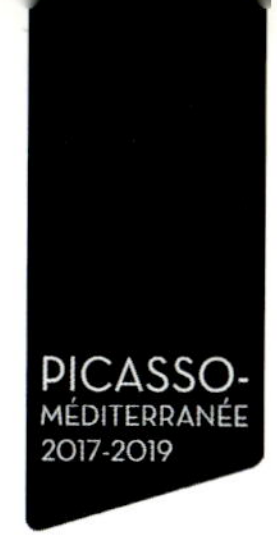

PICASSO

Between Cubism and Classicism 1915–1925

edited by Olivier Berggruen
with Anunciata von Liechtenstein

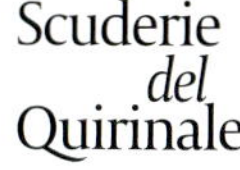

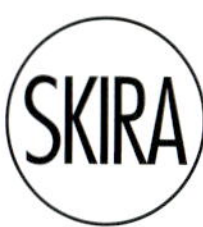

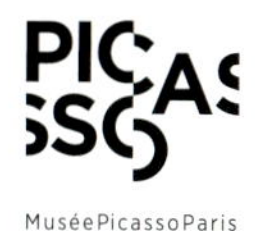

The exhibition will be inaugurated in the presence of the President of the Italian Republic Sergio Mattarella

PICASSO
Between Cubism and Classicism: 1915–1925

edited by Olivier Berggruen
with Anunciata von Liechtenstein

Rome, Scuderie del Quirinale
22 September 2017 – 21 January 2018

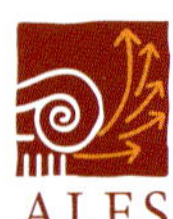

In-house Company of the Ministry of Cultural Heritage and Activities and Tourism

Board of Directors

President and C.E.O.
Mario De Simoni

Councillors
Debora Rossi
Marco Macchia

Board of auditors

President
Paolo Mezzogori

Auditors
Paola Passarelli
Andrea Pirrottina

Director of Private-Public Relations and Financing Projects
Carolina Botti

Administrative Director of Financing Projectso
Gianluca Colabove

Director of Specialized Technical and Operational Services
Alessandra Faini

Director of Personnel, Organization and Development
Giovanni Iannelli

Director of Administration, Finance, Control and MEPA supplies
Fiorentina Russo

Management and Auditing Staff Secretary
Margherita Vitale

Press Office
Nicoletta Ciardullo

Scuderie del Quirinale

Scientific Commission

Mario Botta, *President*
Gabriella Belli
Daniele Manacorda
Ugo Soragni
Alessandro Zuccari
Commission Secretariat
Fabiana Di Donato
Matteo Lafranconi

Ales President
Mario De Simoni

Director
Matteo Lafranconi

Head, Educational and Research Activities and Special Projects
Anna Mattirolo

Head, Exhibition Office
Alexandra Andresen
with Eva Francaviglia, Ludovica Muscettola

Exhibition Registrar
Chiara Eminente

Head, Exhibition Design and Facilities Management
Francesca Elvira Ercole

Head,Marketing and Communication
Chiara Guerraggio
with Francesca Melucci

Head, Editorial Office and Iconographic Archive
Flaminia Nardone

Head, Corporate Events and Ceremonial Office
Barbara Guerrini

Head of Reception and General Affairs
Stefano Natali
with Sandro Capobianchi, Armando Carotenuto, Antonio Iafrancesco, Attilio Muscatello, Insa Ndiaye

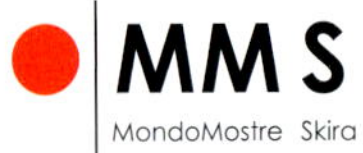

President
Massimo Vitta Zelman

Managing Director
Tomaso Radaelli

Scientific Coordinator of the Exhibition
Thomas Clement Salomon

Production
Benedetta De Pietro
Rosa Fasan
with
Monica Passoni
Francesca Trabattoni
Sergio Tarquinio

Marketing and Communication
Diego Giacomelli
with
Elisabetta Galvagni

Press Office
Federica Mariani
with
Flavia Sciortino

Graphics
Alessandro Mele

Administrative Office
Monica Mihailescu

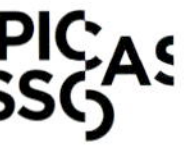

President
Laurent Le Bon

Managing Director
Erol Ok

Special Advisor to the President
Stéphanie Molins

Logistics, Security and Information Technology Systems
Guillaume Gaillard, *Director*

Collections and Production
Claire Garnier, *Director*

Production Department
Sophie Daynes-Diallo, *Director*
Claire Duqué, *Production Manager*
Camille Frasca, *Chargé de mission. Head of the Picasso-Méditerranée Project*
Sarah Lagrevol, *Registrar of the Collections*

Collections Department
Emilie Bouvard, *Conservator of the Heritage, Head of Painting (1938–1972), Publishing, Research and Contemporary Art, Scientific Coordinator of the Picasso-Méditerranée Project*

Communication, Patronage and Privatization
Leslie Lechevallier, *Director*

Public Management and Cultural Development
Guillaume Blanc, *Director*

Administration
Matthieu Chapelon, *Director*

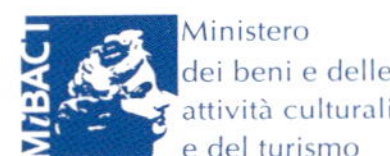

Organized by

ALES

Scuderie del Quirinale

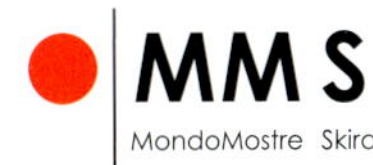

Installation of Parade

BARBERINI GALLERIE CORSINI NAZIONALI

With the support of

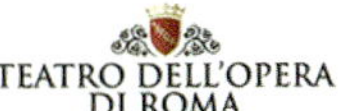

BARBERINI
GALLERIE
CORSINI
NAZIONALI

Director
Flaminia Gennari Santori

Board of Directors
Flaminia Gennari Santori, *President*
Edith Gabrielli
Serena Romano
Paola Santarelli
Claudio Strinati

Scientific Commission
Flaminia Gennari Santori, *President*
Liliana Barroero
Claudia Cieri Via
Valter Curzi
Annick Lemoine

Board of Auditors
Gabriella Maria Salvatore, *President*
Paolo Mezzogori
Davide Rossetti

Head of Educational Activities and Research
Michele di Monte

Head of Exhibition Office
Michela Ulivi

Conservators
Cinzia Ammannato
Maurizia Cicconi
Andrea De Marchi
Michele Di Monte

Registrar
Giuliana Forti

Head of Restoration Laboratory
Paola Sannucci

Head of Administrative Office
Silvana Buonora

Head of Events Office
Simona Baldi

Technical office
Ovidio Casconi
with Gabriele Mari

Heads of Room Assistants
Gioia Costa
Maura Garofalo
Elisabetta Guerriero
Michele Leonetti
Caterina Strappati
Antonio Torre

Room Design
Enrico Quell

Visual Communication
Alberto Berengo Gardin

Press Office
Maria Bonmassar

Digital Media Curator
Nicolette Mandarano

Exhibition curated and catalogue edited by

Olivier Berggruen
with
Anunciata von Liechtenstein

Scientific Committee
Carmen Giménez
Brigitte Léal
Laurent Le Bon
Silvia Loreti
Valentina Moncada
Bernard Ruiz-Picasso
Gary Tinterow

Essays by
Olivier Berggruen
Cécile Godefroy
Silvia Loreti
Valentina Moncada
Anunciata von Liechtenstein
Sarah Woodcock

Exhibition Design
Selldorf Architects,
Annabelle Selldorf,
Dante Furioso, Julie Hausch-Fen

Conservative revision of works on display
Natalia Gurgone
Emanuele Marconi
Tiziana Sorgoni

Communication and Media Relations
Comin&Partners
Gianluca Comin
Elena Di Giovanni

Transport
Montenovi S.r.l.

Insurance
AON SpA Insurance Brokers

Exhibition Staging
Tagi 2000

Exhibition Graphics
SP SYSTEMA

The exhibition was made possible by the exceptional participation of the Bibliothéque historique de la Ville de Paris

Thanks to the support of

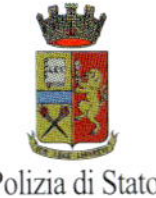

Sponsor

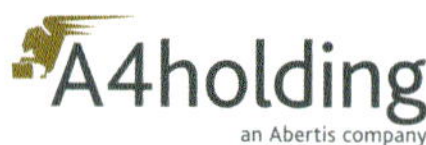

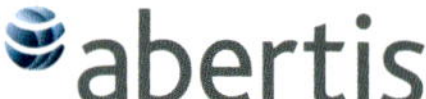

Thanks to
Laurent Le Bon

Colin B. Bailey
Maria Balshaw
Ramona Bannayan
Marcella Beraudo Di Pralormo
Bettina Berggruen
Bernard Blistène
Hans Rudolf Bucher
Thomas P. Campbell
Clarice Cartier
Daniela Cecchini
Caroline Collier
Cécile Debray
Laurence des Cars
Michael Eissenhauer
Ginevra Elkann
Laurence Engel
Ulriche Erbslöh
Larry J. Feinberg
Camille Frasca
Carlo Fuortes
Lukas Gloor
William M. Griswold
Roberto Manuel Guido
Florence Half-Wrobel
Erika Hegewisch
Hiroshi Ishibashi
Sam Keller
Udo Kittelmann
Tim Knox
Serge Lasvignes
Brigitte Léal
Nathalie Léger
Glenn Lowry
Olga Mazure
Felix Meyer
Mary Miller
Stéphanie Monnet
Julie Narbey
Stephen Ongpin
Hermann Parzinger
Paloma Picasso-Thévenet
and Éric Thévenet
Christine Pinault
Daniela Porro
Earl A. Powell III
Felicia Rappe
James Rondeau
Martin Roth
Almine and Bernard Ruiz-Picasso
Stefano Sannino
Esther Schlicht
Georg Schmid
Roberto Antonio Sgalla
Ken Soehner
Guillermo Solana
Andrew Strauss
Sylviane Tarsot-Gillery
Ann Temkin
Emmanuelle Touelet
Mariella Utili
Mario Viola
Sheena Wagstaff
Daniel H. Weiss
Diana Widmaier-Picasso
Maya Widmaier-Picasso
Mirella Zen Gandolfi

A special thank-you to
Marco Fabio Apolloni - W. Apolloni Arte Antica and Monica Cardarelli - Galleria Laocoonte for their help

Lenders

Barcelona, Fundació Museu Picasso de Barcelona
Basel, Paul Sacher Foundation
Berlin, Staatliche Museen zu Berlin, Nationalgalerie, Museum Berggruen
Brussels, Fundación Almine y Bernard Ruiz-Picasso para el Arte
Cambridge, The Fitzwilliam Museum - University of Cambridge
Chicago, Art Institute of Chicago
Cleveland, The Cleveland Museum of Art
London, Tate
London, Victoria and Albert Museum
Madrid, Museo Thyssen-Bornemisza
New York, The Metropolitan Museum of Art
New York, MoMA - Museum of Modern Art
New York, The Morgan Library & Museum
Paris, Bibliothèque historique de la Ville de Paris
Paris, Bibliothèque nationale de France
Paris, Centre Pompidou, Musée national d'art moderne / Centre de création industrielle
Paris, Musée de l'Orangerie
Paris, Musée national Picasso-Paris
Riehen/Basel, Fondation Beyeler, Beyeler Collection
Saint-Germain la Blanche-Herbe, Fonds Erik Satie-Archives de France/Archives IMEC
Santa Barbara, Santa Barbara Museum of Art
Tokyo, Bridgestone Museum of Art, Ishibashi Foundation
Turin, Pinacoteca Giovanni e Marella Agnelli
Washington, D.C., National Gallery of Art
Zurich, Foundation E.G. Bührle Collection

Bill and Donna Acquavella
Ananda Foundation N.V.
Julian Barran, England
Nicolas Berggruen Charitable Foundation
Olivier Berggruen Trust
Gray Collection Trust
Klaus and Erika Hegewisch Kunstsammlung
David Lachenmann Collection
Marlborough International Fine Art

A hundred years ago Pablo Picasso visited Rome, Naples and Pompeii, following in the footsteps of the countless artists and intellectuals who down through the centuries have come to Italy to explore the various cultures that flourished here on the peninsula. Together with his fellow traveller Jean Cocteau, Picasso discovered diverse and multifaceted cultural expressions that combine sacred and profane, ancient and modern, and used these elements to bring a new vein of classicism to his ever-evolving style.

The exhibition at Rome's Scuderie del Quirinale follows the one at the Museo Nazionale di Capodimonte in Naples, and is coupled with a smaller show featuring the huge curtain that Picasso painted for the ballet Parade, *on display in the large hall frescoed by Pietro da Cortona in the Galleria Nazionale d'Arte Antica in Palazzo Barberini, Rome. This unique event – made possible with the collaboration of the Musée national Picasso-Paris and the generous support of many institutions and collectors – has enabled us to celebrate the unbroken links between the great Spanish painter and the multifarious culture of the Mediterranean basin, while showing that even while Europe was being lacerated by the First World War, art continued to be fundamental to an ongoing dialogue between the region's various peoples.*

Dario Franceschini
Minister of Cultural Heritage and Activities and Tourism

Staging a major Picasso exhibition in Italy presents a tremendous challenge, due both to the difficulties any serious project on the artist presents, and to the specific nature of the great master's relationship with Italy. The Italian journey he undertook in 1917 – now one hundred years ago – was pivotal to an ongoing dialogue between tradition and avant-garde, between innovation and museum, that coloured Picasso's entire career. And this dialogue is the critical focus of the exhibition "Picasso. Between Cubism and Classicism: 1915–1925". This ambitious show staged in Rome's Scuderie del Quirinale has had three illustrious precedents: the famous Rome and Milanese exhibitions of 1953, and more recently the Venice show curated by Jean Clair in 1998. But it has also had to contend with the cool reception given to the artist between 1905 – when Picasso was invited and then rejected by the organizers of the 6th Venice Biennale – and 1948, when, at the age of sixty-seven the artist officially participated in the Venice Biennale, thanks to the new climate that emerged after the war.

An exhibition like the present one required lengthy preparation, but we were able to count on the contributions and generosity of many people and institutions, which unfortunately are too numerous to mention here. Their names appear at the beginning of this catalogue, but I must extend special thanks to Olivier Berggruen and Anunciata von Liechtenstein, Laurent Le Bon and the Musée national Picasso-Paris, Flaminia Gennari Santori and Palazzo Barberini, where the Parade *curtain has been put on display, and not least to the staff of Ales-Scuderie del Quirinale and MondoMostre Skira, with whom we shared the difficulties involved in this project from the outset.*

It should be mentioned that this event is an integral part of the international project "Picasso-Mediterranée", brilliantly devised by Laurent Le Bon, and is included in a rich programme of celebrations in which several structures under the MiBACT umbrella will participate, thus making the recent incorporation of the Scuderie in the Ministry network even more significant and valid.

Picasso is an all-time titan of the arts, a name that inevitably attracts a vast and diverse public – that same public that the Scuderie constantly strives to attract. It is aptly described by an attentive observer at the Rome exhibition of 1953 at the Galleria Nazionale d'Arte Modena: there were "ladies, attractive, vivacious young women, men and youths, a politician with his wife, a trader from the north … artists, students. The workers, instead, came on Wednesday and Saturday evening … students arrived at less busy times, from art schools, architecture faculties, universities … Rome had never seen so many people" (Mario De Micheli, "Visitatori di ogni ceto alla mostra di Picasso", in l'Unità, *Turin, 12 June 1953).*

Mario De Simoni
President and C.E.O.
Ales - Arte Lavoro e Servizi spa

Like everyday life, the world of art is full of coincidences and chance meetings that sometimes makes a particular work immensely successful. If there is one artist who has provided an inexhaustible creative resource for exhibitions, and even determined a modus operandi, it is Pablo Picasso.

This is another reason why I enthusiastically agreed to involve the Gallerie Nazionali Barberini Corsini in a major exhibition devoted to Picasso and his initiatory trip to Rome. I realised that the act of displaying a work such as Picasso's outstanding Parade *in the stunning hall frescoed by Pietro da Cortona in Palazzo Barberini, offered a perfect encounter, a meeting of minds that would enable visitors to discover the striking and stimulating coincidences between the two masterpieces, and to view each work in the light of the other, seeing them anew.*

It is of course not just a question of space and dimensions, but above all the fact that the great hall designed by Bernini and the spectacular baroque vault frescoed by Pietro da Cortona share with Parade *a powerful theatrical quality, revealing the two artists' interest in the shifting, illusionistic, and at times illusory, border that is seen as dividing reality and fiction, stage and auditorium, actors and audience. Here Picasso's curtain establishes an original and astonishing dialogue with the majestic hall in Palazzo Barberini.*

A famous art historian once said that you can never really understand a figurative work of art until you "dance it". Now we have the chance to discover how true this is for Picasso as well as Bernini and Cortona. If the idea for Parade *was inspired by Diaghilev's challenging remark to Cocteau, "Etonne-moi!", then there is no better place to admire the outcome of that challenge than Palazzo Barberini, since it was designed to astonish whoever observed it, from any angle and in its entirety.*

Flaminia Gennari Santori
Director, Gallerie Nazionali di Arte Antica di Roma – Palazzo Barberini and Galleria Corsini

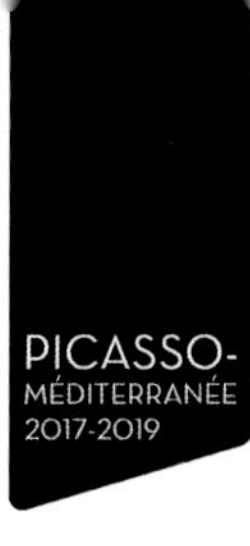

The Picasso-Méditerranée project was born from the desire to explore the many ties between Picasso and the Mediterranean by programming a cycle of dynamic, multifaceted, and interdisciplinary cultural events spanning the period 2017 to 2019. This project involved mapping the different places linked to Picasso's career, and creating a network of institutions connected with that world. The event consists primarily of a series of exhibitions and a research project that combines a thoroughly contemporary approach with the need to safeguard a legacy. The identity of each institution is respected in every sense: the aim is to create a synergy, so that each one can develop its own project and maintain its individuality. The network is currently composed of more than 60 institutions which are liaising to build joint communication, especially through a brand, a graphic style, a website and a publication. The various institutions' steering committees will meet regularly, and the event will feature research seminars designed to bring the Picasso community together. Around forty exhibitions are already on the calendar, each one different: monographic, thematic, shows that create a dialogue with Picasso's contemporaries or the present day, others that focus on a technique, a period, a place where the artist lived or worked. And each one committed to adopting an innovative and unique approach toward Picasso's oeuvre, seen through the lens of the Mediterranean. During the three-year period of the project, Picasso will be the subject of a paper and digital publication. Set in motion by the Musée national Picasso-Paris, this journey through the artist's work and the places that inspired him is a totally new cultural experience, whose aim is to reinforce the ties between the Mediterranean's different shores.

Laurent Le Bon
President, Musée national Picasso-Paris

The year 1917 was crucial in shaping the artistic destiny of the twentieth century. While war gripped Europe, a confluence of individuals and events shifted the cultural perspectives of the new era. First came the founders of Dada – irreverent, iconoclastic, and nihilistic intellectuals – who in 1916 gathered regularly at the Cabaret Voltaire in Zurich. A year later, with the second Dada Manifesto, Tristan Tzara affirmed the movement's stance, one that sought pastiche rather than parody, unabashedly advocating destruction. At about the same time, Picasso joined Diaghilev's Ballets Russes in Rome and in Naples. Away from the battlefield itself, the likes of Cocteau, Diaghilev, Massine, Stravinsky, and Picasso conspired together to forge a less radical but equally influential path for Modernism, one in which the classical paradigm was advanced, not as a betrayal of modern art under the forces of nationalism – as it has sometimes been argued – but as a means to build on Primitivist and Modernist impulses. Its foundation stone was laid in Rome when Picasso devised the costumes, scenery, and curtain for the forthcoming ballet Parade, *which became something of a cause célèbre when first performed a few months later in Paris.*

We may recall several distinguished exhibitions devoted to that crucial period in Picasso's life, one in which the legacy of Cubism does survive, though in a much changed form, most notably Jean Clair's Picasso: The Italian Journey 1917–1924 *held at Venice's Palazzo Grassi in 1998. Yet the present exhibition at the Scuderie del Quirinale – coming one hundred years after Picasso's stay in Rome and Naples – emphasizes not so much the Italian influence; rather, it bears witness to Picasso's agility and genius for transformation, ranging from Primitivism to Cubism and Classicism, according to the demands of the work and its subject matter.*

In broader terms, it will highlight Picasso's experimentation with different styles, from the play of decorative surfaces in the collage-like works executed during the war, to the stylized realism of the Diaghilev years, from cubist-inflected still-lifes to classical portraiture, a grand manner reminiscent of the ancient world. With Parade, *Picasso's cultivation of different stylistic modes emerged as another facet of Modernism, distinct from the efforts of Dada, Italian Futurism, or Russian Constructivism.*

In the wake of his Italian journey, Picasso renewed the traditional depictions of acrobats and circus performers of his youth, the nostalgic portraits of entertainers often caught in meditative situations. The subjects that permeated his Blue and Rose periods now became the models of his artistic stance; thus the figure of the harlequin becomes a metaphor for the artist's creative process. As Brigitte Léal and Yve-Alain Bois have remarked, Picasso became a master juggler of styles, ranging from meditative depictions of bathers and street performers to ironic still-lifes, from decorative Cubist compositions to introverted portraits. In the words of Michael Baxandall, the artist's perceptual process is laid bare, each work reflecting "the serial performance of problem finding and problem-solv-

ing. Picasso became a cognitive acrobat of a conspicuous and dazzling kind."

This exhibition has been in gestation for a long time. Along the way, many have provided invaluable help. I would like to thank them all, and in particular the following: Bill and Donna Acquavella, Gratian Anda, Julian Barran, François Bellet, Bettina Berggruen, Achim Borchardt-Hume, Asya Chorley, Harry Cooper, Ulla Dreyfus-Best, Ginevra Elkann, Andrew Fabricant, Lynn Garafola, Cornelia Grassi, Jodi Hauptman, Erika Hegewisch, John & Paul Herring, Andrew Hochhauser, Eik Kahng, David Lachenmann, Bernardo Laniado Romero, Cristiano Leone, Francesco Libetta, Nina Lobanov, Geoffrey Marsh, Tatiana Massine Weinbaum, Christine Pinault, Jane Pritchard, Felicia Rappe, Sabine Rewald, Katharina Schmidt, Sir Nicholas Serota, Ken Soehner, Andrew Strauss, Anne Strauss, Vérane Tasseau, Ann Temkin, Guidalberto Torlonia, Anne Umland, Elena Valensise, Diana Vishneva and Konstantin Selinevich, Ornella Volta, Sheena Wagstaff and Thilo von Watzdorf.

At Mondo Mostre Skira I would like to acknowledge Tomaso Radaelli, Thomas Clement Salomon; at Skira, Massimo Vitta Zelman and Stefano Piantini. At the Scuderie del Quirinale, I should mention Alexandra Andresen, Chiara Eminente, Francesca Ercole, Flaminia Nardone, and most crucially Mario De Simoni and Matteo Lafranconi.

Flaminia Gennari Santori, director of Gallerie Nazionali di Arte Antica di Roma – Palazzo Barberini e Galleria Corsini, was kind enough to accept our proposal to install the monumental curtain of Parade *in the stately Sala Pietro da Cortona. I am very grateful for her participation in this project.*

Needless to say, I am deeply indebted to the members of the Scientific Committee: Carmen Giménez, Brigitte Léal, Laurent Le Bon, Silvia Loreti, Bernard Ruiz-Picasso and Gary Tinterow. In particular, Carmen Giménez has provided constant and invaluable advice at all stages of this project. In addition I should mention Paloma Picasso-Thévenet and Éric Thévenet, Diana Widmaier-Picasso and Maya Widmaier-Picasso. To all I am deeply indebted.

Further thanks are due to the authors of the catalogue: Cécile Godefroy, Anunciata von Liechtenstein, Silvia Loreti, Valentina Moncada, and Sarah Woodcock.

The exhibition's layout was conceived by Selldorf Architects, and I am grateful to Annabelle Selldorf, Julie Hausch-Fen, and Dante Furioso for coming up with such elegant designs.

Without its institutional and private lenders, this exhibition would be purely imaginary; it is because of their precious support that a project as ambitious as this one succeeded in materializing, and I am grateful to each and every one of them; they are acknowledged above/below.

Last but not least, I would like to express my gratitude to Anunciata von Liechtenstein, who worked tirelessly with me on this project from the moment of its inception.

Olivier Berggruen, July 2017

Cover
Pablo Picasso
Deux femmes courant sur la plage (La course) [Two Women Running on the Beach (The Race)], Dinard, summer 1922
Paris, Musée national Picasso-Paris, Pablo Picasso Donation, 1979, inv. MP78 (cat. no. 167)

Design
Marcello Francone

Editorial coordination
Emma Cavazzini
Eva Vanzella

Editing
Andrew Ellis

Layout
Serena Parini

Translations
Paul Metcalfe for *Scriptum*, Rome

Iconographical Research
Paola Lamanna

First published in Italy in 2017 by
Skira editore S.p.A.
Palazzo Casati Stampa
via Torino 61
20123 Milano
Italy
www.skira.net

Printed and bound in Italy. First edition

ISBN: 978-88-572-3693-3

Photo Credits
© 2017. Digital image, The Museum of Modern Art, New York / Scala, Firenze: fig. 2 (p. 23), fig. 2 (p. 64); cat. nos. 120, 131, 178
© 2017. Image copyright The Metropolitan Museum of Art / Art Resource / Scala, Firenze: cat. nos. 55, 168
© 2017. Foto Scala, Firenze/bpk, Bildagentur fuer Kunst, Kultur und Geschichte, Berlin: cat. nos. 3, 32, 126, 135, 164, 170, 174
© 2017 National Gallery of Art, Washington: cat. no. 189
© 2017. The Art Institute of Chicago / Art Resource, NY/Scala, Firenze: cat. nos. 86, 133, 134
© 2017 The Barnes Foundation: fig. 5 (p. 97)
© Archives Olga Ruiz-Picasso, Fundación Almine y Bernard Ruiz-Picasso para el Arte: cat. nos. 93, 100
© Archives Olga Ruiz-Picasso, Fundación Almine y Bernard Ruiz-Picasso para el Arte. Photographe inconnu, tous droits réservés: cat. nos. 12–19, 42, 94–99, 101–04
© BHVP / Parisienne de Photographie: cat. nos. 20a–b, 21, 22, 24, 46, 155a
© BHVP / Roger-Viollet: cat. nos. 27, 155b
© BHVP / Roger-Viollet / Archivi Alinari, Firenze: cat. no. 27
© BnF, Paris: fig. 4 (p. 82), cat. nos. 35, 36, 37, 38, 39, 40, 41, 149, 153, 157, 169
© British Library Board. All Rights Reserved / Bridgeman Image: fig. 5 (p. 67)
© Cahiers d'Art, Paris: fig. 1 (p. 90)
© Centre Pompidou, MNAM-CCI, Dist. RMN-Grand Palais / Christian Bahier / Philippe Migeat / RMN / distr. Alinari: cat. no. 34
© Jean Cocteau / BHVP / Roger-Viollet / Alinari © ADAGP – SIAE: cat. nos. 23, 25, 26
© FABA Photo: Marc Domage: fig. 5 (p. 31), cat. nos. 7, 123
© FABA Photo: Hugard & Vanoverschelde Photography: cat. nos. 85, 90, 116, 124, 188
© Photo: Equipo Gasull: fig. 3 (p. 24)
© Pinacoteca Giovanni e Marella Agnelli: cat. no. 4
© RMN-Grand Palais (Musée national Picasso-Paris) / Michèle Bellot / RMN distr. Alinari: cat. no. 49
© RMN-Grand Palais (Musée national Picasso-Paris) / Jean-Gilles Berizzi / RMN distr. Alinari: cover, cat. nos. 167, 172
© RMN-Grand Palais (Musée national Picasso-Paris) / Adrien Didierjean / RMN distr. Alinari: cat. no. 142
© RMN-Grand Palais (Musée national Picasso-Paris) / Droits réservés / RMN distr. Alinari: fig. 1 (p. 22); cat. nos. 56, 152, 175
©RMN-Grand Palais (Musée Picasso de Paris) / image RMN-GP / Réunion des Musées Nationaux / distr. Alinari: cat. nos. 57, 58, 77, 78, 104, 109–11, 113, 114
© RMN-Grand Palais (Musée national Picasso-Paris) / Béatrice Hatala / RMN / distr. Alinari: cat. nos. 87, 150
© RMN-Grand Palais (Musée national Picasso-Paris) / Thierry Le Mage / RMN distr. Alinari: figs. 2a and 2b (p. 37), cat. nos. 11, 29, 30, 33, 48, 50, 51, 112, 146, 148, 151
© RMN-Grand Palais (Musée national Picasso-Paris) / Hervé Lewandowski / RMN / distr. Alinari: cat. nos. 144, 145, 147
© Centre Pompidou, MNAM-CCI, Dist. RMN-Grand Palais / Philippe Migeat / RMN / distr. Alinari: cat. no. 129
© RMN-Grand Palais (Musée national Picasso-Paris) / René-Gabriel Ojéda / RMN /distr. Alinari: cat. nos. 2, 115, 117, 128
© Centre Pompidou, MNAM-CCI, Dist. RMN-Grand Palais / Bertrand Prévost / RMN distr. Alinari: fig. 4 (p. 39), cat. no. 8
© RMN-Grand Palais (Musée national Picasso-Paris) / Mathieu Rabeau / RMN / distr. Alinari: fig. 1 (p. 76); cat. nos. 1, 43, 44, 45, 52, 83, 84, 88, 125, 132, 138, 143, 159, 161
© RMN-Grand Palais (Musée de l'Orangerie) / Franck Raux / RMN distr. Alinari: cat. no. 165
© Tate, London 2017: cat. nos. 171, 190
© The Fitzwilliam Museum, Cambridge: cat. no. 81
© The Morgan Library Museum; New York: cat. no. 82
© Victoria and Albert Museum, London: fig. 2 (p. 77); cat. nos. 53, 54, 79, 106, 107, 108
Fonds Erik Satie - Archives de France / Archives Imec: fig. 5 (p. 85), cat. nos. 180–187
Maurice Aeschimann: cat. nos. 10, 179
Bridgeman Images: fig. 4 (p. 28)
Bridgestone Museum of Art, Ishibashi Foundation: cat. no. 141
Fondation Beyeler, Riehen / Basel, Collection Beyeler. Photo: Peter Schibli: cat. no. 162
Fondazione Collezione E.G. Bührle, Zurigo: fig. 1 (p. 35), cat. no. 9
Photography by Heather Johnson, Imaging Department, The Metropolitan Museum of Art: figs. 1 and 2 (p. 47), 3 (p. 49), 4 (p. 50), 5 (p. 57); cat. nos. 59–75
Photo: Kunsthalle Mannheim / Cem Yücetas: fig. 3 (p. 65)
Musée national Picasso-Paris, Paris: fig. 4 (p. 66), fig. 3 (p. 81)
Museo Thyssen-Bornemisza, Madrid: cat. no. 141
Photo © Christie's Images / Bridgeman Images: fig. 3 (p. 92)
Santa Barbara Museum of Art, Gift of Wright S. Lidington: cat. nos. 31, 119
The Cleveland Museum of Art: cat. no. 5
Yale University, New Haven: fig. 2 (p. 91)

Contents

1915–25: Picasso, from *Harlequin* to *Three Dancers*

Cécile Godefroy

For Picasso, the year 1915 can be regarded as one of transition and of deep reflection on his identity. The war deprived the Spanish artist of his companions. The painter Georges Braque and the poet Guillaume Apollinaire had enlisted in the army, and the dealer Daniel-Henry Kahnweiler was forced into exile in Switzerland owing to his German origins and French sympathies. Picasso worked in isolation in his studio on Rue Schoelcher in Paris, and can be seen in photographs displaying the versatility that was part of his image: an experienced artist of multiple identities defying the world of art in the guise of a fighter, a sheet-metal worker, a painter of Montmartre, and a bourgeois Parisian (fig. 1).[1] In December he revived the complex and manifold figure of Harlequin (fig. 2) in a large Cubist composition generally interpreted as a self-portrait in mourning for the death of his lover Eva Gouel, whom he nicknamed "Ma Jolie". The personification of theatrical tragedy, Harlequin also marked the end of a life of bohemian camaraderie, and looked forward to a new era oriented towards the stage. Picasso created sets and costumes for several productions of the Ballets Russes and the Soirées de Paris between 1917 and 1924, and experimented with the idea of total art cherished by the avant-gardes. This unprecedented involvement with the theatre, culminating in his marriage to the Russian dancer Olga Khokhlova and the birth of their son Paul, coloured his work as a painter. During his Neoclassical period Picasso gave Harlequin his own features and resumed his dialogue with the past, especially ancient painting and Antiquity, in a free combination of Cubism and naturalism.[2] The works attest to an extraordinary range of sometimes antagonistic styles, as exemplified by the painting *Études* (1920, Musée national Picasso-Paris, MP65), which juxtaposes figurative elements and Cubist motifs in a Synthetic collage-like, grid-based composition. Picasso stopped working for the stage in 1925[3] and painted *Trois Danseuses* (*Three Dancers*) (Tate, London, T00729), a work of ambitious format where the wild eroticism of the figures and chromatic dissonance herald the end of an era and the birth of a new, more instinctive and violent vocabulary hailed by André Breton as Surrealism. The period of the artist's involvement with the Ballets Russes was over, and his love for Olga on the wane.[4] This essay proposes to look back on the non-linear course of these ten years of Picasso's life and work.

In 1915 Picasso prolonged the experiments of Synthetic Cubism in the use of everyday elements, bringing them to their decorative climax. The citation of Pointillism enabled him to return fully to colour, banished during the Hermetic period, and to express the opacity and transparency of objects. While the *Man by the Fireplace* (1916, Musée national Picasso-Paris, MP54) combines Cubist space (planes of colour) and perspective (the linear

[1] Four of these photographs, dated 1915–16, can be seen in William Rubin (ed.), *Picasso and Portraiture: Representation and Transformation*, exh. cat. (New York, The Museum of Modern Art; Paris, Grand Palais, 1996): 141.
[2] A question examined in depth by Yve-Alain Bois in the exhibition *Picasso Harlequin. 1917–1937* (Rome, Museo Centrale del Risorgimento, 2008) and its catalogue.
[3] While the artist did produce other sets and costumes for ballet and theatre, these works fall outside the chronological bounds of the present study, and were produced for more specific commissions. See Douglas Cooper, *Picasso Theatre* (London: Widenfeld and Nicolson, 1968).
[4] Picasso and Olga lived together until 1935, and were still married when she died in 1955.

contours of the fireplace and the mirror), since 1914 purely figurative drawings – including a whole series of precise, illusionistic portraits – had appeared in his oeuvre. The *Portrait of Max Jacob* (1915–16), published in Amédée Ozenfant's magazine *L'Élan*, is seen in the literature as marking a "return to order" tinged with patriotism.[5] In Picasso's case, the return to figurative art that predominated in Europe during and especially after the war was mainly a dialectical reaction to his work.[6] Abandoning the seclusion of the studio-laboratory, he drew inspiration once again from a reality revisited through the great masters, a pantheon including Jean-Auguste Dominique Ingres. Far from abandoning Cubism, Picasso combined it with forms that were simultaneously more living and more eternal, developing new reflections about representation, which he never ceased to examine during these years.

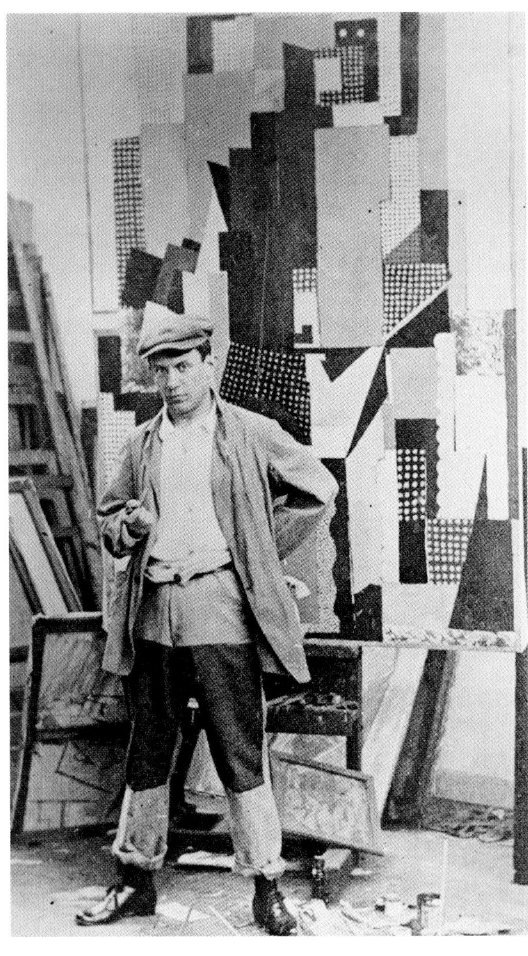

1. Picasso in his studio on Rue Schœlcher, Paris, 1915–16 Paris, Musée national Picasso-Paris, Gift of R. Penrose, inv. FPPH 10

2. Pablo Picasso *Arlequin* [Harlequin], December 1915 Oil on canvas, 183.5 x 105.1 cm New York, The Museum of Modern Art, inv. 76.1950

In 1916 Jean Cocteau invited Picasso to work with Sergei Diaghilev's company. Since 1909, the Ballet Russes thrilled the Parisian stages with performances of the classic repertoire and original creations born out of the combined efforts of modern artists, decorators, composers, and choreographers. In the spring of 1912, *L'Après-midi d'un faune*, the first one-act ballet choreographed by Vaslav Nijinsky for the company to the music of Claude Debussy, established a stylized, sensual body language that broke away from academic ballet in the sophisticated set and neo-Greek costumes of Léon Bakst. One year later, the troupe inaugurated the Théâtre des Champs-Élysées with the "great pagan" *Rite of Spring*, conceived and composed by Igor Stravinsky and choreographed by Nijinsky with sumptuous decor by Nicholas Roerich, which caused a tremendous furore. Based on an idea by Cocteau, *Parade* then combined the music of Erik Satie, the choreography of Léonide Massine, and the scenery and costumes of Picasso, enabling the painter to experiment with arts of the stage, its spatial

[5] *Portrait of Max Jacob*, Paris, 1915, pencil on paper, 325 × 245 mm, Musée national Picasso-Paris, MP1998.307, published in *L'Élan*, no. 10 (1 December 1916): 1. See Kenneth E. Silver, *Esprit de Corps. The Art of the Parisian Avant-Garde and the First World War, 1914–1925* (Princeton, NJ: Princeton University Press, 1989).

[6] Werner Spies, *Picasso: pastels, dessins, aquarelles* (Paris: Herscher, 1986): 31.

[7] See Cécile Godefroy, "Olga Khokhlova, Ballerina, and Pablo Picasso", in Elizabeth Cowling, Richard Kendall (eds.), *Picasso Looks at Degas*, catalogue of the exhibition held at the Sterling and Francine Clark Art Institute, Williamstown, and the Museu Picasso, Barcelona (Williamstown, MA: Clark Art Institute, 2010): 282–97 and 324–27.

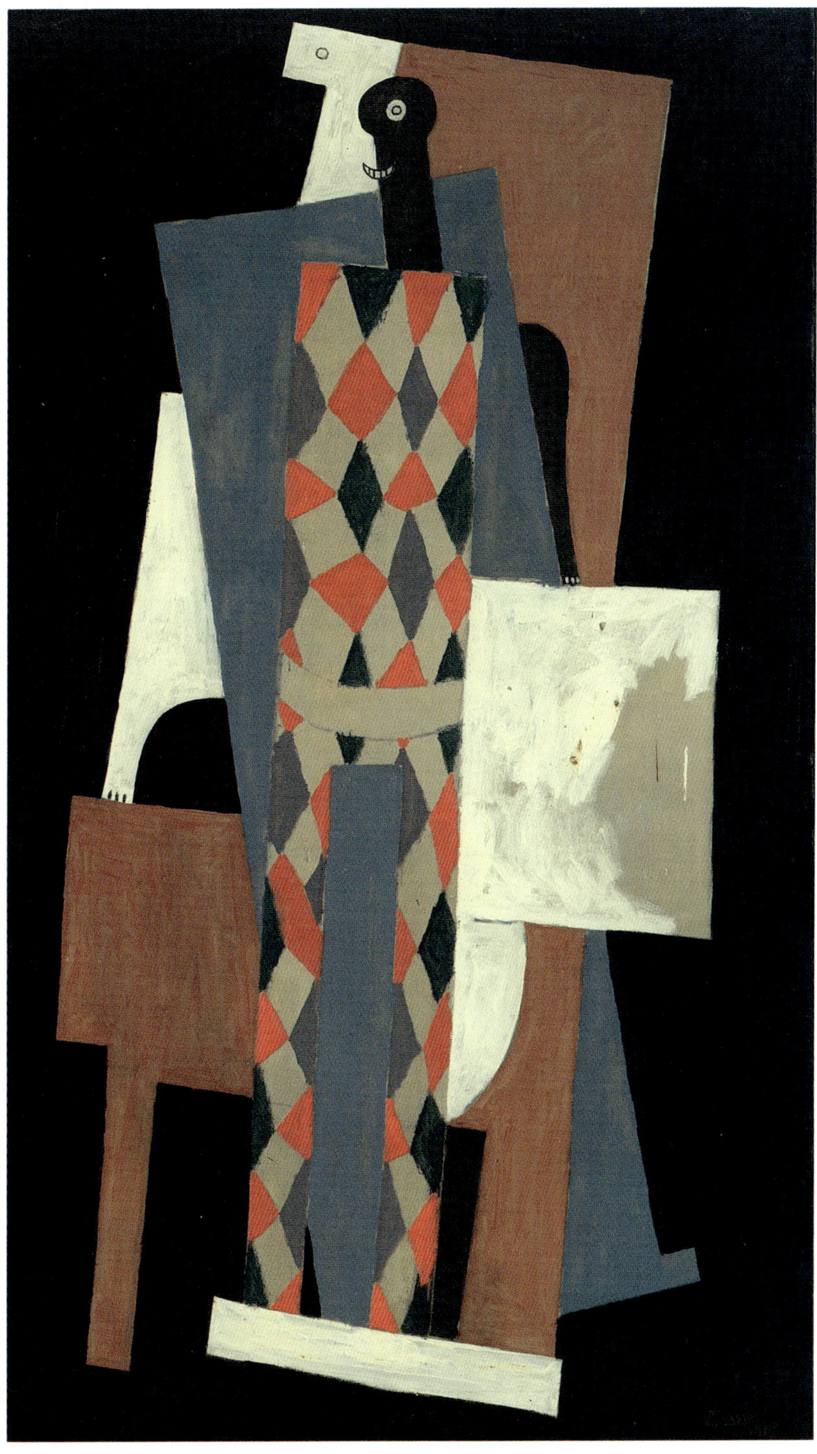

and scenic dimensions, properties unknown to Cubism. Picasso left Paris in the company of Cocteau and Stravinsky in February 1917 to work on *Parade* in Italy. The discovery of Roman antiquities, the ruins of Pompeii and Herculaneum, and Italian folk art, as well as the contact with the company and the meeting with the dancer Olga Khokhlova were sources of aesthetic and affective emotion that would support the artist on the path undertaken in 1914.

When he met Olga in Rome, she was twenty-six and at the peak of her career. Having entered the Ballets Russes in 1911, she developed with talent in the traditional and modern repertoire of Diaghilev's company.[7] A servant in *Thamar*, a sultan's wife in *Scheherazade* (cat. no. 99) and a nymph in *L'Après-midi d'un faune* (cat. no. 100), Olga increased her appearances and began in 1915 to perform her first principal roles in the creations of Massine. A maid of honour in *Las Meninas*, the company's first Spanish ballet to music by Gabriel Fauré, she performed the part of Felicita in *The Good-Humoured Ladies* in Italy. While Picasso has the opportunity to see her dance in various roles as a slave or an oriental princess, he paid more attention to her performance in *Les Sylphides*. Inspired by Filippo Taglioni's *La Sylphide*, the first romantic ballet, Fokine's creation was one of the company's great successes, restoring the iconic ballerina in points and a tutu of white gauze to her place of honour. While

Olga did not play the leading role, her Slavic beauty perfectly epitomized the image of the romantic ballerina. The perfect oval of her face, which Picasso captured in Rome in the first drawings,[8] was lit up by big brown eyes and framed by long auburn hair in a chignon, often with a hairband or chaplet of flowers. A set of photographs taken in New York in 1916 (Clarence H. White studio, Fundación Almine y Bernard Ruiz-Picasso para el Arte [FABA]) to publicize the company show her in the group of Sylphides. While Picasso reinterpreted these images a few years later in Ingres-like drawings (*Three Dancers*, 1919, Musée national Picasso-Paris, MP834), the vision of Olga as a sylphide led him to associate his new muse with the ballerina, the personification of ideal womanhood, and probably prompted the dialogue he recommenced with Classical Antiquity and nineteenth-century French painting.

After a culturally intense stay in Rome, broken by two trips to Naples and one to Florence and Milan,[9] Picasso returned to Paris and attended the premiere of *Parade* at the Théâtre du Châtelet on 18 May 1917. The naturalism of the stage curtain, inspired by the *commedia dell'arte*, contrasted markedly with the Cubist sets, the costumes of the managers and the horse, carried along by the choreography of Massine and the "urban" music of Satie. If the "surrealism" of *Parade* – the term *sur-réalisme* was coined by Guillaume Apollinaire and first used by him in the program of the ballet – heralded the "new spirit abroad today, which will not fail to captivate the elite and promises to transform arts and manners from top to bottom through universal joy",[10] the performance moved the audience and critics to mirth and anger and caused an outcry.[11] As the poet later explained, however, this new spirit reconciling tradition and modernity, both French and Italian, "strives above all to inherit from the classics sound common sense, a sure critical spirit, overall perspectives on the universe and the human heart, and a sense of duty that lays the feelings bare and limits or rather contains their manifestation".[12]

Inebriated by the *succès de scandale* of *Parade* and in love with Olga, Picasso accompanied the Ballets Russes on their various travels in Spain, where the company was received by the king in Madrid and gave several performances in Barcelona. While working with Massine and the composer Manuel de Falla from Cadiz on a new ballet – *The Three-Cornered Hat*, first performed in London at the Alhambra in 1919[13] – he took up the great subjects of his homeland and painted the portrait *Olga in a Mantilla* (1917) (fig. 3), which he symbolically offered to his mother Doña Maria. While the painting of Olga and the portrait of Massine as *Harlequin* (1917) (Barcelona, Museu Picasso, MPB 10.941) are directly related to the Spanish tradition, the bullfighting scenes, focusing on the tragic figure of the dying horse in the arena, the flamenco dancers, and the seated female figures that fill the pages of a sketchbook

3. Pablo Picasso
Olga à la mantille
[Olga in a Mantilla],
summer-autumn 1917
Oil on canvas, 64 x 53 cm
Private collection

[8] See for example the photos of Olga taken in Rome (1917, Fundación Almine y Bernard Ruiz-Picasso para el Arte [FABA]) and the *Portrait of Olga*, 1917, pencil on paper, 275 × 210 mm, private collection, Z. XXIX, 298.

[9] See Jean Clair (ed.), *Picasso. The Italian Journey. 1917–1924* (Venice, Palazzo Grassi, 1998); Olivier Berggruen (ed.), *Picasso and the Theater* (Frankfurt, Schirn Kunsthalle, 2007).

[10] Guillaume Apollinaire, programme of *Parade*, Paris, 18 May 1917; now in *Chroniques d'art 1902–1918* (Paris: Gallimard): 532–34.

[11] See Claire Garnier (ed.), *Parade* (Metz, Centre Pompidou, 2012); Peter Read, "Cubism Breaks Cover: Picasso and *Parade* in 1917", in Harry Cooper (ed.), *The Cubism Seminars* (Washington, DC: National Gallery of Art, 2017): 252–85.

[12] Guillaume Apollinaire, "L'Esprit nouveau et les poètes", in *Mercure de France* 491 (1 December 1918): 385–96.

[13] See Yvan Nommick and Antonio Alvarez Canibano (eds.), *Los Ballets Russes de Diaghilev y España* (Granada, Fundación Archivo Manuel de Falla/Centro de Documentación de Música y Danza-Inaem, 1989), esp. Marilyn McCully, "Picasso and *Le Tricorne*", 97–104.

[14] Sketchbook, Barcelona, summer-autumn 1917, Paris, Musée national Picasso-Paris, MP1866.

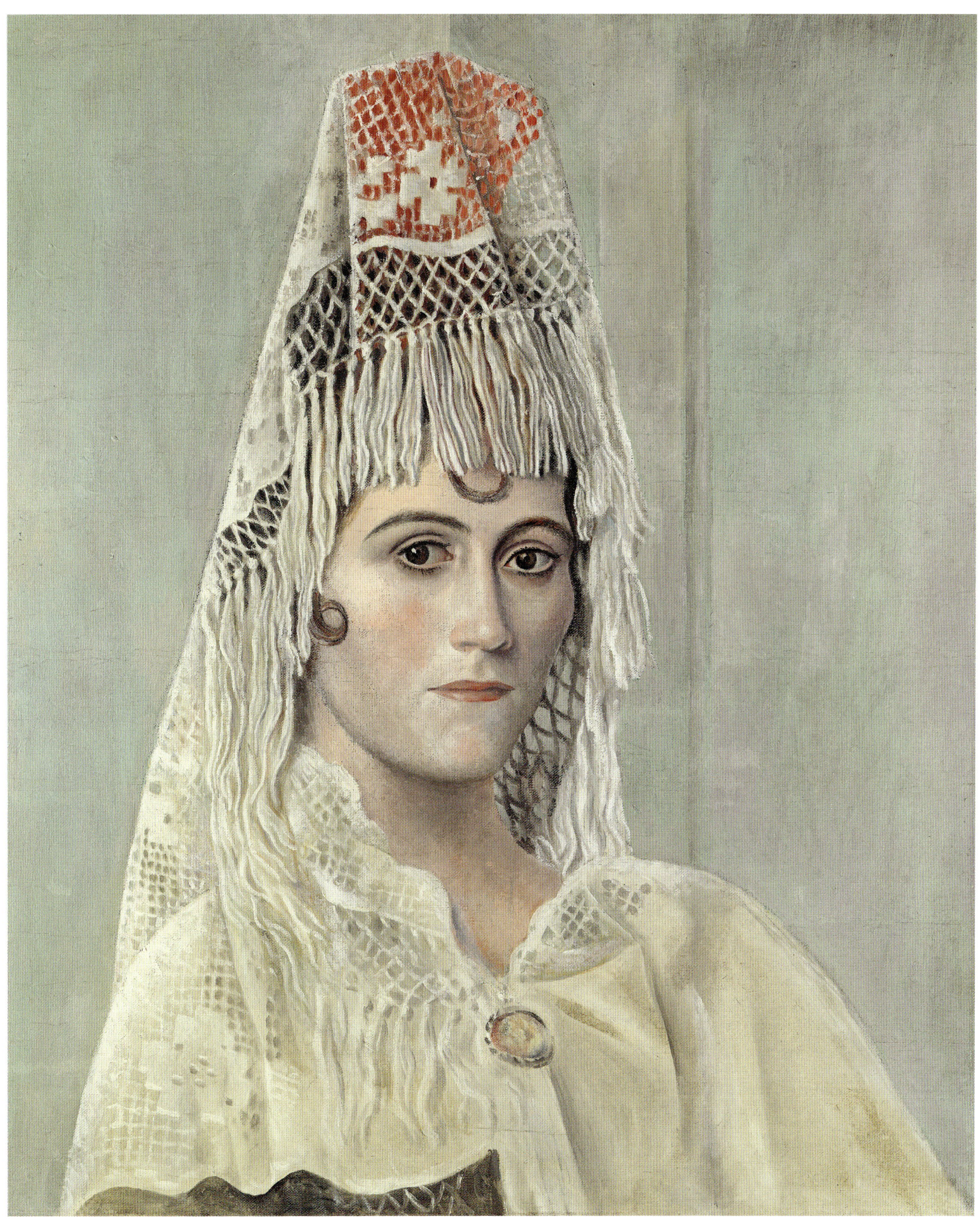

reveal the range of styles practised at the time, from Cubism to illusionistic realism and naturalism.[14]

The portraits of Olga painted by Picasso on his return to France, after she decided to leave Diaghilev's company, recount the first months of their life together between the artist's house in Montrouge and the Hôtel Lutetia (*Portrait of Olga in an Armchair*, 1918, Musée national Picasso-Paris, MP55). Picasso and Olga married in Paris on 12 July 1918, and spent the summer in Biarritz at the home of their friend Eugenia Errázuriz. This stay on the Landes coast established the bather as a figure in Picasso's repertoire (*Bathers*, Cambridge, MA, Harvard Art Museums). With their prosaic quality and agility, the nudes sketched on the beach sometimes meld with the dancers captured by Picasso in repeated motion and at rest. A lunch at the Villa Mimoseraie sealed the contract between the artist and his two new dealers, Paul Rosenberg for France and Europe, and George Wildenstein for the United States. Installed in the smart district of Rue La Boétie, a stone's throw from the Galerie Rosenberg, Picasso was relieved of all material concerns and able to create in complete freedom. His bohemian days were definitively over. His first show at Rosenberg's gallery, held in 1919 with a preface by André Salmon in the catalogue, consisted of 167 drawings and watercolours on subjects including Harlequin and Pierrot, circus and bullfighting scenes, male and female dancers, still-lifes, nudes, landscapes, portraits and some works "after Ingres and Renoir".[15] The series of twenty-five still-lifes in front of an open window at Saint-Raphaël, produced during the summer of 1919 and further developed by Picasso after his return to Paris until the next summer, are midway between painting and set design. Sometimes classical and sometimes Cubist in style, they present powerfully moulded volumes, or decompose the subject into a tangle of lines and planes (*Still Life on a Table in Front of an Open Window*, 26 October 1919, Musée national Picasso-Paris, MP859). These studies are echoed in the Cubists sets Picasso created for Stravinsky's ballet *Pulcinella*, based on music attributed to Pergolese, choreographed by Massine and first performed at the Théâtre national de l'Opéra de Paris on 15 May 1920 (*Study for Scenery for Pulcinella*, 1920, Musée national Picasso-Paris, MP1750r). The still lifes in front of the window and Picasso's sets thus attest to the survival of Cubism after the First World War and its necessary renewal on reappraisal in the light of the movements it inspired, including purism, geometric abstract art, Art Deco, and its flourishing developments in the fields of the applied arts, fashion, and architecture.[16]

The return to reality initiated in 1914 blossomed with his meeting with Olga. The portrait, which is also the earliest application of photography, recalls that this practice was popularized with the appearance of the

[15] See the catalogue *Exposition de dessins et aquarelles par Picasso* (Paris: Paul Rosenberg, 1919).
[16] See Olivier Berggruen, "*Réelles présences - des éléments décoratifs des ballets Parade et Mercure considérés en tant que sculptures*", *Actes du colloque "Picasso. Sculptures"*, Paris, 2016. http://picasso-sculptures.fr/
[17] See Cécile Godefroy, "Olga Khokhlova and the Reign of the Image", in Katharina Beisiegel (ed.), *Picasso and His Muses* (Art Centre Basel/Vancouver, 2016): 40–55.

first portable cameras and accompanied the significant moments in the couple's life. Picasso took amateur photographs of moments of family life between 1917 and 1935.[17] Because the photographic portrait is the likeness of a person drawn by the pencil of light, the Ingres-like drawing that characterizes a number of Picasso's works of the period is described as "photographic", even though it has nothing to do with the reproductive technique of a snapshot. The process whereby Picasso goes from a memory or a visual impression to a study and then to a painting through the medium of photography is a work of artistic synthesis and transformation that owes more to the Cubist episode. This applies to the line drawings and paintings of Olga in pensive or contemplative mood, reading, writing or embroidering (e.g. *Olga Reclining*, March 1921, private collection, (2678 [PiF 1001]). Picasso's realism was enhanced by the birth of their son Paul on 4 February 1921, and the artist's desire to capture all the changes in the child's growth. From mother and child ensembles to portraits of the boy in fancy dress, Picasso's firstborn was the subject of drawn and painted studies produced from memory, life or photographs. *Paul as Harlequin* (1924, Musée national Picasso-Paris, MP83), and *Paul as Pierrot* (28 February 1925, Musée national Picasso-Paris, MP84), following in the line of Renoir's portraits of children, attest to the transformation taking place between the representation of the young model, drawn with virtuoso precision, and the emotion of the moment rendered by the vibrato of the oil paint. This shows, if indeed there were any need, that Picasso's classicism was in no way academic but rather involved a modern reinterpretation of models of the past.

At Fontainebleau during the summer of 1921 in the company of Paul, Olga, and Doña Maria, Picasso walked along the tree-lined avenues of the chateau, whose curiosities afforded an opportunity to revisit the theme of *Women at the Fountain* (Musée national Picasso-Paris, MP74), three timeless, colossal figures drawn in red chalk inspired by classical statuary and the painting of Renoir.[18] Numerous portrayals of Olga attest to this renewed influence of Pompeian art, which transforms the portraits into virginal allegories (e.g., *Female Head*, 1921, Museum Berggruen, Nationalgalerie, Staatliche Museen zu Berlin). All through the year 1922, Picasso continued this exploration of bodies undergoing metamorphosis. During the summer in Dinard, monumental goddesses stand majestically at the water's edge (fig. 4) or frolic on the sand. Two years later the small gouache *Two Women Running on the Beach* (1922, Musée national Picasso-Paris, MP78) served as a model for the stage curtain of *Le Train Bleu* (1924), a ballet to music by Darius Milhaud based on a scenario by Cocteau. While Olga no longer danced in public, the photographs taken by Picasso show the exercises to which she subjected

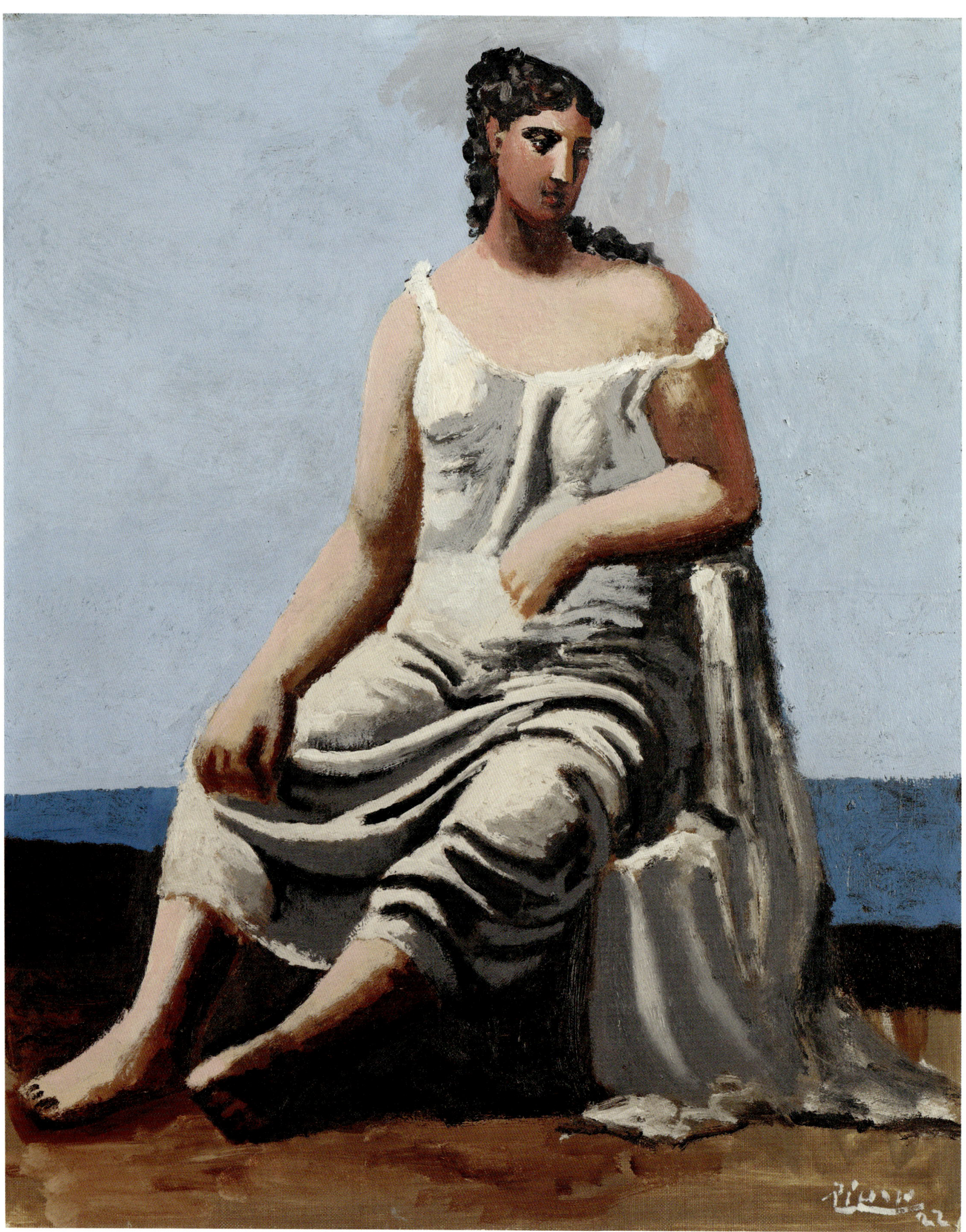

4. Pablo Picasso
Femme au bord de la mer
[Woman by the Sea], 1922
Oil on canvas, 58.42 x 48.26 cm
Minneapolis, Institute of Arts, inv. 61.36.24

herself during the summer holidays.[19] The observation by Picasso of bodies in motion is conducive to the elongation and distortion of line: Werner Spies evokes an "amplification of form starting from the spirit of dance"[20] that leads to the "calligraphic" women of 1924, whose moving contours suggest living matter (*Dancer*, study for the ballet *Mercure*, 1924, private collection).

In 1923 Picasso painted four portraits of the artist Jacint Salvadó as Harlequin (Kunstmuseum Basel, G 1967.9) and the last naturalistic portraits of Olga, already overshadowed by the tragedy to come.[21] During a summer stay in Antibes, once an ancient Greek city known as Antipolis, Picasso plunged fully into Hellenism and painted the *Pipes of Pan* (Musée national Picasso-Paris, MP79), a superb melancholy and strangely silent painting that breaks away from the sensual hedonism of previous works. With the *Three Graces* (1923; fig. 5), the artist takes up the age-old theme of the goddesses of beauty, naked and veiled, and elegantly distorts the figures limned in grisaille. This motif reappeared in the ballet *Mercure*, first performed on 15 June 1924 at the Théâtre de la Cigale within the framework of the Soirées de Paris organized by Count Étienne de Beaumont. In response to the scenario of Cocteau and the music of Satie – his two partners in *Parade* – Picasso created the sets and costumes for *tableaux vivants* that followed one another at the lightning speed of a vaudeville show, in accordance with Beaumont's wishes. Dancers and actors shared the stage with sculpture-paintings of coloured wood and wire in a zany, minimalist setting like a fairground. In the bathing scene, the three goddesses were played by extravagantly made-up and affected transvestites in wigs (photograph: Archives E. Satie).[22] Picasso thus parodied a classical theme that he had celebrated with great sophistication just a few months earlier. The performances – booed by the public, and the attack launched by Breton and his disciples, who praised the painter but were openly critical of Satie's music[23] – were commented on by Louis Aragon in *Le Journal littéraire* on 21 June. Praising the scenery "of superhuman wonder and monstrosity", and asserting that "nothing more striking has ever been presented on stage", the writer argued that *Mercure* was also "the revelation of an entirely new style of Picasso, which owes nothing to Cubism or Surrealism and which surpasses Cubism just as that surpassed realism".[24]

The end of Picasso's involvement with the stage coincided with the moment of a stylistic breakthrough and the beginning of his rift with Olga. Completed in May 1925 on his return from Monte Carlo, where he drew several studies of dancers from life (*Two Dancers*, 1925, private collection), *Three Dancers* (Tate, London, T00729), his last large painting on this subject, inaugurated a new style that André Breton endorsed as surrealist and presented as an illustration in the fourth issue of his magazine.[25] In

[18] See in particular two of the Renoirs bought by Picasso and now in the Musée national Picasso-Paris: *Seated Bather in a Landscape,* 1895–1900, oil on canvas, 116 × 89 cm, R.F.1973-87; and *La Coiffure*, 1900–01, red and white chalk on canvas, 145 × 103 cm, R.F.35793.

[19] Archives Olga Ruiz-Picasso, Fundación Almine y Bernard Ruiz-Picasso para el Arte (FABA).

[20] Werner Spies, op. cit., 33.

[21] See for example *Olga in a Fur Collar*, Paris, autumn-winter 1923, oil on canvas, 116 × 80.5 cm, Lille, Musée des Beaux-Arts, on loan from the Musée national Picasso-Paris, MP 1990.9.

[22] See Brigitte Léal, "Les carnets de *Mercure*", in *Carnets. Catalogue des dessins* (Paris, Musée national Picasso-Paris, vol. 1): 341–44.

[23] "In the light of this exceptional event, Picasso can be seen today, *to a far greater extent than all those around him*, as the eternal personification of youth and the indisputable master of the situation." Louis Aragon, "Pour arrêter les bavardages", *Le Journal littéraire* 9 (21 June 1924): 11.

[24] Ibid., 10.

[25] *La Révolution surréaliste* 4 (July 1925): 17, 26–30.

this Dionysian version of the Three Graces, the female dancer, formerly identified with the idealized, linear image of the beautiful Olga, is an ecstatic, erotic maenad (the figure on the left). The glaring, aggressive colours enhance the disjointed bodies and syncopated rhythm of the three dancers. The flat and ethereal central figure, whose Christ-like pose echoes that of Lydia Lopokova in the photograph of *Les Sylphides* (1916, Fundación Almine y Bernard Ruiz-Picasso para el Arte [FABA]), stands in the embrasure of a window opened onto an abstract blue background. No Mediterranean azure or classical references emerge in this painting, however, the right-hand figure of which is also interpreted, like the *Harlequin* of 1915, as a tribute to a deceased friend, in this case the painter Ramon Pichot.[26] Even though Picasso kept his distance from Surrealism, the eruption of violence and eroticism in his work responds to Breton's call for "convulsive beauty".[27] The rhythmic dissonances of *Three Dancers* liberated the metamorphic power of the painter, who drew on his repertoire of subjects like the seated female figure, the painter and his model, and the bather as from 1925 to produce a whole new order of creatures. As Michel Leiris later observed, "It is far less a question of remaking reality for the sole purpose of remaking it than for the incomparably more important purpose of expressing all its possibilities, all its conceivable ramifications, so as to approach it a little closer and really touch it. Instead of being a vague relation, a panorama of phenomena, reality is thus illuminated in all its pores and penetrated, thus truly becoming a REALITY for the first time."[28]

It is as though the combination of the singular interest taken by Picasso for ten years in classicism – Classical Antiquity, nineteenth-century painting and ballet – and the continuation of his Cubist experiments increased his demonstrative power tenfold. Drawing on two sources, the artist played like Harlequin with the infinite possibilities of his language so as to express reality better and prepare his own departure after 1925 for new formal horizons that were no longer to characterize an "ism" or a given period but Picassian painting as such.

5. Pablo Picasso
Les Trois grâces
[The Three Graces], 1923
Oil and charcoal on canvas, 200 x 150 cm
Private collection

[26] For the biographical interpretation of the paintings as connected with Pichot's death, see Ronald Alley, *Picasso: The Three Dancers* (London, Tate Gallery, 1996). Erik Satie also died on 1 July 1925.
[27] André Breton, *L'Amour fou*, 1937, in Œuvres (Paris: Gallimard, collection Pléiade), vol. 2, 1992, 687.
[28] Michel Leiris, "Toiles récentes de Picasso", *Documents* 2, year 2 (1930): 57–71.

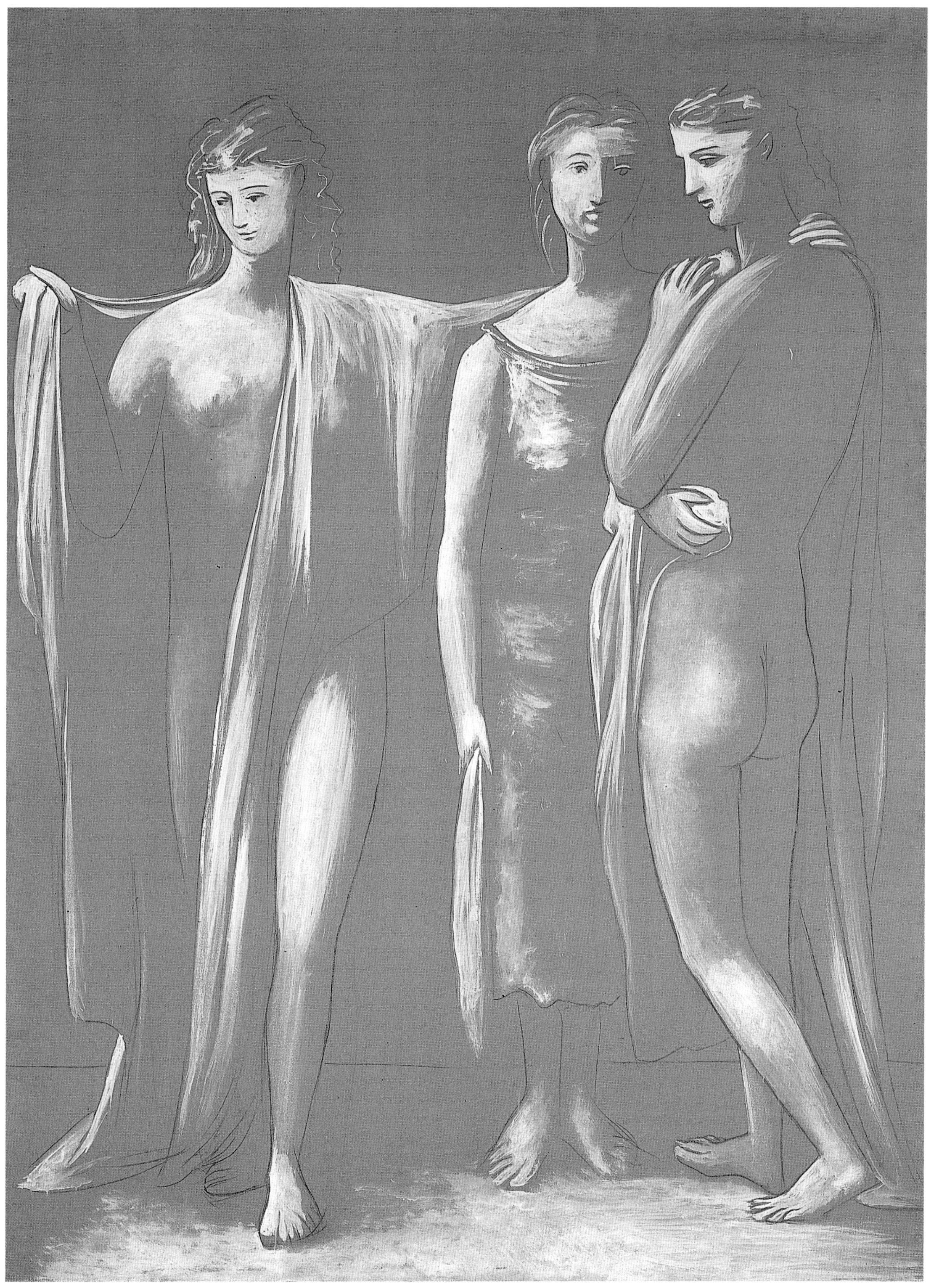

Picasso in Via Margutta: the Studio in Rome

Valentina Moncada

This study addresses works by Pablo Picasso that may have drawn inspiration from the traditions of Via Margutta, a street of artists renowned as the Roman Montmartre, where he rented a studio. Above all, it examines in depth the creative process leading to two masterpieces produced in Rome, namely *L'Italienne* and *Arlequin et femme au collier*, highlighting the key part played by the circulation of the subjects addressed through advertising posters, picture postcards and carte-de-visite photographs.

Picasso arrived in Rome on 17 February 1917 with Jean Cocteau and Sergei Diaghilev's Ballets Russes. Work was under way on *Parade*, the first Cubist ballet in history, with costumes and sets by the Spanish artist. He and Cocteau stayed at the Hotel de Russie on the corner of Via del Babuino and Piazza del Popolo, one of the most exclusive areas of Rome, just a stone's throw from Via Margutta, the street of artists *par excellence*. Picasso then rented a studio there at number 53b, as attested by a note in pencil in a sketchbook now in the archives of the Musée Picasso in Paris: "Mon atelier 53b Via Margutta".[1] Further confirmation is provided by documents such as letters from Cocteau to his mother, as from 23 February, and from Picasso to Apollinaire.[2]

Having arrived in Rome, the artist may have heard of the possibility of renting a studio in the vicinity of his hotel and precisely in the Studi Patrizi opposite the seat of the Associazione Artistica Internazionale. This was then a quiet, secluded area by comparison with the "Trident" of Via di Ripetta, Via del Corso, and Via del Babuino.

The Studi Patrizi at 53-54-55 Via Margutta, on which building started in 1858, was a monumental complex whose studios, flooded with light from the large windows still visible from the street today, attracted numerous artists from all over the world. Midway through the nineteenth century, while Italy was achieving unification with Rome as its capital, the particular interest developed in the founding of foreign academies had led in just a few years to the creation of a vibrant international community of artists. They gathered at the Associazione Artistica Internazionale,[3] which organized a host of courses, exhibitions, meetings, concerts and lectures that marked an important and exciting chapter in the cultural history of Rome, as well as parties, banquets and the famous carnival celebrations, for which the artists created spectacular *tableaux vivants* and fancy-dress parades.[4]

When Picasso arrived in Rome, Europe was at war and the exhibitions of the Associazione Artistica Internazionale were devoted exclusively to this subject.[5] Many artists were at the war front, and the atmosphere in the streets was certainly less festive, even though the historical traditions were still maintained.

[1] Carnet 19, page 1, verso, 1917, note in pencil (Paris, Musée national Picasso-Paris); previously published in V. Moncada, *Picasso a Roma* (Milan: Electa, 2007). The presentation of this book in the courtyard of the Studi Patrizi coincided with the unveiling of a plaque commemorating the artist's stay there.

[2] See *Picasso a Roma*, op. cit. A new document recently appeared on the market at a Sotheby's auction, namely an unpublished Picasso drawing of Villa Medici with the inscription "atelier via Margutta". The drawing is signed and dated "Rome Février 1917, Hotel de Russie".

[3] For further information on the history of the studios in Via Margutta and the activities of the Associazione Artistica Internazionale, see *Atelier a via Margutta. Cinque secoli di cultura internazionale a Roma*, ed. V. Moncada di Paternò (Turin: Allemandi & Co, 2012). The presentation of this book was also marked by the installation of a plaque commemorating the most important events.

[4] For the spectacular *tableaux vivants*, see V. Moncada, "Luigi Ontani: maschere d'artista e artisti in maschera", in *"mar' DEI guttAvi". Luigi Ontani*, ed. R. Meucci Reale (Turin: Umberto Allemandi & C., 2009): 22–28. This book was published in conjunction with the performance of the same name by Luigi Ontani in Via Margutta in 2009, where the artist paid tribute to this historical tradition.

Picasso produced two large works. *L'Italienne* and *Arlequin et femme au collier*, and the associated studies in just over two months as well as various sketches of the façade of Villa Medici, the costumes for *Parade* – the preparatory drawings already made in Paris underwent original and indeed revolutionary reworking after his Italian stay – and the design for the stage curtain, then produced in Paris in the space of two weeks.

The models of Via Margutta: the Ciociara, an icon of the Italian tradition

Working in Via Margutta, Picasso could hardly avoid depicting a Ciociara. The female models in traditional costume known as Ciociare (plural) had been a very popular subject for over a century with the artists who lived and worked there. The Ciociara was indeed not only an icon in the Roman environment where he was working, but a popular subject at the national and international level. One of the masterpieces created in Rome, preceded by a Pointillist watercolour now in the Hakone Open-Air Museum, is *L'Italienne* (*Italian Woman*), a work in the synthetic Cubist style now in the collection of E.G. Bührle in Zurich (fig. 1). Apart from the evident stylistic differences, the elements distinguishing the initial watercolour from the definitive work include the addition of a view of St Peter's, almost as though to specify the location.

The subject represented has a centuries-long iconographic tradition including Italian but above all foreign artists, not only in Rome but also in other countries.

Piazza di Spagna, a few steps away from the more secluded Via Margutta, was in fact the haunt of beautiful young flower sellers in traditional costume, who took advantage of this vogue to serve the artistic community as models. While waiting to be hired, they would distribute carte-de-visite photographs and picture postcards, which became a further channel of circulation for their image, above all in other countries, where they enjoyed great popularity.

The traditional costume was that of Ciociaria, a pastoral area south of Rome that was an enormously popular setting for Italian genre scenes. Ciociari in traditional dress were in fact so common in the capital – above all from midway through the nineteenth century – as to be identified as the authentic Roman population and hence to be depicted by all the foreign artists resident in Rome, who were particularly attracted not only by the extraordinary beauty of the Eternal City but also by local folklore. The subject was widely addressed in particular by the important and numerous colony of Spanish artists resident in Via Margutta, as exemplified by José Benlliure with his portraits of what he called *campesinas romanas*,[6] or women from the Roman countryside, and Mariano Fortuny y Marsal with his *Teresina* in traditional costume.[7]

The subject enjoyed great success outside Italy too, as attested by the presence

1. Pablo Picasso
L'Italienne [Italian Woman], 1917
Oil on canvas, 149.5 x 101.5 cm
Zurich, Foundation E.G. Bührle Collection, inv. 78

See http://www.valentinamoncada.com/mostre/it/2009_Ontani_marDei.html for further details.

5 See "La mostra d'arte della guerra all'Associazione Artistica Internazionale", in *Il Giornale d'Italia* (18 January 1917): 2; "La mostra di guerra all'Associazione Artistica Internazionale", in *Piccolo Giornale d'Italia* 63 (4–5 March 1917).

6 J. Benlliure, *Campesinas romanas en fiestas* (Valencia, Museo des Bellas Artes). See *Atelier a via Margutta*, op. cit.

7 Mariano Fortuny y Marsal, *Teresina*, private collection. See *Atelier a via Margutta*, op. cit.

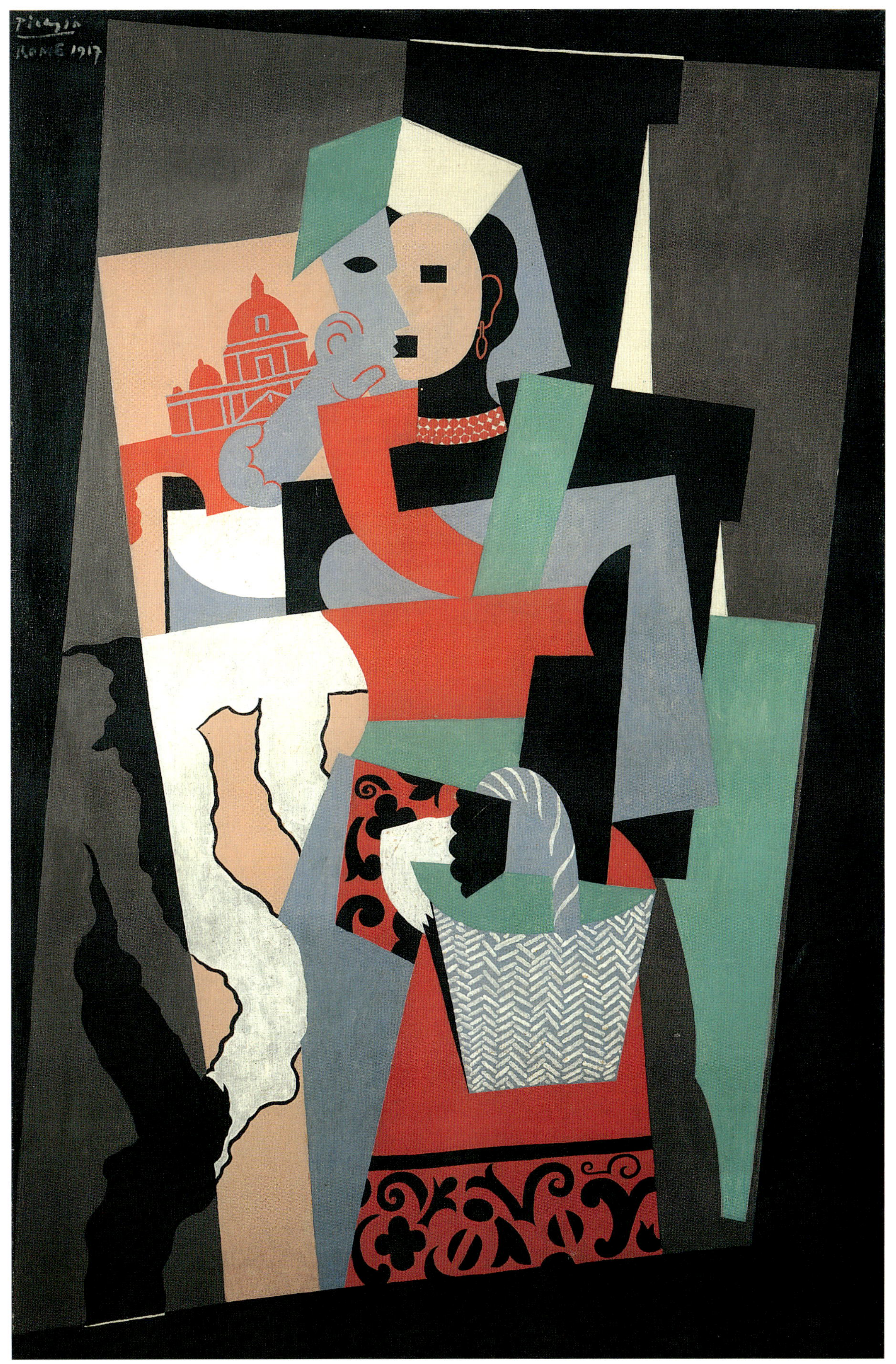
ROME 1917

of Ciociare in Paris around 1850,[8] not only in works of art but also as waitresses serving in traditional costume. One example is the model Agostina Segatori, owner of the Café du Tambourin at 27 Rue de Richelieu, the poster of which shows a Ciociara. Segatori posed for numerous artists of the period, including Édouard Manet, Jean-Baptiste-Camille Corot, a painter Picasso greatly admired,[9] and Vincent van Gogh, and was portrayed in celebrated masterpieces as *L'Italienne*. The traditional costume was indeed so widely known as to be identified as Italian rather than peculiar to Ciocaria. The fact that the untranslatable term "Ciociara" would have been difficult for non-Italians to pronounce also contributed to the common adoption of the more general label "Italian".

When Picasso arrived in Rome the subject was still very popular, above all in Via Margutta, where it was by no means rare to encounter women in traditional costume.[10] The souvenirs of his Roman trip include two watercolour picture postcards of Ciociare now in the archives of the Musée national Picasso in Paris (figs. 2–3).[11] The fact that Picasso worked precisely on Via Margutta suggests that he may have depicted the women in traditional dress from life, as well as from the postcards in his possession, which also circulated widely in black and white photographic reproductions. In-depth study of period postcards, photographs, and posters could reveal that Picasso drew on various sources for *L'Italienne* but preserved only two items of this material, which he faithfully reproduced in two sketches now in the archives of the Musée national Picasso in Paris.[12]

In the creation of his masterpiece, Picasso combined various elements from his sources, like the presence of the basket, the pose with the head resting on one hand and the elbow on the railing, sometimes reversed as in a mirror image. The female figure, her head resting on her closed right hand, wears the traditional costume of the Lazio region with a colourful apron, a basket of flowers, a form of hanging headgear (*mantilla*), in the shape of an inverted V, and a conspicuous red necklace (or *curagli*), as can be seen not only in the sketches but also in the more traditional iconography of the subject in the various reproductions of the period.

Intense iconographic research on this subject has led to the discovery of an advertisement for the Rome Express train (Paris–Rome) by Rafael de Ochoa y Madrazo,[13] a Spanish artist active in Paris and little known today. The poster shows the typical figure of a Ciociara selling flowers in the foreground with a view of St Peter's in the background, the very detail that Picasso added to the final version of *L'Italienne*. Other similarities include the typical headgear and the traditional dress, especially the lower part of the apron, the overlapping neckline and the characteristic red necklace (fig. 4).

It is therefore possible that Picasso already knew this poster, dated 1900, not only

[8] See M. Santulli, *Ciociaria sconosciuta* (Casamari di Veroli: Tipografica "La Monastica", 2002): 58.

[9] See B. Léal, "'moi Hotel Vesuvio Naples chambre 11' (Les Carnets italiens de Picasso)", in *Picasso 1917–1924, Le Voyage d'Italie*, ed. J. Clair (Paris: Gallimard, 1998): 58.

[10] A. Jandolo, *Studi e modelli di via Margutta (1870–1950)* (Milan: Casa editrice Ceschina, 1953). The book contains numerous photographs of Ciociare, like Palma and Lisetta, two models very well known in Via Margutta. Further documentation of this tradition is provided by a photo taken by Giuseppe Primoli, entitled *Modelli a Piazza di Spagna* and dated 1890, discovered in the Primoli archives in Rome. See *Picasso a Roma*, op. cit.

[11] Ibid.

[12] For a comparison of the postcards kept by the artist and his sketches, see *Picasso a Roma*, op. cit. See P. Picasso, *Italian Woman with Flower*, 1917, watercolour on paper, 27 × 20 cm, collection of Marina Picasso; and *Italian Woman with Flower* (Dresden: Stengel & Co, 1900), chromolithograph, Paris, Musée national Picasso-Paris, Archives Picasso.

[13] Rafael de Ochoa y Madrazo (1858–1935) was a Spanish artist active in Paris after a period in the studio of his uncle, the painter Raimundo de Madrazo, whose daughter Cecilia married Mariano Fortuny i Marsal, resident in Via Margutta. The son of Carlota de Madra-

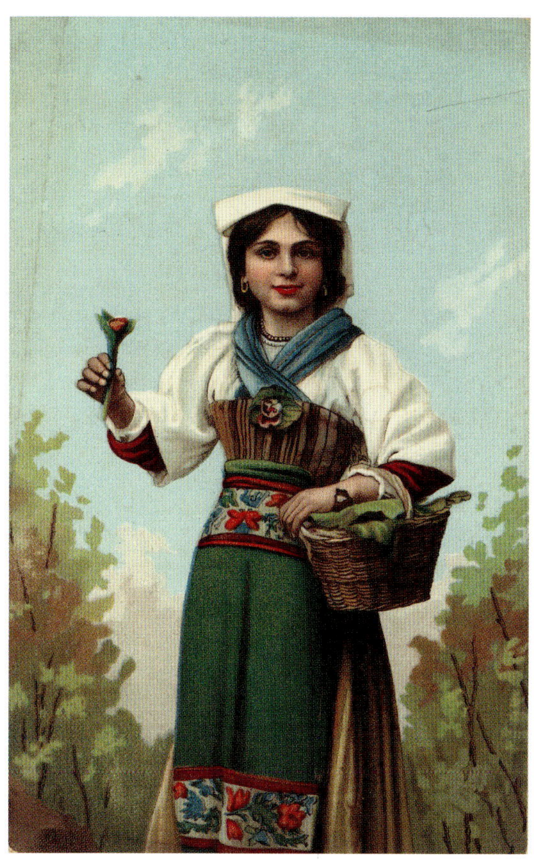

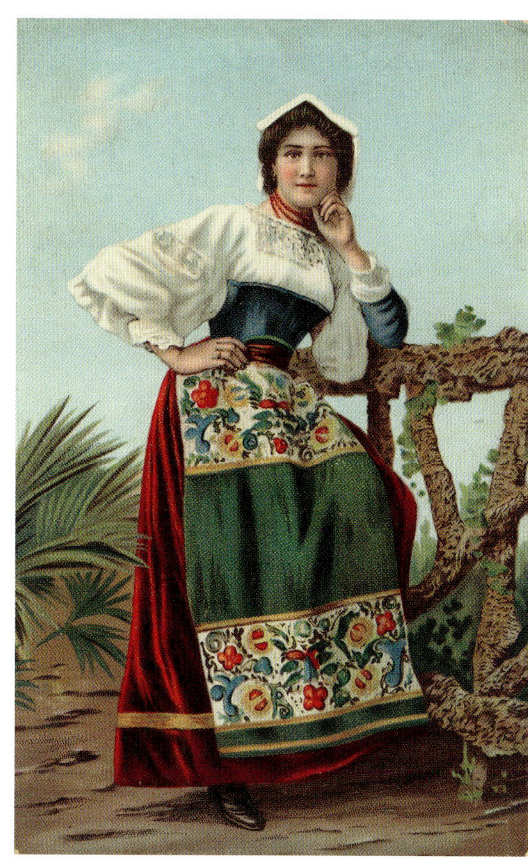

2. *Italienne en costume traditionnel avec une fleur à la main* [Italian Woman in Traditional Costume Holding a Flower (Flower Seller in Piazza di Spagna)], c. 1900
Postcard, 14 x 9 cm
Paris, Musée national Picasso-Paris, Donation of Picasso's heirs, 1992, inv. APPH2762

3. *Italienne en costume traditionnel* [Italian Woman in Traditional Costume], c. 1900
Postcard, 14 x 9 cm
Paris, Musée national Picasso-Paris, Donation of Picasso's heirs, 1992, inv. APPH14388

because of the extraordinary similarities but also because the Rome Express line was the one he took in his journey to Italy, first to Rome and then to Naples in the company of Léonide Massine, Igor Stravinsky, Jean Cocteau, and Sergei Diaghilev.

One enigmatic detail is to be found on the left side of *L'Italienne* just below the arch of the Sant'Angelo bridge, beneath which the Tiber appears in white. It is interesting to note that while the poster shows three arches of the same bridge, Picasso presents three somewhat ambiguous vertical lines of white that suggest the delta of a river. Careful observation of the second postcard in his possession (fig. 2) reveals the extraordinary similarity between the railing and two of these enigmatic elements, to which the artist added a third that can be read as a continuation of the railing or as an anthropomorphic element.

Rafael de Ochoa's poster presents an advertising image of the Italian ideal as circulated above all outside the country, and on such a scale as to be reproduced as though it were a postcard of Rome.

zo and nephew of the better-known José de Madrazo and of the writer Eugenio de Ochoa y Montel, Rafael presumably lived in Paris at the beginning of the twentieth century. There is little biographical information about the artist, who was, however, a friend of Jacques-Émile Blanche, a French writer and painter known above all as a portraitist, and appears beside him in his self-portrait. Blanche's closest friends also include Marcel Proust and Jean Cocteau. Blanche produced portraits of many important figures of the period, including Stravinsky, who was in close contact with the Ballets Russes. Rafael de Ochoa's poster was printed by the Imprimerie Lemercier in Paris (active 1803–1901).

Further evidence of the possible connection between Picasso's works and popular representations include the present author's discovery of a very similar period postcard showing Ciociari in front of St Peter's, which is therefore a possible iconographic source, and a sketch of a Ciociaro and child made by the artist in Rome.[14]

We might therefore surmise that Picasso spent some time seeking out these postcards and photographs, different elements of which he then combined in one image capable of encapsulating all the more popular aspects of the representation of an Italian woman in traditional costume, deliberately distancing the final work from its sources and diverting the viewer into an attempt to interpret a number of intentionally ambiguous elements.

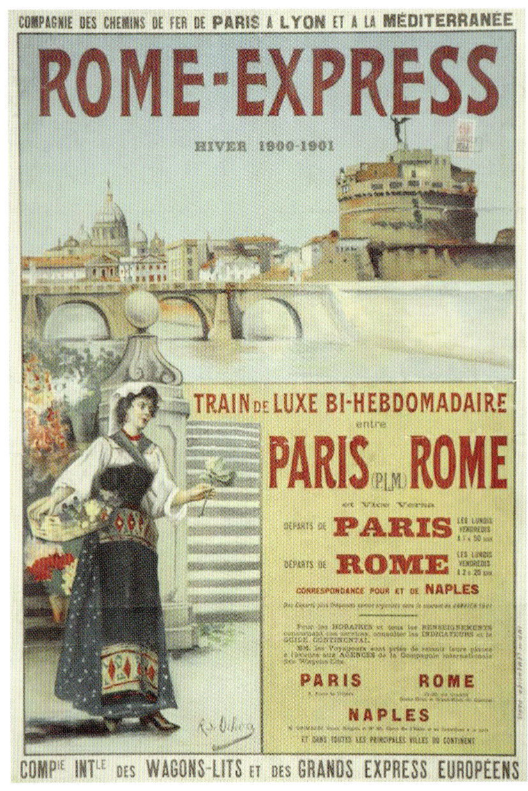

4. Rafael de Ochoa y Madrazo
Poster advertising
the *Rome-Express* train,
Imprimerie Lemercier, Paris 1900

Who is the woman with a necklace?

The second masterpiece produced by Picasso in Rome is *Arlequin et femme au collier* (*Harlequin and a Woman with a Necklace*), again in the synthetic Cubist style (fig. 5).

The artist Gino Severini, who saw the canvas in Paris and admired it greatly, described it as a "work of pictorial poetry at the utmost level of transposition and abstraction [...] entitled *Maschere*".[15] It is necessary to understand that the word *maschera* (singular) can mean *mask* but also *fancy dress, costume, disguise*.

Observation of the work immediately suggests that the *femme au collier* is Columbina, the mistress and female counterpart of Harlequin, both *maschere* or stock characters of the *commedia dell'arte*.

Unlike *L'Italienne*, this work has, to the best of my knowledge, no preparatory drawings or direct iconographic sources in the form of photographs or picture postcards in Picasso archives.

The subject of Harlequin is a topos of Picasso's artistic production from the outset and the artist produced numerous drawings of this character during 1916.[16]

The woman with a necklace is instead an innovation in some respects. But who precisely is this female figure? While examination of Picasso's production in 1916

[14] See *The Online Picasso Project*, E. Mallen, Sam Houston State University. 1997–2016 (https://picasso.shsu.edu/); see J. Palau i Fabre, *Picasso 1917–1926. Des ballets au drame* (Cologne: Köneman, 1999).

[15] G. Severini, *Tempo de l'Effort moderne. Vita di un pittore*, vol. II, ed. P. Pacini (Florence: Vallecchi, 1968; (actually written in 1943–46): 15–20; quoted by G. Carandente, "Il viaggio in Italia: 17 febbraio 1917", in *Picasso. Opere dal 1895 al 1971 dalla collezione Marina Picasso*, exh. cat. (Venice, Palazzo Grassi, 3 May–26 July 1981; Florence: Sansoni, 1981): 48.

[16] *Online Picasso Project*, cit.

[17] Ibid.

[18] Tarenghi's possession of studio in Via Margutta is documented from 1872 to at least 1931. For further details and for the Società degli Acquarellisti, see *Atelier a via Margutta*, op. cit. See also R. Mammucari: *Ottocento Romano* (Rome: Newton & Compton, 2007); and *Acquarellisti romani: suggestioni neoclassiche, decadentismo bizantino, esotismo orientale, realismo borghese* (Città di Castello: Edimond, 2001): 378.

and 1917 reveals various drawings of interest in this connection,[17] it is in fact possible to suggest that the necklace with round beads, whose insertion as the principal element identifying the figure constitutes the real innovation in this masterpiece, is also an iconographic element distinguishing the Ciociara. The necklace and the typical headgear are indeed the hallmarks of the traditional costume. Picasso's *femme au collier* does not appear to wear the usual hanging form of headgear, but is shown in profile with an ambiguous blue rectangular shape on her head. Iconographic research on the Ciociara has, however, revealed the existence of two different types of *mantilla*, one hanging or inverted V shape and the other flat, as can be seen in some period photographs (fig. 6).

Examination of hundreds of representations of this subject has brought to light one in particular that appears directly related to Picasso's female figure (fig. 7). This is a watercolour by the artist Enrico Tarenghi (1848–1938), a member and subsequently a director of the Rome Association of Watercolourists, who had a studio at 48 Via Margutta[18] in the Studi Nardi, quite near the Studi Patrizi at no. 53b. As we can see, the two images bear great similarities in the headgear, which has slipped down onto the shoulders,

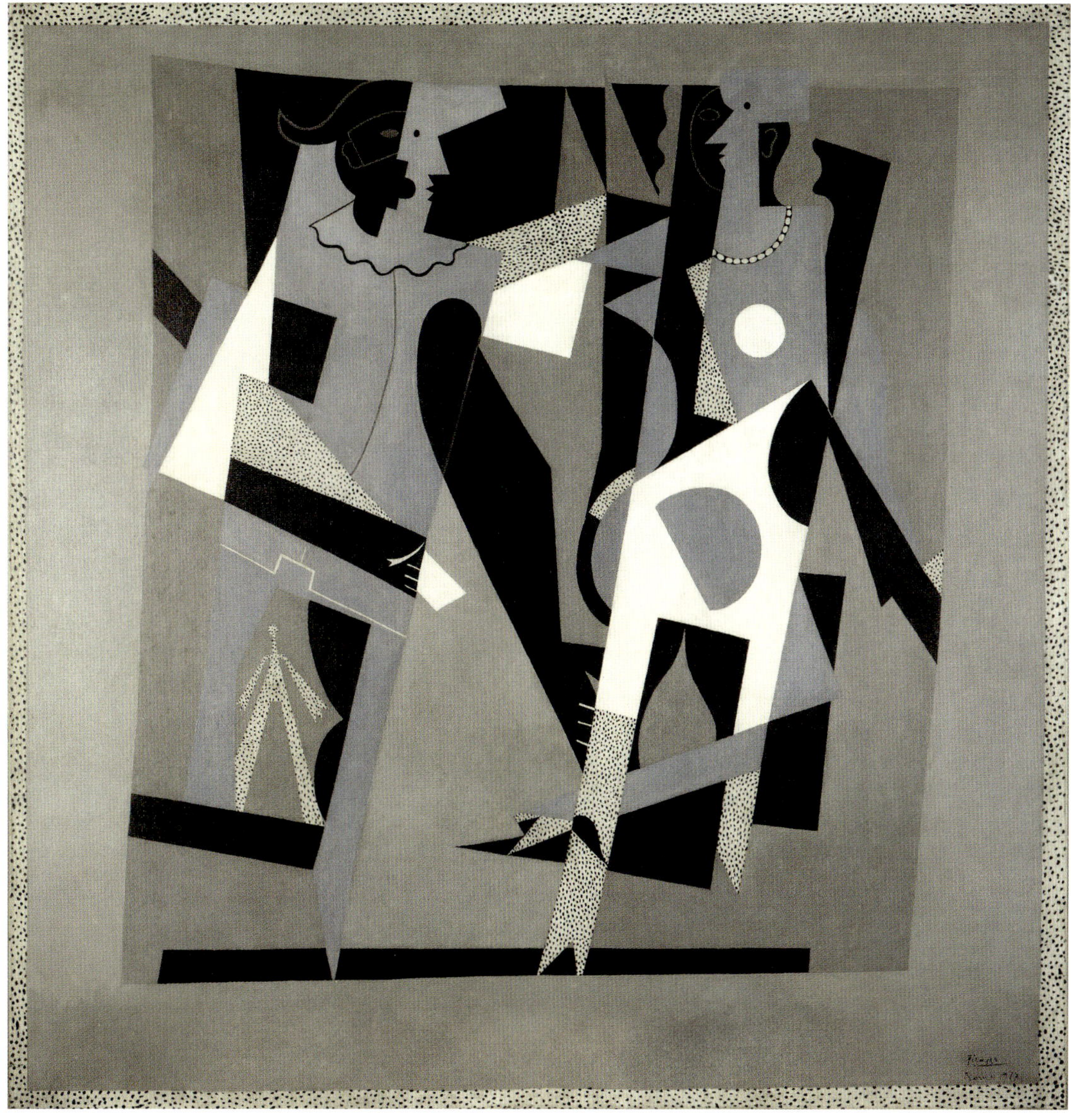

5. Pablo Picasso
Arlequin et femme au collier
[Harlequin and Woman with a Necklace], Rome, 1917
Oil on canvas, 200 x 200 cm
Paris, Georges Pompidou, Musée National d'Art Moderne / Centre de création industrielle, inv. AM 3760

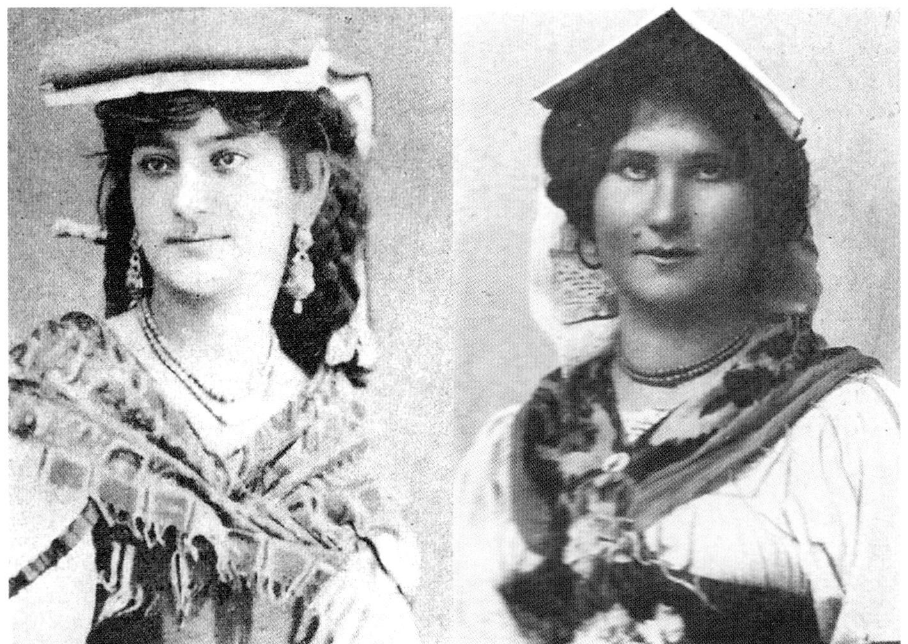

6. Checca Blasi and Luisa Palma, models in traditional costume on Via Margutta

the hair, the pose in profile and of course the necklace. To complete the iconography of the typical costume, the attribute of the basket can be discerned in the curved elements by the left hip of the *femme au collier*, which appear to suggest the presence of a round object. The artist indicates its perimeter with a circle, partly in black and partly dotted, and a blue shape that looks like the bottom of a receptacle.

Another interesting element to emerge from a close study of the subject depicted is Picasso's handling of the lower part of this female figure. The legs appear to be crossed in what is almost a position of rest with the knee bent, as though the figure were leaning all its weight on some support to the right. All these elements can be traced back to one of the postcards that the artist kept and faithfully reproduced in one of his sketches of Italian women (fig. 3).

Picasso focuses on another detail – the feet –, "synthetically" represented by two simple pointed shapes that recall a pair of *ciocie*, the typical traditional footwear of the Lazio region and the source of the term *ciociaro*, meaning wearer of *ciocie*.[19] This too can be seen in Tarenghi's work, where the position of the feet also seems to correspond to that of the *femme au collier*.

It can therefore be deduced that the woman with Harlequin is a female figure in traditional costume and not Columbina.

Moreover, if Harlequin can be identified as a possible alter ego of Picasso in the artist's numerous representations, then *Arlequin et*

[19] M. Santulli, *Ciociaria sconosciuta*, op. cit., 155.
[20] Gerald Hugh Tyrwhitt-Wilson, Lord Berners, was an eccentric figure in English literature in the first half of the 20th century. The photo is published in V. Moncada, *Picasso a Roma*, op. cit., 77, to which readers are referred for further information.

femme au collier can also be traced back to another of his favourite themes, namely the artist and his model, connected in this case with his studio in Via Margutta, a street of artists full of models in traditional costume. The figure of Harlequin, characterized here by his hat, mask, and collar, holds a rectangular object in one hand, represented by white lines to indicate fingers, while the other appears to touch the leg of the *femme au collier*, as though to emphasize a real and direct relationship with the models in the street. *Arlequin et femme au collier* therefore appears to draw not only on the *commedia dell'arte* but also on the artist's first-hand experience of working in Via Margutta.

The only photograph of the artist in his studio at no. 53b shows him with Lord Berners[20] and Stravinsky in front of this masterpiece.

It can thus be concluded that Via Margutta, with its long history and strong traditions, played an important part in Picasso's stay in Rome, and served him as a source of inspiration, just as it has for centuries for all the artists who have lived, worked and produced memorable masterpieces on this important street.

7. Enrico Tarenghi
Traditional Costume of Ciociaria
Alatri, private collection

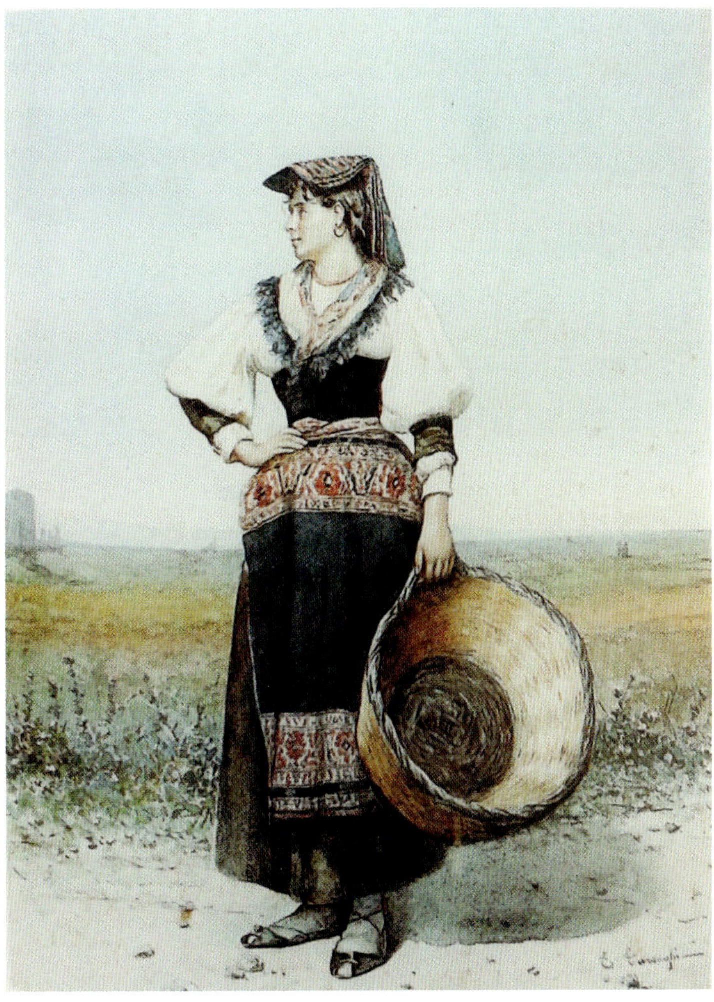

The Genesis of *Parade*

Anunciata von Liechtenstein

Introduction

It was against the backdrop of Paris in the First World War that Jean Cocteau arrived at Pablo Picasso's studio dressed as a harlequin. His hope was to convince his friend not only to paint his portrait, but to collaborate on "a realistic one-act ballet" called *Parade*, "the greatest battle", as he was to describe it, "of the war".[1] The visit coincided with Picasso's painting of *Harlequin* (1915), one of his first attempts at combining figuration with Cubism.

Having always identified with the solitary figure of the Harlequin, Picasso had recently shown new interest in the classical theme of the *commedia dell'arte*. Ever-attentive, Cocteau seized the opportunity to interest him in his latest project. Cocteau's romantic (and, he felt, misunderstood) personality was similarly drawn to the idea of the travelling fair with its references to the human condition, and to the outcast in particular. He must have assumed (rightfully, as it turned out) that *Parade*'s theme of the *forain*, or "low" entertainment, would draw Picasso in.

Picasso's scheme of offsetting the classical with the ground-breaking fitted perfectly with Cocteau's desire of bringing radical Modernism to the traditionalist genre that is ballet. *Parade* would not only act as a playing-field for Picasso to transpose his latest impulses while popularizing his avant-gardist work, but it would do so in the large, three-dimensional scale of a theatrical event. As for Cocteau, it was his third attempt at producing a fairground-themed ballet, which incorporated the everyday to create a Modernist visual language – hence his relentless efforts to bring in the painter whom he believed to hold the keys to *Parade*'s success.

The Build-up

The seeds of *Parade* lay in Cocteau's desire to work with Serge Diaghilev, founder of the Ballets Russes, with the aim of fulfilling the latter's challenge: "étonne-moi" (astound me). Determined to mix classical ballet with a contemporary dialogue in an interdisciplinary approach, Diaghilev was unafraid to use painters with no previous theatrical experience, allowing them to express themselves by means of large-scale three-dimensional works. For Cocteau, the ultimate multi-disciplinarian, Diaghilev's vision coincided perfectly with his own:

> The first time I attended one of Serge Diaghilev's productions – they were dancing Le Pavillon d'Armide – I went with my family. Everything took place far away, behind the footlights, in the midst of that great burning bush that the theatre is for people who are not of its world. Later I met Diaghilev at Madam Sert's. From then on I was a member of the troupe.[2]

Since childhood Cocteau had developed what he would refer to as "theatre-itis," a fascina-

[1] Francis Steegmuller, *Cocteau: A Biography* (Boston: Little, Brown, 1970): 82.
[2] Cocteau quoted in Francis Steegmuller, *Cocteau: A Biography* (Boston: Little, Brown, 1970): 68–69.

tion with the action – as much onstage as off, be it in the wings or among the audience.[3] *Parade* was focused on this interest. The trope of the "parade" was meant as a teaser – a sort of theatrical trailer – designed to seduce the audiences into the performance. Cocteau's piece was to be an inversion of the traditional idea: since the drama, per se, never materializes, the parade itself becomes the performance. (Interestingly, the ballet prefigured such works of high Modernism as Luigi Pirandello's *Six Characters in Search of an Author* [1921] – in which the protagonists look for a playwright who never turns up.) Cocteau's first commission for the Ballets Russes, *Le Dieu Bleu* (1912), was poorly received, and considered too folkloric and traditional by the troupe, which was striving for more experimental horizons. It was soon afterwards, while walking back from a performance together, that Diaghilev threw down the challenge to "Astound me!"[4] This was to lead to the revolutionary work that is *Parade*.

Cocteau's first attempt at a circus-themed ballet was *David*. The setting was a booth in a fairground, outside which an acrobat would be performing a parade for a spectacle to be held inside. This scenario, which would serve as the basis for *Parade*, followed Stravinsky's ballet, *Rite of Spring* (1913). Later to be associated with the violence and barbarism of the First World War, it reflected the search for a new artistic expression in response to a world in turmoil. As a result Cocteau asked Stravinsky to write the score for *David* so that he could "astound" Diaghilev by means of his own Modernist language. In the end, however, Stravinsky declined, seeing the project as too complicated and too close to his own ballet *Petrushka*. Though their relationship floundered as a result, it had shown Cocteau the war offered an opportunity for artistic renewal. This would lead him to *Parade* and his collaboration with both Picasso and the composer Satie.

It was in this context that Cocteau began to seek out Cubists in the hope of getting them to collaborate on his second circus-themed project, a modern French adaptation of Shakespeare's *A Midsummer Night's Dream*. This, too, would prove inspirational to *Parade*. The production was to be staged at the Cirque Médrano in Montmartre, and would star the Fratellini brothers, internationally renowned circus clowns. The scenario was based on the transfiguration of everyday life into a fantastical fairground universe. Transposition from one world to the other occurred as soon as the characters crossed the magical circle of the stage, as per Cocteau's obsession with blurring the lines between auditorium and spectacle. The decor and costumes were to be Cubist in line with his idea of incorporating avant-garde with dance. As for the music, it was his wish to "astound" Diaghilev that led him to Eric Satie. The eccentric and idiosyncratic composer had spent part of his career playing at the Montmartre cabaret venue Le Chat Noir, thus developing his sense for popular ditties and interaction with the audience. This made him ideal for Cocteau. The theme

[3] Franck Ries, *The Dance Theatre of Jean Cocteau* (Dance Books Ltd., March 2, 2015): 2–3.
[4] Steegmuller, 82.
[5] Deborah Menaker Rothschild, *Picasso's "Parade": from street to stage: ballet by Jean Cocteau, score by Erik Satie, choreography by Léonide Massine* (New York: in association with the Drawing Center, 1991): 44.
[6] Steegmuller, 136.

of *A Midsummer Night's Dream* allowed the collaborators to mix the "low" art of the circus and the "high" art of Shakespeare's play, originally set in classical Athens but transposed by Cocteau to the circus. This prefiguration of *Parade* in *A Midsummer Night's Dream* is perhaps most clearly demonstrated in Satie's papers. A manuscript score entitled *Five Grimaces for A Midsummer Night's Dream*, found after Satie's death, showed the composer applying the same combination of classical and popular orchestration that he would later use in his score for *Parade*.[5]

Meanwhile, whatever the reason for the project's abandonment, Cocteau had begun developing another project, sparked by his meeting with Satie. In a letter to a friend he describes it as "more modern and original than *Midsummer Night's Dream* could ever be". The letter also contains the first mention of Picasso in association with "a much transformed *David*" – namely *Parade*.[6]

The Met Documents

In 2016 a series of documents relating to the conceptual development of *Parade* and Picasso's involvement in its inception were rediscovered at New York's Metropolitan Museum of Art. Their provenance is the archive of William S. Lieberman, curator at the Modern Department. Forgotten since his death in 2005, they are now housed at the museum's Watson Library.

A notebook headed in Cocteau's hand with the *Dictionnaire Larousse*'s definition of the word parade – "Parade: scène burlesque, jouée à la porte d'un théâtre forain pour attirer le monde" (a burlesque scene played outside a sideshow booth to entice spectators inside) – lays out the foundation for the work. A similar such notebook, now at the New York Public Library, was given to Satie during Cocteau's leave in April-May 1916 with the same handwritten inscription on its cover. However, it is blank inside, suggesting his wish for Satie to include his own ideas. The Met version, on the other hand, has Cocteau's libretto of *Parade* followed by descriptions of its three characters.

The setting is the *forain*, a form of travelling fair which had been popular in France since the seventeenth century. The resulting incongruity allows not just for the juxtaposition of different artistic styles and mediums, but for a culture clash between the "high art" of ballet and "low art" of the travelling fair. The curtain rises to a fair-booth in front of which Cocteau's three characters – a Chinese conjurer, a little American girl, and an acrobat – will perform their parade with the aim of luring the public inside. Mistaking the parade for the actual performance, the audience never gets to see the show itself. From an offstage megaphone disembodied voices praise the qualities of the performers. Inspiration for this came from the vulgarity of fair promoters (managers, or "carnival-barkers", as they were known), as well as the advertisers of the day, basically people paid to bellow out announcements in the streets. Cocteau's emphasis on the "drama that occurs inside" and the "the drama that is missed by those that have stayed outside" has a twofold objective. On the one hand it symbolizes the real-life drama playing out in the artist's mind; on the other, it leaves the spectacle itself to the audience's imagination, thereby turning the latter into active participants of the show. In this notebook, which represents the early stages of *Parade's* development, Cocteau already bills himself with Picasso. "The drama which did not occur for the people having stayed outside," says the libretto's last page, "was by Jean Cocteau, Erik Satie, Pablo Picasso." A preliminary draft for this libretto includes several versions of a poem addressed to Picasso, thus further stressing the artist's involvement in the work's nascent stages.

Two sets of further notes written on large tissue-papers, no doubt from the bundle of work given to Satie during Cocteau's leaves of absence from the war front, give more detailed descriptions of the characters and the Modernist elements envisaged for the work. The barkers' announcements were to be delivered in two voices, a contralto and a child's, thereby adding to the dramatic effect. Numerous references are made to Cocteau's *trompe-l'oreille* (a pun on *trompe-l'œil*), a sort of aural transposition of Cubist collages. They include sounds from every-day life, among them a siren, a dynamo, a typewriter, an express train, and an airplane. Eventually, disapproving of such notions as artificial, Picasso would replace the carnival barkers by onstage "managers" dressed as Cubist constructions. Their aim would be to introduce the acts of the three performers: the Chinese conjurer, the little American girl, and the Acrobat, without shedding their vulgar promotional imagery.

A second notebook, handwritten by Cocteau and entitled "*Études pour Parade*", reveal the production's unfolding. For the first time, reference is made to three black (on-stage) Managers instead of the original disembodied voices. Allusions to a Red Plan, a Plan of the Harlequins and a Theatre Curtain in Prelude invoke what would end up being Picasso's masterpiece theatre curtain. As for the Plan for a Reduced Stage, it might be a reference to Picasso's Cubist-inspired set. However, the frequent mention of sounds throughout the notebook reveal Cocteau's insistence on their being included. As with all collaborations, Cocteau's initial ideas were improved upon and altered by his partners. Another example of this is the musical score, also to be found in the Met documents. Dated 1917 and entitled "Parade, ballet réaliste" (most likely a copyist's manuscript), it came later than the original score at the Bibliothèque nationale de France, and shows the initial role of Cocteau's Chinese Conjurer as having been abridged in favour of Picasso's first Manager.[7]

Picasso and Cocteau: A Fractious Relationship

As the Met documents make clear, Cocteau's conception of *Parade* included Picasso – hence his relentless pursuit of the artist throughout 1915–16. Midway through this

[7] Christopher Schiff, Music and Arts Librarian, The George and Helen Ladd Library, Bates College.

[8] "Dear friend – do not be afraid: it works. What a great subject! I think I am there and well! What luck! Where are you putting up? A word if you would? Your old accomplice: ES. P.S. Valentine Gross tells me you are scared. No? When are you coming to Paris? I would like to see you. There are so many things to do that alone I am dumbfounded. It's crazy! Bravo! Long live Cocteau!" Documents concerning *Parade*, Watson Library Special Collections.

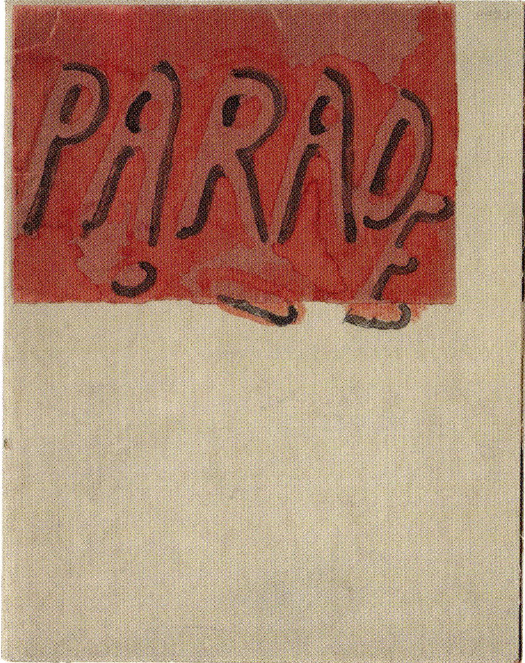

1. Manuscript of Jean Cocteau for the libretto of *Parade*, 1916–17
New York, The Metropolitan Museum of Art, Thomas J. Watson Library, Bequest of William S. Lieberman

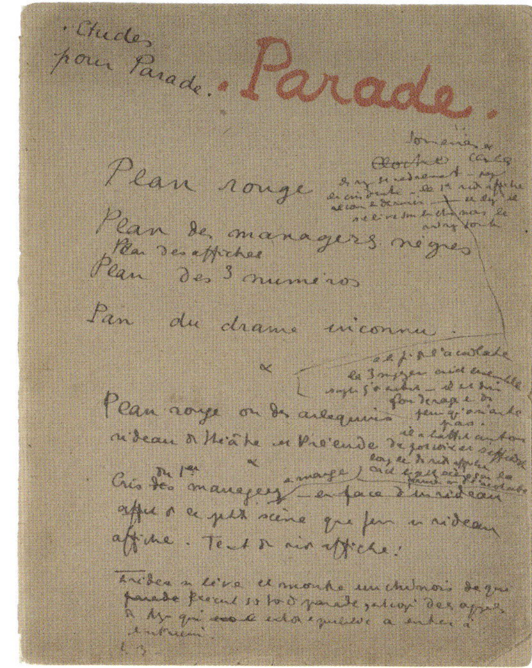

2. Notebook with Cocteau's handwritten notes on *Parade*, 1916–17
New York, The Metropolitan Museum of Art, Thomas J. Watson Library, Bequest of William S. Lieberman

charm offensive, Cocteau had to return to the front, where he was stationed in an ambulance unit. His main preoccupation (as his letters home and the *Parade* documents from this period bear out) lay in convincing both Picasso and Diaghilev that *Parade* was a project worth their while. A further concern was his own developments for the project, especially its musical aspect with Satie. As we have seen from the Met documents, the lyrical and realistic "*trompe-l'oreille*" sounds, sourced from the everyday, were of particular importance to him.

Satie to Cocteau, 18 May 1916:

Cher ami – N'ayez pas peur: ça marche. Quel chic sujet! Je crois que j'y suis et bien! Veine! Ou donc perchez-vous?
Un mot voulez-vous? Votre Vieux Complice: ES
P.S. Valentine Gross me dit que vous avez la frousse. Non? Quand passez-vous à Paris? J'aimerais vous voir, il y a tellement de choses à faire que tout seul, j'en suis baba. C'est fou et chic! Bravo! Vive Cocteau![8]

Throughout this period Cocteau dedicated his leaves of absence to a twofold mission. The first was to lure Picasso into a venture that would imply the abandonment of his closely-knit bohemian left bank (*rive gauche*) group in favour of what many of the latter would see as the bourgeois glitters of the Ballets Russes; its second, to convince Diaghilev to push the boundaries of his productions towards a truly avant-garde work.

(At the time of *Parade*'s beginnings in Paris, the artistic *rive gauche* and the bourgeois *rive droite* were intellectually and artistically divided. It was this that led Cocteau to call *Parade* the biggest battle of the war: "There was no political left or right, there existed only an artistic left and an artistic right, and we were in the patriotism of art… coaxing the Cubists out of their isolation, persuading them to abandon their hermetic Montmartre folklore of pipes, packages of tobacco, guitars, and old newspapers…"[9])

Initially irritated by Cocteau's pushiness and dandyism, Picasso eventually yielded to the distraction and amusement he offered. Indeed, with the outbreak of war Picasso had been separated from many of his closest friends. Apollinaire and Braque, for instance, were at the front, whilst others, such as his German-born dealer Daniel-Henry Kahnweiler, had been expelled as enemy aliens. Eva Gouel, too, the first woman whom Picasso had considered marrying, had died after a long and painful illness. By 1916 Picasso had began seeing Paquerette, a model of Paul Poiret very much in vogue at the time, as well as such people as the wealthy Chilean socialite Eugenia Errazuriz, a patron of the arts and a great friend of Cocteau's. As for the latter's friendship with Satie (who swung from group to group), it grew with the emergence of *Parade*.

Picasso's rapprochement with Cocteau and introduction to the avant-garde further encouraged the latter's interest in including avant-gardist and Cubist elements into the work. "Picasso," declared Cocteau, "was my great encounter."[10] The Spaniard's collaborative input stems from his ability to strip down Cocteau's ideas and translate them into a Modernist idiom.

Picasso to Cocteau, October 1916:

> *Mon cher Jean, J'ai vu Kisling hier soir au cinéma. Si vous voulez me voir venez toujours les matins. (Encore dans déménageurs) Bien à vous et à toi, Picasso.*[11]

Artistically speaking, Cubism's growing intellectualism had started to put a strain on Picasso. Furthermore, having been controversial even before the war, Cubism was now being dragged into the discourse of patriotism, becoming associated with the German enemy. For all Picasso's concern with artistic renewal, this disapproval could hardly have left him indifferent. Never having abandoned figuration and his painting's classical roots, he was now considering them through different eyes while continuing to draw on his Cubist discoveries, often mixing these diametrically different genres in a single canvas. He began his return to figuration through smaller-scaled still-lifes, slowly moving towards monumentality and the human figure as in *Seated Man* (1915). Furthermore, as Elizabeth Cowling notes: "Picasso made innumerable drawings which appear to be plans for figurative Cubist constructions, but apart from a tiny paper *Guitarist,* he had taken none of them beyond the sketch stage."[12]

[9] Steegmuller, 139.
[10] Steegmuller, 137.
[11] "My dear Jean, I saw Kisling yesterday night at the cinema. If you would like to see me come any time in the morning. (Still with the movers) Ever yours, Picasso." Documents concerning *Parade*, Watson Library Special Collections.
[12] Elizabeth Cowling, *Picasso: Style and Meaning* (London: Phaidon, 2002): 296.
[13] Steegmuller, 165.
[14] "My dear Jean, let's see each other at my place tomorrow afternoon at six, and if you can we will dine later together at Diaghilev's. Your friend, Picasso." Documents concerning Parade, Watson Library Special Collections.
[15] Steegmuller, 169.
[16] "Dear friend – "Parade" is composed entirely, Great! It is while coming home during the night that "Parade" saw the light of day – the "first day of the year" – on paper. "Parade" music, of course. My role is finished, dear friend; yours is beginning. It starts well. It will be – and it is – the first time that a ballet is really done by a poet. It is justice. The spirit (poetry) dominated the material (music). The same will take place on the side of the painter, believe me. I had the vision of it a few days ago. And I saw it well. Your old: ES." Documents concerning *Parade*, Watson Library Special Collections.

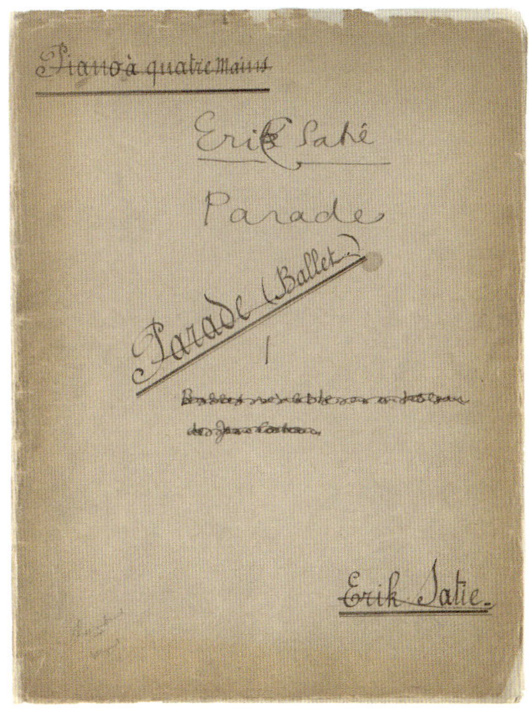

3. Satie's Musical score of *Parade, Ballet réaliste*, 1916–17
New York, The Metropolitan Museum of Art, Thomas J. Watson Library, Bequest of William S. Lieberman

The introduction of the stage, with its large-scale, three-dimensionality, offered him a break from the increasingly restrictive aspects of Cubism whilst allowing him to explore a new and tempting theme. On 24 August 1916 Cocteau and Satie were finally able to wire their friend and supporter Valentine Gross the good news that "Picasso is doing *Parade* with us".[13]

Cocteau's next campaign was to target Diaghilev.

Picasso to Cocteau, 6 October 1916:

> *Mon cher Jean, Venez demain après midi à six heures chez moi et si vous pouvez nous dînerons ensemble après chez Diaghilev – votre ami, Picasso*[14]

The dinner was a great success. It gave Picasso and Cocteau the opportunity to meet their third collaborator Léonide Massine, who had been chosen to dance the Chinese Conjurer and choreograph the ballet.[15] Massine, who had studied acting and dancing in Moscow but for whom *Parade* would be a first venture into choreography, was a novice to contemporary Western culture, making him the ideal artist for the project. By combining his lack of choreographical training with the traditions of classical dance, Picasso and Cocteau would inspire him to a new choreographical language. Finally, at the start of 1917 Diaghilev came on board, at which point a trip was planned to his headquarters in Rome. More good news was to follow in a letter from Satie to Cocteau dated 1 January 1917:

> *Cher Vieux – "Parade" est composé entièrement, Chic! C'est cette nuit en rentrant que "Parade" a vu le jour – le "jour de l'an" – sur le papier. "Parade" musique, bien entendu. Mon rôle est terminé, cher gros; le votre commence. Il commence bien. Ce sera – et c'est – la première fois (foie de veau*) qu'un ballet est réellement fait par un poète. C'est justice. L'Esprit (poésie) domine la Matière (musique) Le même évènement aura lieu du côté du peintre croyez-le. J'en ai eu la vision il y a quelques jours. Et j'ai bien vu. Votre vieux: ES *Excusez cette plaisanterie.*[16]

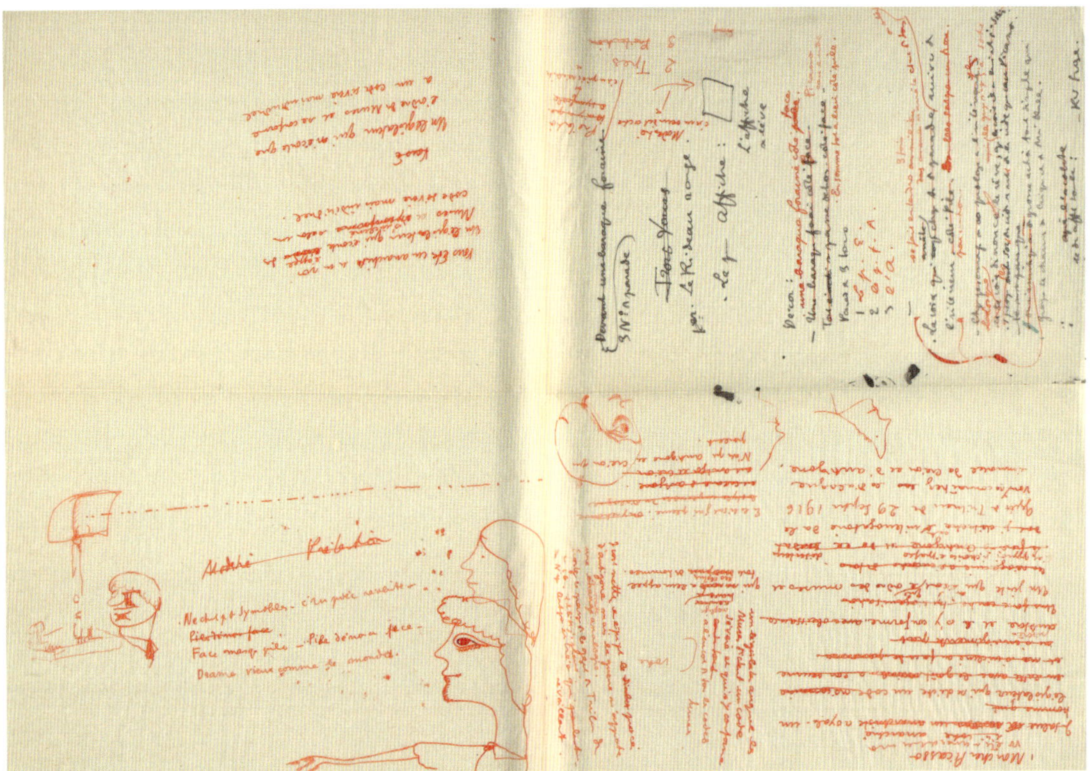

4. A preliminary loose-leaf draft by Jean Cocteau for the libretto of *Parade*. Included are several versions of a poem addressed to Picasso, 1916–17
New York, The Metropolitan Museum of Art, Thomas J. Watson Library, Bequest of William S. Lieberman

Satie's letter is ambiguous. Although it announces the accomplishment of *Parade*'s musical aspect and highlights its collaborative element, many changes to Cocteau's original conception had occurred and more were to come. The importance of poetry and the poet's role, which he underlines, is followed by the equal weight of Picasso's art on the production. Whether Cocteau knew it or not, his contribution would soon be overshadowed by Picasso's.

Trouble for Cocteau

Once Picasso had decided to join in, he did so wholeheartedly, reassessing those among Cocteau's original ideas which he deemed over-complicated, overly-narrated, or excessively lyrical – especially the verbal and aural enhancements referred to in Cocteau's notebooks, with their free associations evoking what the viewers would never see. As the Met documents show, Cocteau's collaboration with Picasso led him to rein in his tendencies towards the exotic and the alien. This is best seen in the progression of the Managers, who, after starting off as voices meant to reflect a modernist language followed by onstage black characters illustrating a theme of universality, were finally replaced with Picasso's Cubist managers. By liberating them from their literary and cultural associations, Picasso was able to create a jarring new Cubist visual.[17]

No doubt irked by the obstruction of Cocteau's music and set-designs in *Parade's* advance towards the truly avant-garde, a similar fate to his voices befell his gimmicky *trompe l'oreille,* the extra-musical sounds comparable with the Cubist notion of "auditory scraps". Eventually a compromise was reached, and though the voices were removed Cocteau's sounds were kept for the time being. Later, writing about one of his first encounters with Picasso, he gushes about the painter's influence on him.

> Lying around were lowly bits of scrap which Picasso was gradually rehabilitating by incorporating them into his works. Picasso has much more admiration for what he can make use of than for the finished product... From him I learned to waste less time gaping open-mouthed at things that are of no use to me, and to understand that a ditty sung by a street-singer, if listened to for what one can get out of it, may prove more rewarding than Götterdämmerung.[18]

In the end, having finished the first draft of *Parade*'s music, Satie decided not to join the Roman trip, preferring to continue his work in the quietness of his home. However, the numerous letters to be found among the Met documents show frequent requests for updates and changes to the sound with the aim of adapting the score – and commensurate satisfaction at the shape the project was taking.

Satie to Cocteau in Italy on 29 March 1917:

> *Cher Jean – Mais oui les changements me vont. Je leur reproche une chose très grave pour la* partition *d'orchestre: leur manque d'exactitude; car je ne saisis point l'endroit précis où ils se manifestent. Soyez donc, cher vieux, très précis sur ce point... P.S. Écrivez vite mon travail d'orchestre est suspendu.*[19]

A further, undated letter from Satie to Cocteau in Rome, tells him that the orchestration is finished but requests details on future changes and asks about the typewriter (whose sound Cocteau had wanted to include).[20]

Italy

On 17 February 1917 Picasso and Cocteau left Paris from the Gare de Lyon to continue their work in Rome, where Diaghilev and his Ballets Russes were stationed during the war. "Long live our followers!" Picasso would later remark to Francis Poulenc. "It's thanks to them that we seek novelty."[21] In addition to providing the source of such renewal, Italy would usher Picasso into a new artistic phase. It was in Rome, a city rooted in Classical Antiquity whilst contributing to Modernism through the Futurist movement, that *Parade* came to life. Having booked them in the Grand Hotel de Russie, Diaghilev had arranged for Picasso's use of one of the Patrizi studios on Via Margutta: "I cannot forget Picasso's studio in Rome", Cocteau would later

[17] Rothschild, 24.

[18] Steegmuller, 137.

[19] "Dear Jean – Indeed the changes suit me. I reproach them one very grave thing for the orchestra score: their lack of exactitude; for I do not understand the exact point where they manifest themselves. So, old friend, be very precise on that point... P.S. write quickly my orchestra work is in suspense." Documents concerning *Parade*, Watson Library Special Collections.

[20] Documents concerning *Parade*, Watson Library Special Collections.

[21] Francis Poulenc, *Moi et mes amis* (Paris and Geneva: La Palatine, 1963); English edition *My Friends and Myself* (London: Dobson Books, 1978): 82.

write. "A little box contained the model for *Parade* – the houses, the trees, the booth. On a table, looking out towards the Villa Medici, Picasso had painted the Chinese magician, the managers, the American girl, the horse."[22]

As Picasso's first trip outside Spain and France, Rome was to leave a lasting impression on him. Inspiration would come to him at every street corner, from the Renaissance and Baroque churches to the traditionally-dressed flower girls on the Spanish Steps. It also marked his first contact with the Ballet Russes. Only when confronted with its classical dance roots was he able to juxtapose its high art against his avant-gardist ideas. Much of their time was spent at the Cantina Taglioni, the basement dance studio where Massine was providing an air of renewal and Modernism not only in the company's choreography but also its repertoire, with the introduction of three new ballets. It was during the rehearsals of one of the latter that Picasso laid eyes on the dancer Olga Khokhlova, who would become his first wife. While he had already been sketching the dancers with the aim of getting to know the workings of the ballet, this would further draw him into their world. In addition Diaghilev had brought two avant-garde Russian artists, Natalia Goncharova and her husband Mikhail Larionov, to work on the set designs of another of Massine's choreographical works, *Les Contes Russes*. By assisting them in their decor and costumes Picasso was able to gain access to the workings of the stage. In March the rest of Diaghilev's company arrived from New York, where they had been touring, while Stravinsky came over from Switzerland to conduct the *Firebird*. It was through their common search for "regenerating Classicism with Modernism" that Picasso and Stravinsky developed a life-long friendship.[23] Meanwhile Cocteau's letters to his mother attest to a homesickness aggravated by jealousy over his idol's new-found bond with Stravinsky.

It was in the Cantina Taglioni that *Parade*'s choreography came to life along with Cocteau's characters, who until now had only existed in his lengthy and cryptic descriptions. Given Massine's lack of familiarity with of Western popular culture, it was left to Cocteau to demonstrate the variety of acts and movements of the music-hall performers. Massine's training as an actor and his study of *commedia dell'arte* proved vital for the miming element so essential in bringing the characters to life, especially since the removal of the aural enhancements. The collaborators' reliance on Cocteau's free associations resulted in a stylization and exaggeration of the gestures and routines inspired by popular spectacles and everyday life, thereby creating a set of completely novel movements. The acrobat act was the only one nearer in form to traditional ballet, and Massine insisted on the addition of a second female acrobat, to enable a pas de deux.

The Little American Girl's choreography harked back to the American movie stars Pearl White and Mary Pickford. As such, she was to dance to a jazzy ragtime tune appropriated by Satie from Irving Berlin, and first seen by him in the Parisian cabarets. The Chinese Conjurer's choreography was based on similar real-life acts, greatly in vogue at the time. As for the Managers by which Picasso replaced Cocteau's voices, to the delight of the others and Diaghilev's support, they finally took shape as giant Cubist constructions. Each was to draw on a mix of cultural and personal imagery to bring out his characteristics. Thus the American Manager, who was to introduce the Little American Girl, would be dressed as a cowboy with a skyscraper on his back. He holds a megaphone and a small poster-board reading "PA/RA/DE". The French Manager, who was to introduce the Chinese Conjurer, was conceived as a caricature of Diaghilev. Embodying a sort of pompous elegance, he would wear a top-hat and tails and holds a baton. A third Manager, a minstrel in blackface on horseback, would introduce the acrobats. Given their restrictive costumes, a suitable dance had to be composed by Massine, its stomping and shaking delighting Cocteau for its novel form of choreography. "When Picasso showed us his sketches," he would later write, "we understood how effective it would be to exploit the contrast between the three "real" characters as "chromos" pasted on a canvas, and the more solemnly transported inhuman, or superhuman, characters who would become, in fact, the false reality on stage, to the point of reducing the real dancers to the stature of puppets."[24]

The jerky and flickering movements were drawn from the burgeoning moving film genre and from marionettes. Rome's puppet theatres proved of great inspiration, not to mention the local cinema. (Italian Futurism had created one of the first cinematic avant-garde movements, with films such as Enrico Guazzoni's *Quo Vadis* [1913] and Giovanni Pastrone's *Cabiria* [1914]). This would doubtless fuel Cocteau's already established use of cinema as exemplified in his little American girl. Cubism, too, played an informative part. Through Picasso, Massine had developed a growing interest in it, owning several Cubist works in his art collection. In parallel, Cocteau's ever increasing use of Cubist ideas going back to his Medrano project, had reached new heights through his proximity with Picasso.

The walls of Rome, too, with their graffiti commingling the classical and the vulgar, played their parts. *Soyons vulgaires!* (Let us be vulgar!), observes Cocteau in his Roman notebook, a sensibility he shared with Picasso – the search for poetry in the everyday.[25] This self-exhortation, which twice appears in Cocteau's Roman notebook, is confirmed in a letter to Massine. "My dear Massine," he wrote, "you will never be sleazy, partake therefore of sleaze. Long live sleaze… Don't forget *Parade* is in the street."[26]

Within the busy atmosphere of the Ballets Russes, life in Rome was mostly about work. Nevertheless, when time allowed, Picasso, Stravinsky, and Cocteau – and occasionally Massine (when free of work commitments

[22] Steegmuller, 177.
[23] John Richardson, *A Life of Picasso*, Vol. II (New York: Random House, 2007): 23.
[24] Cocteau translated in Rothschild, 90.
[25] Rothschild, 61.
[26] Cocteau in Rothschild, 61.

and of Diaghilev) – would set out to discover the city's many museums and churches as well as its street life. Accounts vary but it can be assumed that they visited the Vatican and the Sistine Chapel. While Picasso recorded his impressions of the Villa Borghese sculptures, Cocteau wrote vivid commentaries on Raphael and Michelangelo. Renaissance and Baroque art could be seen in every public space, be it in the streets or the countless churches of the Eternal City. Such was the mark left on him by Bernini's sculptures that Picasso would draw from them in future set designs. Among others, he admired his *Elephant and Obelisk* on the Piazza della Minerva, as well as Michelangelo's *Risen Christ* in the eponymous church.[27] (The square was the site of the dancers' hotel, where Picasso would attempt in vain to sneak into Olga's room.)

Through Stravinsky, the collaborators of *Parade* were also introduced to a Roman vaudeville theatre, "a dirty little music-hall" with "a variety program and an orchestra à *tout crever*," which fitted with their intended atmosphere.[28] Another such inspiration was the Teatro dei Piccoli, a marionette theatre favoured by Cocteau and Picasso, and referred to in their postcards. In one such missive to his mother, Cocteau wrote: "The puppets made fairyland much more convincing than human performers ever could."[29] Massine, too, would draw from the marionette shows, especially for the movements of the little American girl. For Picasso an outcome of this lay in the relationship between the giant Cubist Managers, whose dwarfing of the "realistic" characters made them appear like puppets.

According to Picasso, one of a stage-designer's most important tasks is the modifying, magnifying or intensifying of a line, colour, or pattern according to its impact at a certain distance from the stage.[30] This would be reflected in the clean-cut lines, bold designs, and bright colours of his decors and costumes. Fortunato Depero, a Futurist hired by Diaghilev to assist in the creation of the giant Cubist constructions of managers and the papier-mâché horse, had been trained as a puppeteer, thereby helping to consolidate Picasso's budding stage know-how.

Barely a month into their Roman stay, the group went to Naples, a city that was to prove even more stimulating to Picasso. He felt at home in this Mediterranean port city, reminiscent as it was of his Spanish roots. The bustling streets and haphazard architecture would provide a source of inspiration for the set designs situated by Cocteau in an urban setting. At the end of his Italian stay, Picasso would pay Naples a second visit, this time without Cocteau and for a longer duration, to attend a performance of the Ballets Russes at the San Carlo Opera House.

The collaborators' fascination with Neapolitan street life stemmed from both its suitability for *Parade* and Picasso's attraction to both the mundane and the city's rich theatrical tradition, steeped as it was in the *commedia dell'arte*. In search of this heritage they visited the San Martino Museum with its collec-

[27] Cowling, 317.
[28] Richardson, 8.
[29] Cocteau quoted in Richardson, 10.
[30] Richardson, 11.
[31] Cowling, 302.
[32] Rothschild, 53.

tions of popular culture, such as the nativity *crèches*, puppets, masks and costumes relating to Pulcinella and the *commedia dell'arte*. On his second visit, with Stravinsky, he continued this search for relics of the city's great theatrical past, seeking out old Neapolitan watercolours and prints. It is probably during this trip that Picasso bought a reproduction of a tavern scene by the nineteenth-century painter Achille Vianelli, which is considered to be one of the most direct inspirations for *Parade's* drop-curtain.[31] Most influential of all were the improvised performances riddling the Neapolitan streets and crowded "one-room theatres", whose impact lay in the brevity of the works and their ploy of interaction with the audience. Similarly, with its emphasis on mime and reliance on improvisation, the *commedia dell'arte* provided a source for Massine's choreography. As Deborah Menaker Rothschild notes, the spirit of the *commedia* – to which nearly all forms of anti-authoritarian street entertainment trace their origin – is present in every Diaghilev production to which Picasso contributed.[32]

From Naples they visited Herculaneum and Pompeii, further awakening Picasso's enthusiasm for Antiquity. Their fragmented columns contributed to his set design for *Parade* alongside Naples's decaying rococo architecture. His greatest thrill was the discovery of the vulgar and erotic elements pre-existing the brothels of Naples, borne out by the Pompeian objects, paintings and murals which he reproduced in his notebooks and wrote home about. Perhaps his greatest revelation, however, was the Farnese collection of Greek and Roman sculptures, whose monumentality would be used as an inspiration for *Parade*'s set design.

Cocteau's Torments and the Theatre of the Mind

However, trouble was brewing. The modernistic, frivolous, and self-promotional elements that Cocteau wanted to integrate into *Parade* had been irritating Picasso throughout the partnership. Back in Rome they ended up annoying Diaghilev to such an extent that he sent the Frenchman back to Paris to do what he did best, namely drum up publicity for *Parade*. The Met documents bear out the metaphor that Cocteau was trying to bring across, namely that the artist's creative process is as inaccessible as the spectacle in *Parade* is to its audience. Cocteau's conception of *Parade* was very much a metaphor for his own identity as an artist, unable as he was to be taken seriously due to his failings as an artist and pursuit of fame. The work is thus a bid to look beyond the fun and flashiness of the parade into something more serious and profound. By creating an inverted drama played both onstage and off, he was representing the unattainable reality of the creative process: the actual show, in other words, never takes place, not just because the audience fails to join the parade, but because it is constricted by the reality of the theatre itself. His return to Paris did in effect cut him off from the creative process, and he aborted his aspirations for the work's end result. "Our parade," he wrote referring to the opening performance, "was so far from what I would have wished that I never went to see it in front. I made it a point to stay in the wings..."[33]

With Cocteau out of the way, back in Rome the finalized conception of Picasso's onstage Cubist managers could finally be put in place. Their role was to advertise the performance and expand on the characters of the performers. Ironically Cocteau a born propagandist, which is what had attracted Diaghilev to him in the first place, had been sent back to Paris to do just that.

Cocteau to Massine:

> *Mon très cher Massine, Pourquoi Diaghilev me donne t-il tant de mal et ne s'adresse-t-il jamais à moi? J'en dirais de me supprimer complètement même sur l'affiche de* Parade *– mes aspirations dépassent le journalisme, comme les vôtres. J'ai fait écrire la partition mots par mots à Satie, j'ai amené Picasso contre tous ses principes (quoi qu'il puisse dire) j'ai amicalement, joyeusement et loyalement collaboré avec vous, imprimant un sens qui m'est cher à votre travail superbe – je ne demande rien de plus. C'est par justice que je m'étonne et non par petitesse. Je ne regrette qu'une chose c'est que ces "drames" empêchent, dans la suite des collaborations dont Parade ne prouve l'efficacité. Vote ami Cocteau P.S Si je ne poussais pas le goût de perfection scénique jusqu'à l'effacement de moi même, j'aurais laissé la parole. Tout cela vous le savez vous en êtes certain.*[34]

On 18 May 1917, in the Théâtre du Châtelet, *Parade* was launched as a matinée premiere on behalf of the War Fund. The house curtain rose onto Picasso's drop-curtain depicting the members of a travelling circus enjoying a picnic: measuring ten by seventeen metres it was Picasso's largest-ever painting. It was raised to the strains of a solemn and meditative prelude by Satie. Because the curtain was only displayed for a few minutes, the audience had little time to appreciate its rich narrative. This brief glimpse was a deliberate ploy to defy audience expectations, a notion that would run throughout the performance. The characters featured on the curtain seemed to have been caught offstage during a break or at the end of a performance. However, having materialized onstage at the *start* of the performance, they thus became part of the performance itself. Picasso framed his own curtain with red draperies, thereby making this classic theatre device appear to hang both at the front and the rear of the stage, confounding the spectators' sense of position, as if they were simultaneously behind the scenes and among the audience.[35] Subtle Cubist features include the flattened characters and the condensed perspective orchestrating all the figurative elements.

The juxtaposition of styles is heightened once Picasso's drop-curtain rose to reveal the

[33] Steegmuller, 189.

[34] "My dearest Massine, Why does Diaghilev give me so much trouble and never addresses me directly? I will tell him to supress me completely from *Parade's* bill – my aspirations surpass journalism, as do yours. I got Satie to write the score, word by word. I brought Picasso against all his principles (regardless of what he may say), I amicably, joyfully and loyally collaborated with you, imprinting a direction to your superb work which is dear to me – I ask for nothing more. It is by justice that I am upset and not small-mindedness. The one thing I regret is that these 'dramas' will bar the future collaborations necessary to *Parade*. Your friend, Cocteau..." Documents concerning *Parade*, Watson Library Special Collections.

[35] Rothschild, 209.

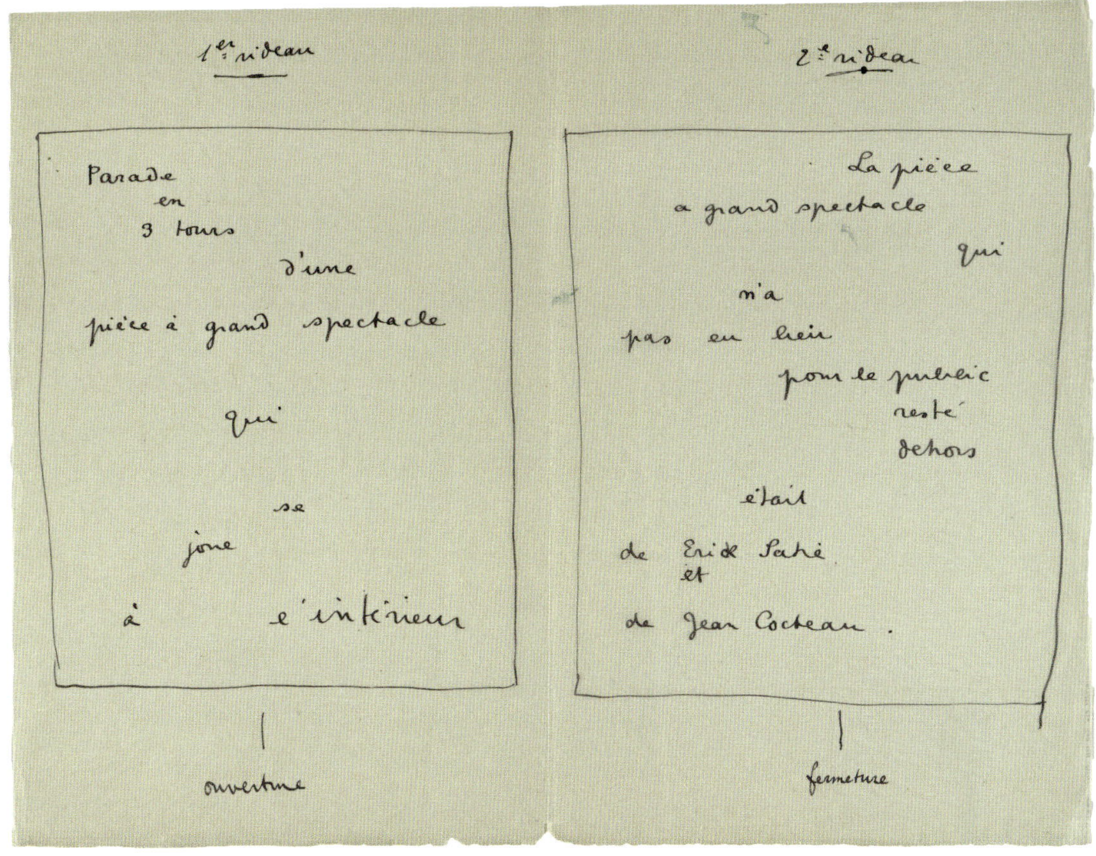

1er rideau

Parade
en
3 tours
d'une
pièce à grand spectacle
qui
se
joue
à l'intérieur

ouverture

2e rideau

La pièce
à grand spectacle
qui
n'a
pas eu lieu
pour le public
resté
dehors
était
de Erik Satie
et
de Jean Cocteau.

fermeture

5. Autograph notes of Jean Cocteau on *Parade*, 1916-17
New York, The Metropolitan Museum of Art, Thomas J. Watson Library, Bequest of William S. Lieberman

set, in effect a Cubist conception. Sketches by Picasso show that initially the Cubist elements were meant to be starker. In the end, however, they were toned down to include more figurative/classical elements. The classical elements had a Modernist slant with Cubist underpinnings. The pillars holding up the booth, for instance, are crooked, their angle destabilizing rather than supportive. The balustrade at the front has an inverted perspective and a pseudo-illusionistic quality. The outsize Baroque adornments and the Pompeian mural offer a parodic element, joshing with the set's classical components. Interestingly, the resulting whole was in line with Cocteau's initial vision: a fair-booth in a cityscape. Meanwhile, the deliberately vague and unidentified setting was intended to generate a sense of universality, leaving it to the audience's imagination to identify a geographical context, subjectively.

The Cubist element was heightened by the arrival Picasso's two giant Managers, the Frenchman and the American, each measuring over three metres in height. Rightly sensing that they would be shocking to the audience, Diaghilev had arranged for the printed programme to include an apologia about them. The third Manager, now in the form of a riderless horse (since the dummy rider had repeatedly fallen off during rehearsals!), failed to amuse the audience despite its vaudeville look and comical choreography. Furthermore, the last-minute alteration meant that Satie's music no longer matched the action, and so the horse was obliged to dance without any musical accompaniment. As the scene progressed, the audience became increasingly outraged at having paid to see a ballet, when what unfolded seemed merely popular entertainment. The contrast between the three "realistic" performers – the Cubist Managers and the pantomime horse – further heightened the jarring effect. The fact that the Little American Girl's costume had been bought in a Parisian sporting goods store – not to mention the scraps and cardboards that made up the Managers' costumes – only added to the play's fragmented reality.

It was in this circus atmosphere that the collaborators were able to demonstrate their reflections on contemporary life and modernity and introduce the audience to Cubism through satire and humour. In an article that appeared on the day of the premiere Cocteau wrote:

> *Our wish is that the public may consider Parade as a work concealing poetry beneath the coarse outer skin of slapstick. Laughter is natural to the Frenchmen: it is important to keep this in mind and not be afraid to laugh even at this most difficult time. Laughter is too Latin a weapon to be neglected.*[36]

For many, *Parade* was shocking for a number of reasons: it aligned street life and popular entertainment with the high realm of ballet, and moreover included avant-garde aesthetics. But the outrage it caused must be understood in its historical context. The premiere took place while some of the worst battles of the war were raging merely two-hundred and fifty kilometres from the Théâtre du Châtelet. Hence, the audience was in no mood for light-heartedness and frivolity. This clash of mood resulted in the ballet's opening night going down in history as a scandal. Some sources claim that a riot broke out in the theatre: feeling cheated by the spectacle, the largely bourgeois audience began booing and yelling. Furthermore, they were incensed by what they saw as disrespectful of the prevailing mood of patriotism and the war effort, an affront which only the appearance of the war-wounded poet Guillaume Apollinaire – complete with bandaged head – was able to quell. Characteristically, Cocteau would later delight in these reactions, and even exaggerated the fracas for an article he wrote for *Vanity Fair* later that year (of which a draft edit exists in the Met documents). He would associate the *scandale* with the reaction provoked by the *Rite of Spring* and concluded by saying: "Finally, in 1917, at the opening night of *Parade*, I did astound him!" meaning Diaghilev.[37]

[36] Quoted in Silver, *Picasso: The Great War, Experimentation, and Change* (New York: Scala, 2016): 123 (Cocteau's article was published in *L'Excelsior*, 18 May 1917).
[37] Steegmuller, p. 82.
[38] Conrad Debold, "Parade" and "le spectacle intérieur": the role of Jean Cocteau in an avant-garde ballet, Thesis (Ph.D.), Emory University, 1982, 12.

That said, in the eyes of the writers, painters, and musicians of the *Esprit Nouveau* who attended the show it *was a success*. Parade had achieved the unimaginable feat of bringing the avant-garde to the realm of ballet. The uproar in the theatre and the violence of the public reaction emphasized *Parade*'s temporal and subjective nature as a stage drama that demanded direct interaction with and from its audience. The historical context was critical to its impact. While some of the startling effect and rawness of the piece is lost today, there is little doubt that *Parade* represents a watershed in the dissemination of Modernist ideas. Its execution offered a unique confrontation between the new emerging ideas of the day and the obsolescing aesthetic sensibilities dear to the bourgeoisie.

Parade confronted the audience with the avant-garde concepts being explored at that time, concepts that came to embody the dramatic changes rocking Europe.[38] In the end, what gave *Parade* its radical impact is the collaborative nature of the work. Far from being an isolated pictorial event for the fruition of an artistic and intellectual elite, *Parade* was a total work of art, a *Gesamtkunstwerk* that shook bourgeois society to its core. The Met documents highlight the extent of the collaboration, how each artist fed off the other, thereby in effect creating a new artistic language. It is the interdisciplinary nature of *Parade* that ultimately caused Guillaume Apollinaire – who was asked to write the notes in the opening programme – to coin the word "*sur-réalisme*". His praise goes to Picasso, Satie and Massine whilst only mentioning Cocteau as the author of *Parade*'s sub-title "a realistic ballet", to which he alludes tongue-in-cheek. In many ways, however, the end result must have surpassed Cocteau's wildest dreams, shedding the production's precious or gimmicky aspects and turning them into a veritably avant-garde work of art.

Stravinsky and Picasso: Elective Affinities

Olivier Berggruen

In a drawing from 1917, Picasso offers us an impression of Igor Stravinsky, the celebrated composer of the *Rite of Spring*. Stravinsky is shown draped in his armchair, fingers intertwined, looking self-assured, aloof even, in his oversized suit (fig. 1).[1] This is the first of three portraits, all executed in pencil, that are a testament to the enduring friendship between the two great artists.[2] Stravinsky had arrived in Rome on 5 April 1917, just as the sets for the ballet *Parade* were being completed. Less than a fortnight later, Picasso, Stravinsky, and the Swiss conductor Ernest Ansermet travelled to Naples where the Ballets Russes was due to perform. While walking in the city's Forcella quarter, they chanced upon *commedia dell'arte* puppet shows, traditional outdoor theatrical representations of the masked Pulcinella, who was, according to Stravinsky, "a great drunken lout whose every gesture, and probably every word, if I had understood, was obscene."[3] For both artists, the modest spectacle provided by the Neapolitan theatre reaffirmed their taste for popular and traditional forms of art; it offered proof that the simplest of artistic expressions could have a universal appeal. Disparate sources of inspiration, ranging from high to low, could be integrated into their works, just as the Roman landscape offered a vision wherein Antiquity, Renaissance churches and Baroque architecture seemed to coalesce.

Sergei Diaghilev, the founder of the *Ballets Russes*, had just invited Picasso to Rome to work on a new production, *Parade*, in an effort to revive his reputation after a failed American tour. As for Stravinsky, he was already a celebrated member of Diaghilev's circle, the composer of the *Firebird* and the *Rite of Spring*. Apart from their friendship, Picasso and Stravinsky had much more in common: their uneasy relationship with the aggressive Modernism of Dada and the Futurists, their rejection of Expressionism, their embrace of vernacular forms of art, a dislike of organized artistic movements, and, above all, a similarity of artistic conceptions. Both men shared a comparable background in Symbolism. For Picasso, it was the art of Toulouse-Lautrec and Arte Juvens; for Stravinsky, it was Russian Symbolism fused with Debussy and French influences.

When Picasso and Stravinsky first met in Rome, the battles of the Avant-garde – whether Picasso's heroic cubist years or Stravinsky's epic scores for Diaghilev – were behind them; now their modernist tendencies were somewhat tempered by a classicizing influence. Both artists felt uneasy with the Avant-Garde's rejection of historical traditions. Unlike the Futurists and Dadaists, their work looks at the past for inspiration. In that sense Stravinsky, in particular, was closer to Cocteau, Valéry, Eliot and Pound, all of whom were innovators, albeit conservative ones.[4] Broadly speaking, their attitude towards prevailing fashions and movements was one of distant amusement.

I am indebted to Mebrak Tareke, Silvia Loreti, John Seilern, and Tobias Berggruen for commenting on earlier drafts of this essay.

[1] *Portrait of Stravinsky*, Paris, Musée national Picasso-Paris, cat. no. 87. According to Robert Craft, "Picasso's Stravinsky is more real, even literally, than the thousands created by photographers." (Igor Stravinsky, *Selected Correspondence*, ed. Robert Craft [New York: Alfred A. Knopf, 1985] III: 521.)

[2] Picasso executed a further two pencil drawings of Stravinsky, one in profile, one of his face, with what looks, at first glance like a monocle, but is actually the salvaged lens of a broken pair of spectacles. Cf. Douglas Cooper, *Picasso Théâtre* (Paris: Éditions Cercle d'Art, 1967), plate no. 271; and *Portrait of Stravinsky*, 1917, private collection, cat. no. 80.

[3] Eric Walter White, *Stravinsky: The Composer and his Works* (Berkeley: University of California Press, 1984), 62.

[4] See Christopher Butler, "Stravinsky as Modernist", in *The Cambridge Companion to Stravinsky*, ed. Jonathan Cross (Cambridge: Cambridge University Press, 2003), 19.

The Aftermath of the War

A new political and social situation emerged after the war. The struggles of the Avant-garde were replaced by Cocteau's more accessible version of Modernism, as displayed in the idiosyncratic *Parade*. There was also, at least on Picasso's part, a desire to appear more "French", given his absence from the battlefield during the war, and the Cubists' association with the German art-dealer Daniel-Henry Kahnweiler. Nationalism is one explanation for this retreat. But these factors do not explain Picasso's path, in which he retained, again and again, a Cubist sensibility. Let us remember that the Cubism of Picasso was not meant to serve as rigid syntax, as a way of bending the world to fit a particular vocabulary.[5] Instead, this so-called Synthetic Cubism, which came out of the *papiers collés,* allowed Picasso to see the pictorial surface as autonomous fragments, which could be articulated and assembled in a variety of ways. This playfulness, then, became an essential part of Picasso's strategy.

The portrait of Stravinsky is a striking example of Picasso's rejection of stylistic purity. Though at first glance it appears to be classical and academic, it bears the hallmarks of a stylistic ambivalence; the exaggerated contours succeed in establishing an expressive autonomy that competes with the artist's mimetic ambitions. It is therefore not surprising that Picasso's seemingly classical drawings never fail to reveal a corrupting element: the slight disfigurement of a face, a sudden shift in perspective, as in some of the beach drawings; the careful, sensitive rendering of a face at the expense of the body; exaggerated limbs in monumental paintings such as *Trois femmes à la fontaine* (1921; fig. 2).

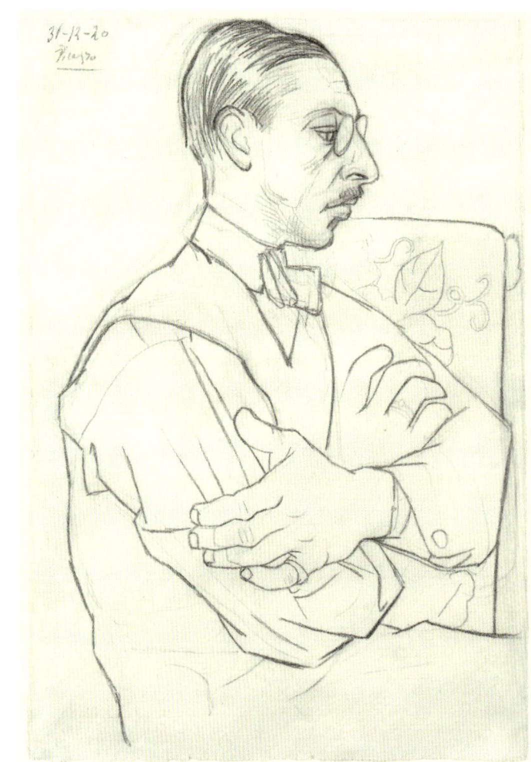

1. Pablo Picasso
Portrait d'Igor Stravinsky
[Portrait of Igor Stravinsky], 1920
Pencil on paper, 34.3 x 23.5 cm
New York, private collection

Stravinsky's modernist tendencies had emerged with the visceral, primitivist *Rite of Spring* (1913). A year later, in *Three Pieces for String Quartet,* the composer created a tapestry of clashing tonal orientations and rhythms; it amounts to a disruption of linearity, a discontinuity that endeavours to create more space in the listener's imagination.[6] As Jonathan Butler writes, "Juxtaposition is preferred to logical order."[7] Often, works from this period succeed in juxtaposing or fusing

[5] This explains, in part, why Picasso abandoned the "heroic" Cubism of 1910–11 when it became a kind of international *lingua franca* after the war.

[6] William R. Everdell identifies "the collapse of ontological continuity" as a central tenet of Modernism in *The First Moderns: Profiles in the Origins of Twentieth-Century Thought* (Chicago: University of Chicago Press, 1997): 11.

[7] Butler, "Stravinsky as Modernist", p. 26.

together high and low artistic modes, ranging from the classical to the vernacular.

In April of 1917, on a piece of hotel stationery, Stravinsky composed a few bars of music for clarinet, creating a witty musical equivalent to Picasso's Cubism. Stravinsky certainly knew that the clarinet was the musical instrument featured in many of Picasso's canvases, including the two versions of *Three Musicians*.[8] In the sketch's five bars, rhythm and metre are subverted – the time signature oscillates between 5/8 and 6/8 – much as Picasso stretches visual representation. In it, Stravinsky demonstrated how traditional musical structures could be toyed with and re-configured without compromising the piece's overall coherence. In his dedication to the Spanish Master, the composer broke apart the words, no doubt acknowledging the painter's ability to create new meanings and polysemy (fig. 4).

A couple of years later, Picasso drew the cover for Stravinsky's piano transcription of *Ragtime* (published in January 1920). He worked on the cover more than once, as he was unhappy with his initial design.[9] The score featured dotted notes and triplets and the rhythmic syncopation characteristic of ragtime. Picasso's single continuous line (done in one swooping motion) in the shape of two musicians gave the cover the appearance of a swirling, but at times stalled, movement; he also incorporated the motif of a treble clef in his portrayal of the instrumentalist on the right (fig. 5).

Stravinsky's *Octet* was first performed in 1923 to the public's general dismay, since the Parisian audience did not expect such a radical departure from the composer's visceral, earlier style; they could not understand how certain "rococo" mannerisms could be juxtaposed with an ironic, slapdash waltz. Overall, the composition features simple melodic lines, devoid of Stravinsky's earlier polytonality, and repeated rhythmic patterns reminiscent of Baroque music. The composer's gradual embrace of clear, transparent structures should not be seen as a retreat from Modernism, even though the material is steeped in classical repertoire. Fantasy, not to mention local, romantic colour, now became things of the past. Purified of emotion and flourish, the elegant tonal blocks of *Symphonies of Wind Instruments* (1921) disclose stripped-down structures, creating a musical counterpart to Picasso's cubist scaffolding.

Whereas Stravinsky's formal concerns became all-important in later works such as *Les Noces* and the *Octet*, Picasso kept on cultivating disruption – witness the humour and irreverence of his design for the ballet *Mercure* (1924), with music by Erik Satie. It was described in the programme as a series of "poses plastiques en trois tableaux" in which the dancers wear strange accoutrements that look like papier-mâché sculptures. Not only are they stripped of the conventions of traditional ballet, but they take on the guise of awkward-looking burlesque caricatures.[10]

[8] For a discussion of Picasso and musical instruments, see Simon Shaw Miller, "Instruments of Desire: Musical Morphology in the Early Work of Picasso", *Musical Quarterly* 76, no. 4 (Winter, 1992): 443–64.

[9] Stravinsky, *Selected Correspondence*, ed. Robert Craft (New York: Alfred A. Knopf, 1984) vol. II, 188.

[10] Another ballet in a similar vein was *L'Homme et son désir* by Claudel, produced by the Ballets Suédois in 1921 with music by Darius Milhaud, and originally performed by the Ballets Russes with Nijinsky in Rio de Janeiro in 1916. This was to be one of Nijinsky's last performances. Costumes were made by Audrey Parr, who treated the dancer's bodies like sculptures. In accordance with Claudel's wishes, the costumes were cut out of coloured boards making the dancers look like exotic birds.

[11] For early depictions by Picasso of *commedia dell'arte* characters, see Brigitte Léal, *Carnets: Catalogue des dessins, 1899–1924* (Paris: Réunion des musées nationaux, 1996) vol. I, 256–57, 259.

[12] Igor Stravinsky and Robert Craft, *Expositions and Developments* (Garden City, New York: Doubleday & Company, 1962): 127–28.

[13] Ibid. "*Pulcinella* was my discovery of the past," Stravinsky says in *Expositions and Developments*, "the epiphany through which the whole of my late work became possible. It was a back-

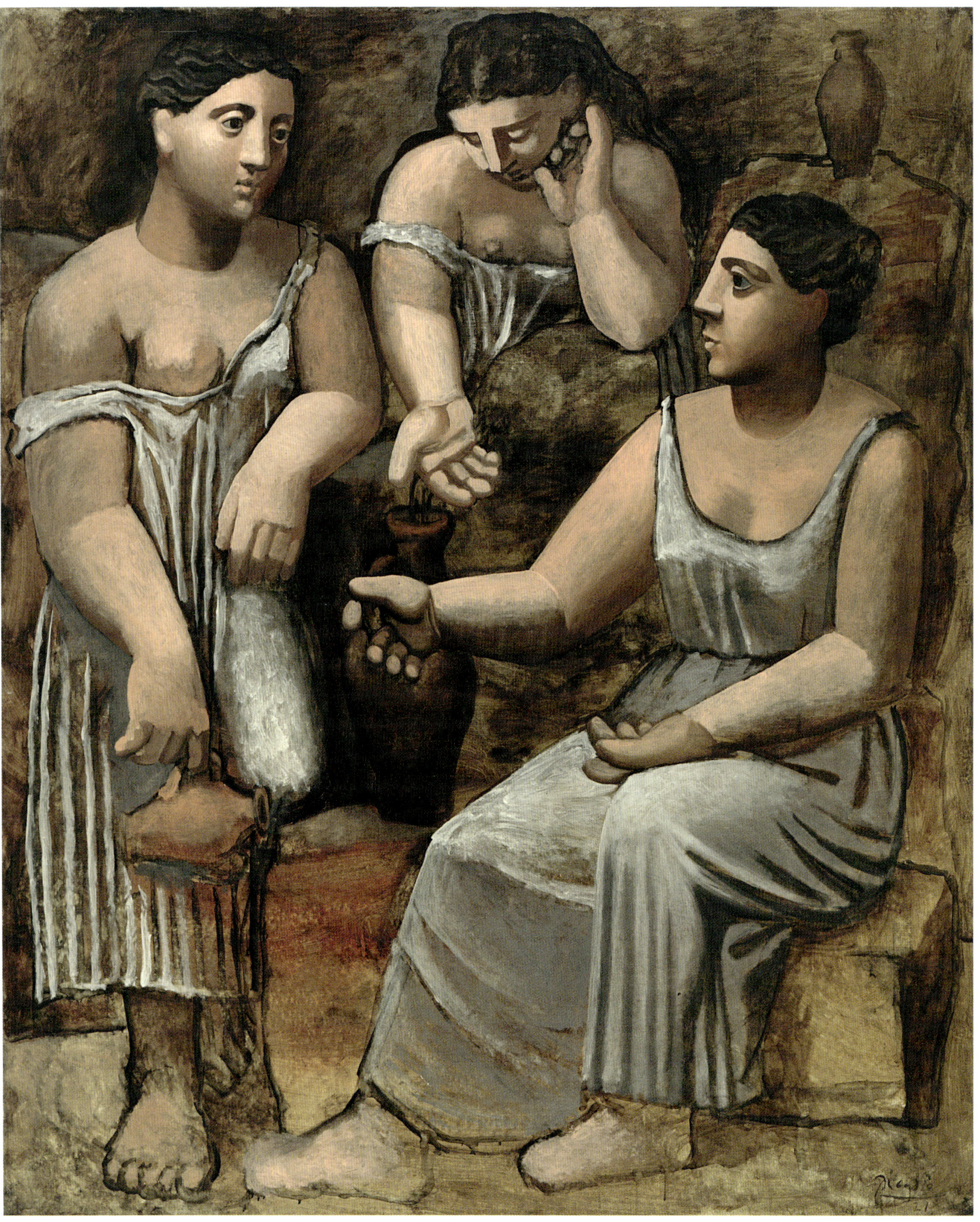

2. Pablo Picasso
Trois femmes à la fontaine
[Three Women at the Spring], 1921
Oil on canvas, 203.9 x 174 cm
New York, The Museum of Modern Art, Gift of Mr and Mrs Allan D. Emil

A historic collaboration: Pulcinella

As we have seen, in 1919 Diaghilev embarked on *Pulcinella*, a new ballet inspired by the *commedia dell'arte*. The seeds of *Pulcinella* were planted in April 1917, when Picasso and Stravinsky witnessed the traditional puppet shows in the streets of Naples. They delighted in the bawdy, slapstick vulgarity of the masked Pulcinella, the central character of the Neapolitan *commedia dell'arte*. The idea for the ballet came originally from Ansermet. Diaghilev entrusted the libretto and choreography to Léonide Massine, the score to Stravinsky, and the design of the sets and costumes to Picasso.[11]

Stravinsky began *Pulcinella* in the late summer of 1919, and completed it in April of the following year. Diaghilev then urged Stravinsky to look at some eighteenth-century scores; and Massine read several *commedia dell'arte* libretti at the Naples Royal Library during that summer.

Initially, Stravinsky was reluctant to follow Diaghilev's idea, for he had a scant regard for Pergolesi (1710–36), a relatively unknown Neapolitan composer on whose compositions the new production was based. It has since been established that not all compositions were by Pergolesi. The poster for the premiere announced "musique de Pergolési arrangée et orchestrée par Igor Strawinsky." "I began by composing on the Pergolesi manuscripts themselves, as though I were correcting an old work of my own," Stravinsky later wrote. "I knew that I could not produce a 'forgery' of Pergolesi because my motor habits are so different; at best, I could repeat him in my own accent."[12] The composer retained the eighteenth-century bass lines and melodies, but the inner harmonies, the rhythms, and the sonorities were his own. "The remarkable thing about Pulcinella," Stravinsky said, "is not how much, but how little has been added or changed."[13]

Diaghilev expected a score not unlike Respighi's recent, somewhat conventional, tribute to Rossini, *La boutique fantasque*. When *Pulcinella, Ballet in One Act with Song*, was

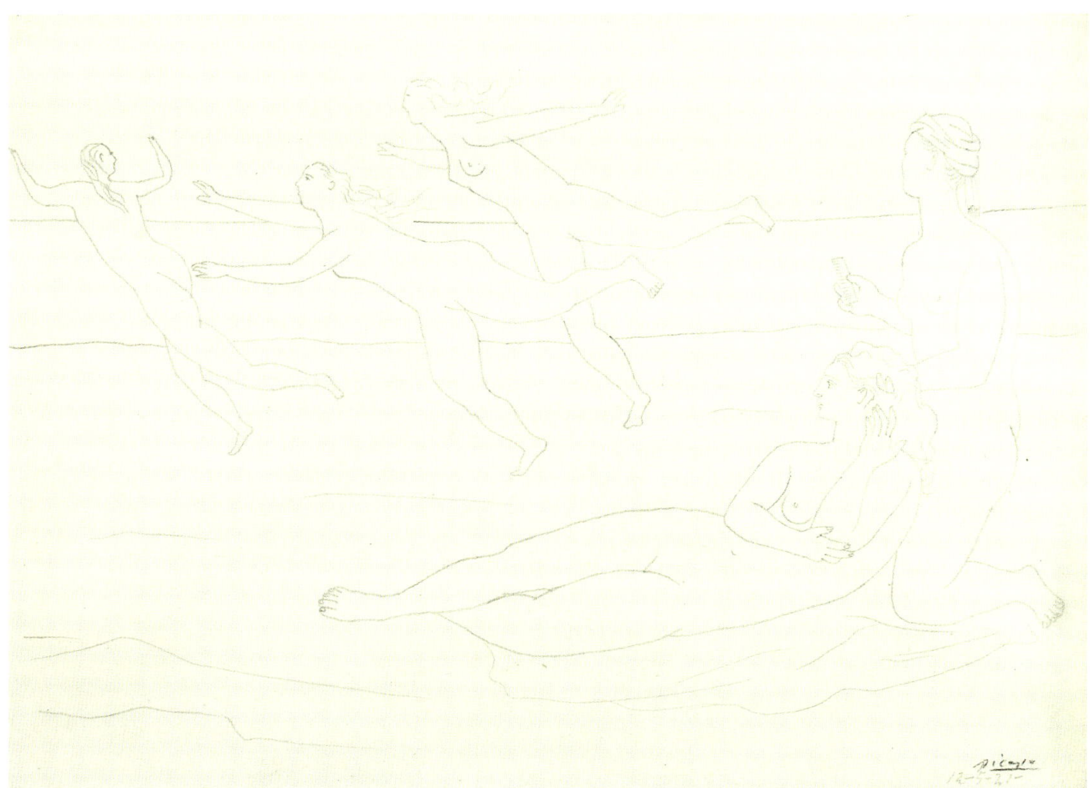

3. Pablo Picasso
Femmes au bord de la mer
[Women at the Seaside], 1921
Pencil on paper, 24 x 34 cm
Mannheim, Kunsthalle

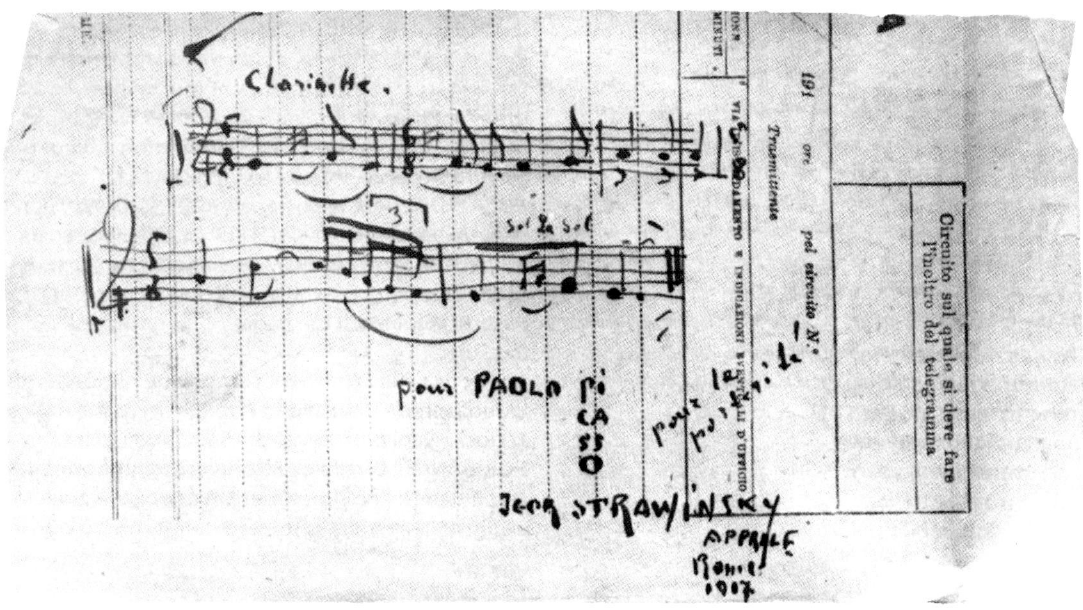

4. Igor Stravinsky
Sketch for Music for the Clarinet,
13 April 1917
Paris, Musée national Picasso-Paris

first performed on 15 May 1920 at the Paris Opera, its reinvented Baroque style came as a complete shock to the public, for whom the Russian composer was primarily the author of the *Rite of Spring*.

The collaboration between Picasso and Diaghilev was fraught with tension. Initially, Picasso played with the idea of making a theatre out of the stage, with theatre boxes flanking a view of Naples and Vesuvius in the background. This mirror-image of a *théâtre à l'italienne*, with cartoon-like balconies and tiers, was no doubt reminiscent of the puppet shows he had so much enjoyed on his visit to Naples. Picasso wanted to highlight the artificial character of the situation. Diaghilev asked him to redo the designs twice, and at one point threw Picasso's drawings on the floor, angrily treading them underfoot. The final design was less radical yet more Cubist. It displayed a Neapolitan street with a view of the bay, a boat, and Vesuvius framed by white houses, painted in shades of blue, grey, dark brown, and white. The costumes were influenced by *commedia dell'arte,* with Pulcinella in the traditional white bouffant dress and black mask with a beaked nose. Picasso's costumes provided a playful contrast to the Cubist set, displaying his modernist take on Classicism. Yet, as Stravinsky remarked later, it was "one of those productions where everything harmonizes, where all the elements – subject, music, dancing, and artistic setting – form a coherent and homogeneous whole."[14]

What is interesting about the much-decried *Pulcinella* is that it has the feel, at least superficially, of a late Baroque composition. It involves three vocalists, a solo string quartet,

ward look, of course – the first of many love affairs in that direction – but it was a look in the mirror, too. No critic understood this at the time, and I was therefore attacked for being a *pasticheur*, chided for composing 'simple' music, blamed for deserting 'modernism,' accused of renouncing my 'true Russian heritage.' People who had never heard of, or cared about, the originals cried 'Sacrilege! The classics are ours. Leave the classics alone.' To them all, my answer was and is the same, You 'respect,' but I love." Ibid., 128–29.

[14] Igor Stravinsky, *An Autobiography* (New York: W.W. Norton & Company, 1962), 85.

[15] *Three Musicians,* 1921. Oil on canvas, 204.5 × 188.3 cm. Philadelphia Museum of Art, A.E. Gallatin Collection. *Three Musicians*, 1921. Oil on canvas, 200.7 × 222.9 cm, New York, The Museum of Modern Art, Mrs Simon Guggenheim Fund.

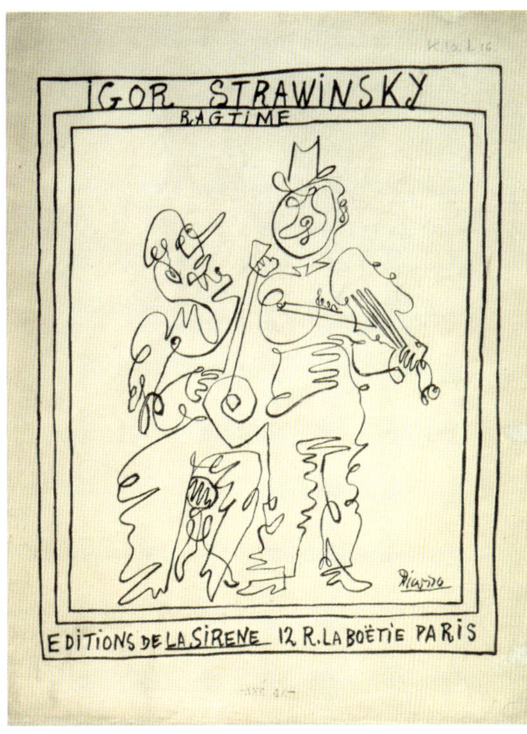

5. Pablo Picasso
Design for the cover
of *Ragtime* by Stravinsky
Éditions de la Sirène, Paris 1920

and a small orchestra, instead of Stravinsky's previous scores for large orchestras.

The composer remained close to the spirit of the original scores, keeping their structural development, bass lines, and melody. However, he altered certain rhythmic elements and harmonies, thereby achieving an altogether unexpected outcome, which was neither old or new but different.

By re-arranging fragments he re-created each phrase, every sound – foreshortening, stretching – introducing unexpected harmonies to reach a work that bore the hallmarks of the Russian composer's treatment of timbre and instrumentation. Furthermore, the appearance of occasional dissonant chords in such a classical context created an element of surprise, a departure from its eighteenth-century model. However, Stravinsky's score was criticized (most forcefully by Diaghilev), for introducing freedoms that were too slight, too whimsical, compared to the shock and force of *Petrushka* and *The Rite of Spring*.

Pulcinella was to be the last collaboration between Picasso and Stravinsky. It was also the last time he collaborated with the quarrelsome Diaghilev. Yet the whimsical production clearly resonated with him, and Picasso would pay his homage to Pulcinella with two versions of *Three Musicians* in 1921: notably, the clarinet player is Pulcinella himself, recognizable from his traditional white dress.[15]

Stylistic fluidity

During his adolescence and early twenties, Picasso was increasingly drawn to the ways in which the artificial nature of a situation was represented and exposed, particularly on stage, including the popular theatre of his early Parisian years. He also realized that theatre – and more specifically, decorating a stage – provided him with a metaphor for assembling his paintings and other works, a method he first devised for his Cubist constructions. For Picasso, the technique of set design, derived from his Cubist experiments, was employed to bring together various compositional elements.

Already, during the First World War, we see works in which various motifs or single works are executed in a variety of styles, as in the playful series of *Arlequins à la batte*.[16] On numerous occasions, Picasso displayed a real aversion to the notion of *style*: "Down with style", he once declared. "Does God have a style? He made the guitar, the Harlequin, the dachshund, the cat, the owl, the dove. So did I. He made paint. So did I."[17] If Picasso were to be considered a painter without style, he was nonetheless deeply marked by his years of relentless quest for a distinct form of expression, a quest that led to Cubism. He quickly realized that Cubism was not just a style, and as soon as it risked becoming one, it was already dead (which is why Picasso quickly distanced himself from his followers).

Picasso's preoccupation with Cubist still life – the emblematic motif of bottle and glasses arranged on a café table – is presented and dramatized over and over again. It is almost as if – albeit in a somewhat iconic manner – Picasso had deliberately wanted to enshrine the one style that was so dear to him, namely Cubism, through elaborate staging and re-staging. In his celebrated *Études* (1920), Picasso's different representational modes all co-exist without any sense of hierarchy, each constituting its own theatre set, all different styles frozen in space as though they were a dictionary of possible idioms and subjects.[18]

Picasso was well known for his willingness to change styles or even to incorporate various styles within a single work. The same could be said of Stravinsky, who made extensive use of popular sources, such as jazz as early as 1918 (in his *Ragtime for 11 instruments*); these were put together through a method of construction not unlike Picasso's – in contrast with the slow, structural development typical of the German musical tradition. At the time they first met, both Picasso and Stravinsky embraced a certain form of stylistic pluralism, which may not have been a complete coincidence. Let us consider Stravinsky's *Ragtime*, or Picasso's mix of heterogeneous elements in his still-lifes of Saint Raphaël (1919).[19] In these works, there is a continued effort to synthesize Cubist principles with classical ones, both of which, as we have seen, are realistic. Picasso, in a playful mode, does not shy away from representing a Cubist still-life as though it were painted in a traditional manner.[20] Here I would like to emphasize that despite their great differences, these stylistic modes did not always clash.

Particularly relevant to our discussion is the relationship that Jean Cocteau establishes between Cubism and Realism. That Cocteau underscored Realism is well known, especially given his tendency to advocate for a more traditional French art in the aftermath of the war. "French" was usually understood to be Neoclassical in inspiration, as opposed to Cubism, which was said to be "'German", perhaps owing to its connection to the art dealer Daniel-Henry Kahnweiler. Yet Cocteau seized the connection between these seemingly opposite movements. For instance, in the programme notes for the opening performance of *Parade*, Apollinaire writes, "Jean Cocteau calls it a realistic ballet. The Cubist decor and

[16] See Christian Zervos, *Works From 1917 to 1919*, vol. II**, *Pablo Picasso* (1942; repr., Paris: Éditions Cahiers d'Art, 2013), nos. 908–921.

[17] Quoted in Mary Ann Caws, *Picasso* (London: Reaktion Books, 2005): 12.

[18] *Études* (1920), Paris, Musée national Picasso-Paris, cat. no. 115. For a thorough discussion of Picasso, Cubism and style, see Rosalind E. Krauss, "Picasso/Pastiche" in *The Picasso Papers* (Cambridge, MA: MIT Press, 1999): 89–210. For Picasso's own pronouncement on cubism, see Pablo Picasso, "Statement by Picasso: 1923", in *Picasso: Fifty Years of his Art*, by Alfred H. Barr, Jr. (New York: The Museum of Modern Art, 1946): 270–71, previously published as "Picasso Speaks", *The Arts* (May 1923): 315–26.

[19] See for example *Still Life in front of a Window, Saint Raphaël*, 1919, Berlin, Staatliche Museen zu Berlin, Nationalgalerie, Museum Berggruen, cat no. 126.

[20] For a discussion of the still-lifes at Saint Raphaël, and the extent to which they are painted in a naturalist mode, see Yve-Alain Bois, "Picasso the Trickster", in *Picasso Harlequin: 1917–1937*, ed. Yve-Alain Bois (Milan: Skira, 2008): 33.

[21] Guillaume Apollinaire, "*Parade* and the New Idea". Quoted in *Picasso The Italian Journey 1917–1924*, ed. Jean Clair (New York: Rizzoli, 1998): 321.

[22] Quoted in John Richardson, *A Life of Picasso: The Triumphant Years, 1917–1932* (New York: Alfred A. Knopf, 2007): 29.

costumes by Picasso testify to the realism of his art. This realism – or Cubism, if you prefer – is what has most profoundly stirred the arts in the last ten years."[21] Cubism is realistic to a degree because it takes inspiration from everyday life. Conversely, a Cubist still-life can be given a theatrical presence. In his Saint Raphaël compositions, Picasso gave everyday things the weight and elaborate *mise-en-scène* usually reserved for set design on stage. Indeed, Synthetic Cubism created visual shortcuts that were common currency among set designers. Various objects were displayed in such a way that they unfold before our eyes in a rhetorical rather than a veridical manner.

Classicism, on the other hand, has always consciously and openly cultivated illusion. The fiction of art is inevitable – there is an old and venerable tradition of using skill in manipulating scale, of using artifice in order to create a greater sentiment of reality. That is to say, Classicism is not incompatible with a modernist vision. Furthermore, the classical tradition is never as pure as we might think, and Picasso was well aware of that. For example, Picasso admired the marbles from the Farnese collection he saw at the Museo Nazionale in Naples. The sheer size of the Hercules underscores the pathos of what the painter Fuseli called the "gigantism in the disproportion of the parts".[22]

Both artists' work reveals different strands, impulses, and voices – the painter's fluid lines caught between flow and break, thereby echoing the movement of the ballet dancers; the stylized realism of his theatre designs, the monumental manner of the large nudes; the aesthetics of fragmentation in the cut-and-paste, clashing decorative surfaces; and the collision of musical planes in the work of Stravinsky, as in the waltz in the *Octet*'s second movement.

At more or less the same time in the early 1920s, Picasso and Stravinsky turned away from Neo-Primitivism and embraced a language of purified emotions, as embodied by Stravinsky's ballet *Apollon Musagète* and Picasso's large composition *La Flûte de Pan*, painted in a grand manner reminiscent of Poussin and classical Roman art, albeit devoid of the allegorical and narrative aspects of earlier painting.[23] Hieratic and perhaps withdrawn, Picasso's monumental figures hark back to late Roman reliefs and Etruscan drawings he discovered while travelling in Italy.[24] The core principles of art and architecture of Antiquity, the noble simplicity of Greek statuary, provided a foundation for both artists in the wake of the tragedy of war.

It is worth noting that for both artists, "period Modernism" emerged in an effort to confound public expectations; but more importantly, it is a response to profoundly personal circumstances and desires.[25] I would like to argue that the stylistic shifts of Picasso and Stravinsky are not simply a formal conceit, a play between different art historical or musical strands. They are a reflection of a particular stance the artist has taken towards a work of art. For both artists, this constant

[23] *La Flûte de Pan*, 1924, Paris, Musée national Picasso-Paris, see cat. no. 172.
[24] See Cooper, *Picasso Théâtre*, 66.
[25] "Period Modernism" is Lynn Garafola's expression. See Lynn Garafola, *Diaghilev's Ballets Russes* (New York: Oxford University Press, 1989): 90ff.

reinvention and continuous interweaving of sources is the result of deeply subjective and personal processes. It is not merely intellectual. The artist proceeds by associating images or sounds freely, where deposits of memory – and personal experience – are allowed to grow together into a scheme that was never preordained.

The Artist as Performer

It is well known that Picasso was fond of depicting himself in the guise of a harlequin; it is indicative of his fascination with theatre, particularly in its low, popular forms such as vaudeville and circus. It is also a metaphor for the vulnerability of the artist. Picasso identified with this bohemian crowd of jugglers and musicians, for he depicted himself disguised as a harlequin as early as in 1905 in *Au Lapin agile*.[26] The theme of *Parade* is that of a performance, reminiscent of popular vaudeville theatre. The artist can be seen as a conjurer, and the harlequin, with his multi-faceted, diamond-shaped costume, acts as a metaphor for stylistic diversity.[27] The forlorn acrobats and performers he depicted, often in meditative situations, become the model of his artistic stance, one of a juggler of styles and of the renewal of dramatic action. They reappear in the 1920s as well, most strikingly in the *Arlequin au Miroir* (1923), a nostalgic portrayal of a youth whose appearance in the guise of a performer lets him imagine the intoxicating powers of art.

What is the position of the artist with regard to his work? Does his creative output occupy a space before him that would parallel what tricks mean to the entertainer? That is an essential question at the forefront of Picasso's artistic practice. Furthermore, what are the impulses at the root of the work? And to what degree does the artist control them? These are perhaps the most important questions Picasso asks by engaging in stylistic transformation. At the core of his practice is a commitment to realism, to making the outside world intelligible through figurative means; yet there's no privileged method or style for absorbing this sentiment of reality, of a tangible world; and sometimes parody is the best way to articulate the artist's elusive pursuit, his dilemma in facing the weight of reality. In *Parade* and *Mercure*, parody is the artist's weapon of choice for contaminating the legacy of the art historical canon. Yet, Picasso's practice reaffirms a constant commitment to painting, and to its enduring rhetorical powers.

Stravinsky, for his part, said to Robert Craft: "... composers and painters are not conceptual thinkers; what a Picasso or a Stravinsky has to say about painting or music is of no value whatever from *that* side. (We do certainly love *talking* conceptually, though.) The composer works through a perceptual, not a conceptual, process. He perceives, he selects, he combines, and he is not in the least aware at what point meanings of a different sort and significance grow into his work. All he knows or cares about is his apprehension of the contour of the form, for the form is everything. He can say nothing whatever about meanings."[28]

[26] *Au Lapin Agile*, 1905. Oil on canvas, 99.1 x 100.3 cm. New York, The Metropolitan Museum of Art, The Walter H. and Leonore Annenberg Collection.

[27] Yve-Alain Bois refers to Picasso as a "trickster" in the title of his essay "Picasso the Trickster".

[28] Stravinsky and Craft, *Expositions and Developments*, 116.

[29] With respect to Picasso's cubism, Michael Baxandall writes, "At the same time the earlier narrative themes were appropriated by Picasso's own performance; what he had formerly depicted on the canvas he now enacted on the canvas as an acrobatic post-dramatic, occasionally jokey meditation on his own perceptual process." The cubist pictures "act out Picasso's own serial performance of problem finding and problem-solving. Picasso became a cognitive acrobat of a conspicuous and dazzling kind." (Michael Baxandall, *Patterns of Intention: On the Historical Explanation of Pictures* [New Haven: Yale University Press,1985]: 71–72.)

[30] In the *Poetics of Music*, Stravinsky writes: "What is important for the lucid ordering of the work – for its crystallisation – is that all the Dionysian elements which set the imagination of the artist in motion and make the life-sap rise must be properly subjugated before they intoxicate us, and must finally be made to submit to the law; Apollo demands it." (Igor Stravinsky, *Poetics of Music in the*

The composer's words articulate a point of view different from Picasso's. He points to a practice that is at first glance more spontaneous and instinctive; yet Picasso was all of those things as well – not self-conscious, as opposed to the manipulations of Dada and later conceptualists; but nevertheless willing to adopt different styles suited to various purposes, such as a grand manner for portraits, and "theatrical" Cubism in the still-lifes he executed in Saint Raphaël; or a kind of proto-Surrealism for large compositions. Thus, the artist cannot be identified with his style, but by the underlying gesture that brings all together, a dramatic gesture through which the artist creates a sense of astonishment, bewilderment, contemplation.[29] Stravinsky was drawn to clear structures, even though stylistic modes would change from time to time, as in the Serialism of his later years. For him, the exercise was of a purifying kind, whereby structures are laid bare, a way to reject one's ego and depart from individual expression in favour of a more universal approach to art. Stravinsky's classicism takes inspiration from structural, harmonic and mathematical principles; and in fact, these notions are based on universal aesthetic principles that cut across time and culture.

After 1925, Picasso's relentlessness meant that often what he had done and conceived had to be destroyed figuratively by pursuing other formal paths. Yet his commitment to the rhetorical powers of painting remained intact; whereas for Stravinsky, an increasingly intellectualized approach meant that structural clarity became an overriding concern. Compositional craftsmanship is laid bare by the artist; the idea of raw, barely mediated, instinctive artistic expression is eschewed in favour of a world of controlled emotions. With Stravinsky, the path led resolutely from Primitivism to Classicism. The forces of Apollo have vanquished those of Dionysos (to use Nietzschean terminology).[30] Not so in the works of Picasso. If dance – the overarching trope of Stravinsky and Picasso's post-war practice – is synonymous with creation and regeneration, in *Trois Danseuses* (*Three Dancers*, 1925), the convulsive, frenetic action of the left-hand figure can be seen as a metaphor for creative impulse; one that contains the seeds of disintegration and rebirth.[31]

Form of Six Lessons, trans. Arthur Knodel and Ingolf Dahl [Cambridge, MA: Harvard University Press, 1947]: 80.) For Picasso's engagement with the writings of and response to Nietzsche, see T.J. Clark, *Picasso and Truth: From Cubism to Guernica* (Princeton: Princeton University Press, 2013).
[31] *Trois Danseuses*, 1925, London, Tate, cat. no. 190.

Diaghilev, Picasso and Painters in Performance

Sarah Woodcock

Today Picasso's stage designs are known as art works in galleries and from academic studies, divorced from the theatre for which they were created. How successful were they as theatrical designs, illuminating the ballets for which they were created, and where do they stand in the history of the Diaghilev Ballets Russes and in relation to the rest of the repertory? Diaghilev has always been hailed for his commissioning of artists, but how successful were they in adapting to a very different medium?

When Picasso first worked with the Diaghilev Ballets Russes the company was at a crossroads. From its Paris debut in 1909, the Russian Ballet became the most exciting and innovative theatrical experience of its day. It had grown out of a young generation's dissatisfaction with Russian art's outworn realism and their promotion of new and European ideas through their excellent periodical, *Mir iskusstva* (World of Art). When they met dancer and choreographer Michel Fokine, they adopted ballet as another medium ripe for reform. Fokine rebelled against the stultified, formulaic full evening ballets of the Imperial Theatres, mostly full of empty virtuosity, where everything was subservient to the ballerina in her pointe shoes and tutu; the scores were simple, the design realistic. In Fokine's ballets, the subject dictated the style, demanding that choreographer, composer, and designer work closely together towards a common end, and that concept of collaboration remains the most important legacy of the Diaghilev Ballets Russes. Ballet became fully expressive and, shorn of dance for its own sake, Fokine's works were short, so each programme was made up of three or four contrasted works.

The specialist trained theatre designer is a twentieth-century phenomenon. In the nineteenth century, scenery was realistic, usually contrived by the scene painters, and costumes were stylized and standardized. Needing a new approach for the new ballet, Diaghilev and Fokine turned to their colleagues in the *World of Art*. Léon Bakst and Alexandre Benois distilled the mood and emotion of each individual ballet, an imaginative recreation of reality in service of the whole.

The state theatres in Russia regarded Fokine's ballets as dangerously modern. However, Diaghilev knew that new ideas would find a sympathetic audience in Paris, even though ballet was no longer considered a significant art form in Europe. On 18 May 1909 the Parisian public first saw *Le Pavillon d'Armide, Polovtsian Dances*, and *Le Festin*, and from that moment dance in Europe changed forever. Fokine revealed ballet's expressive potential, and audiences thrilled to the full-bloodied performances and designs. The following year Bakst's opulent, exotic, sensuous designs for *Schehe-*

razade captivated (and still captivate) audiences, and his influence spilled out into fashion and interior design.

Nothing in the company's history matched the impact of those first seasons when Fokine created the ballets that would form the bedrock of the company's repertoire, and become the foundation on which twentieth-century ballet was built. They covered myriad subjects: themes seen through Russian eyes like *Polovtsian Dances from Prince Igor*, *Thamar*, *Petrouchka*, and *The Firebird*; *Scheherazade* and *Cléôpatre* reinvented the Orient and near East, just as *Narcisse* and *Daphnis and Chloe* did Greece. *Les Sylphides* and *Le Spectre de la rose* embodied romanticism, while *Carnaval* mocked social behaviour. No less importantly, the artist as stage designer gained currency because, although artists had occasionally designed productions in Europe (notably Vuillard and Munch), they were working in small theatres, whereas the Ballets Russes was a high profile company and touring to major European cities.

In 1911 Diaghilev broke with Russia and formed the first ballet company independent of a state theatre, dependent on the box office for survival. He needed to keep the company in the public eye, especially in Paris, whose audiences Diaghilev regarded as arbiters of taste (although his most loyal audience and longest seasons would actually be in London). To stay on top, he had to appeal to the Parisians' love of novelty and the new. His new choreographer, Vaslav Nijinsky certainly raised the bar with ballets that shocked audiences – *L'Après-midi d'un faune*, with its angular style inspired by Greek vases and contentious final movement as a faun made love to a nymph's scarf; the shortlived *Jeux* (three tennis players searching for a lost ball); and *Le Sacre du printemps*, which provoked one of the most famous theatrical riots of all time.

Then Nijinsky unexpectedly married, and he was dismissed. In one of the greatest talent-spotting feats in theatrical history, Diaghilev discovered in Moscow a young dancer – acclaimed by actor Mikhail Sadovsky as "a boy who has God's spark". The eighteen-year-old Léonide Massine had extraordinary charisma and theatrical sensibility, becoming a great star and a superb choreographer, taking the company in a new direction.

Upon the outbreak of war in 1914 the troupe was forced to disband, but Diaghilev continued Massine's education as dancer and potential choreographer, and gradually rebuilt the company. On 20 December 1915 he was rewarded with *Soleil de nuit,* Massine's amazingly assured first work, designed by Mikhail Larionov. Based on Russian folk traditions, Massine's bold translation of folk dance and Larionov's deceptively sophisticated brightly coloured folkloristic designs looked fresh and new. In 1916 he produced two short works, *Kikimora*, based on a Russian folk tale, and *Las Meninas* designed by the Spanish painter José-Maria Sert. The company spent much of the years 1916 to 1918 touring in North and South America, and in Spain.

The company was moving on from the fluidity of Fokine, the lushness of Bakst and the precision of Benois. Massine's style leaned towards *demi-caractère*, which, while requiring a classical base is more earth-bound and allowed the introduction of new themes and sharply observed characters; his choreography embraced angularity, dynamism and speed, characteristics he shared with Futurism. His next ballet exploited these attributes, showing that the Russian Ballet would be now looking to Europe for inspiration, but it also kept faith with the past. Premiered on 12 April 1917 in Rome, *Les Femmes de Bonne Humeur* (*The Good-Humoured Ladies*) was based on a comedy by the Italian playwright Carlo Goldoni, with a score derived from the works of Domenico Scarlatti. Bakst's costumes were influenced by the French painter Antoine Watteau's *fêtes galantes,* but the sets were conceived as though seen in a glass ball; these were rejected by Diaghilev in favour of a more realistic setting to fit Massine's comedy of manners.

On the same evening came the first work inspired by Diaghilev's interest in contemporary art – not a dance work, but a visual accompaniment by Giacomo Balla to Stravinsky's early work *Feu d'artifice* (*Fireworks*, 1908). Balla produced a curtain of transparent red-and-blue cones and rectangles that blinked on and off in time to the music; the audience was bemused, and even more so when the artist took his call and activated a device that made his necktie do tricks. During the second performance, a technical problem occurred and the work was never seen again.

The Good-Humoured Ladies and *Fireworks* were pointers to the future. Cut off from Russia by war and then the October Revolution, Diaghilev had no option but to seek inspiration and collaborators elsewhere, and, although the company never lost its roots, Russian influence would no longer be paramount.

Travelling with Diaghilev in Italy was Pablo Picasso, who was working on one of Jean Cocteau's "étonne-moi" ideas for a new ballet which would feature Cubism. Picasso's first experience of theatrical design, therefore, came when Massine was still widely unknown as a choreographer, and indeed Picasso himself was hardly a name outside art circles. It was in Rome and Naples that Picasso was first exposed to the Classical world – so as he made his first foray into theatre design, working in the Cubist style, the foundations were being laid for the next development of his art, and for his personal life, for it was during rehearsals for *The Good-Humoured Ladies* that he met dancer Olga Kokhlova, who would become his wife. Helping Bakst out on the production, the novice theatre designer absorbed the practicalities of this new direction, aided by his insatiable curiosity, willingness to embrace new experiences, and extraordinary powers of concentration. His fascination with the Ballets Russes found another outlet in innumerable drawings of the dancers and personalities connected with the company.

In an extraordinary bout of creative energy, Massine was working not only on *The Good-Humoured Ladies* but on two other works, both due to be premiered in Paris, barely a week apart in May 1917 – *Contes russes* on 11 May (designed by Larionov and Natalia Gontcharova, and based on Russian children's tales), and *Parade* on 18 May.

Parade was Cocteau's brainchild; from the first European seasons, he had attached himself to Diaghilev, becoming his link into avant-garde Paris and supplier of ideas to "étonne-moi"; he designed posters for *Le Spectre de la rose* and provided the libretto for the short-lived *Le Dieu bleu*, more a costume parade than a ballet, but which left a legacy of superb costumes, proving how brilliantly Bakst's designs translated into fabric, texture, and surface decoration.[1]

Cocteau developed *Parade*'s scenario and brought Picasso and composer Erik Satie on board with Massine. A *parade* was a sampling of a performance given to attract an audience, and reflected the Paris intellectuals' interest in circus and music hall. Cocteau wanted to glorify everyday banalities, Massine to create something new and representative of the age; hence the references to modern developments like jazz and cinema.

On 18 May 1917 Picasso's drop curtain for *Parade* gave little away – it showed circus performers grouped around a table, with a ladder and winged horse balancing on a sphere (he had painted in the details himself using a toothbrush). The curtain rose to reveal a streetscape, Cubist in style, mostly

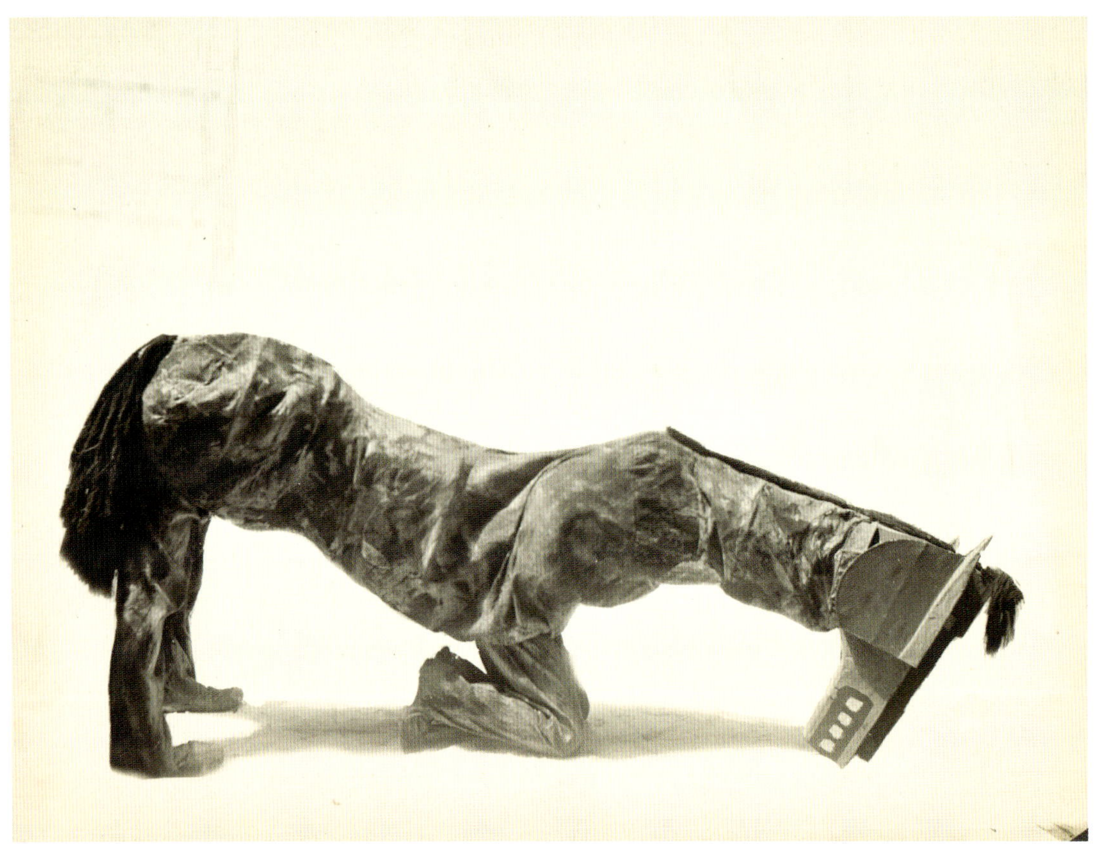

1. Anonymous
The Horse bowing in the ballet *Parade* with dancers Edmund Novak and George Oumansky, 1917
Paris, Musée national Picasso-Paris, Pablo Picasso Donation, 1979, inv. APPH4821

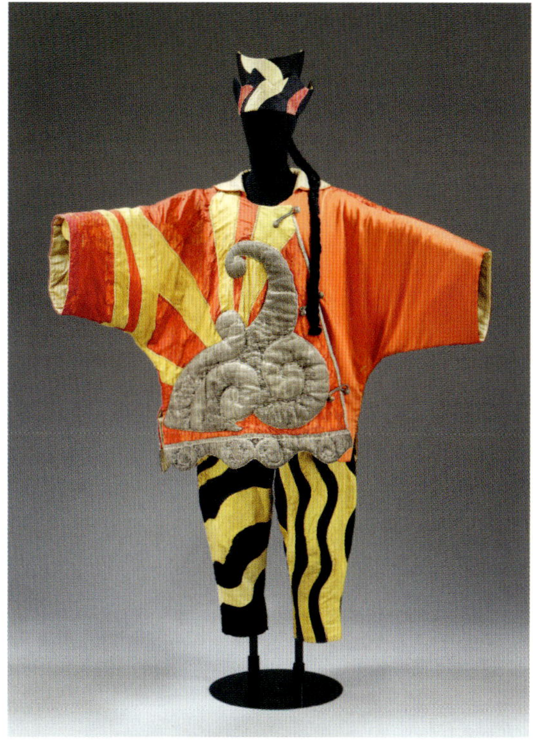

2. Costume for the Chinese Conjurer designed by Picasso for the ballet *Parade* choreographed by Massine, 1917
London, Victoria and Albert Museum, Department of Theatre and Performance, inv. S.84-1985

in ochres and greys, with dull green trees; in the centre was an improvised booth outlined by barley-sugar columns. Two figures entered to drum up the public's interest, their upper bodies encased in high Cubist constructions, one suggesting an American businessman with skyscraper and cowboy motifs, the other suggesting a French manager, elegant with hat and stick and a hint of trees; the constructions rendered the wearers incapable of any normal movement except stomping around and miming shouting through their megaphones. A third figure was a pantomime horse, its elongated face like an African mask, astride which was a black figure (which initially fell off, but evidently was later restored). Then came the performers: a Chinese Conjurer (Massine) swallowed an egg and retrieved it from his shoe; the Little American Girl (Marie Shabelska)'s solo recalled Chaplin and Pearl White movies – jumping on a train, swimming a river, firing a pistol; two Acrobats (Nicholas Zverev and Lydia Lopokova) executed pirouettes and arabesques and pretended to walk the tightrope. All then joined together in a rapid ragtime dance. The audience failed to materialize, leading to the collapse of the Managers.

Introducing the Managers to announce the acts in dumb-show was Picasso's suggestion, as was executing their costumes in Cubist style and thus transforming them into animated bill-boards to suggest the vulgarity of show-business promoters. The audience was confused, some feeling these figures were some kind of depersonalized scenery, others that they were more "real" than the three soloists. Satie's score was deliberately provocative; and to annoy the public further, Cocteau wanted everyday sounds to be added, such as typewriters clicking, sirens, and aeroplanes, although the more extreme noises – and the suggestion that the Managers speak lines – was vetoed by Diaghilev. All these, Cocteau explained, "were in the spirit of cubism, and helped to portray the feverish inanity of contemporary life."[2]

Although pigeon-holed as a Cubist ballet, *Parade* also displayed Futurist elements

[1] It is, of course, costumes from failed works that survive. Costumes for the popular ballets fell apart through overuse, and had to be remade.
[2] Cocteau, *Nord-Sud* quoted in Douglas Cooper, *Picasso Theatre* (New York: Harry N. Abrams): 103.

– concrete gesture and sound, variety material, alogical structure, mechanistic movement and constructed costume. While the Managers are clearly Cubist, the Chinese Conjurer, one of the most memorable of all theatrical costumes, prefigures Art Deco, in its bold scarlet and yellow and the sunray motif which, independent of *Parade*, would become a defining decorative motif of the 1920s and 1930s. This superb costume became familiar as the company emblem in the 1920s, when the design appeared on posters and programmes. Its survival is remarkable: Leon Woizikovsky, who succeeded Massine in the role, was living in Poland during the Second World War and buried the costume to keep it safe. Curiously, the Chinese Conjurer is one of the few costumes for which a design also exists for the back; costume-makers usually have to work out the back from the design for the front.

For the Little American Girl, Picasso designed a short frilled dress, but in the end she wore a sailor suit, bought off the peg; while the Acrobats' costumes followed the traditional uniform for such performers, based on fleshings but decorated with star and whorl designs in blue and white. All-overs were not new in ballet – for example, the costume for *Le Spectre de la rose* comprised all-overs with petal additions – but they were certainly not yet ubiquitous. Famously Picasso painted the design on the female Acrobat's costume and also provided details for the make-up.

In the programme notes, Bakst praised Picasso for discovering a new branch of his art, and while Apollinaire foresaw that the ballet would likely upset the audience, they would also be surprised and charmed by the "unimagined grace of modern dance movements". However, by 1917 audiences were exhausted by the ongoing war, and in no mood to be charmed. The ballet's premiere was disrupted both by those who perceived connections between Cubism and German atrocities, and by intellectuals objecting to Picasso working for an organization they considered "establishment". Yet Picasso himself had never envisaged *Parade* as an intellectual manifesto for modern art and, indeed, his compatriot Juan Gris described it as a sort of "musical joke in the best taste, and without high artistic pretensions".[3] When performed in London, *Parade* was described as "A Merry Display", and so later audiences seem to have accepted it, although the *Daily Telegraph* did point out that even if "Picasso's simple, though definitely unconventional, art [supplied] a setting that required no label ... the rest was of an oddity so extravagant, a conception so grotesque ... that without the informing synopsis it would have been impossible to have made head or tail of it."[4]

Few theatre productions have attracted as much analysis, speculation and comment as *Parade* which has spawned numerous books, articles and exhibitions. Feeding

[3] Juan Gris to Maurice Raynal, 18 May 1917.

[4] Anon., *Daily Telegraph* (London), 15 November 1919.

[5] He clearly antagonized his collaborators: as Satie wrote to Valentine Gross in 1920: "Cocteau is sticking to the boring 'tricks' of 1917. He's worn Picasso and myself down to a pulp. It's a mania with him – *Parade* is by himself alone. All right, I say. Why didn't he do the decor and costumes, or write the music for this wretched ballet."

[6] Anon., *Liverpool Daily Courier*, 2 August 1928.

the legend was that arch-publicist Cocteau himself through his own writings,[5] but the extraordinary fame of *Parade* is also due to Picasso's numerous drawings that chart the evolution of the designs, which makes the piece a fascinating study for historians of art and theatre; Picasso's outpourings are a tribute to his curiosity and willingness to learn and collaborate. Yet this is a ballet that was only performed thirty-four times in ten years – sixteen performances in Paris (seven in 1917, three in 1920, two in 1921, 1923, 1924 and 1926), one in Madrid, one in Barcelona, and sixteen in London (fourteen in 1919 and two in 1926), and while the number of performances is not in itself an indicator of quality, *Parade* never formed a regular part of Diaghilev's repertory, suggesting that after the initial wave of shock or amusement there was nothing to sustain further viewings. The British artist and friend of Picasso, Roland Penrose stated that with each production, *Parade* won more respect while recognizing that "it remained a ballet for the elite and a victory in the campaign of the *avant-garde*". If *Parade* aroused controversy and drew attention to Cubism and Picasso, this was rather a triumph for the art world and it was through writings rather than through the theatrical experience itself that *Parade* became so widely known.

In performance, *Parade* lasted only fourteen minutes, and so was staged with two or three other works from the repertory. It was this juxtaposition of works within a single evening that enabled Diaghilev to introduce so many new works, with the old favourites buoying up the novelties. New works were important, but in embracing the avant-garde (or a section of the avant-garde, since the term includes many different factions, largely at war with each other), Diaghilev had to be careful not to alienate more conservative elements in his audience; as a theatrical enterprise comprising a large company, orchestra (always a drain on resources) and support services, he had to preach to as wide an audience as possible, and he was extraordinarily successful in achieving a precarious balance between public acceptance and remaining in the vanguard. In fact, the Diaghilev Ballet did not so much initiate artistic trends as home in on them when they were ripe for transmission, translating the new tendencies into theatrical terms and laying them before a wider audience. Although rarely on the cutting edge, to the general public this was avant-garde. 'Russian Ballet ... probably illustrates modernism in art in a way more intelligible to the man in the street and the woman in the shop than any other medium (e.g., Cubism) ... ballet dancing not only largely explains itself, but helps to explain the music which accompanies it (e.g., Stravinsky).'[6]

Despite being hailed as a new beginning and an influential work, little direct influence can be traced to *Parade*, unlike *Scheherazade* which had an impact on fashion and interior decoration, and even spawned the immensely popular musical comedy *Chu-Chin Chow* (whose box-office rewards inspired Diaghilev to mount his own spectacular *Sleeping Princess*, albeit with less financial success). While *Parade* had no apparent influence on mainstream theatre, elements of it may be found in 1920s revues, but it's immediate importance was to show that Diaghilev was now looking to Europe for inspiration, and new designers would be sought from among important European painters.

Parade was created at a time when Diaghilev was rebuilding his company, and the dancers had yet to regain their pre-war standards, so there was a danger that the troupe would come to rely more on design and music than on dancing. Tamara Karsavina was concerned that "*Parade* projected so far into the topical as to strip it of ballet's essential virtue – its own creative material", she noted, while admitting that to embody the Little American Girl had been "tremendous fun".[7]

It was two years before the next new ballet when, on 5 June 1919, Diaghilev introduced another major painter to the theatre. Having rejected Bakst's designs for Massine's *La Boutique fantasque* as lacking the necessary charm and gaiety, he turned to André Derain, who brought "pure painting" into the theatre. His fantastical toy-shop was seen as if through the eyes of a child, with bright colours and *trompe-l'œil* tables and chairs (painted by Derain) that perfectly matched the wit and sparkle of Rossini's music and Massine's brilliant choreography, with its cast of strongly conceived characters. It was the first major hit of the post-war period, and remained popular for decades.

With Diaghilev needing two new works a year to appease his Paris audience, Massine was already at work on another ballet to be premiered six weeks later. Again, the designer was Picasso, but, unlike *Parade* there was no intention to be overtly avant-garde or *épater la bourgeoisie*. *Le Tricorne* was a tribute to Spain – where the company had found refuge during the war –based on a play by Pedro Antonio de Alarcón, and with a score commissioned from Manuel de Falla. Massine would have been familiar with a balleticized version of Spanish dancing in nineteenth-century Russian ballets, but now he immersed himself in authentic Spanish dance, which he then translated seamlessly into a form that was perfectly credible in balletic terms while losing nothing of its essential character. *Le Tricorne* was a much bigger production than *Parade*, requiring forty costumes and a enough stage space to accommodate the larger ensembles. Unlike *Parade* – in which Diaghilev had uncharacteristically hardly intervened, in this case he kept a keen eye on the whole, and Picasso was now working

[7] Tamara Karsavina, "Dancers of the Twenties", *Dancing Times* (February 1967): 252.

[8] Vladimir Polunin, *The Continental Method of Scene Painting* (London: Beaumont 1927).

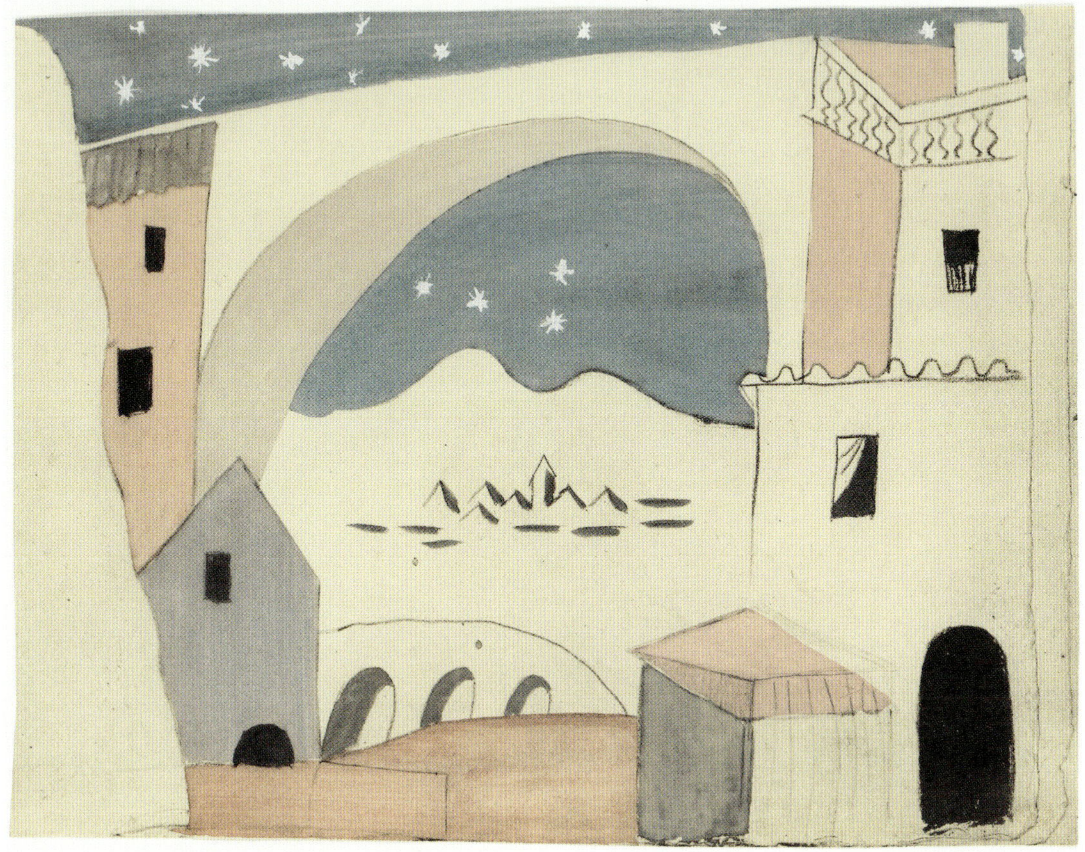

3. Pablo Picasso
Final sketch for the set design of the ballet *Le Tricorne*, 1919
Paris, Musée national Picasso-Paris

in close collaboration, accepting Diaghilev's suggestions and producing innumerable sketches in a quest for the perfect solution.

Picasso's major contribution to theatre design lay in showing how a subject can be reduced to essentials. In *Le Tricorne*, a few strokes conjured up a sun-baked Spanish village nestling beneath a mountain range under a blue starlit sky; to either side of the stage was a house, the two linked by a background arch, beneath which ran a low bridge. Any Cubist elements were unobtrusive – such as the twist of structural features to reveal more than the eye would see, the play of angles creating volumes – and the simple realism made the designs easy to realize in stage terms. The scenery painter Vladimir Polunin recalled how he was astounded by the "austere simplicity" of Picasso's designs after the complexities and ostentation of Bakst's scenery.[8] The drop curtain – illustrating a bull-fight from the perspective of spectators in a theatre box – was mostly painted by Picasso himself.

The set gave the costumes space to breathe. The women wore Goyasque cos-

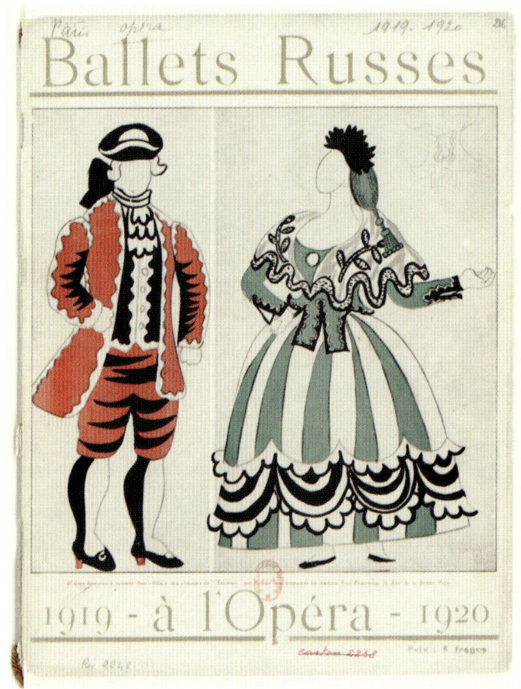

4. *Ballets Russes / 1919 – à l'Opéra – 1920*, frontispiece of the program of three ballets: *Petrushka*, *Le Sacre du printemps* and *Le Tricorne*
Paris, Bibliothèque nationale de France

tumes with high headdresses executed in bold coloured stripes decorated with simple motifs; the men sported bold colours. Against them, the Miller's Wife stood out in pink silk trimmed with black lace that was intentionally symbolic of Spanish dress, rather than a meticulous reproduction. One idiosyncratic touch – highly stylized but realistic – was the introduction of curves in the male costume designs to suggest creases in the fabric. Picasso also oversaw the performers' make-up, and in one case he painted blue, green, and yellow dots on a character's chin to give him the appropriate sinister appearance.

Le Tricorne was premiered on 22 July 1919 to great enthusiasm. It is a perfect collaborative ballet, seamlessly blending music, choreography and design. Picasso's designs are a joy to behold on stage, and not mere designs for their own sake – they enhance the choreography without detracting from it, and Massine himself acknowledged how they had inspired his choreography for the ballet. Over the next decade *Le Tricorne* was one of the Diaghilev Ballet's most popular works, and it enjoyed a long after-life.

Not all Diaghilev's commissioned painters were as successful in submitting to the demands of theatre. The artist commissioned to design Massine's next ballet *Le Chant du rossignol* (premiered on 2 February 1920) was Henri Matisse. Unlike Picasso and Derain, the French artist was less open to the collaborative process and to the needs of the theatre. Matisse saw the stage as a painting, and envisaged the dancers posed vertically to disguise the depth of the stage, and devised costumes grouped as stage pictures; he was horrified when he discovered that stage pictures were the choreographer's job, and the dancers would have to move.

Picasso's last major designs for Diaghilev were for Massine's *Pulcinella* premiered on 15 May 1920. The ballet was inspired by the *commedia dell'arte* performances that Massine had seen in Naples in 1917, and Diaghilev selected the score from works by Pergolesi, which were orchestrated by Stravinsky. Picasso at first conceived the designs in modern terms, then as a stage within a stage to underline the artificiality of the action. He then devised an 1880s-style theatre flanked by painted stage-boxes peopled with figures; Diaghilev rejected the scheme in no uncertain terms, actually throwing the designs on the floor. For all Diaghilev's reliance on the publicity value of renowned artists as designers, they had to know their place. Picasso took umbrage, but, realizing Diaghilev was right, he produced a much simpler set which cleverly suggested improvised screens used by a troupe of strolling players. Using only black, blue-grey, and white, he suggested a moonlit street overlooking the Bay of Naples, the moonlight effect enhanced by painting the stage floor white and only lighting from above. The costumes in traditional *commedia* style, provided splashes of colour – Pulcinella in white and black with red at neck, wrists and ankles, the other characters introducing red, green, plum pink, pale blue, and jade green.

The ballet was full of disguises and high-speed pursuits, but the choreography lacked the spontaneity of *The Good-Humoured Ladies*. Although enjoyed by the dancers and early audiences, the busy plot became tedious after a few viewings. The designs were too advanced for some, and when the company performed in Barcelona, the theatre manager asked for another ballet to be performed instead. *Pulcinella* would be performed sixty-one times over the next eight years, but had no life beyond the Diaghilev Ballet.

Massine left the company in 1920. Without a choreographer or star dancer, the emphasis and publicity shifted even more to the painter-designers. The only work in production was *Chout,* choreographed by dancer Theodore Slavinsky in collaboration with Larionov, who was also the designer. This was another excursion into Russian life, this time the rumbustious national peasantry. Larionov's costumes were daringly experimental – a mix of folkloristic and Constructivism, with added features of cane and canvas extending up and out from the body. Despite their ingenuity, these costumes obscured the wearer's movement and, anyway, could hardly be seen against the frenetic Rayonnist set.

Diaghilev's need for a second new work for the Paris season was solved when he met the English impresario (or showman, as he preferred to call himself) C.B. Cochran on holiday in Spain. Diaghilev urged Cochran to present him in London, and Cochran agreed with the stipulation that Diaghilev should present a Cuadro Flamenco performed by authentic Spanish dancers drawn from all over the country. To give some unity, Picasso designed realistic, colourful costumes, took the rejected *Pulcinella* decor showing a nineteenth-century theatre with painted audience in stage boxes and added a central rostrum, cleverly suggesting the interior of a cabaret. *Cuadro flamenco* premiered on 17 May 1921 and guaranteed gratifyingly full houses whenever it was performed in Paris and London.

As the dancers then dispersed back to Spain, the ballet was never performed again, so, when Diaghilev fell on financial hard times, he cut up and sold the set, along with the drop curtain for *Le Tricorne*. Thus Picasso ensured the survival of the Diaghilev Ballets Russes.

In 1924 Picasso gave permission for his painting *Deux femmes courant sur la plage* to be used as a drop curtain for Bronislava Nijinska's topical ballet *Le Train bleu,* which showed the smart set indulging in various sports on a fashionable beach. The curtain was executed by Prince Schervashidze, and Picasso was so pleased with the result that he signed it as a genuine Picasso. The curtain probably had the greatest impact of any of Picasso's work for Diaghilev, exerting a profound influence on the early artistic development of sculptor Henry Moore.

In 1924 Satie, Massine and Picasso reunited, but not under Diaghilev. *Mercure* was produced on 15 June 1924 by Comte Étienne de Beaumont's "Soirées de Paris" and, as all three names had become more famous since *Parade,* Diaghilev was distinctly nervous. Described on programme as "Poses Plastiques", the production was a series of tableaux depicting the (mostly inauthentic) deeds of Greek gods and goddesses. "Poses plastiques" were the nearest music halls got to nudity; the performers, wearing all-over fleshings, posed in tableaux usually depicting famous statues, which lent them a spurious respectability.

Entirely Picasso's conception, *Mercure* was more an installation than a dance work. His moving cardboard and rattan constructions competed for attention with the dancers (who also had to move them about). Ironically, the dancers in some photographs look strangely ungraceful and lumpy against the fluidity of Picasso's lines.

Why Diaghilev decided to present it in 1927 is unclear. He only scheduled three performances in Paris and one in London, and critics and audiences were unenthusiastic, although, in London there was enough interest among a section of the audience for him to announce a second performance. The avant-garde supporters of *Mercure* claimed it showed a way forward from classical ballet, which they felt had become a restrictive convention depriving dance of expressive possibilities. Why they felt this could be achieved by diminishing dance itself is unclear. The Diaghilev Ballets Russes had shown just how expressive and creative dancers trained in the classical style could be, and they would continue to explore and expand its possibilities throughout the 1920s.

Diaghilev continued to commission leading painters, with variable success on ballets which varied widely in quality. While not every new ballet could be a masterpiece, a number of exceptional works produced in the 1920s showed that seamless blending that was a hall mark of a Diaghilev ballet. Besides *The Good-Humoured Ladies, La*

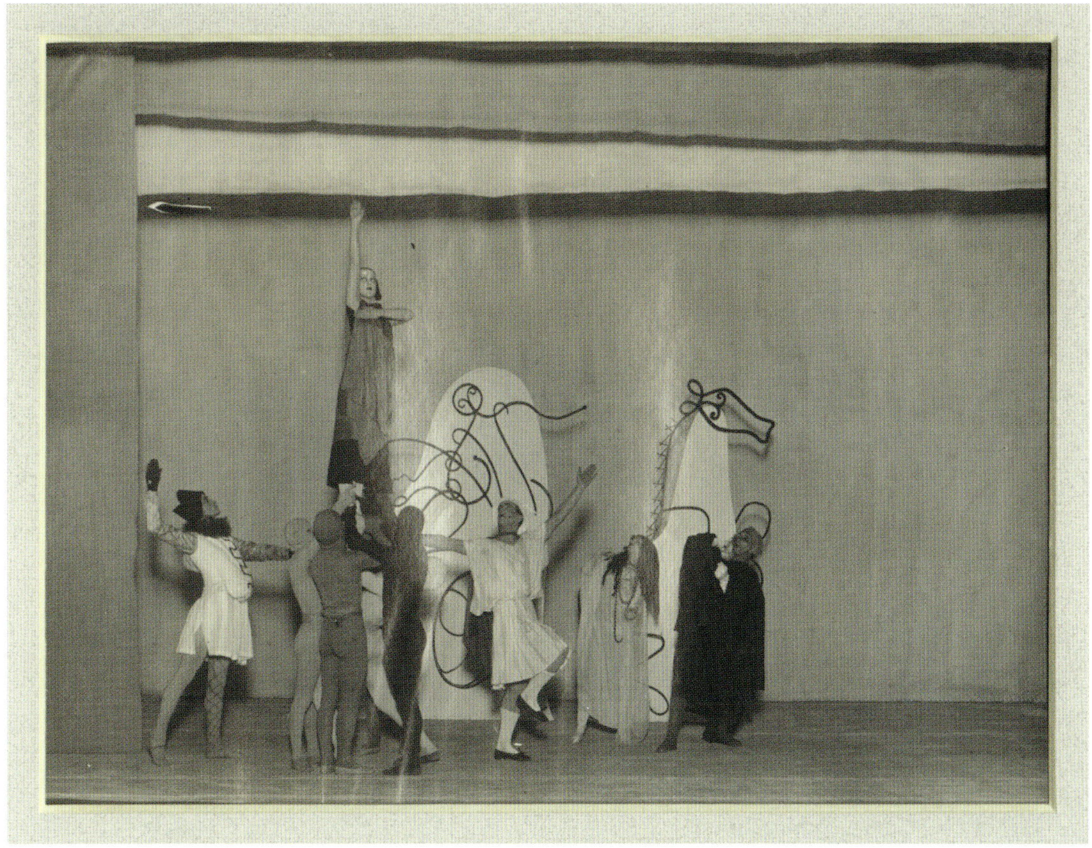

5. *Mercure*, Feast in the home of Bacchus, Spring 1924
Saint-Germain la Blanche-Herbe, Fonds Erik Satie – Archives de France / Archives IMEC, 165SAT/153/0

Boutique fanasque and *Le Tricorne,* there were two ballets by Bronislava Nijinska, *Les Biches*, a caustic look at 1920s society with cool, sophisticated Marie Laurencin designs, and her masterpiece, *Les Noces,* a Russian peasant wedding designed by Nathalie Gontcharova. *Les Matelots* designed by Pedro Pruna, was Massine's engaging romp about three sailors and their girls; while in contrast was George Balanchine's *La Chatte* with its bewitching Perspex and American cloth set (billed as "architecture and sculpture") devised by Naum Gabo and Antoine Pevsner, which was among the most popular new ballets produced in the last two years of the company's life; then came *Prodigal Son,* designed by the French painter Georges Rouault, created just before Diaghilev died in 1929. The major mismatch where a design failed to capture the essence of a masterpiece was André Bauchant's designs for Balanchine's production of Stravinsky's *Apollon Musagète*.

Other painters were either less suited to theatre or less lucky on the productions on which they worked. For example, Maurice

Utrillo contributed to the lacklustre *Barabau*; Pavel Tchelichev created designs for Stravinsky's orchestral piece *Ode*, in which he mingled bodies and light; Max Ernst and Joan Miró designed Nijinska's modern *Romeo and Juliet* with the action transferred to a rehearsal room, which evoked a satisfactorily uproarious first night when the designers' colleagues demonstrated against their association with Diaghilev. Georges Braque created a charming costume for Flore in *Zéphyr et Flore* with a tiny half tutu and his idea of decorating only the front of costumes in *Les Facheux was* ingenious but neither ballet was particularly successful. *Le Pas d'acier* with Yakulov's constructivist machine set reflected Soviet trends and like *Les Noces* refutes the idea that Diaghilev no longer looked to Russia for inspiration. Giorgio de Chirico's surreal costumes for *Le Bal* encumbered the dancers with architectural mouldings, overshadowing Balanchine's choreography.

All the attention given to Diaghilev and the artist-designers, does, however, obscure an important point. It is clear from a study of the nightly repertory, that audiences in the 1920s went to see the company primarily for the dancing. The most performed ballets were the Russian works from the first seasons – *Polovtsian Dances from Prince Igor*, *Les Sylphides*, *Le Carnaval* and *Petrushka; Scheherazade* gradually dropped out of the repertory, but *Cléôpatre* and *Thamar* were still popular as was *L'Après-midi d'un faune*, *Le Spectre de la rose*, and *The Firebird*; from post-war *The Good-Humoured Ladies, La Boutique fantasque, Le Tricorne, Les Biches, La Chatte,* and *Les Matelots* were good box office. Indeed, the appetite for dancing was growing: two of the most performed ballets in the 1920s which have merited little attention were the 1922 production of *Aurora's Wedding* (Act III of *The Sleeping Beauty* augmented with choreography taken from earlier acts) and *Cimarosiana* (1924) a divertissement created by Massine for the opera *Le astuzie femminili* in 1920. Neither could be classed as "novel", and neither were distinguished for their designs, but they were full of dancing.

Throughout the 1920s the pendulum was swinging back. Both Picasso and Stravinsky were moving towards Neoclassicism, the impetus coming from their work with Diaghilev – Picasso's exposure to Italy while working on *Parade* and Stravinsky's discovery of the past ("the epiphany through which the whole of my late work became possible") in his work on Pergolesi for *Pulcinella*. Similarly Diaghilev's last great choreographer, George Balanchine, returned the company to the roots of classical ballet which had nourished Fokine's choreography at the beginning.[9] Diaghilev himself recognized the shift and was planning to revive *Swan Lake* and *Giselle* before he died in 1929.

Ultimately, the legacy of the Diaghilev Ballets Russes lay not in advanced mod-

[9] Balanchine's later preference for austere design may have been a reaction to his experiences with Diaghilev, where he saw the danger of the designer usurping the dancer and the *raison d'être* for ballet, dance itself.

ernism, but in restating the power and expression of classical dance. This legacy was followed up in America by Balanchine in New York City Ballet, and in Britain by his former dancers Marie Rambert in Ballet Rambert, and Ninette de Valois in what is now The Royal Ballet.

Yet nothing can obscure the spell cast by the artist-designer, especially Picasso – the elegance and fluidity of his drawing, streamlining of detail, the wonder of his colour and the theatrical effectiveness of his imagination. His designs cross the barrier between working blueprints and art, and his imaginative development can be traced as the designs on paper become painted canvas, fabric, and texture. The pity is that they can now so rarely be experienced where they were meant to be seen – in the theatre.

Diving Deep into a Mediterranean Affair: *The Pipes of Pan*, Nature and Culture

Silvia Loreti

> The satyr, like the idyllic shepherd of our more recent age, is the product of a longing for the primordial and the natural. ... Nature, still unaffected by knowledge – that's what the Greeks saw in their satyr. ... Modern man's idyllic shepherd is nothing but a counterfeit of the sum of cultural illusions that he takes to be nature.
>
> Friedrich Nietzsche[1]

From La Toilette de Vénus *to* The Pipes of Pan*: Art and Life*

During the summer of 1923, while on holiday in Antibes, or after his return to Paris the following autumn, Picasso painted a solemn canvas, *The Pipes of Pan* (cat. no. 172) over an existing large-format mythological scene known as *La Toilette de Vénus* (fig. 1). The original painting was seen in Picasso's studio at the time, is documented by numerous studies and its presence is confirmed by X-ray analysis of *The Pipes of Pan*.[2]

La Toilette de Vénus had a timeless character, perhaps as the result of its long and gradual evolution. It began as a group composition in which a couple – likely Venus and Mars – danced to the music of Pan under the watchful eye of Cupid. Subsequently, the couple was represented in tender embrace.[3] Eventually, Picasso introduced the mirror that gave *La Toilette de Vénus* its title, experimenting with an eighteenth-century costumed dancer as mirror-holder to Venus, before settling on the naked Mars.[4] The sketches show that the scene could take place either outdoors – against what appears to be a seaside horizon – or within a modern bourgeois interior reminiscent of Picasso's Paris studio on the elegant Rue de la Boétie. *La Toilette de Vénus* was thus as an allegory of sensual and contemplative love unravelling in the liminal spaces of nature and culture.

Such straightforward allegorical readings are lost in *The Pipes of Pan*. Picasso maintained the reference to mythology in the theme and title of the final painting, choosing a Mediterranean setting that amplified the ancient dimension of the previous work.[5] Yet the two survivors from *La Toilette de Vénus*, with their short hair, lean bodies and sporty loincloths, look more like remnants of Cézanne's bathers than mythological characters. Confined between walls that look like theatre sets and separated by a solid sea, the youths interact as immobile actors in a frozen *tableau vivant*. Their generic features, cool detachment and theatricality mark them as representations of a modern loss of identity, depth, intimacy and authenticity as opposed to the assumed state of nature of a dreamed antiquity.

No wonder *The Pipes of Pan* has been considered emblematic of a phase in Picasso's career and in the history of the avant-garde that is largely regarded as an anti-modernist "call to order", with the two bathers embodying the humanist ideal of the western male body pre-

I wish to thank Rachel Sloan and Talia Kwartler for their assistance during my research and their comments on this text.

[1] Friedrich Nietzsche, *The Birth of Tragedy Out of the Spirit of Music*, Engl. trans. Shaun Whiteside, ed. Michael Tanner (London: Penguin, 2003): 40–41.

[2] Drawings related to *La Toilette de Vénus* are documented in Christian Zervos, *Pablo Picasso, 1895-1972* (33 vols), 1932–78, Paris, Editions Cahiers d'art, vol. 5, *Oeuvres de 1923 à 1925* (hereafter Z) and in the Musée Picasso, Paris (hereafter MP) Sketchbooks nos 1868 (Paris 1922) and 1990–101 (Dinard, Paris, Antibes, 1922–23) in Brigitte Léal (ed.), *Carnets. Catalogue des dessins*, Réunion des musées nationaux, Paris, 1996, vol. 1, cat. nos 24–25, pp. 319–21 and 331–32. The rediscovery of *La Toilette de Vénus* underneath *The Pipes of Pan* was the work of Danielle Giraudy and the Laboratoire de Recherche des Musée de France: Giraudy, "Pablo Picasso: *The Pipes of Pan*", in *Canto d'Amore: Classicism in Modern Art and Music*, Kunstmuseum Basel, 1996, 266–78. John Richardson (*A Life of Picasso*, 1991, vol. III: *The Triumphant Years, 1917–1932*, London: Cape, 2007, 224) has noted that Picasso left for Antibes on 23 July 1923, and likely left *La Toilette de Vénus* in Paris. The painter Jacinto Salvadó, who visited Picasso's studio in Paris after the Soirée du Cœur à Barbe on 6 July, recounted seeing a "painting of a perfect classicism" entitled

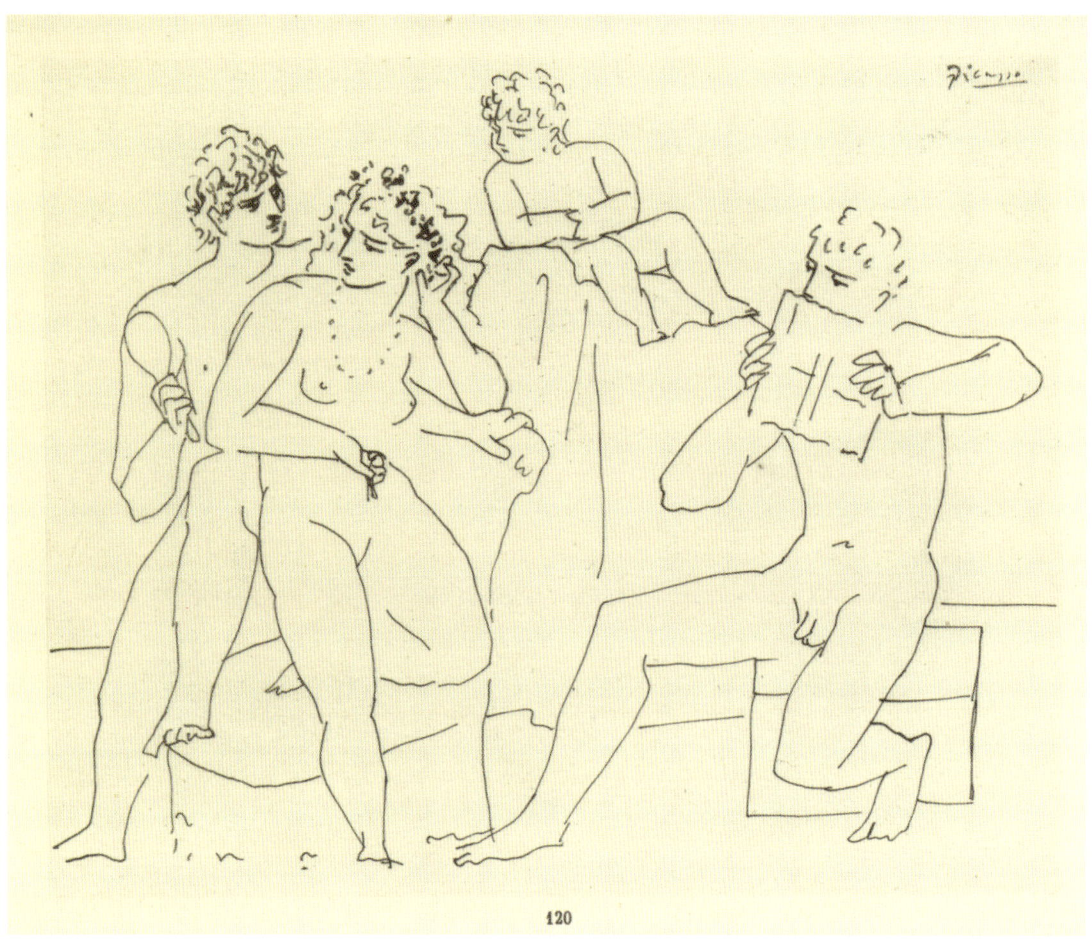

1. Pablo Picasso
Jeune homme au miroir, nu, jouer de flûte de Pan, enfant
[Young man with a mirror, nude playing the pipes of Pan, child]
[Study for The Toilet of Venus],
1923
India ink on paper, 22.5 x 32 cm

siding over nature. According to T.J. Clark, *The Pipes of Pan* stands for "the true seriousness of – the massive ambition – of [Picasso's] style of the 1920s, which had gone on fighting for an epic space made out of Cubist materials".[6]

At the same time, the rediscovery of *La Toilette de Vénus* prompted biographical readings of the changes that occurred between this work and *The Pipes of Pan*. In this context, the two paintings have been read through the prism of Picasso's private life in the early 1920s, a time when the artist bathed more in the spotlights of his theatrical collaborations than in the Mediterranean sun. According to a romantic narrative devised by William Rubin, *The Pipes of Pan* is the denouement of *La Toilette de Vénus*. In the earlier work Picasso would have represented his unconsummated passion for the married American heiress Sara Murphy. It was she who, with her husband Gerald, invited the Picassos to spend the summer of 1923 in Cap d'Antibes (fig. 2).[7] Gerald

La Toilette de Vénus on an easel. Picasso also showed Salvadó a series of studies: Salvadó, "Chez Picasso", *Paris-Journal* (14 March 1924): 5.

[3] M.P. 1868, 36R and 44R. The pan-piper has often been associated with Apollo, but the presence of a shepherd rod in Z V, 107 and of a goat in a drawing dated 4th February 1923 (M.P. 983) distinctly mark this figure as the Pan of the title.

[4] Respectively Z V, 118–20 and Z V, 114–16 and 121–2, 125 and 127.

[5] The painting appears as *The Pipes of Pan* in the large 1932 Picasso retrospectives at the Galerie Georges Petit (Paris, 16 June–30 July 1932, cat. no. 138, p. 48, illustrated) and Kunsthaus Zurich (11 September – 13 November 1932, cat. no. 129, p. 9, as *Die Pansflöte*). With thanks to Laura Bruni for confirming this information.

[6] T.J. Clark, *Picasso and Truth. From Cubism to Guernica* (Princeton and Oxford: Princeton University Press, 2013): 252.

[7] William Rubin, "*The Pipes of Pan*: Picasso's Aborted Love Song to Sara Murphy", *Artnews* 93, no. 5 (May 1994): 138–47.

[8] Calvin Tomkins, *Living Well is the Best Revenge* (originally published 1971; New York: The Museum of Modern Art, 2013): 15–16.

[9] Kenneth E. Silver, "The Murphy Closet and the Murphy Bed", in Deborah Rothschild (ed.), *Making it New. The Art and Style of Sara & Gerald Murphy* (Williamstown, MA: Williams College Museum of Art, Yale University Art Gallery and Dallas Museum of Art, University of California Press and Williams College Museum of Art, 2007/8): 107–18.

[10] For example, François Boucher, *La Toilette de Vénus*, 1751, oil on canvas, 108.3 x 85.1 cm, New York, The Metropolitan Museum of Art.

[11] Christopher Green, "Classicism of Transience and of Transcendence. Maillol, Picasso and de Chirico", in Elizabeth Cowling and Jennifer Mundy (eds.), *On*

was a talented painter, and he and his wife Sara had worked as curtain restorers for the Ballets Russes.[8] Though happily married with three children, Gerald was a closeted homosexual.[9] Sexual frustration and repression would explain the imagery of *The Pipes of Pan*, with Picasso playing the piper to Gerald's bather at rest. Key to this argument are a number of idealized female portraits that Rubin identified with Sara, as well as the presence in *La Toilette de Vénus* of a long pearl necklace, a trademark of Sara's outfit that she made fashionable as a beach accessory. Pearls, however, are a traditional attribute of the goddess of love, and pearl necklaces often feature in depictions by the Old Masters of Venus at her toilette.[10]

So, on the one hand *The Pipes of Pan* is considered to be a document of the period's regression into the Classical past, despite its present-tense dimension.[11] On the other, it is viewed as the translation of life events despite the fact that its imagery clearly derives from the classical tradition. This essay attempts to reconcile Classicism and modernity, biography and history, nature and culture in the interpretation of *The Pipes of Pan* and to rethink Picasso's Neoclassicism beyond gossip and pastiche.

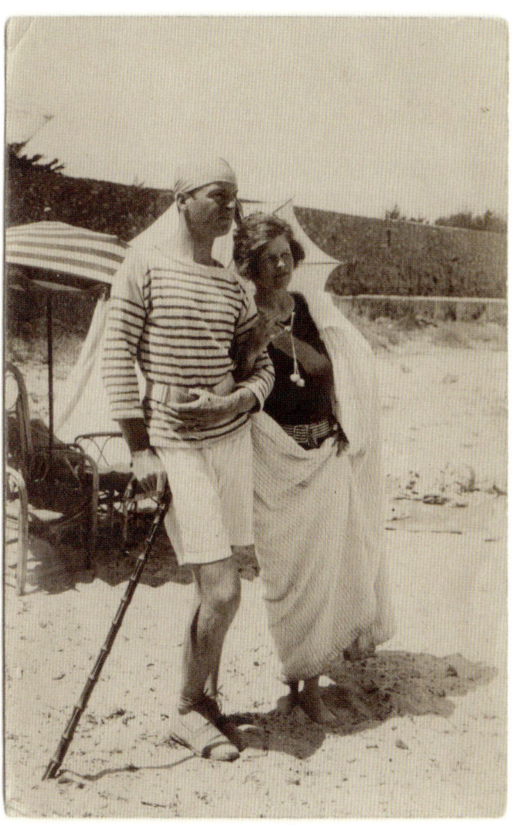

2. Gerald and Sara Murphy, on the Garoupe Beach, Cap d'Antibes, 1923
New Haven, Yale University, Beinecke Rare Book & Manuscript Library, Sara and Gerald Murphy Papers

Ballet and the Italian Journey: The Youth of Antiquity

The four-figure composition of *La Toilette de Vénus* already appears in a sketchbook of 1922. In fact, the original nucleus of the scene lies in drawings dating back to 1917–18 of two *commedia dell'arte* characters serenading first a female dancer, then Venus at her toilet with Cupid, which Picasso made in the wake of his stay in Italy with the Ballets Russes and the creation of the *Parade* drop-curtain (cat. nos. 34, 134).

The concomitant experiences of the ballet and Italy are key to an understanding of Picasso's Neoclassical work. With the exception of a spell of interest in the Louvre's antiquities in 1905–07, prior to 1917 Picasso saw classical antiquity as the source of his academic studies, which – like many of his generation – he rejected in favour of avant-gardism. His work with the Ballets Russes revealed to him the possibilities of an alliance between avant-garde iconoclasm and the academic, aristocratic, and highly codified art of ballet. Working alongside musicians and choreographers, Picasso was able to subvert established theories that

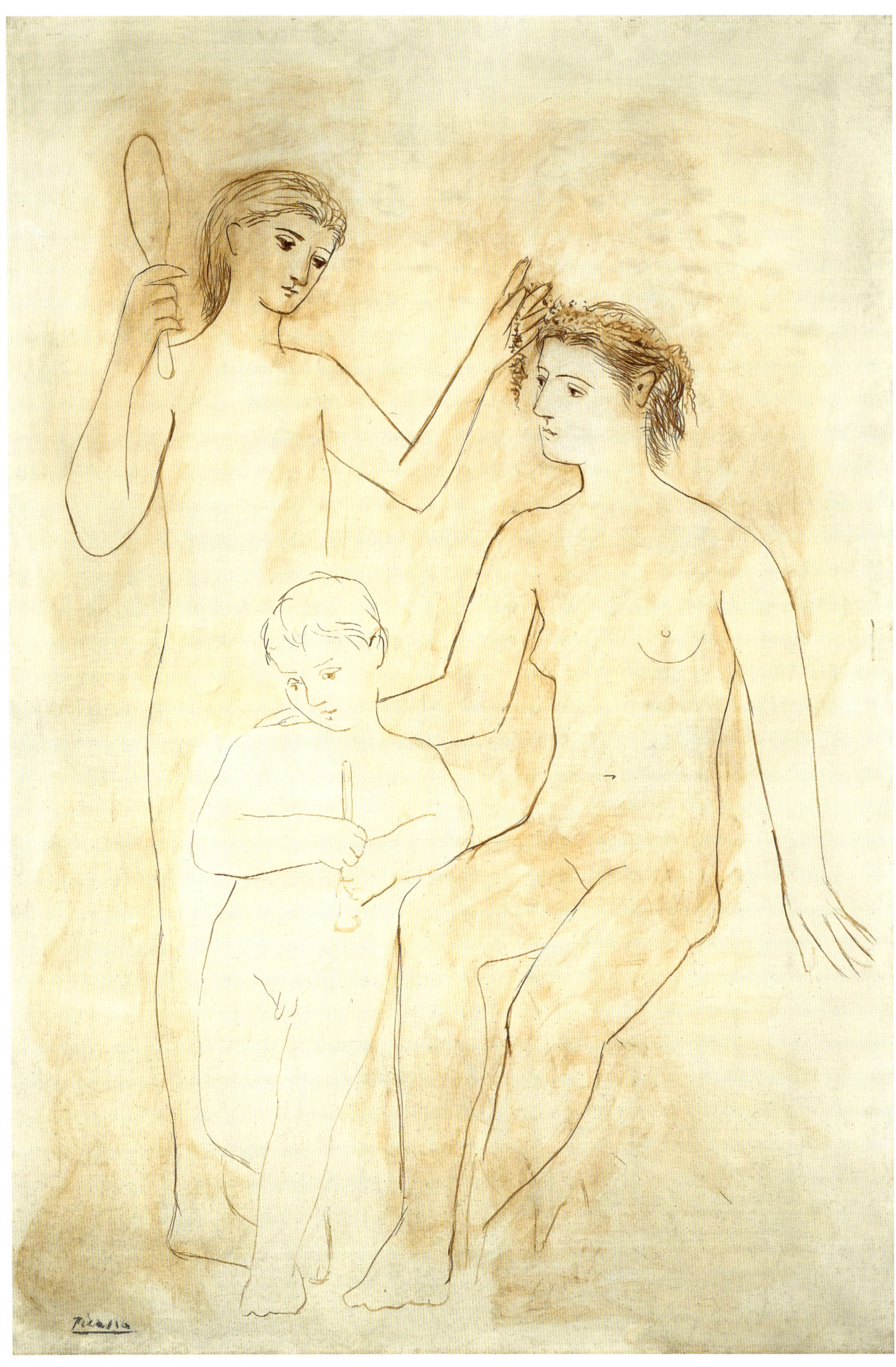

3. Pablo Picasso
Deux femmes et enfant
[Two Women and Child],
Paris, winter 1922
Oil on canvas, 189 x 129.2 cm
Private collection

forced a distinction between the fine arts, music and dance.

In Italy, the land of Classicism's most enduring tradition, Picasso also became aware – to paraphrase Rodin – of "the youth of Antiquity".[12] Together with the Ballets Russes' choreographer Léonide Massine, with whom he worked on *Parade*, Picasso explored not only the museums but also the theaters and brothels of Rome, Naples and Pompeii. The two collaborated again in spring 1923 on a lost theatrical piece that provided the starting point for the grotesque *Mercure* (1924), their last work together, and Picasso's very last contribution to the ballet.

It has been noted that Massine's stocky build and strong facial features resemble those of the standing youth in *The Pipes of Pan*.[13] The goliardic character of his and Picasso's adventures in Italy – which can be surmised from the queer disposition of the two youths in the painting – reflected in the artist's rediscovery of antiquity and Classicism. With Massine, the Ballets Russes' impresario Serge Diaghilev and the poet Jean Cocteau, Picasso also experienced the popular and post-classical traditions of Rome and Naples, such as the carnival and the miniature sculptures of the Neapolitan Christmas crib, which were on display in the city all year round. Classicism emerged from these experiences as incredibly close, alive, and authentic, and at the same time spurious, staged and anachronistic – revealing to Picasso the complex, fluid, playful and ultimately elusive nature of the meeting between Classicism and Modernity.

Salomon Reinach's Repertoires: Antiquity by Type and the Indeterminacy of Visual References

In 1922 Picasso transformed the original *commedia dell'arte* group into the properly classical *La Toilette de Vénus*. The passage took place through a series of coiffure scenes of the same year. These scenes mirror a section of the pictorial cycle of the Villa of the Mysteries (Villa dei Misteri), in Pompeii, depicting the wedding preparation of a bride accompanied by Cupid (fig. 3). The coiffure is a theme that Picasso had already explored during his Rose period, but the groomed seated woman in the 1922 version, who was to be reproduced, alone, in a number of Ballets Russes brochures, has undergone a process of classicization (cat. no. 108).

During his Italian journey, Picasso saw Roman frescoes in Rome, Naples and Pompeii. At some point, he bought postcards and prints of wall paintings in the Museo Archeologico Nazionale in Naples.[14] We do not know with certainty whether he visited the Villa of the Mysteries, but it seems possible. It was, after all, the only suburban structure in Pompeii in which extensive high-quality painting had been left *in situ* and travel guides of the period indicated how to obtain access through the doorman of a nearby hotel.[15]

Classic Ground: Picasso, Léger, de Chirico and the New Classicism, 1910–1930 (London: Tate, 1990): 267–82.

[12] "Antiquity is my youth", Rodin said: Auguste Rodin, "Vénus. À la Vénus de Milo", *L'Art et les Artistes*, no. 10 (March 1910): 243–55.

[13] Anne Baldassari, "Pompeian Fantasy: A Photographic Source of Picasso's Neoclassicism", in Jean Clair (ed.), *Picasso: The Italian Journey, 1917–1924* (Venice: Palazzo Grassi, 1998): 79–86.

[14] Baldassari 1998, 81–83.

[15] The decorative cycle of the Villa of the Mysteries was first brought to light at the beginning of the century and then excavated systematically in the late 1920s: Elaine K. Gazda, "Replicating Roman Murals in Pompeii: Archaeology, Art and Politics in Italy of the 1920s"; and Bettina Bergmann, "Seeing Women in the Villa of the Mysteries: A Modern Excavation of the Dionysiac Murals", in Victoria C. Gardner Coates and Jon L. Seydl (eds.), *Antiquity Recovered. The Legacy of Pompeii and Herculaneum* (Los Angeles: Getty, 2007): 207 and 241–44 respectively. My thanks to Silvio Lapaglia for discussing this topic with me. For more on the possible links between the Pompeii frescoes and Picasso's so-called Rose Period, see *Conceptión Boncompte Coll, "Iconografía picassiana entre 1905–1907. Influencia de la pintura pompeyana"*, PhD thesis, Universitat de Barcelona, 2009.

Incidentally, in 1922 the entire pictorial cycle of the Villa of the Mysteries was reproduced in a repertoire of ancient painting by the French scholar Salomon Reinach, in a section dedicated to representations of the mythological couple Dionysus and Ariadne (fig. 4).[16] The repertoire of Greek and Roman painting was the last of Reinach's three encyclopaedic dictionaries that illustrated ancient works of art, classed by media and by subject matter, through small and approximate engravings. Pocketsize handbooks rather than catalogues raisonnés of antiquities, Reinach's volumes were addressed as much to travellers and artists as to scholars and curators. Their role in the rediscovery of ancient subjects and the development of a modern linear Classicism, not least Picasso's classical prints of the 1930s, should not be underestimated.[17]

4. Salomon Reinach
Répertoire de peintures grecques et romaines
E. Léroux, Paris 1922
(Villa of the Mysteries)

Reinach's illustrations, which often derived from photographs, have the cumulative, mechanical quality of modern mass-media images. They reproduce perspectival paintings as well as sculptures and reliefs through flat, linear engravings that confound media distinctions. Interestingly, Picasso produced a number of grisailles of *La Toilette de Vénus*.[18] With their suggestion of volume through sfumato, the grisailles reveal that the artist was thinking of sculpture while working on *La Toilette de Vénus*, although at the time his sculptural production was restricted to theatrical sets and costumes. Above all, it is the vast number and reduced scale of Reinach's illustrations that seem significant for a Modernist appraisal of classical antiquity, as they converge in erasing the notion of the individual classical masterpiece. Instead, ancient art is presented as a consumable stock of types that bring together different media, periods and regions.

The visual references of *The Pipes of Pan* have a similar character. They are never punctual or individual and they range across time, subjects and media. The list includes ancient sculptures as disparate as the colossal Farnese heroes and the pederastic group *Pan and Daph-*

[16] Salomon Reinach, *Répertoire* de *peintures* grecques et romaines (Paris: Leroux, 1922).

[17] A discussion of Reinach's work in relation to Picasso is to be found in Cowling 2002, 145 and 416–17.

[18] He said to Salvadó (1924 above): "I search the composition in grisaille before adding any colour."

[19] For a discussion of possible iconographical references in *The Pipes of Pan*: Elizabeth Cowling, *Picasso. Style and Meaning* (London: Phaidon, 2002): 431–38. Picasso owned homoerotic pictures of southern Italian boys by Wilhelm von Plüschow: Anne Baldassari, *Le Miroir noir: Picasso sources photographiques, 1900–1928* (Paris: Réunion des musées nationaux, 1997): 62–64. See also Robert Judson Clark and Marian Burleigh-Motley, "New Sources for Picasso's *The Pipes of Pan*", *Arts Magazine* 55 (October 1980): 93–94.

[20] In 1922 Picasso produced the decor for Cocteau's new version of Sophocles' *Antigone*.

[21] Richardson III, 382.

[22] Ovid, *Metamorphoses*, I, 687–713.

[23] Charles Andler, *Nietzsche, sa vie et sa pensée*, 6 vols. (Paris, 1920–31). Volume three was published in 1922 and analyzed ideas contained in *Human All Too Human* and *The Gay Science*: Andler, *Nietzsche et le transformisme intellectualiste: la philosophie de sa période française*, (Paris: Bossard, 1922).

nis – both seen by Picasso in the Museo Archeologico Nazionale in Naples – Old Master paintings from the Louvre, such as Perugino's *Apollo and Marsyas*, nineteenth-century homoerotic photography of Mediterranean boys – which Picasso possessed – and his own classical period of 1905–06.[19]

Ovid and Nietzsche: The Metaphoric Power of Classicism

The everyday, intimate character of the 1922 female toilette scenes contrasts sharply with the monumental dimension of the male *Pipes of Pan*. Here Picasso seems to privilege a more literary mode, perhaps a consequence of his friendship and collaboration with Cocteau at the time.[20] At the end of the 1920s Albert Skira commissioned Picasso with the illustrations for Ovid's *Metamorphoses*. It seems that, while in Rome in 1917, Picasso had already been fascinated by the Ovidian couple Apollo and Daphne that he saw represented in Bernini's sculpture in the Galleria Borghese.[21]

The imagery and title of *The Pipes of Pan* show knowledge of the section of the *Metamorphoses* that follows on from the tale to Apollo and Daphne, when Ovid digresses into the origins of the panpipes. The instrument derives, we learn, from the metamorphosis of Syrinx, the nymph who was turned into reeds to escape the sexual assault of Pan. To console himself Pan turned the reeds into pipes, for which the word syrinx is a synonym.[22] In Ovid, then, the panpipes function metonymically to signify the solitary satisfaction of Pan's unfulfilled sexual desire. Ovid's erotic tale of Pan and Syrinx seems to bring us back full circle to Rubin's interpretation of *The Pipes of Pan*. However, like the characters of the *Metamorphoses*, the two youths of the painting have no fixed identity, but function as metaphors for the mutability of human nature.

The individual embodiment of universal human conditions finds a parallel in Friedrich Nietzsche's conception of life and art through the Greek gods Apollo and Dionysus, the former the expression of control, reason, sight and painting, the latter of man's communion with nature, sexuality and music. The two youths of *The Pipes of Pan* seem to be the pictorial translations of these two principles – the standing figure, derived from the mirror-holder of *La Toilette de Vénus*, all outward sight, the seated character a musician inwardly absorbed. Nietzsche had always been popular with Picasso and fellow avant-garde artists, who in time picked up on different aspects and interpretations of the German's thought. In France after the Great War, the philosopher's first lengthy biography in French pitched him as the unlikely herald of a national rationalism.[23]

Via Nietzsche, art and life are again confounded. The philosopher located universal principles in Apollo and Dionysus, but also interpreted his own life through them. After his falling-out with Richard Wagner, whose operatic work had been the initial stimulus behind the conception of the Apollonian and the Dionysian, Nietzsche related his infatuation for Wagner's wife Cosima to Dionysus's salvific role for the abandoned Ariadne. In similar ways, *The Pipes of Pan* can be viewed as the coming together of flesh-and-blood figures and universal and timeless principles that are given tangible forms as vestiges of real-life experiences.

The Modern Mediterranean: Constructed Idylls and Fluid Identities

During the spring prior to his 1923 in Antibes, Picasso gave an interview in which he released an uncharacteristically articulate, and evidently Nietzschean commentary on his Neoclassical work. Here is an extract of it: "Art is a lie that allows us to approach truth, at least the truth that is accessible to us. [...] People oppose modern painting to naturalism. But has anyone ever seen a *natural* work of art? Nature and art, being two different things, cannot be ruled by the same object. Art allows us to express our conception of what nature does not represent in one fixed way."[24]

This preoccupation with the relationship between art, nature and truth finds a parallel in *The Pipes of Pan*, a painting that belongs, by virtue of its title, to the genre of the idyllic. Deriving from the classical myth of the Golden Age, the idyllic enjoyed renewed fortune in France at the end of the nineteenth century. The modern idyllic, as Margaret Werth has analyzed, represents "desire binding individual and cultural fantasies".[25] It was an attempt to reconnect modern culture to a lost original state of nature through a depiction of time outside history. Within Modernism the genre found its most complete expression in Matisse's *Bonheur de vivre* (1905–06, fig. 5), a pictorial utopia composed by figurative vignettes that verge on abstraction. *The Pipes of Pan* is the nemesis of *Le Bonheur de vivre*, not least in its use of a monumental Neoclassicism to represent modern man's loss of touch with the natural world.[26] Moreover, Picasso's transposition of the pastoral onto a modern beach setting breaks the Golden Age's ideal (and idyllic) unity between man and nature and discloses modernity's pretension to naturalness.

When Picasso discovered the Côte d'Azur, the Riviera was undergoing a fast and irreversible transformation from *locus naturae* to *locus culturae*, for which the Murphys became two of the principle actors. Importing North-American beach culture to the Mediterranean through their festive and generous hospitality, they determined the transformation of the Riviera into a site of new-world reinvention, both physical and social. Their introduction to the French littoral of the seasonal rites of tanning, beach sports and mundane entertainment, transformed the Côte d'Azur into a modernist Eden – a carefully constructed idyll at the same time accessible and remote. In 1923,

[24] Florence Fels, "Propos d'artistes. Picasso", *Les Nouvelles littéraires*, no. 41 (4 August 1923): 2.

[25] Margaret Werth, *The Joy of Life: The Idyllic in French Art circa 1900* (Berkeley, CA: University of California Press, 2003): 10.

[26] *The Joy of Life* was sold to the American collector Alfred Barnes in 1922, thus marking Matisse as *the* modern European master in the United States. It is likely that, as ever, Picasso had the Nice-based Matisse much on his mind while in Antibes in 1923 and that the older master's success in the United States was deeply felt by the Spanish artist during the preparation of his own first American retrospective the following autumn.

[27] Deborah Rothschild, "Masters of the Art of Living", in Rothschild (ed.) 2007–08, 45–56. Richardson 2007, 233.

[28] Picasso's brochure for the 1924 Paris season of the Ballets Russes was already used for their 1923 summer season in Monte Carlo.

[29] Oliver Winchester, "Diaghilev's Boys", in *Diaghilev and The Golden Age of the Ballets Russes 1909–1929*, ed. by Jane Pritchard, Victoria & Albert Museum, London, 2010, 46–47.

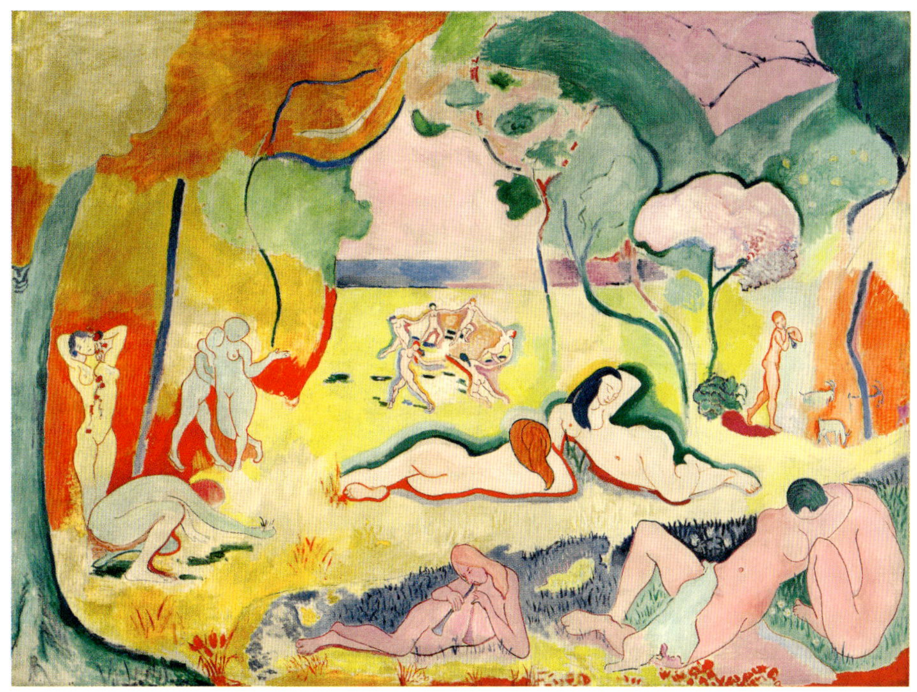

5. Henri Matisse
Le Bonheur de vivre
[The Joy of Life], 1905–06
Oil on canvas, 176.5 x 240.7 cm
Philadelphia, The Barnes Foundation

the Murphys and their entourage effectively endorsed the fashion for summers on the Riviera, whose later mass-cultural appeal Picasso decried in the post-War years.[27]

The search for an apparent natural state is central to the myth of the Murphys. Sara and Gerald were lively and sincere personalities but their continuous effort to shape their life as a work of art and their association with the culture of disguise – both in recurrent fancy-dress parties and in the everyday construction of sophisticated identities – could easily transform them into artful characters. This is how they appear in Scott Fitzgerald's *Tender is the Night* (1934), which took them as the initial inspiration for the two protagonists.

Artfulness was prominent in the Ballets Russes. Picasso's wife, Olga, had been a ballerina with Diaghilev, whose company spent the summer of 1923 in Monte Carlo, near Antibes.[28] Ballet and opera share the place of honour for ambiguity and artificiality among the theatrical arts. Onstage disguise, quibbles and pastiche, as well as backstage promiscuity, feuds and jealousies are the staples of ballet. Moreover, ballet entails a rigorous physical practice whose transformative powers on the body can underscore sexual fluidity. Given their sensual nature, relationships among company members can easily slip from the professional to the sexual and become a means to advance (or impede) careers, as it repeatedly happened to Diaghilev's choreographers, including Massine.[29] The intersection between avant-garde and elite cultures operated by Diaghilev's project implied broader social fluidity too. Picasso experienced this transformative aspect of the Ballets Russes first hand, as the riches and fame that he acquired in the 1920s were largely the result of his collaborations with the impresario.

In conclusion, the presence of real people in *The Pipes of Pan*, is not about the representation of specific individuals and circumstances. Rather their spirit expresses a desire to bridge the gulf between that profound communing with nature attributed to a primordial antiquity and the seductive but fleeting appearances of Classicism in modern culture.

Works

I. Cubism Goes on Stage

1. Pablo Picasso
Homme à la pipe
[Man with a Pipe], 1914
Oil and printed fabric on canvas,
138 x 66.5 cm
Paris, Musée national Picasso-Paris,
Pablo Picasso Donation, 1979,
inv. MP39

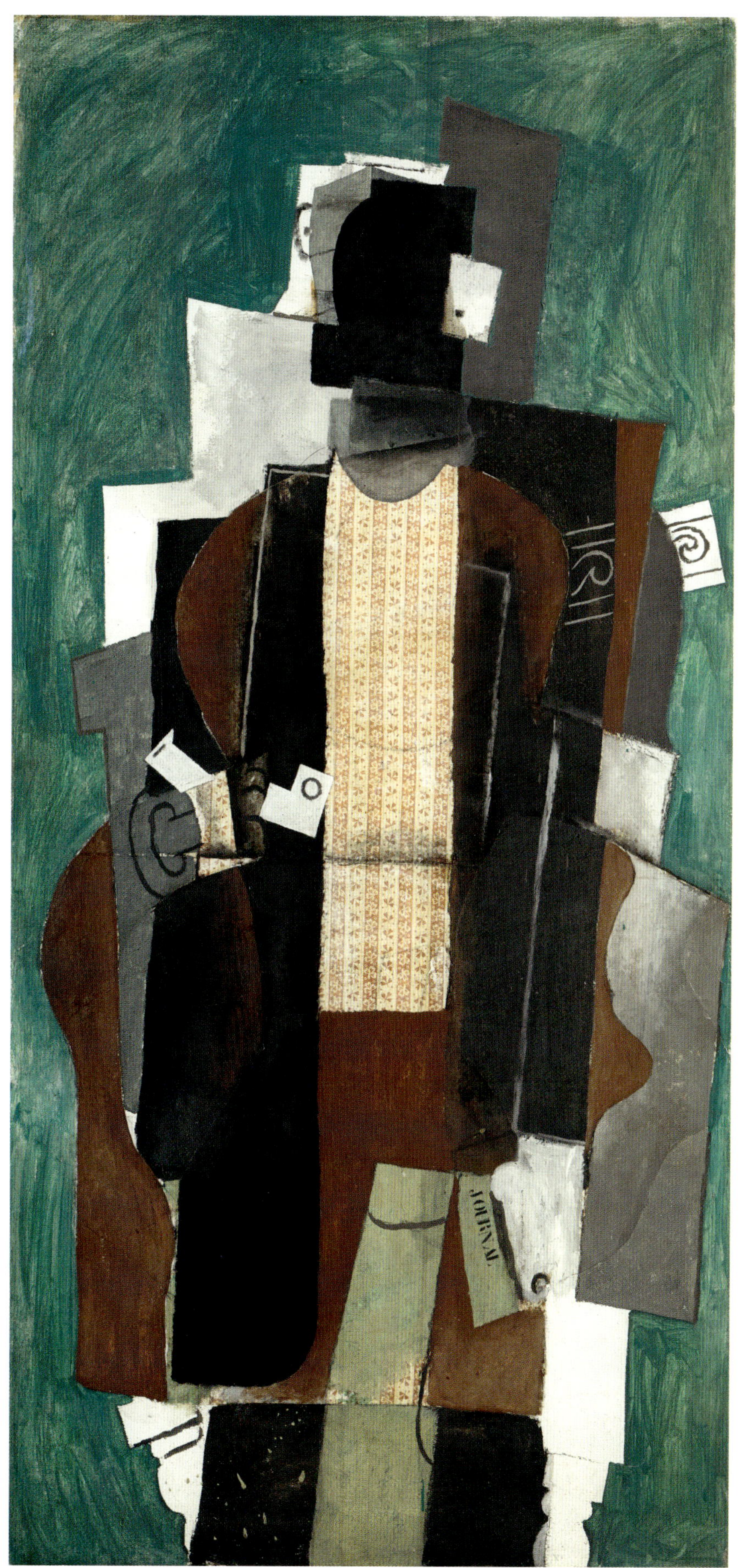
JOURNAL

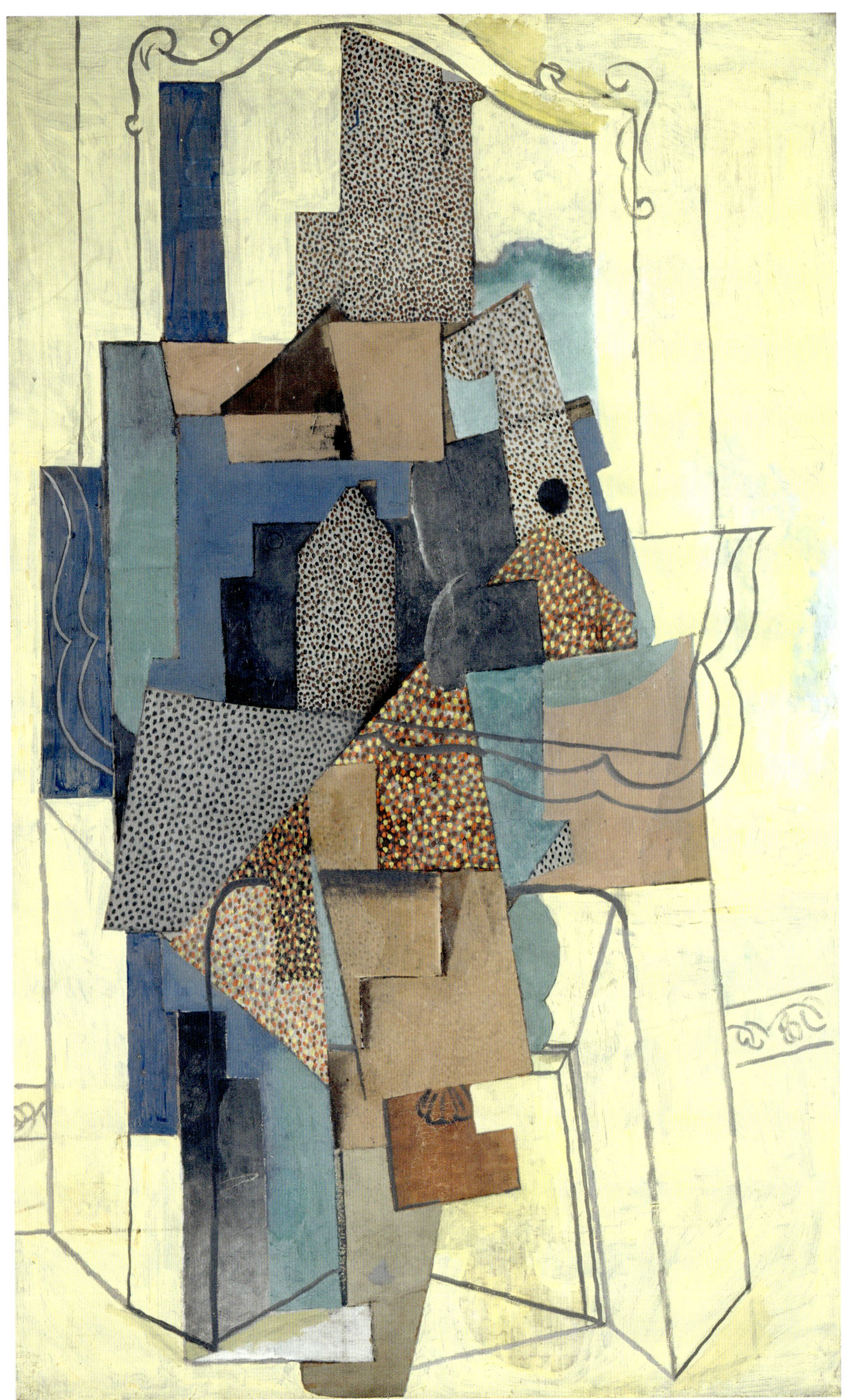

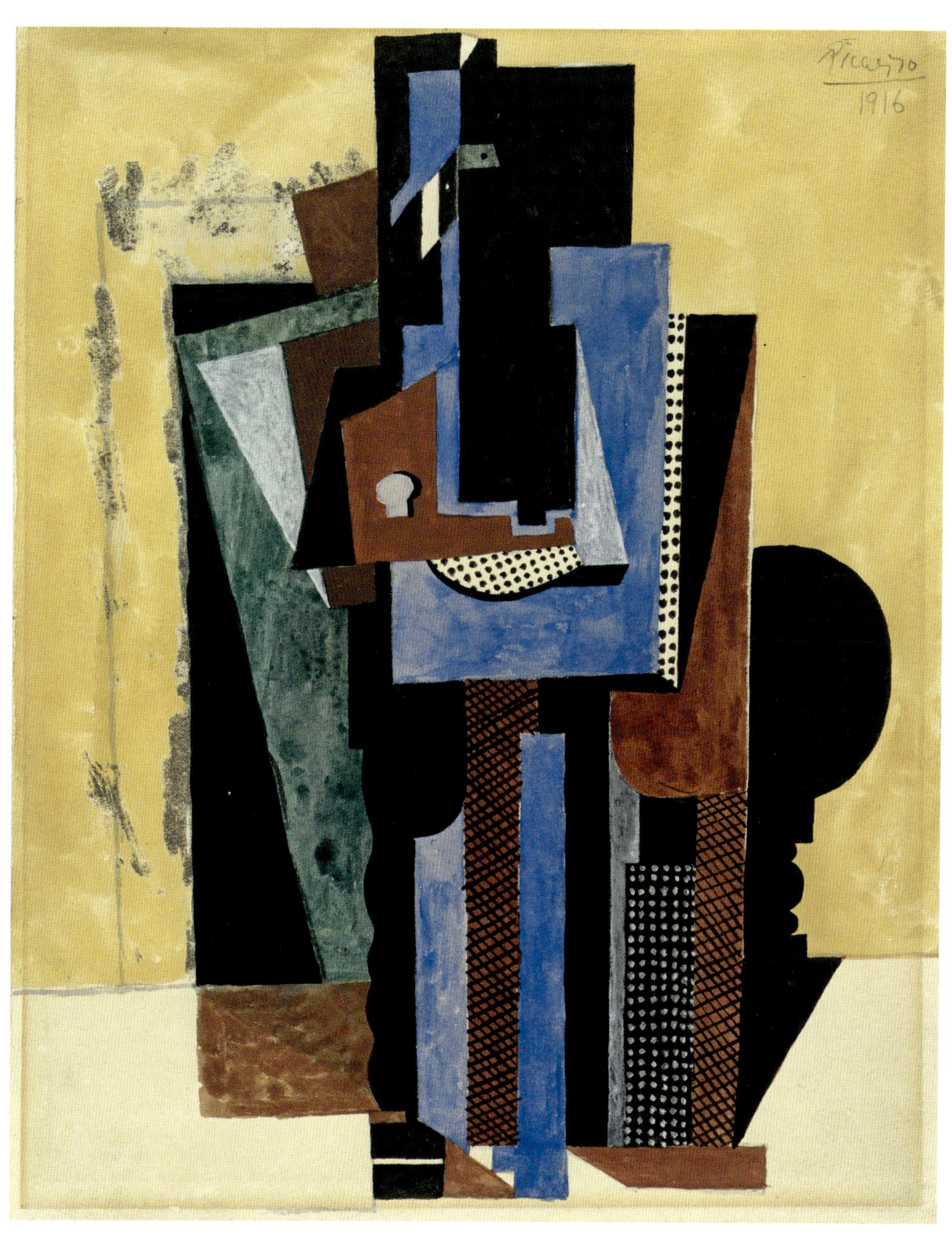

2. Pablo Picasso
Homme à la cheminée
[Man at the Fireplace], 1916
Oil on canvas, 130 x 81 cm
Paris, Musée national Picasso-Paris,
Pablo Picasso Donation, 1979,
inv. MP54

3. Pablo Picasso
Homme accoudé à une table
[Man Leaning on a Table], 1916
Gouache, pen and ink on paper,
27.5 x 21.7 cm
Berlin, Staatliche Museen zu Berlin,
Nationalgalerie, Museum Berggruen,
inv. NG MB 29/2000

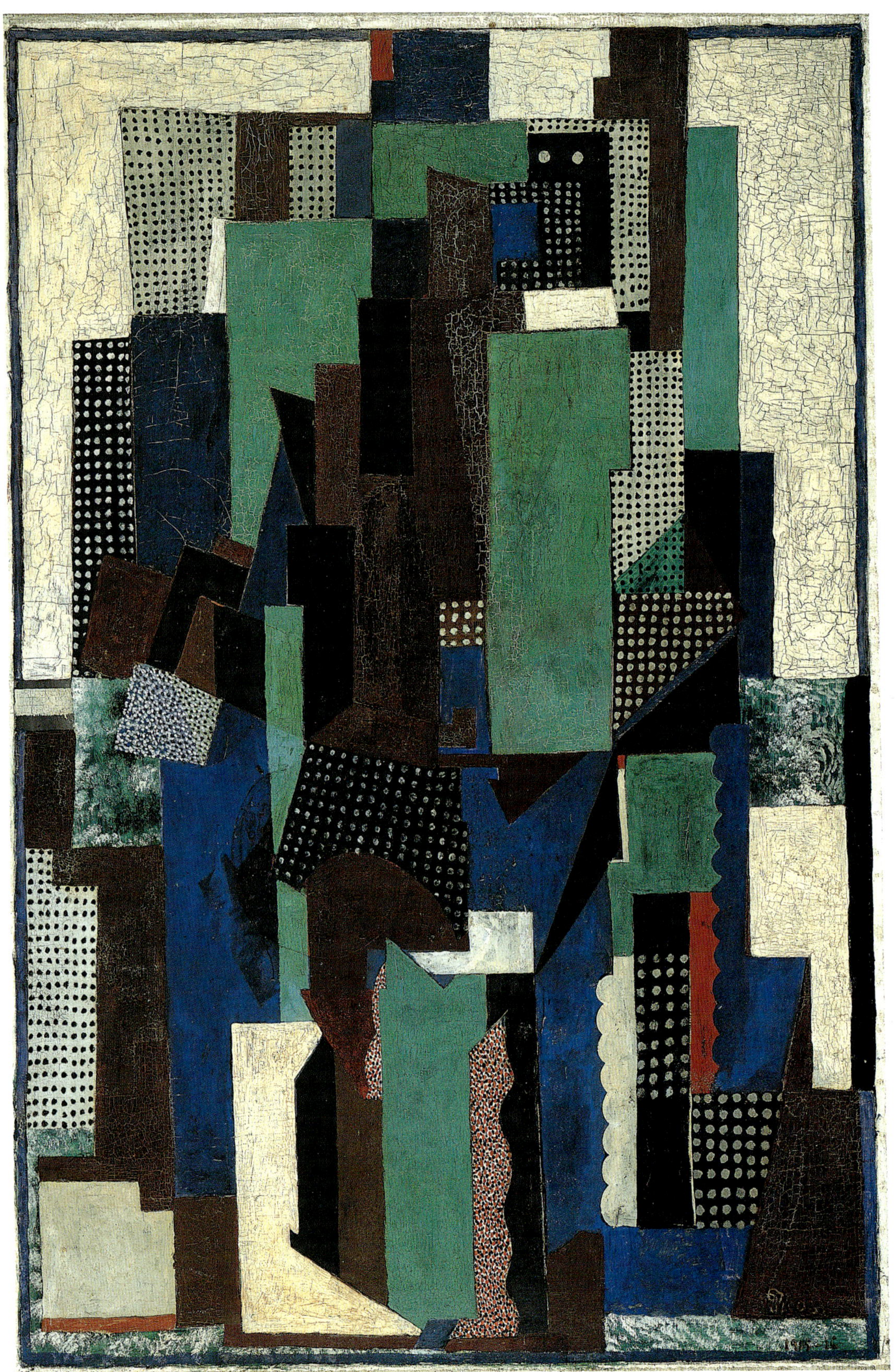

4. Pablo Picasso
Homme accoudé à une table
[Man Leaning on a Table], 1916
Oil on canvas, 197 x 132 cm
Turin, Pinacoteca Giovanni
e Marella Agnelli

5. Pablo Picasso
Arlequin au violon
[Harlequin with a Violin],
Montrouge, 1918
Oil on canvas, 142.2 x 100.3 cm
Cleveland, The Cleveland Museum
of Art, inv. CMA 1975.2

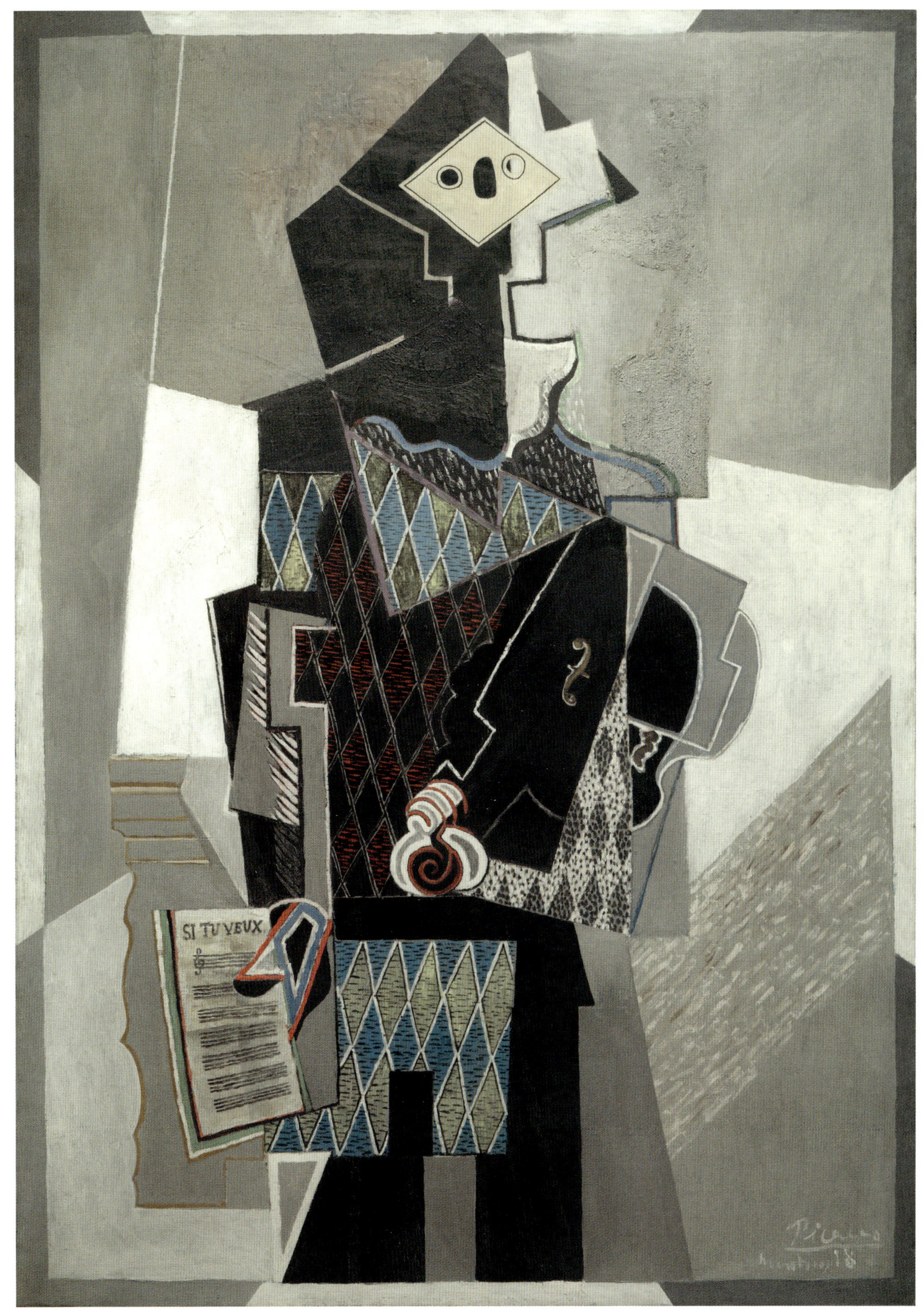
SI TU VEUX

II. Journey Diary: Rome and Naples [1917]

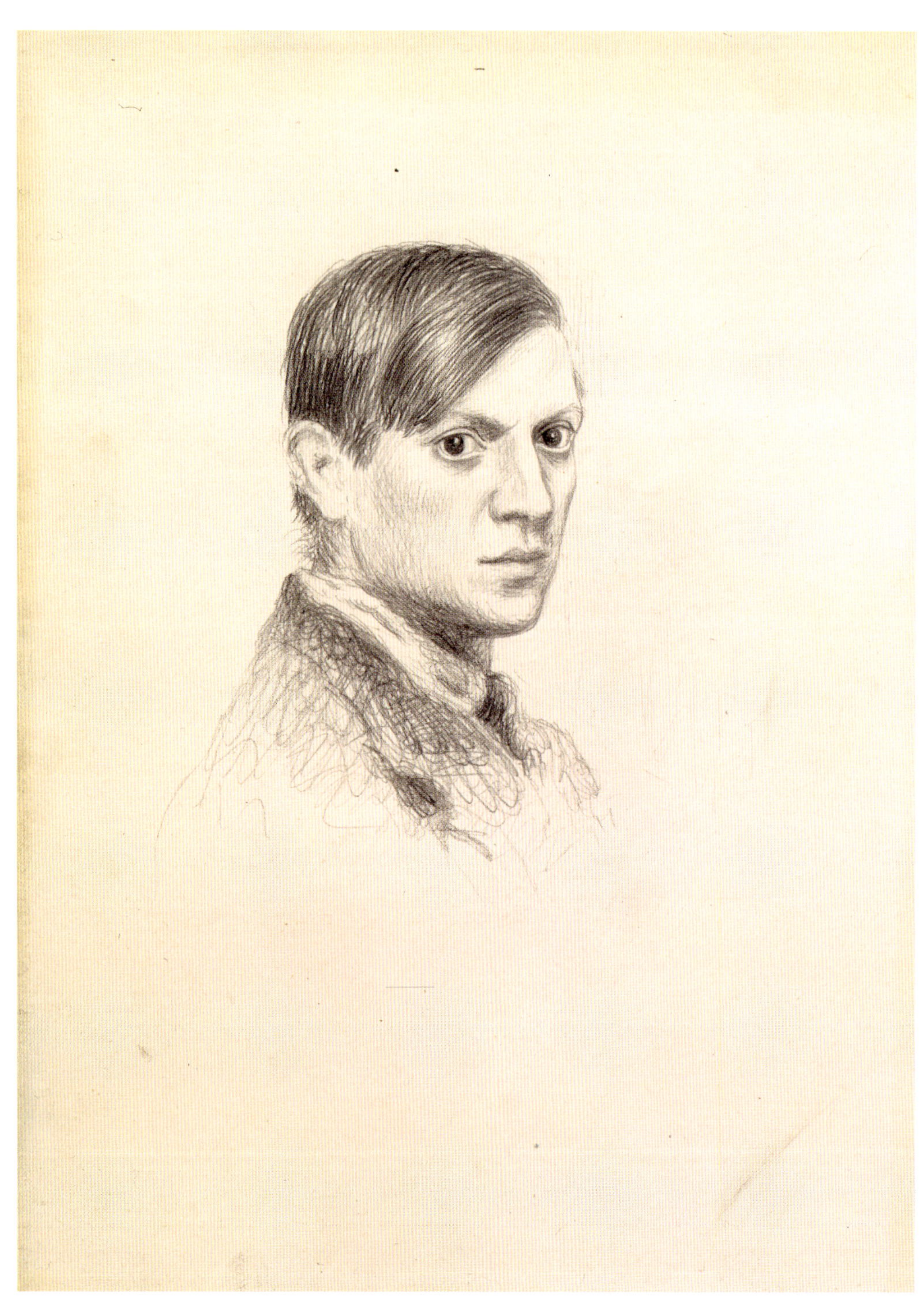

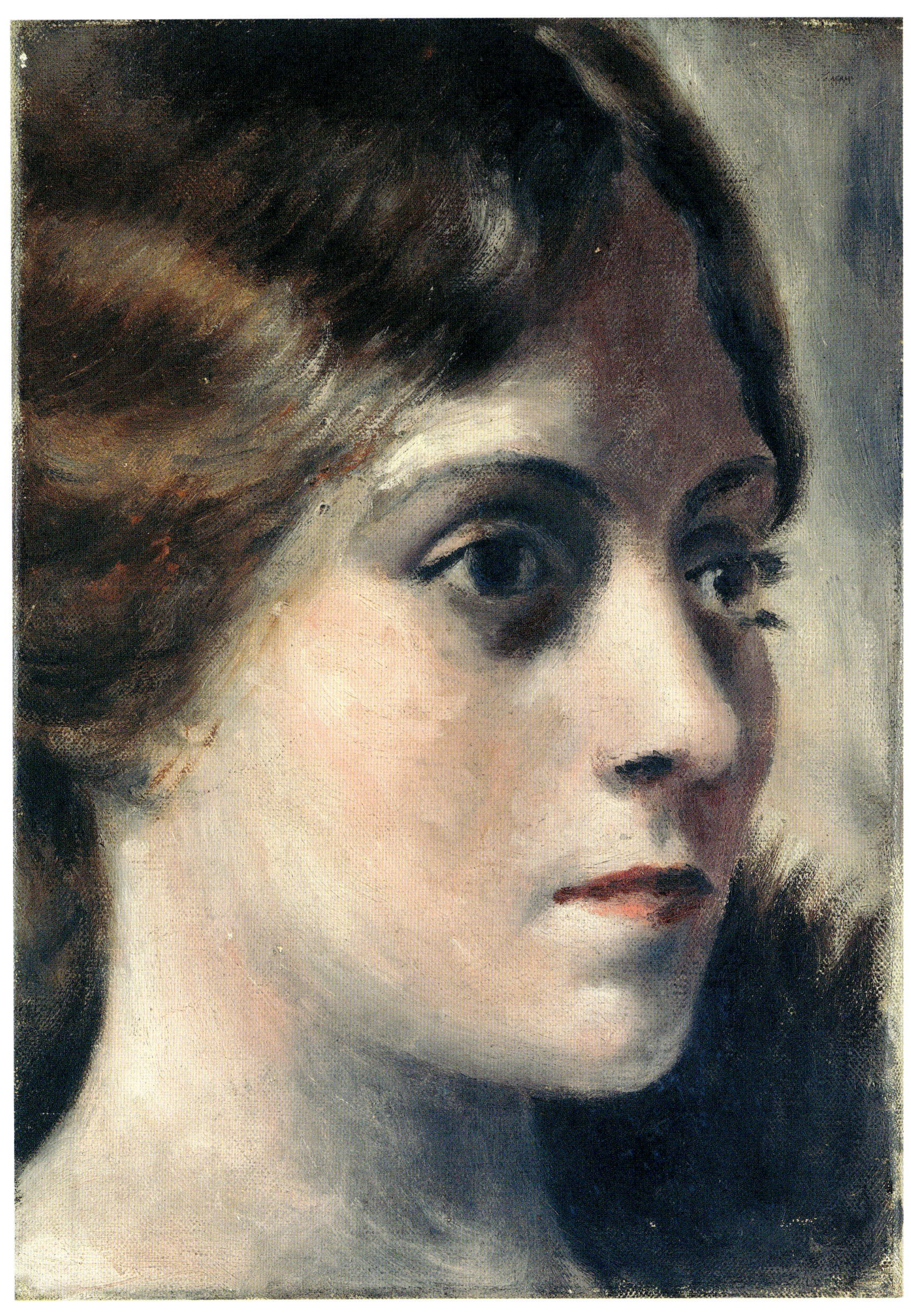

6. Pablo Picasso
Autoportrait [Self-Portrait], 1917
Pencil on paper, 34 x 26 cm
Private collection

7. Pablo Picasso
Tête de femme (Olga) [Head of Woman (Olga)], Montrouge, 1917
Oil on canvas, 22 x 16 cm
Brussels, Fundación Almine y Bernard Ruiz-Picasso para el Arte, inv. 12176

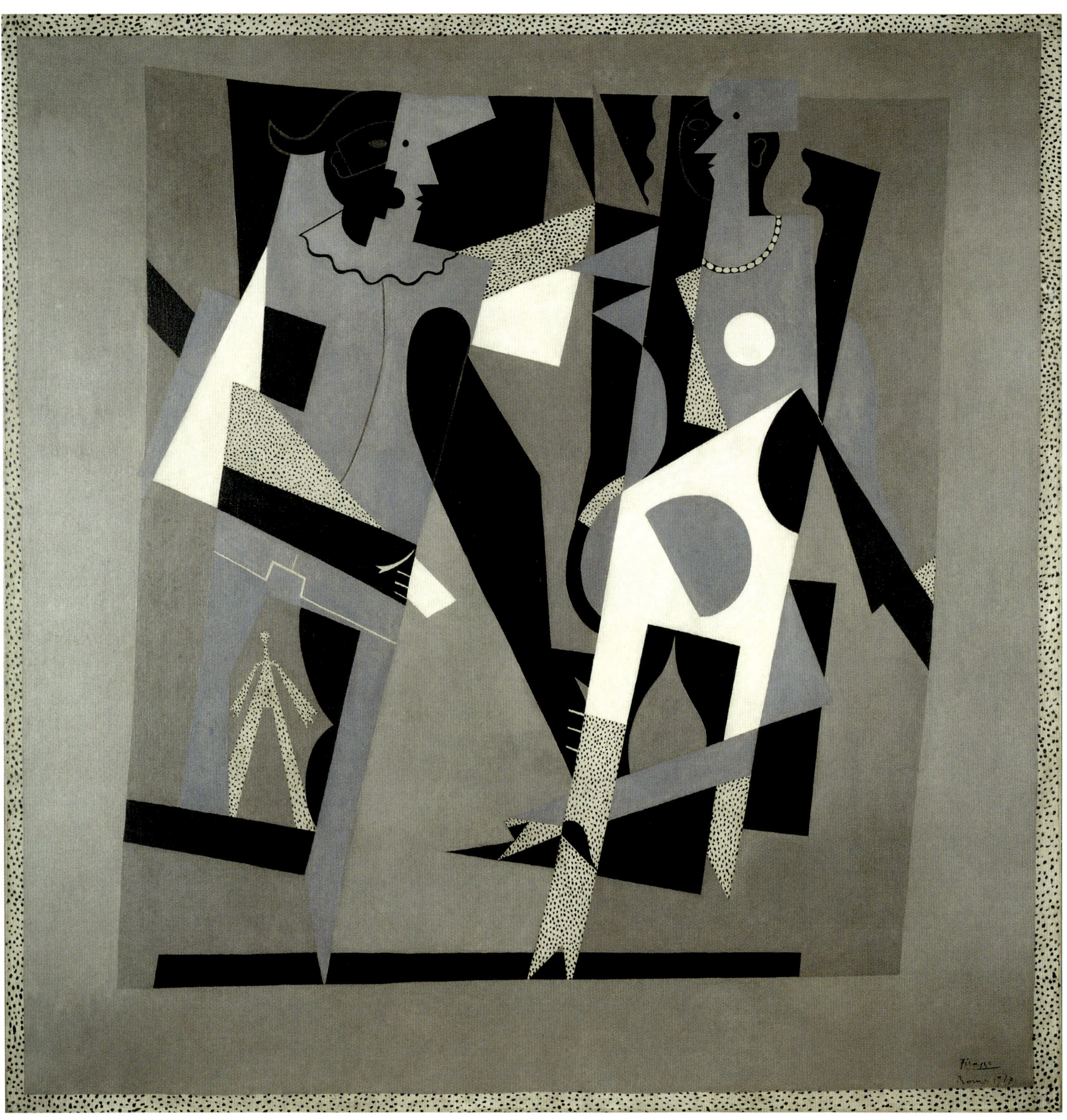

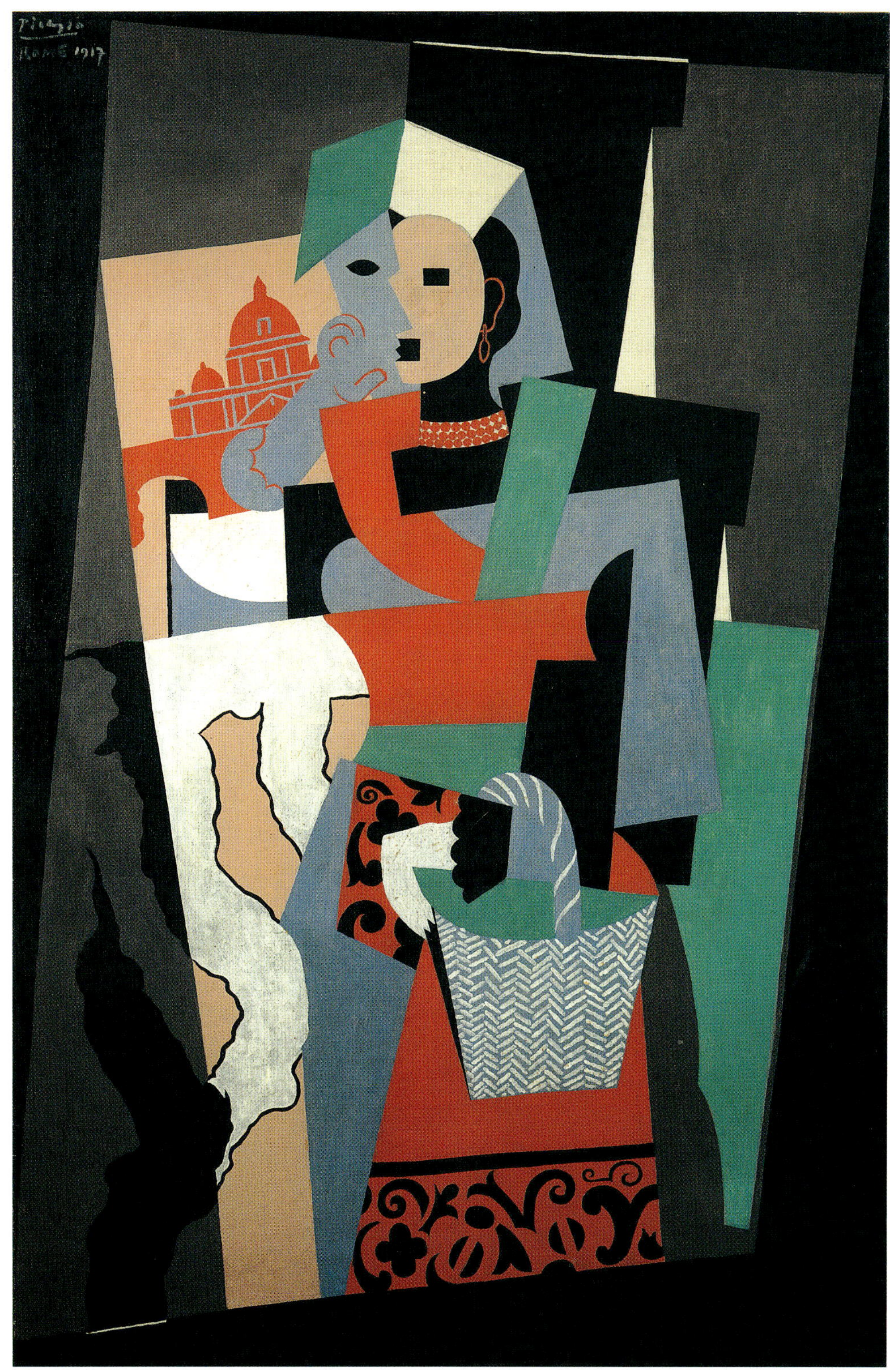

8. Pablo Picasso
Arlequin et femme au collier
[Harlequin and Woman
with a Necklace], Rome, 1917
Oil on canvas, 200 x 200 cm
Paris, Centre Georges Pompidou,
Musée National d'Art Moderne /
Centre de création industrielle,
inv. AM 3760

9. Pablo Picasso
L'Italienne [Italian Woman], 1917
Oil on canvas, 149.5 x 101.5 cm
Zurich, Foundation E.G. Bührle
Collection, inv. 78

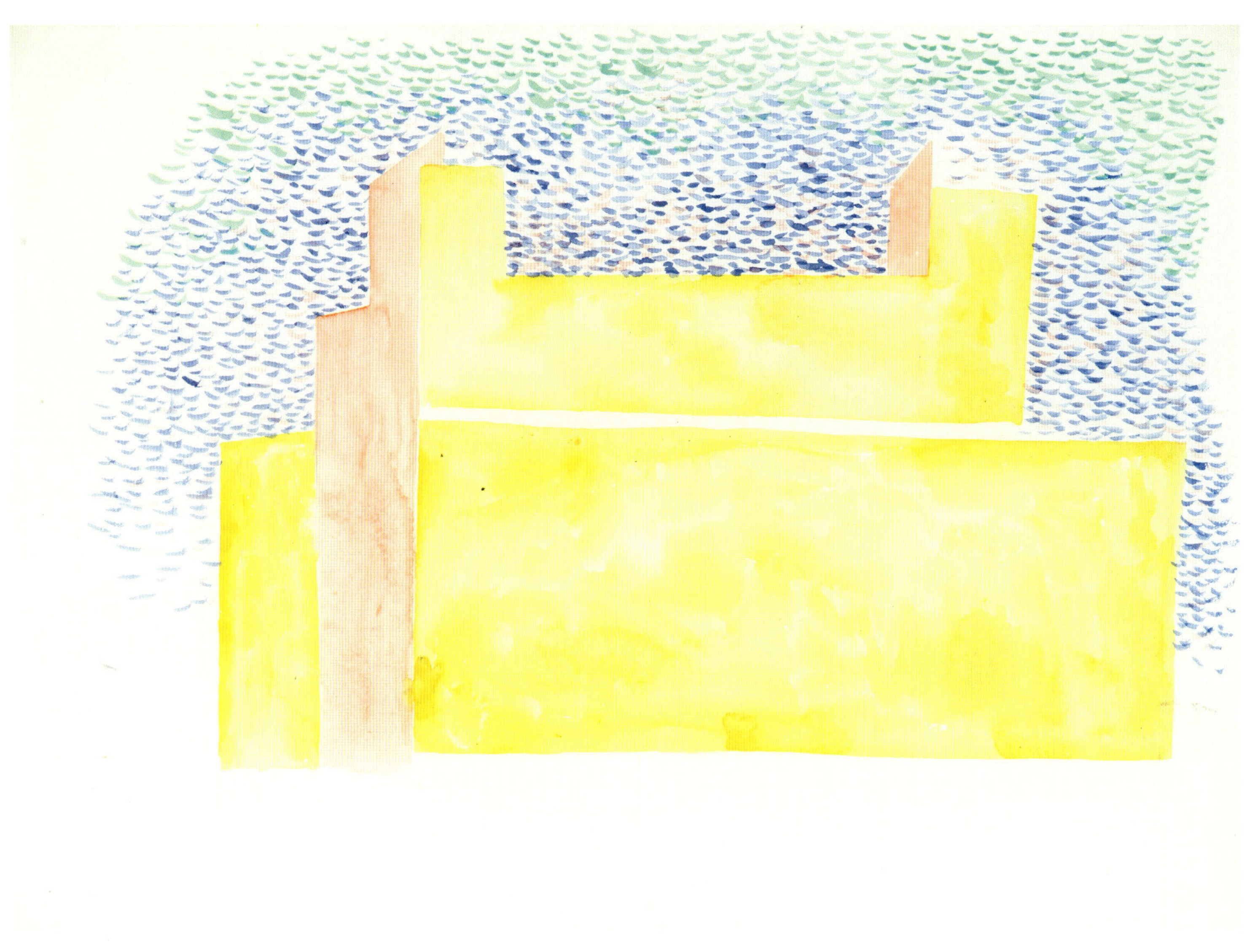

10. Pablo Picasso
Villa Médicis à Rome
[Villa Medici in Rome], Rome, 1917
Watercolour on paper folded in two, 21 x 27 cm
Private collection

11. Pablo Picasso
Villa Médicis à Rome
[Villa Medici in Rome], Rome, 1917
Pencil on Fabriano vellum drawing paper, 20.9 x 28.1 cm
Paris, Musée national Picasso-Paris, Pablo Picasso Donation, 1979, inv. MP783 (r)

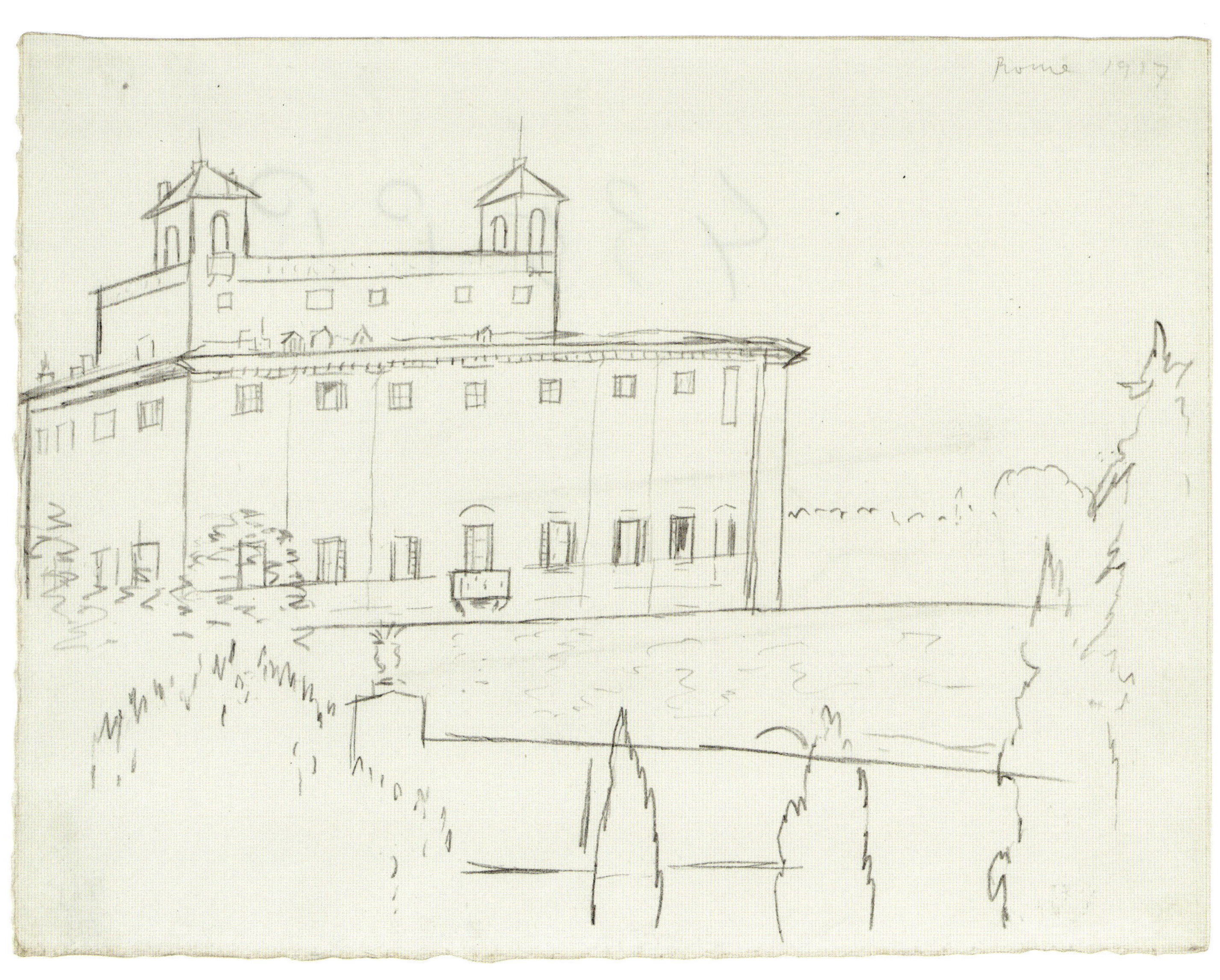
Rome 1917

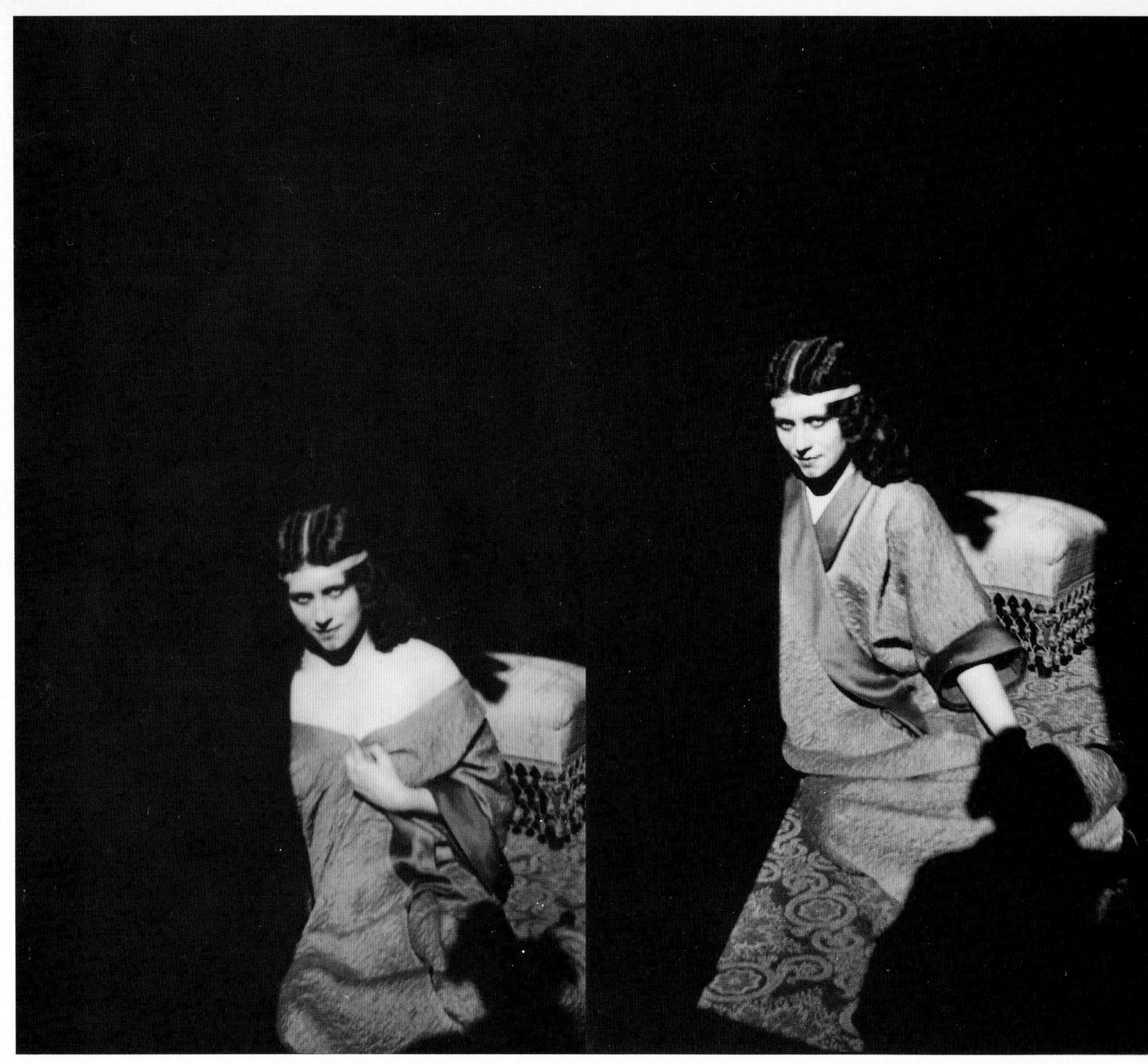

12. Olga Khokhlova, Rome (?), 1917
Gelatin silver print, 11.2 x 6.8 cm
Bruxelles, Fundación Almine y
Bernard Ruiz-Picasso para el Arte,
inv. 103072

13. Olga Khokhlova, Rome (?), 1917
Gelatin silver print, 11.1 x 6.5 cm
Brussels, Fundación Almine y
Bernard Ruiz-Picasso para el Arte,
inv. 103079

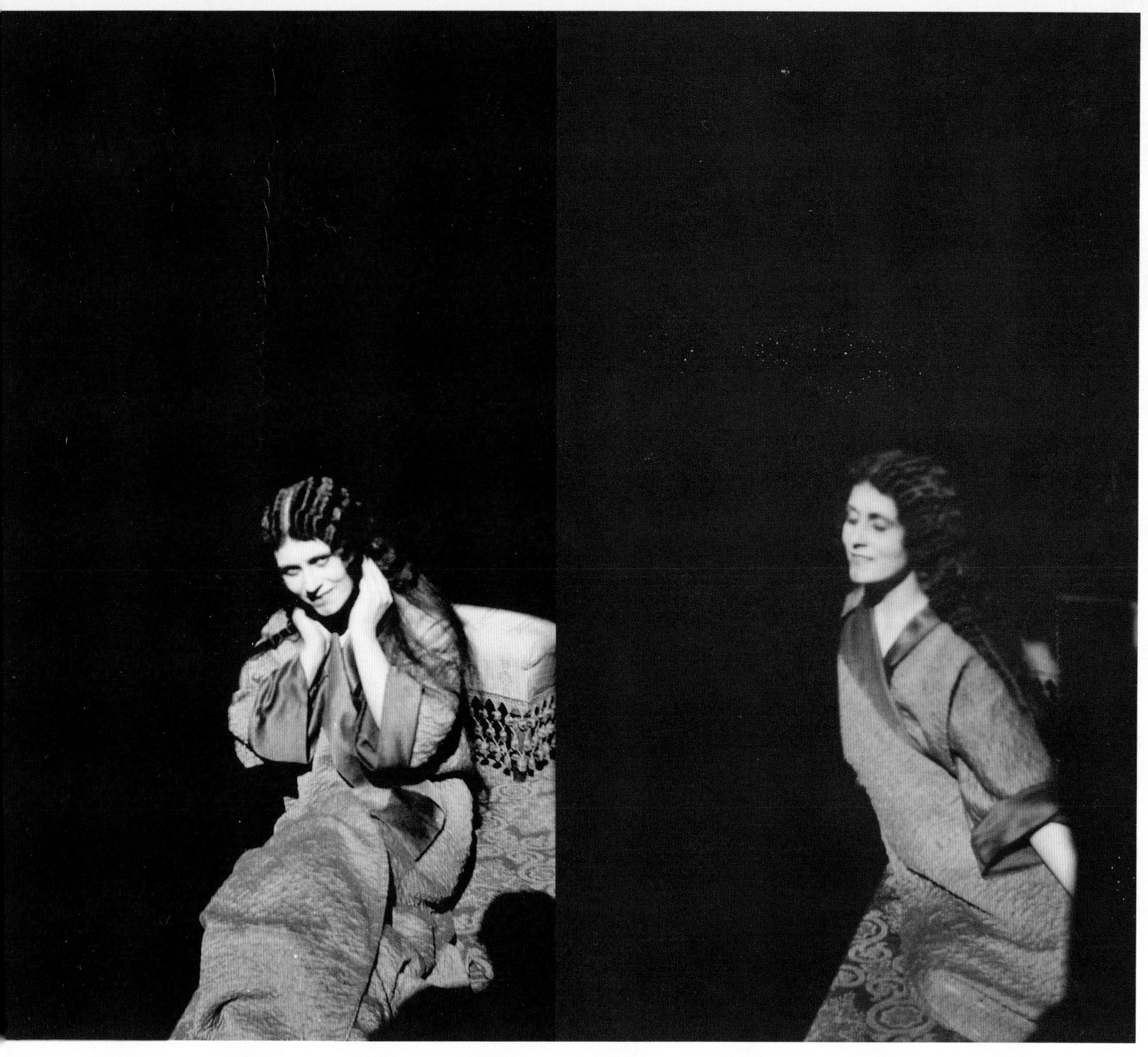

14. Olga Khokhlova, Rome (?), 1917
Gelatin silver print, 11.1 x 6.5 cm
Brussels, Fundación Almine y
Bernard Ruiz-Picasso para el Arte,
inv. 103071

15. Olga Khokhlova, Rome (?), 1917
Gelatin silver print, 11.2 x 6.8 cm
Brussels, Fundación Almine y
Bernard Ruiz-Picasso para el Arte,
inv. 103077

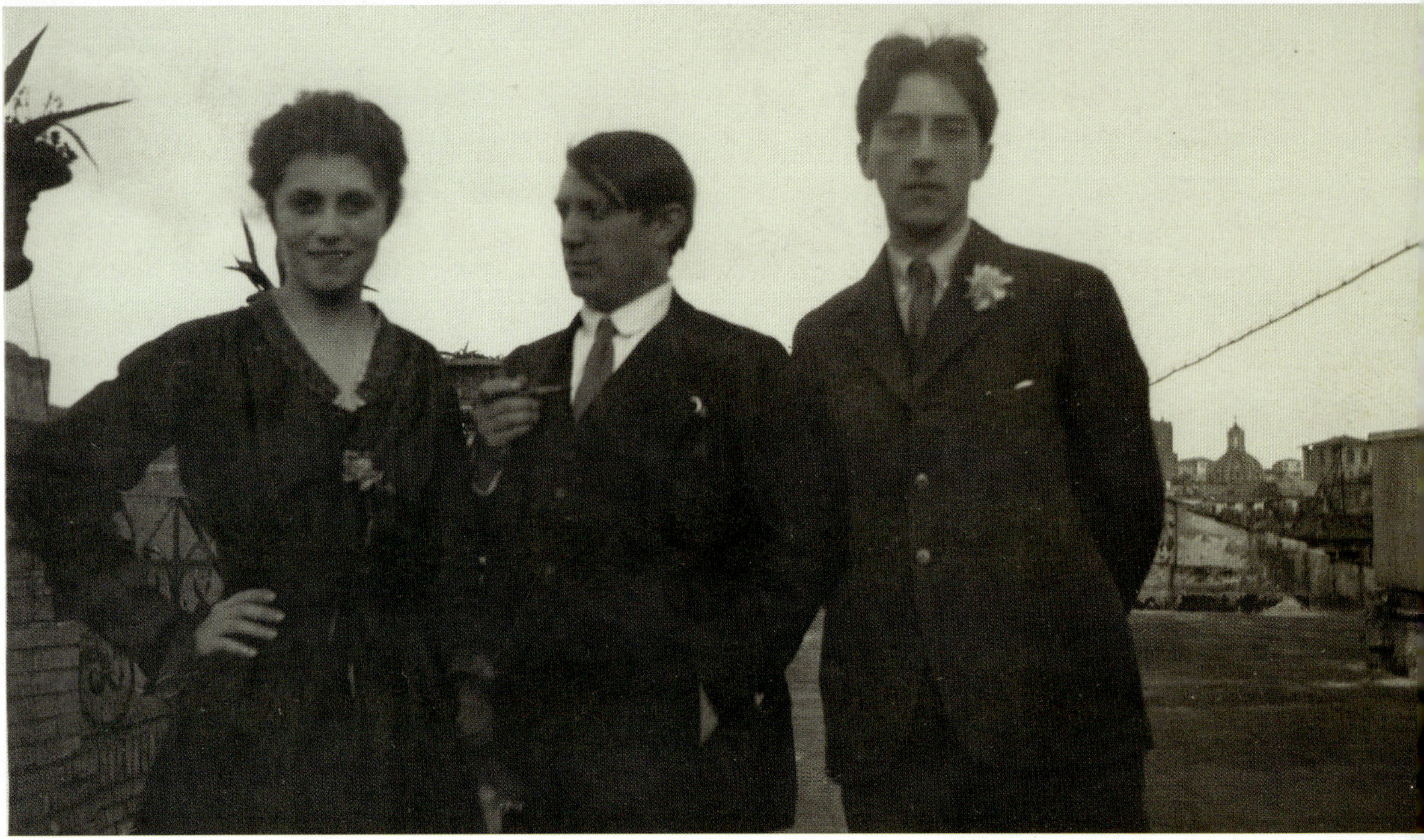

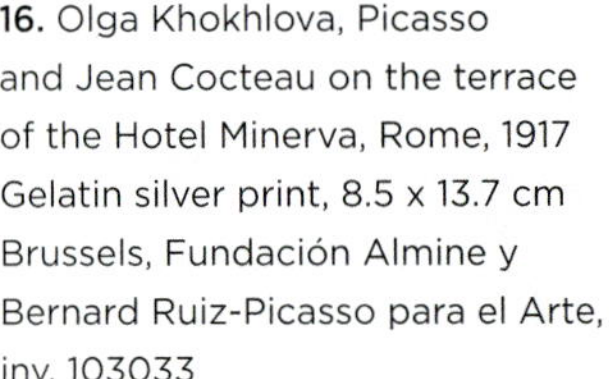

16. Olga Khokhlova, Picasso and Jean Cocteau on the terrace of the Hotel Minerva, Rome, 1917
Gelatin silver print, 8.5 x 13.7 cm
Brussels, Fundación Almine y Bernard Ruiz-Picasso para el Arte, inv. 103033

17. Olga Khokhlova on the terrace of Hotel Minerva, Rome, 1917
Print from the original glass plate negative, 11.7 x 6.9 cm
Brussels, Fundación Almine y Bernard Ruiz-Picasso para el Arte, inv. 101357

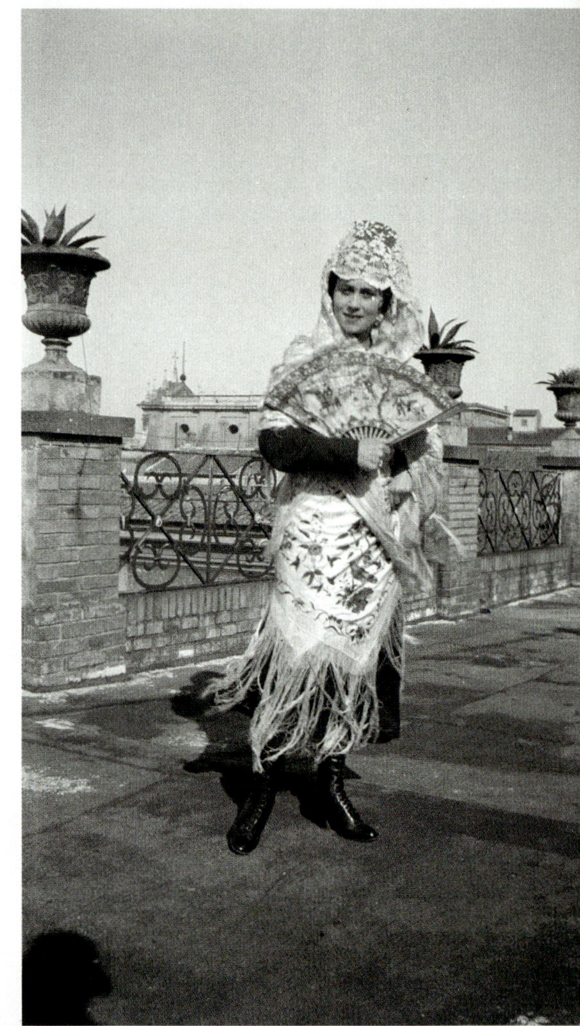

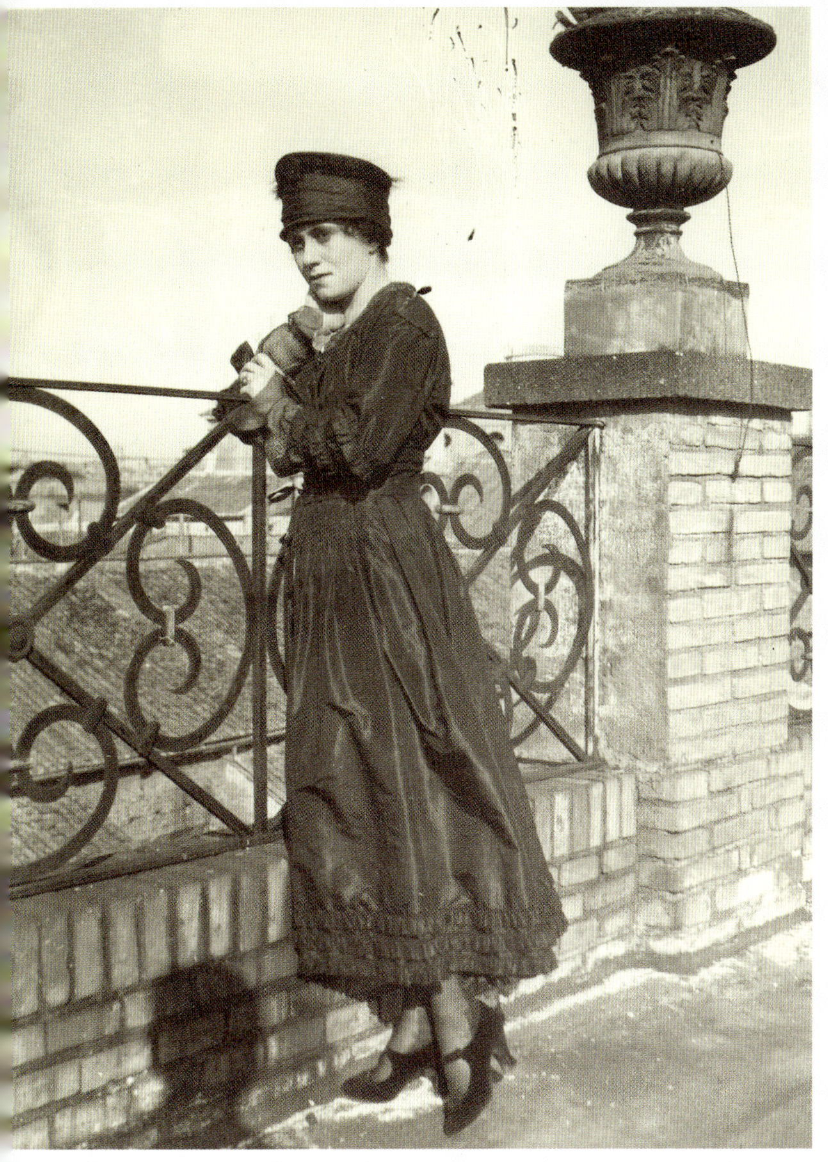

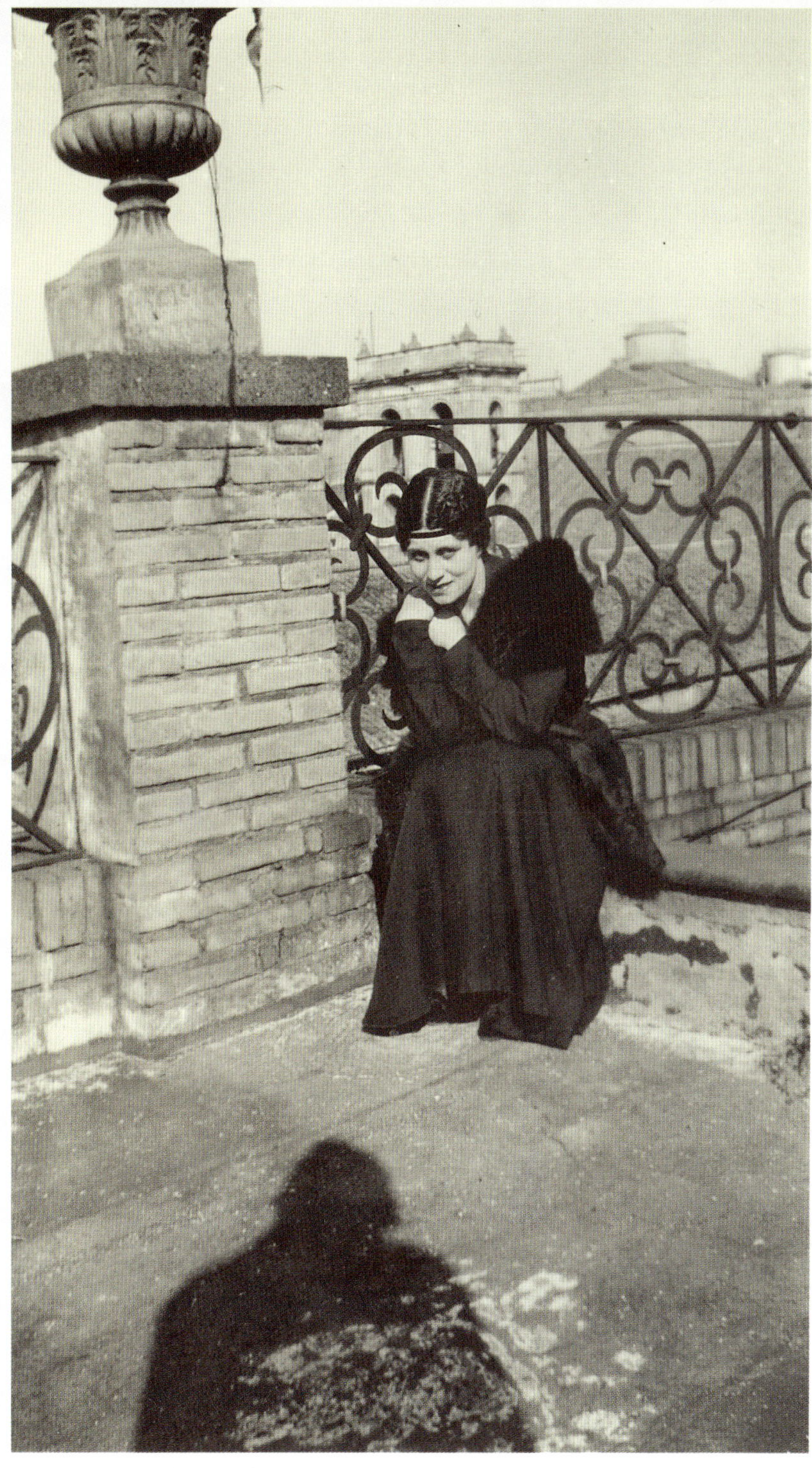

18. Olga Khokhlova on the terrace of the Hotel Minerva, Rome, 1917
Print from the original glass plate negative, 11 x 8.1 cm
Brussels, Fundación Almine y Bernard Ruiz-Picasso para el Arte, inv. 103038

19. Olga Khokhlova on the terrace of the Hotel Minerva, Rome, 1917
Gelatin silver print, 11.2 x 6.8 cm
Brussels, Fundación Almine y Bernard Ruiz-Picasso para el Arte, inv. 103060

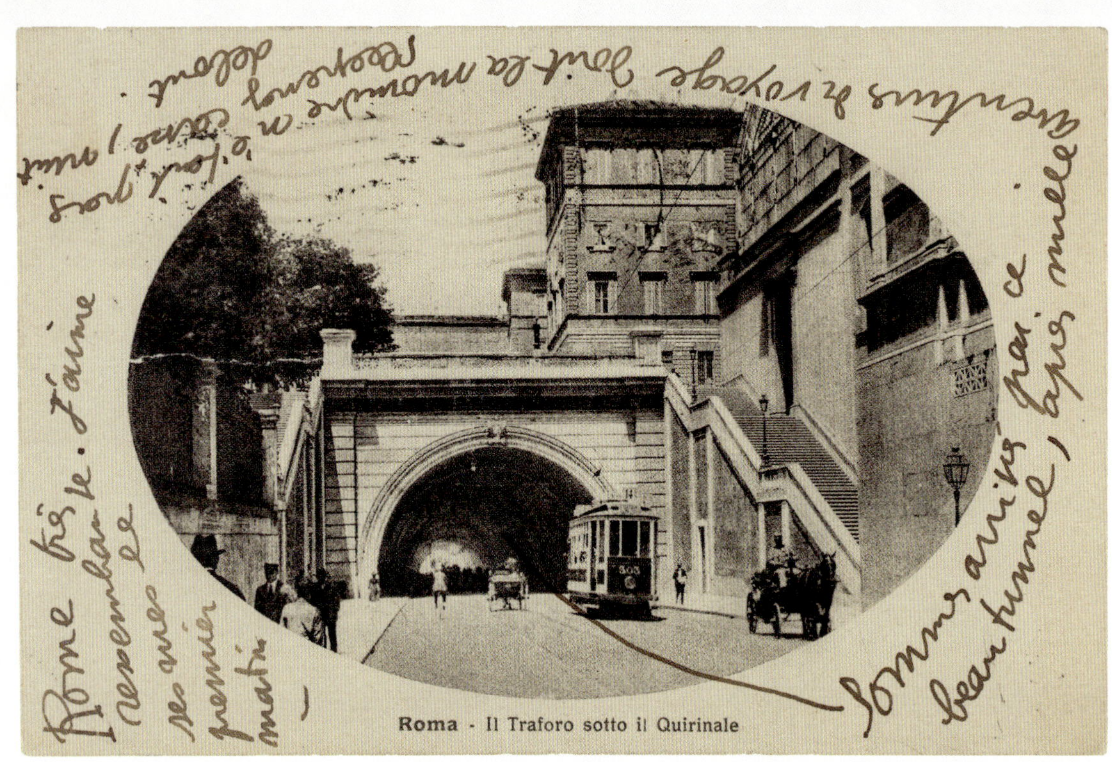

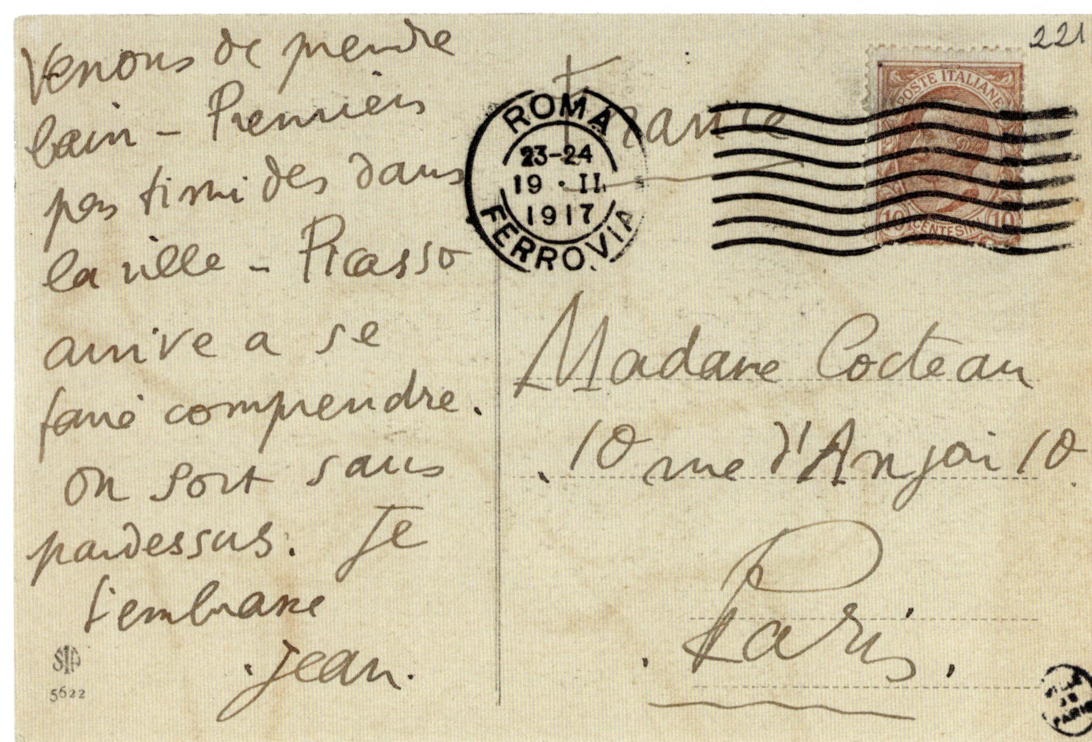

20a-b. Postcard of the tunnel beneath the Quirinale, April 1917
Paris, Bibliothèque historique de la Ville de Paris, Fonds Jean Cocteau, inv. 2-MS-FS-05-0330

21. Jean Cocteau
Picasso and Massine in the ruins of Pompeii, 1917
Gelatin silver print, 6.2 x 8.2 cm
Paris, Bibliothèque historique de la Ville de Paris, Fonds Jean Cocteau, inv. Coc-1944

22. Jean Cocteau
Massine, Cocteau and Picasso in front of a mirror, Naples, 1917
Gelatin silver print, 6.4 x 8.4 cm
Paris, Bibliothèque historique de la Ville de Paris, Fonds Jean Cocteau, inv. Coc-1934

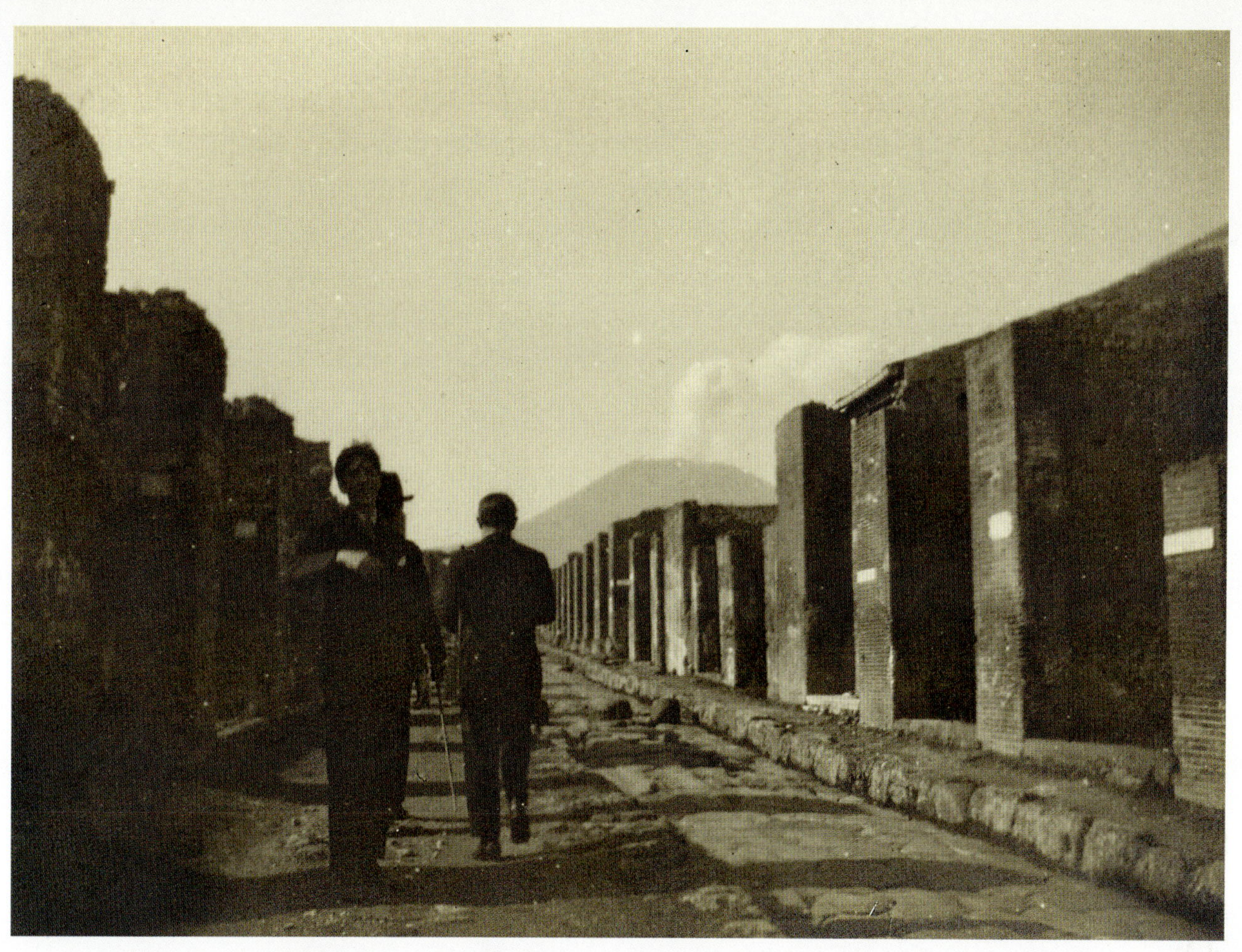

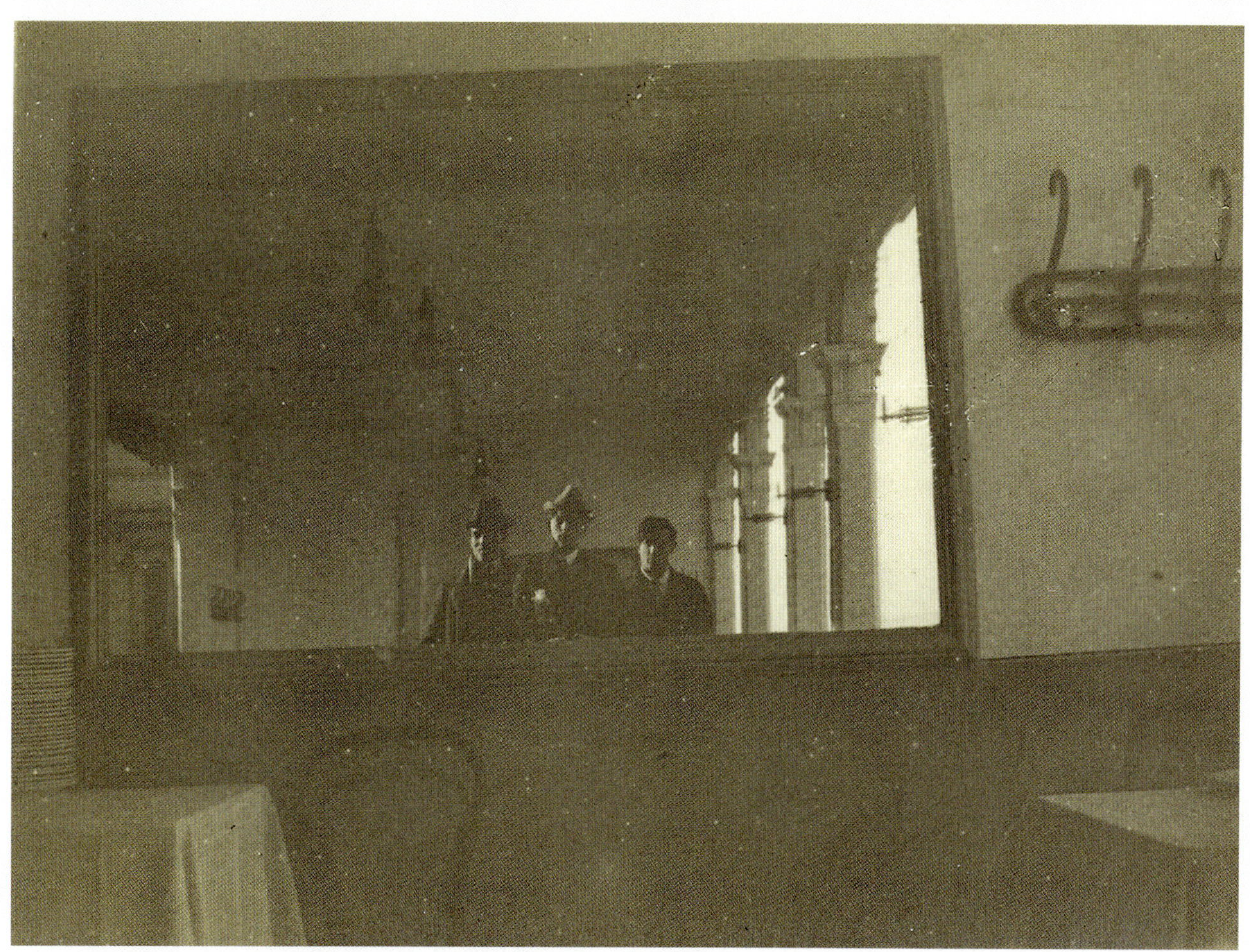

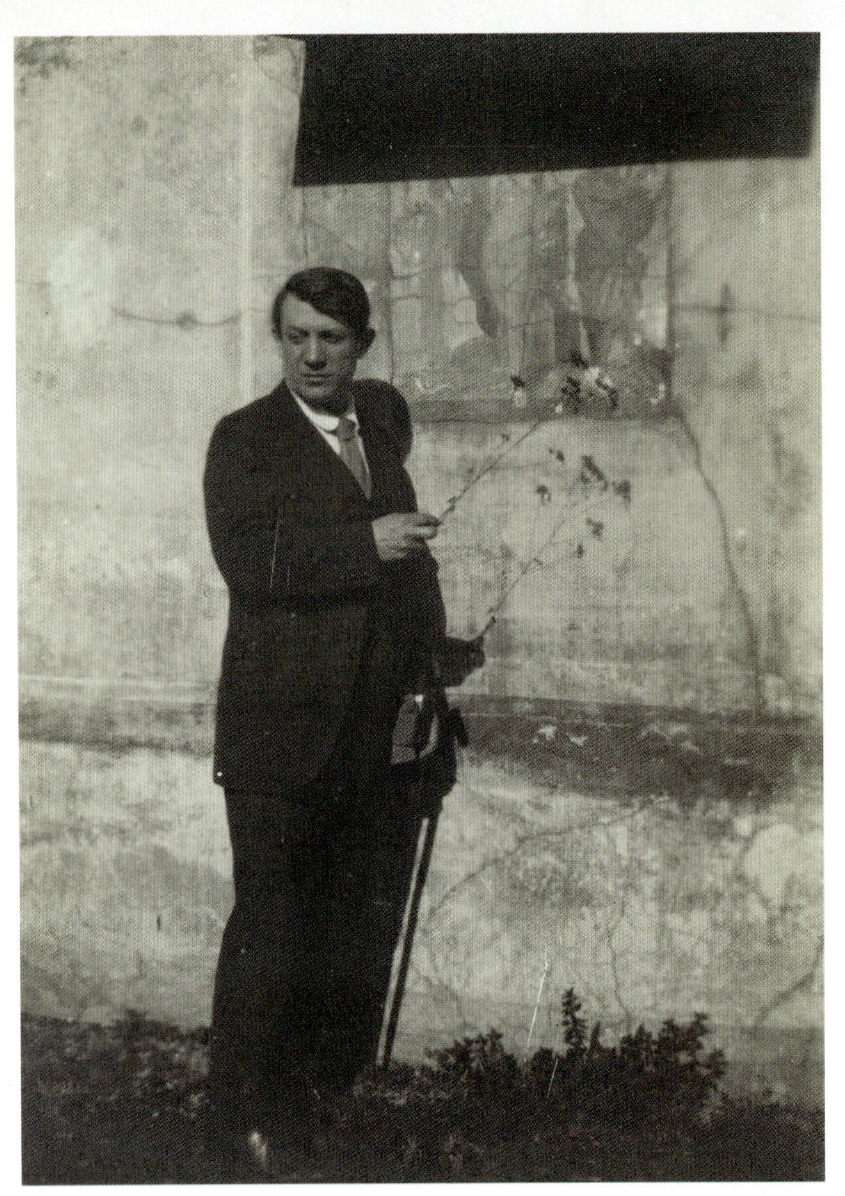

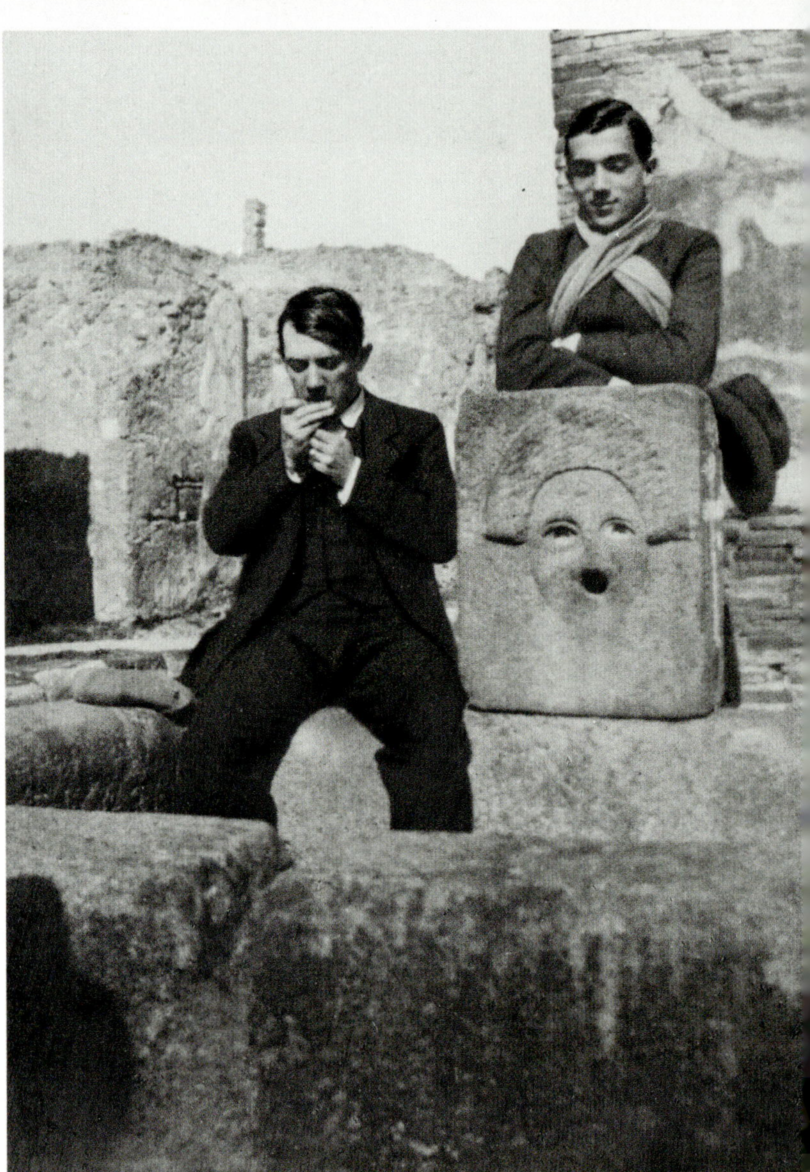

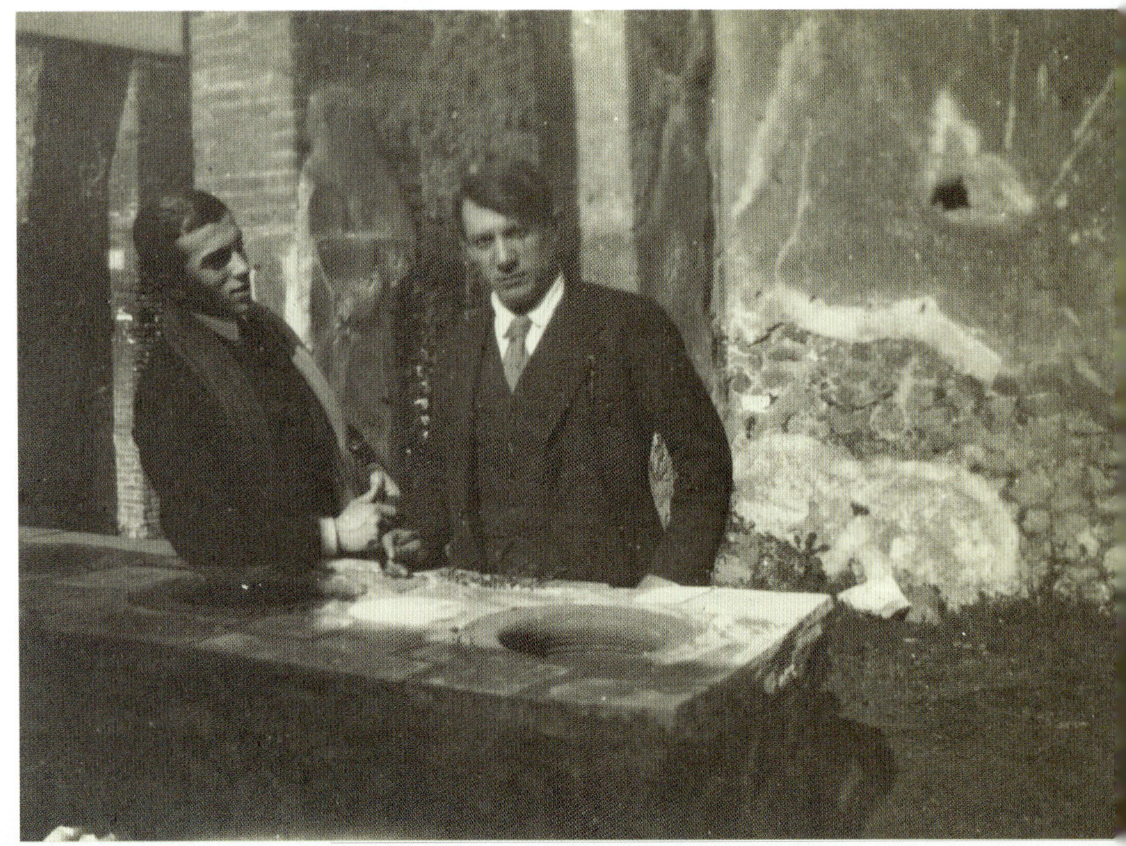

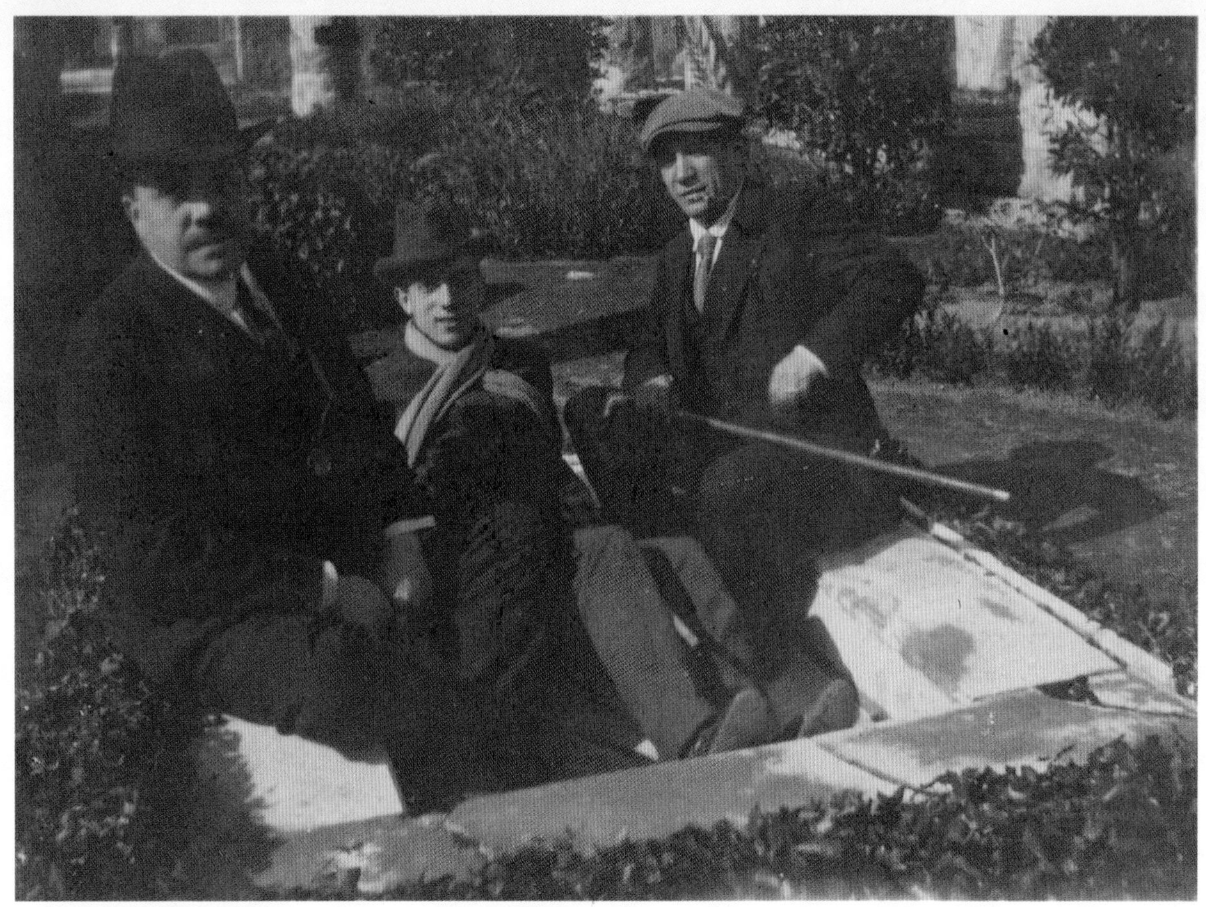

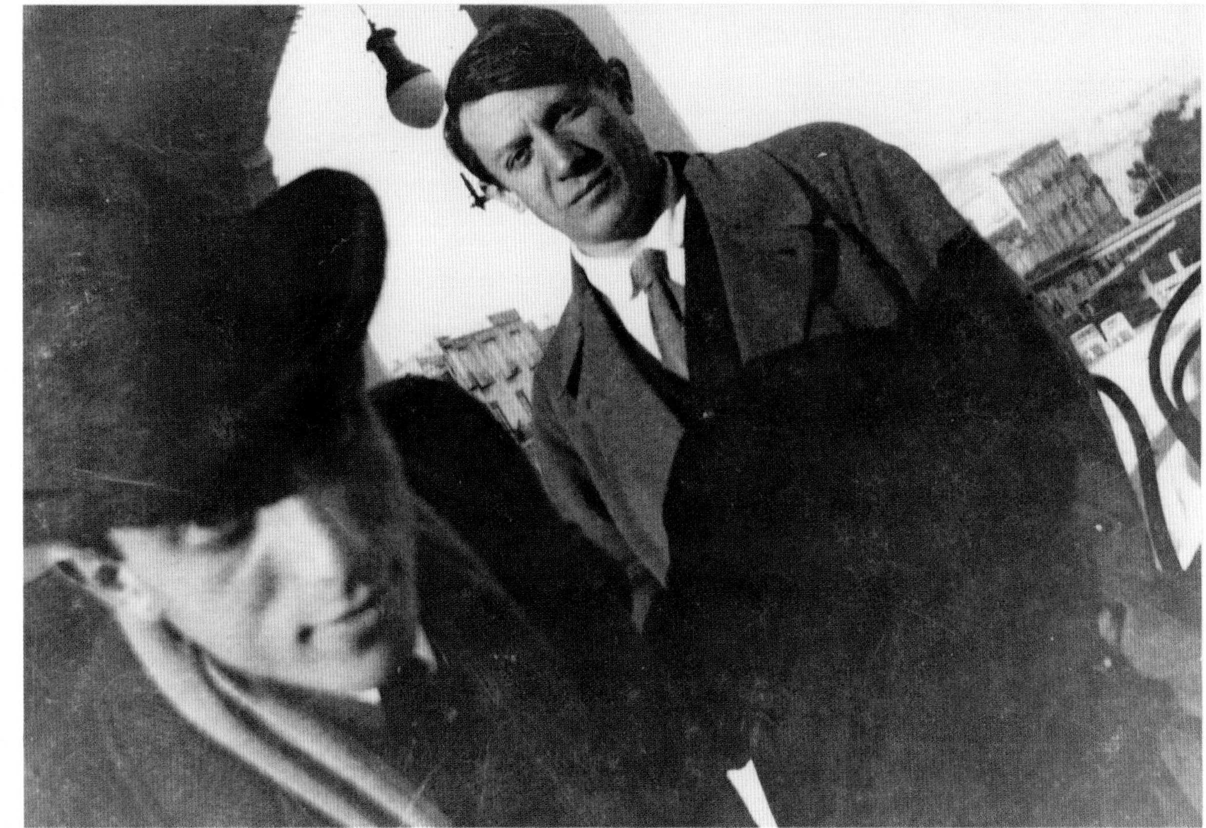

23. Jean Cocteau
Picasso in Pompeii, 1917
Gelatin silver print, 8.2 x 6.2 cm
Paris, Bibliothèque historique de la Ville de Paris, Fonds Jean Cocteau, inv. Coc-1948

24. Jean Cocteau
Picasso and Massine in the ruins of Pompeii, 1917
Gelatin silver print, 8.8 x 6.3 cm
Paris, Bibliothèque historique de la Ville de Paris, Fonds Jean Cocteau, inv. Coc-1931

25. Jean Cocteau
Picasso and Massine in the ruins of Pompeii, March 1917
Gelatin silver print, 6.2 x 8.2 cm
Paris, Bibliothèque historique de la Ville de Paris, Fonds Jean Cocteau, inv. Coc-1939

26. Jean Cocteau
Picasso and Massine in the ruins of Pompeii, 1917
Gelatin silver print, 6.2 x 8.3 cm
Paris, Bibliothèque historique de la Ville de Paris, Fonds Jean Cocteau, inv. Coc-1936

27. Picasso and Massine in Rome, 1917
Gelatin silver print, 9 x 12.5 cm
Paris, Bibliothèque historique de la Ville de Paris, Fonds Jean Cocteau, inv. Coc-1931

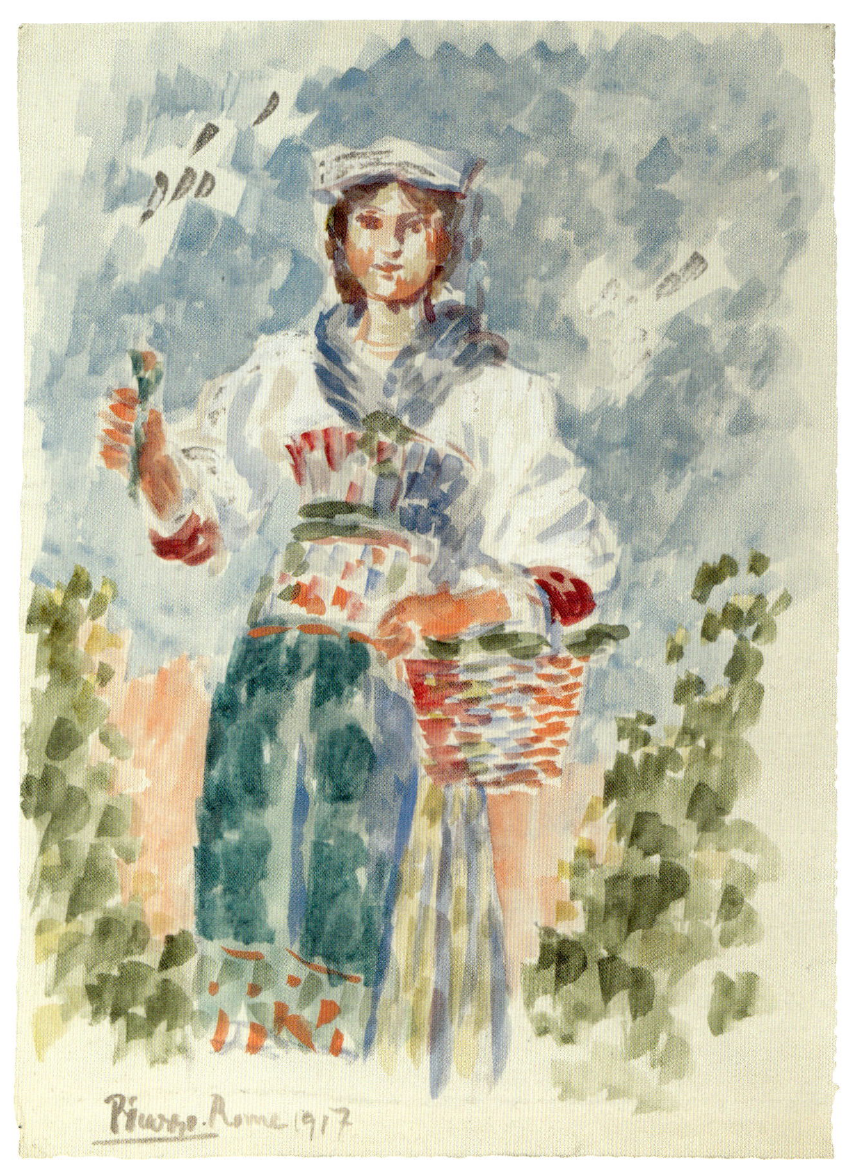

28. Pablo Picasso
Italienne à la fleur [Italian Woman with Flowers (Flower Seller in Piazza di Spagna)], Rome, 1917
Watercolour and tempera on pasteboard, 26.5 x 19.5 cm
Private collection

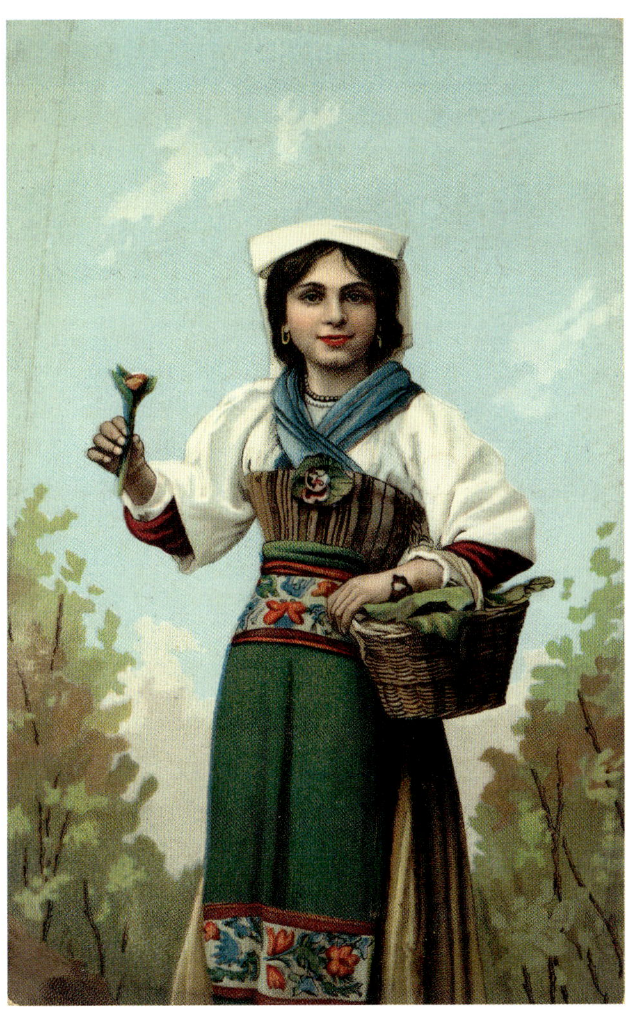

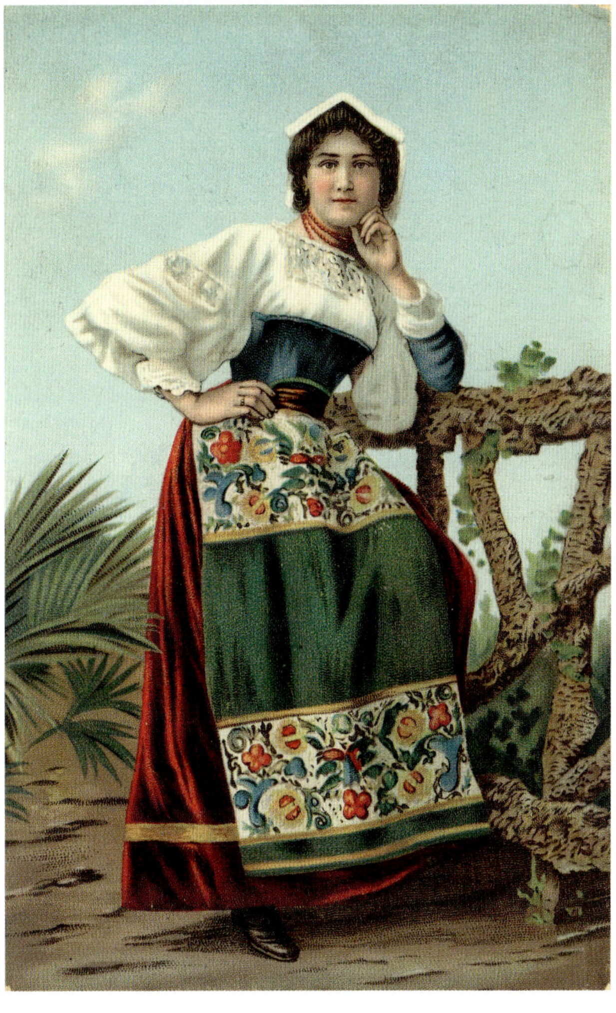

29. *Italienne en costume traditionnel avec une fleur à la main* [Italian Woman in Traditional Costume Holding a Flower (Flower Seller in Piazza di Spagna)], c. 1900
Postcard, 14 x 9 cm
Paris, Musée national Picasso-Paris, Donation of Picasso's heirs, 1992, inv. APPH2762

30. *Italienne en costume traditionnel* [Italian Woman in Traditional Costume], c. 1900
Postcard, 14 x 9 cm
Paris, Musée national Picasso-Paris, Donation of Picasso's heirs, 1992, inv. APPH14388

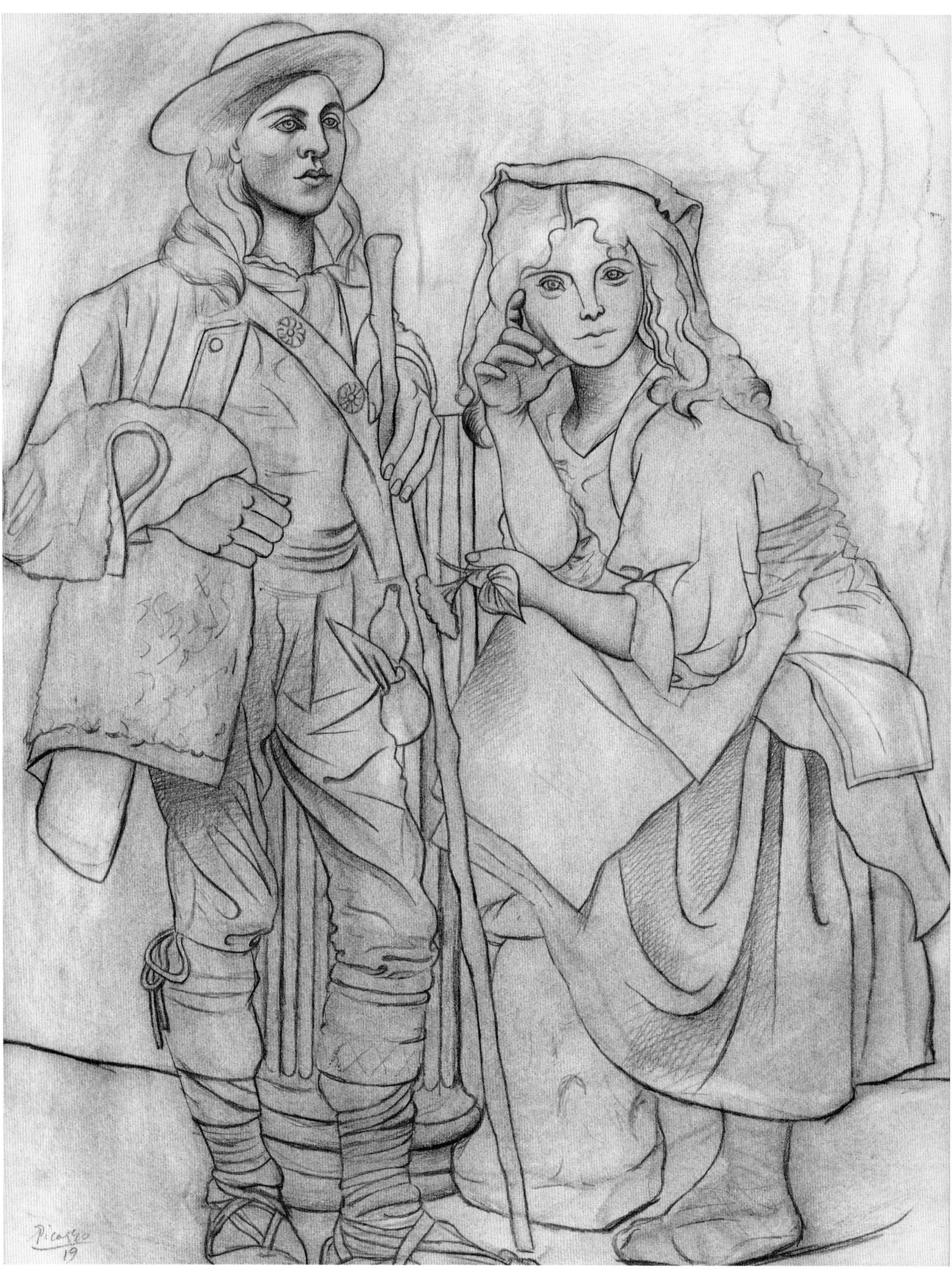

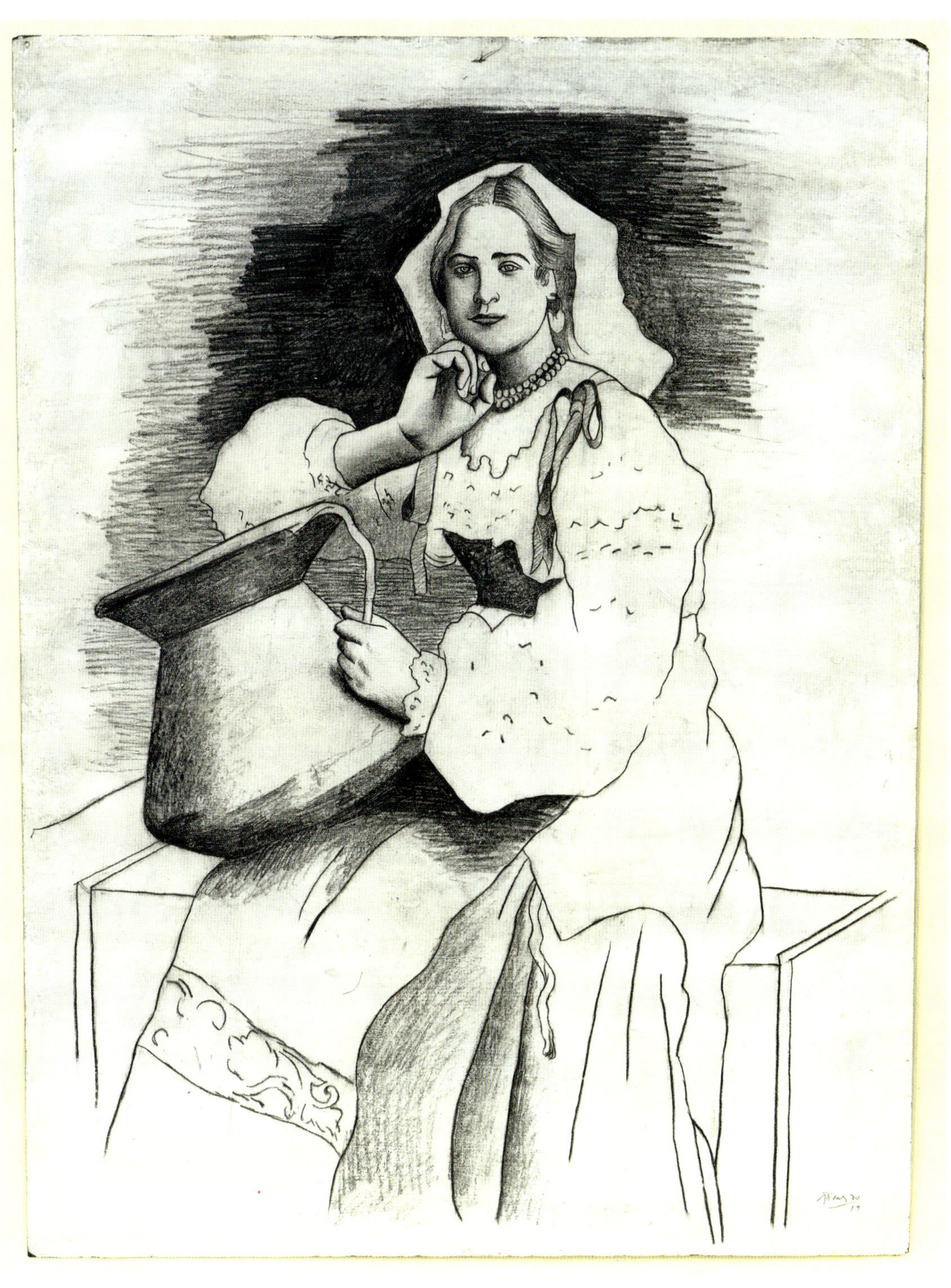

31. Pablo Picasso
Paysans italiens [Italian Peasants], 1919
Pencil and charcoal on paper, 61.3 x 49.5 cm
Santa Barbara, Museum of Art, Gift of Wright S. Ludington, inv. 1946.10.2

32. Pablo Picasso
Femme italienne à la cruche [Italian Woman with Jug], 1919
Pencil on paper, 66 x 48 cm
Private collection, on loan to Staatliche Museen zu Berlin, Nationalgalerie, Museum Berggruen

III. *Parade* [1917]

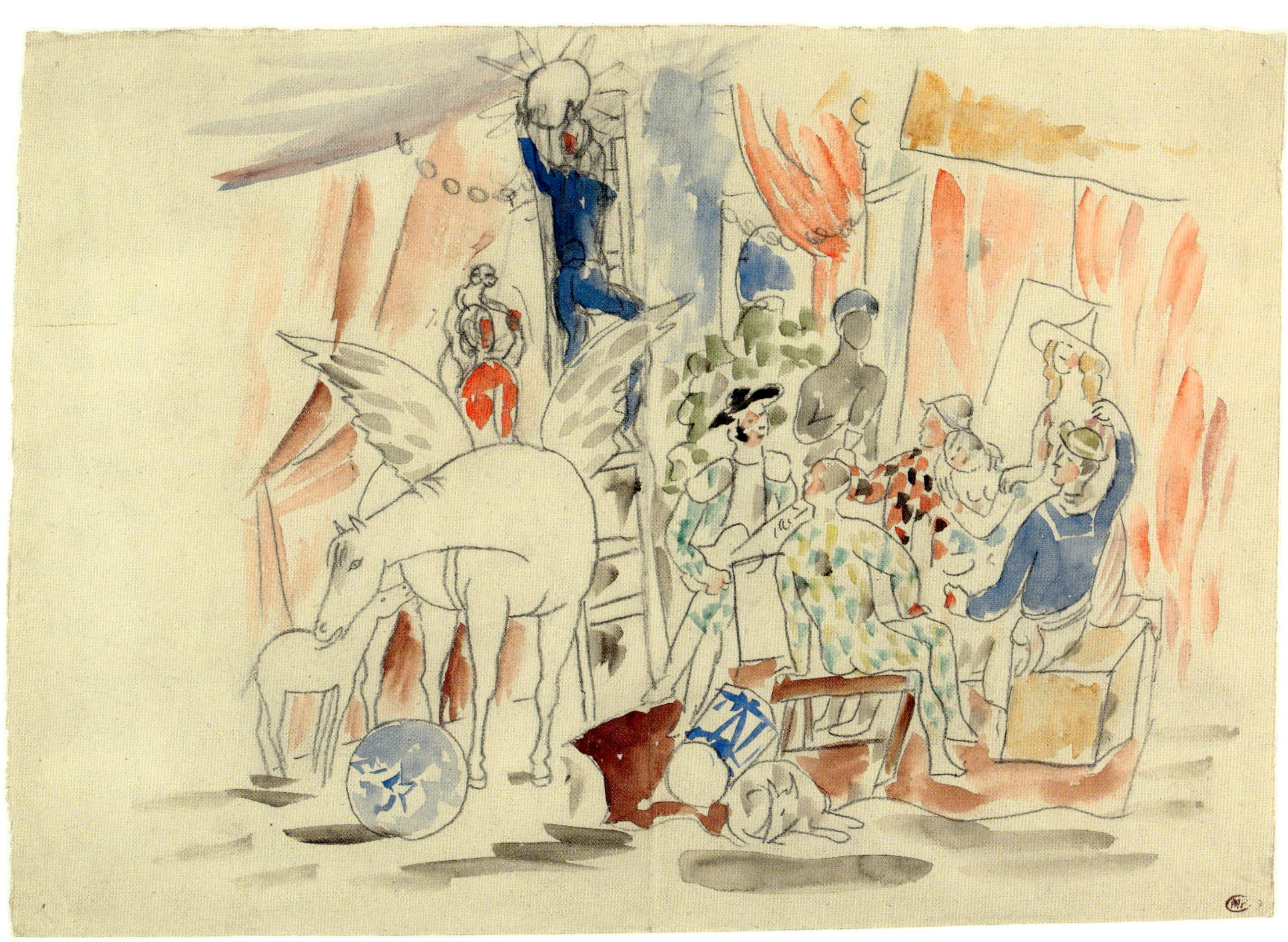

33. Pablo Picasso
Projet pour le rideau de scène du ballet "Parade" [Sketch for the stage curtain of the ballet *Parade*], Paris–Rome, 1916–17
Pencil and watercolour on vellum paper, 27.7 x 40 cm
Paris, Musée national Picasso-Paris, Pablo Picasso Donation, 1979, inv. MP1557

Following pages
34. Pablo Picasso
Stage curtain for the ballet *Parade*, 1917
Tempera on canvas, 1050 x 1640 cm
Paris, Centre Georges Pompidou, Musée National d'Art Moderne / Centre de création industrielle, inv. AM3365 P
(work on display at the Gallerie Nazionali d'Arte Antica - Palazzo Barberini, Salone Pietro da Cortona)

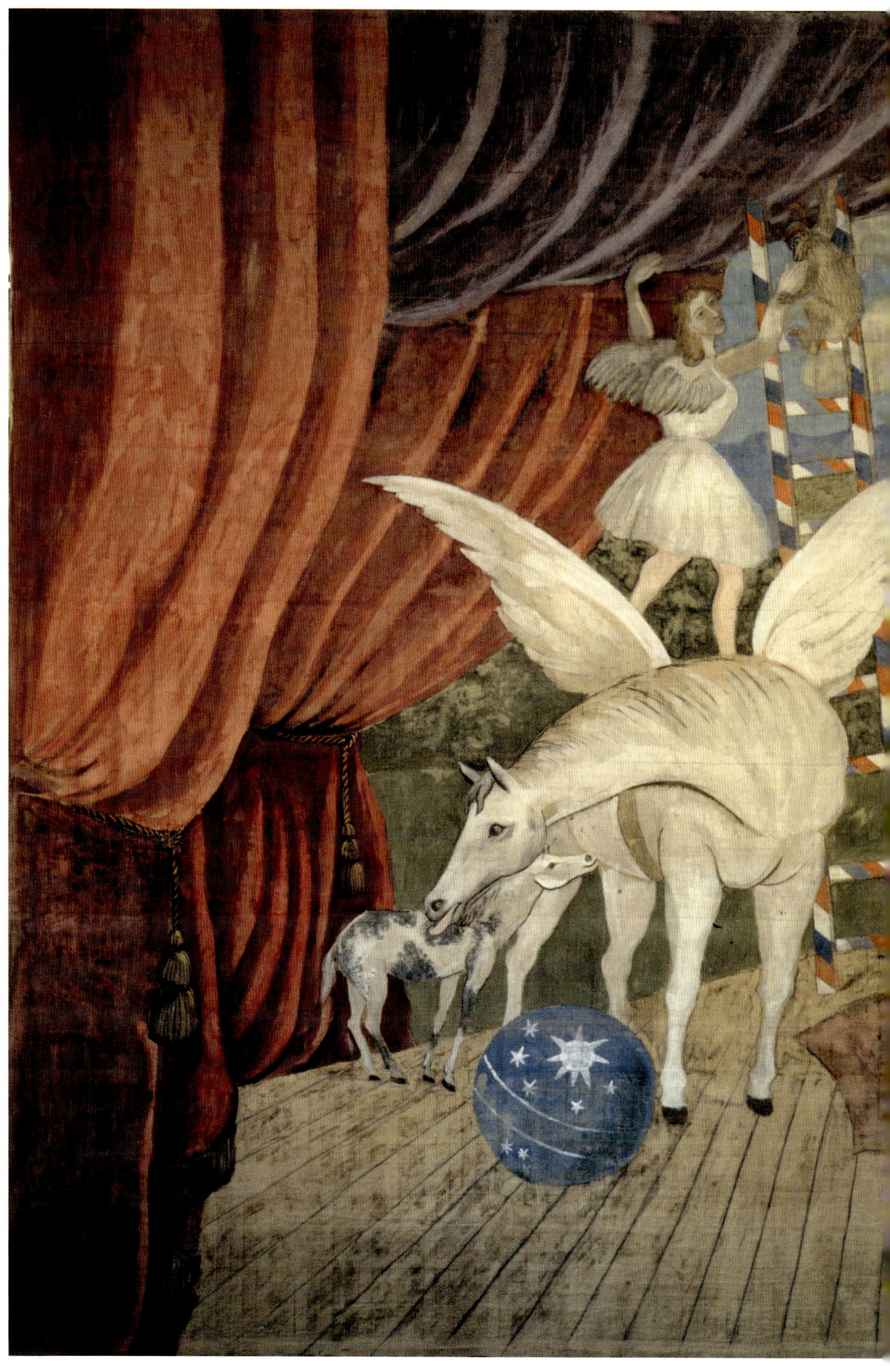

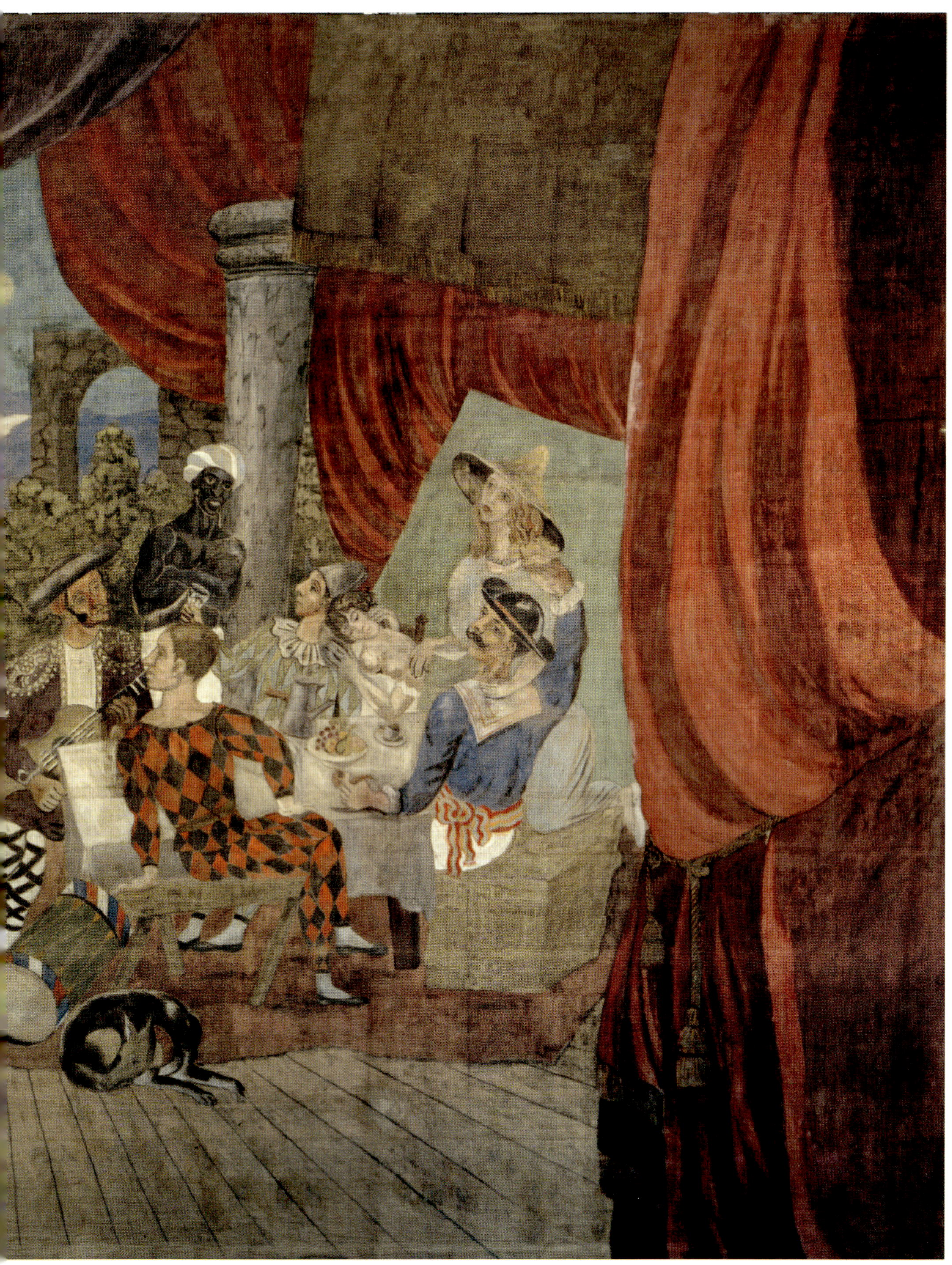

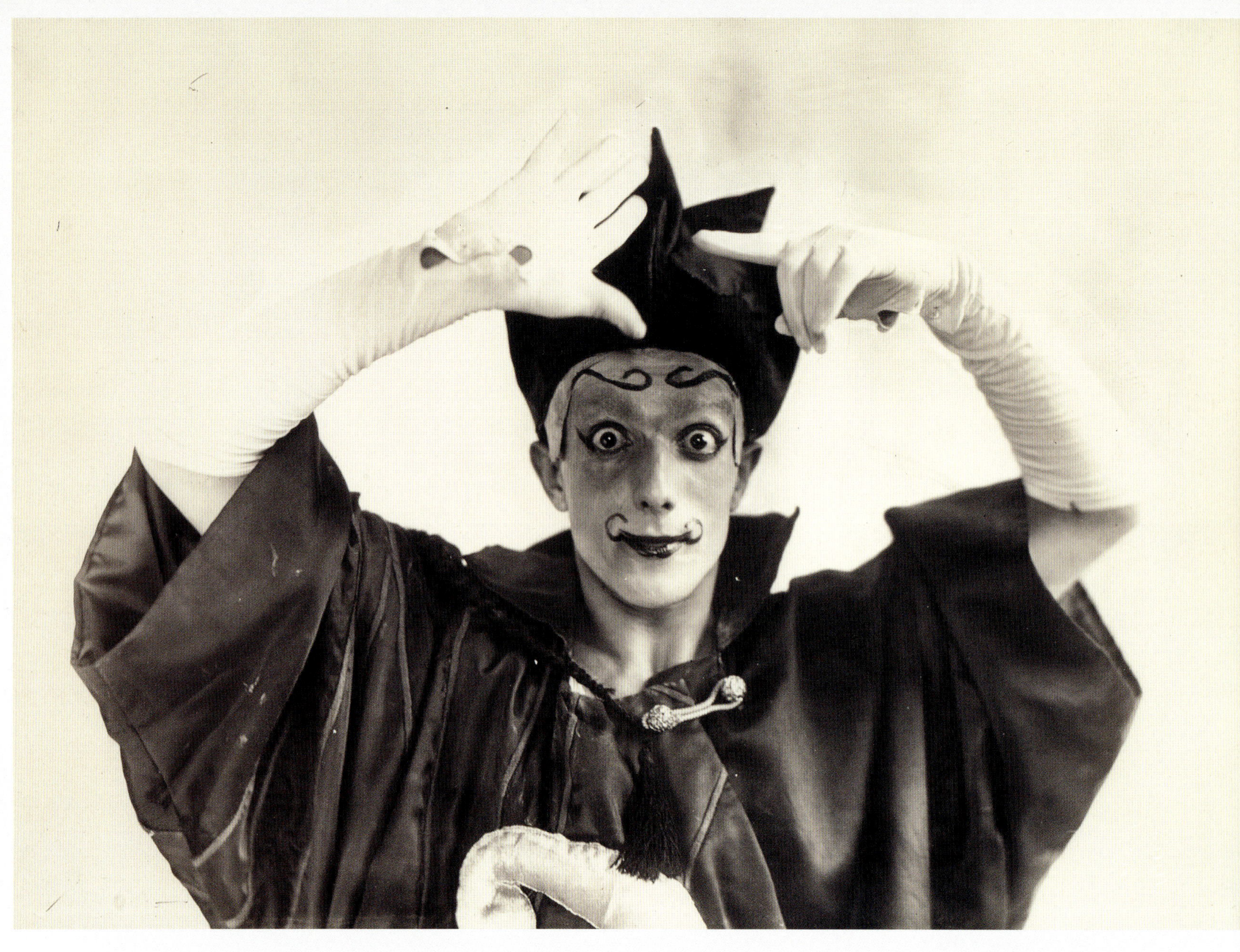

35. Harry Lachman
Léonide Massine in the role
of the Chinese Conjurer, 1917
Gelatin silver print, 18 x 24 cm
Paris, Bibliothèque nationale
de France, Alb.Ph.Kochno "Parade",
Bl./pl.19

36. Harry Lachman
Léonide Massine in the role
of the Chinese Conjurer, 1917
Gelatin silver print, 18 x 24 cm
Paris, Bibliothèque nationale
de France, Alb.Ph.Kochno "Parade",
Bl./pl.12

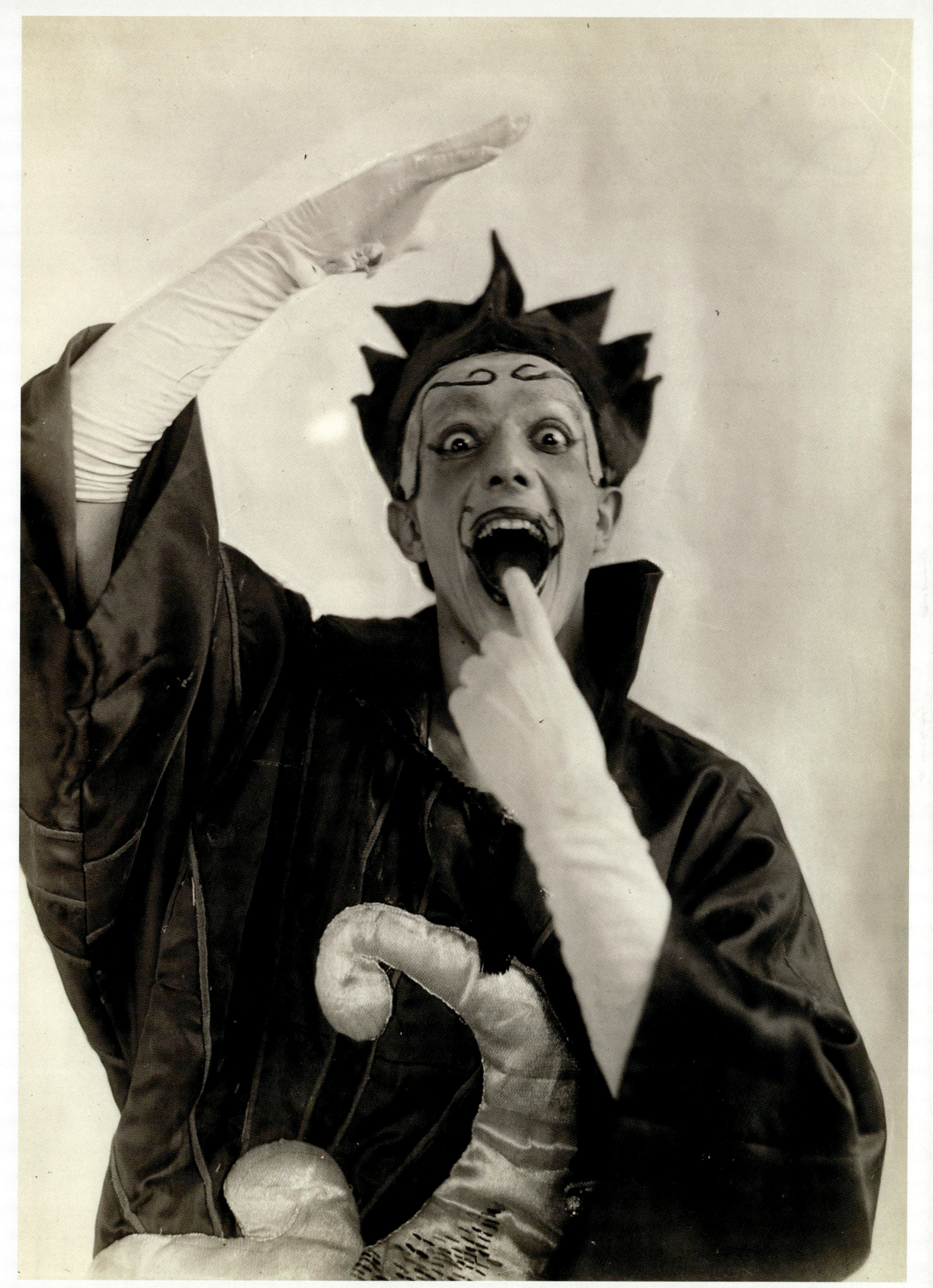

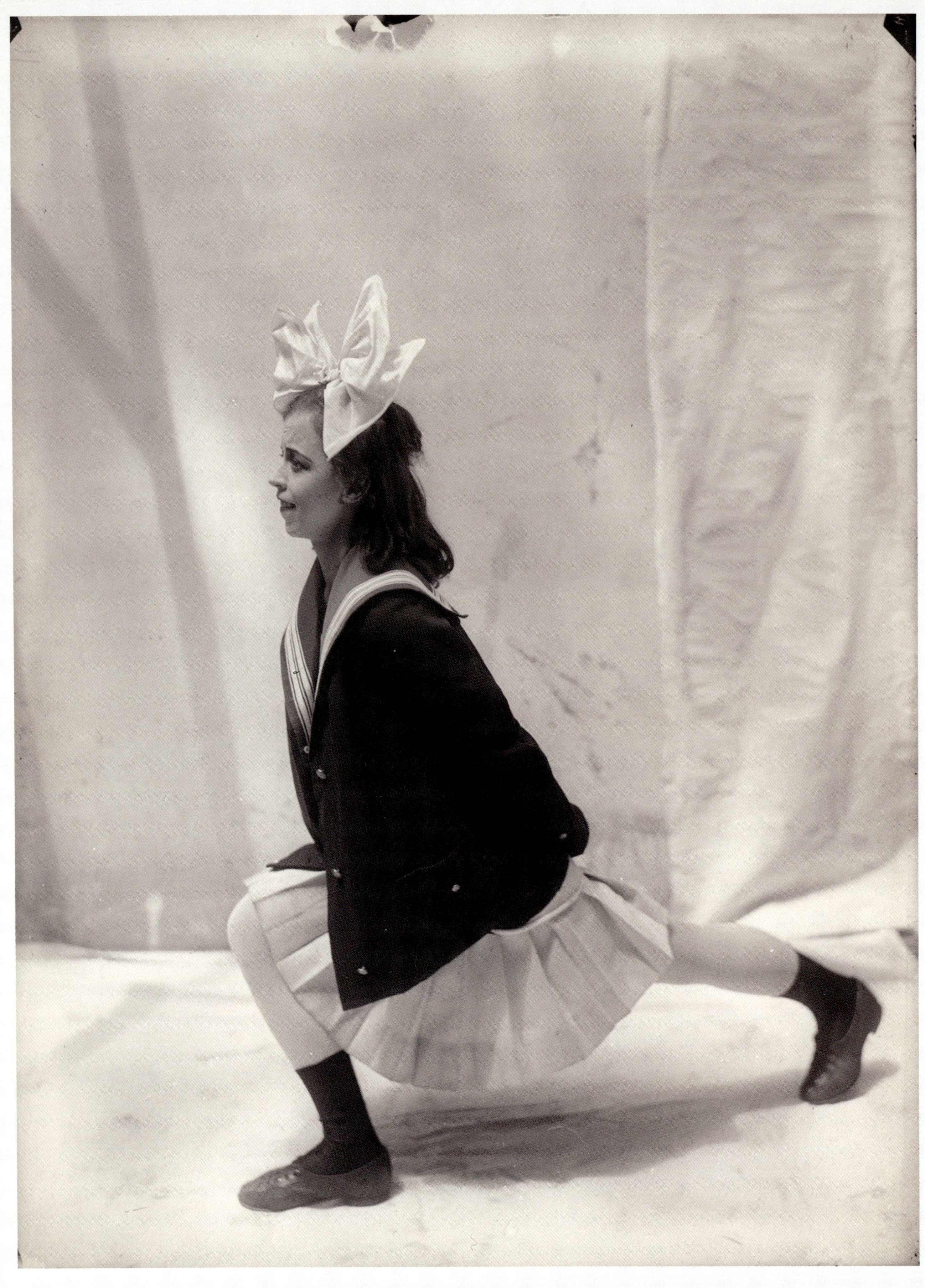

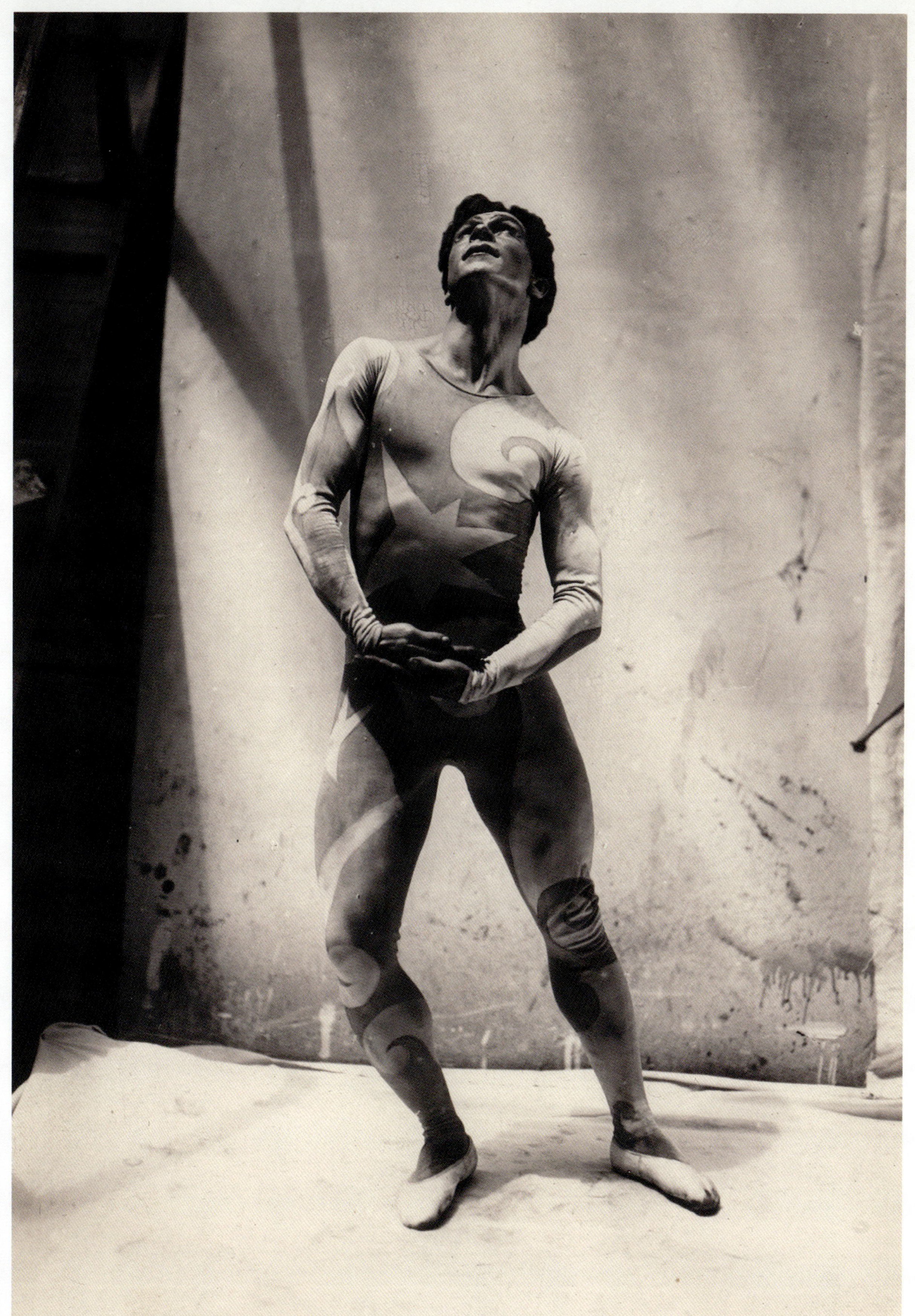

37. Harry Lachman
Marie Chabelska in the role
of the Little American Girl, 1917
Gelatin silver print, 23.5 x 18 cm
Paris, Bibliothèque nationale
de France, Alb.Ph.Kochno "Parade",
Bl./pl.26
(work not exhibited)

38. Harry Lachman
Nicholas Zverev in the role
of the Acrobat, 1917
Gelatin silver print, 17 x 12.5 cm
Paris, Bibliothèque nationale
de France, Alb.Ph.Kochno "Parade",
Bl./pl.40

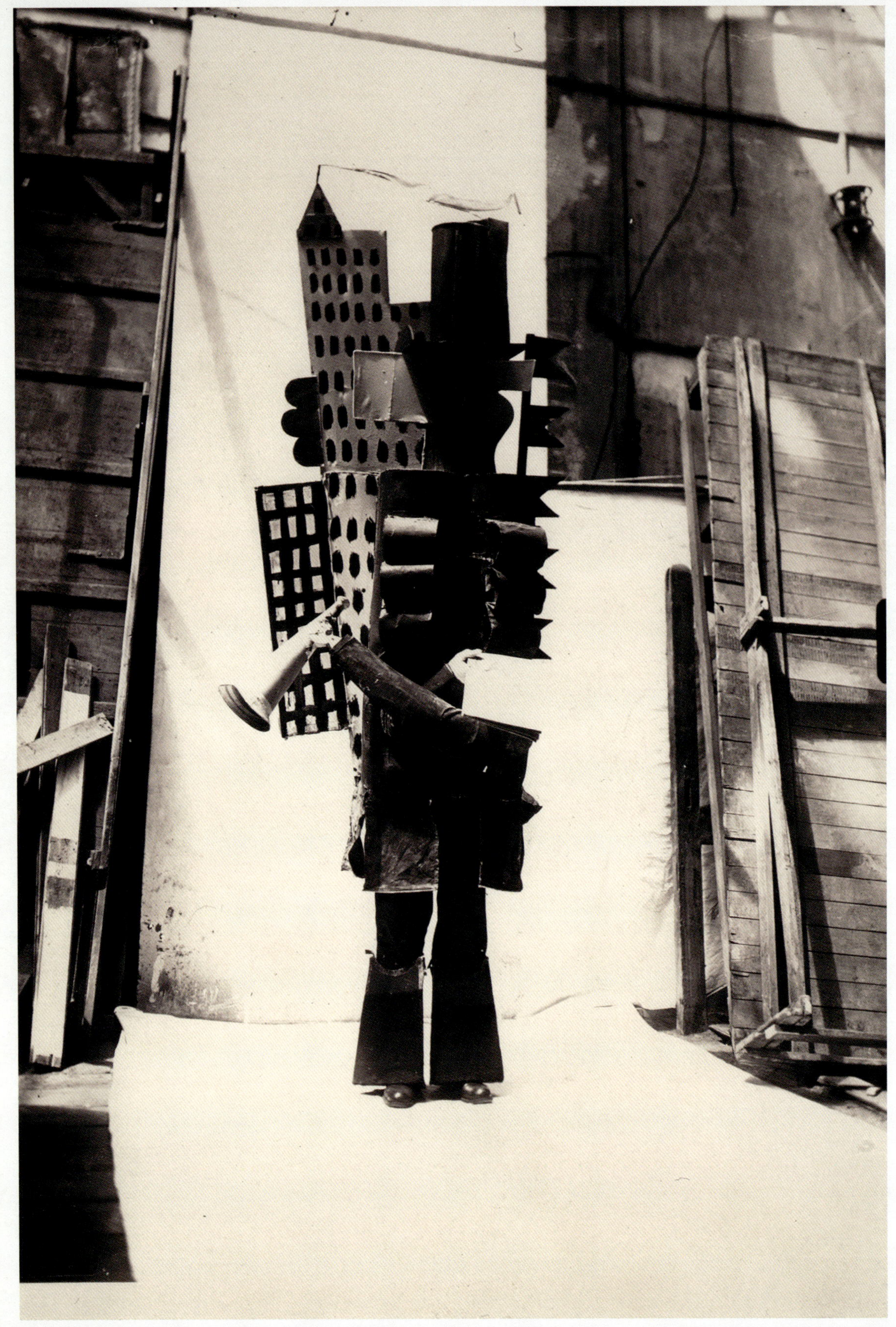

39. Harry Lachman
The American Manager, 1917
Gelatin silver print, 18 x 13 cm
Paris, Bibliothèque nationale
de France, Alb.Ph.Kochno "Parade",
Bl./pl.48

40. Harry Lachman
The American Manager, 1917
Gelatin silver print, 24 x 18 cm
Paris, Bibliothèque nationale
de France, Alb.Ph.Kochno "Parade",
Bl./pl.56

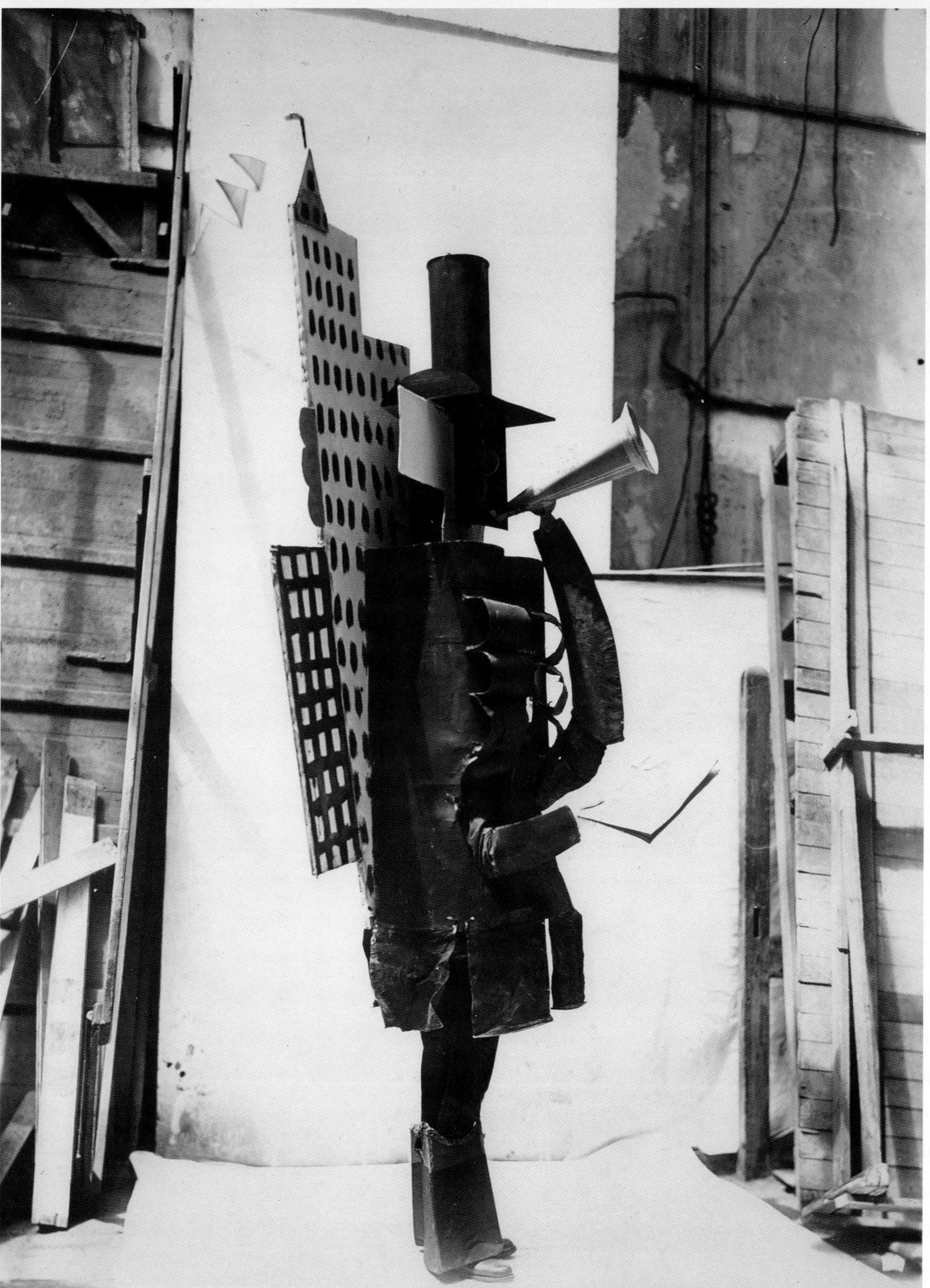

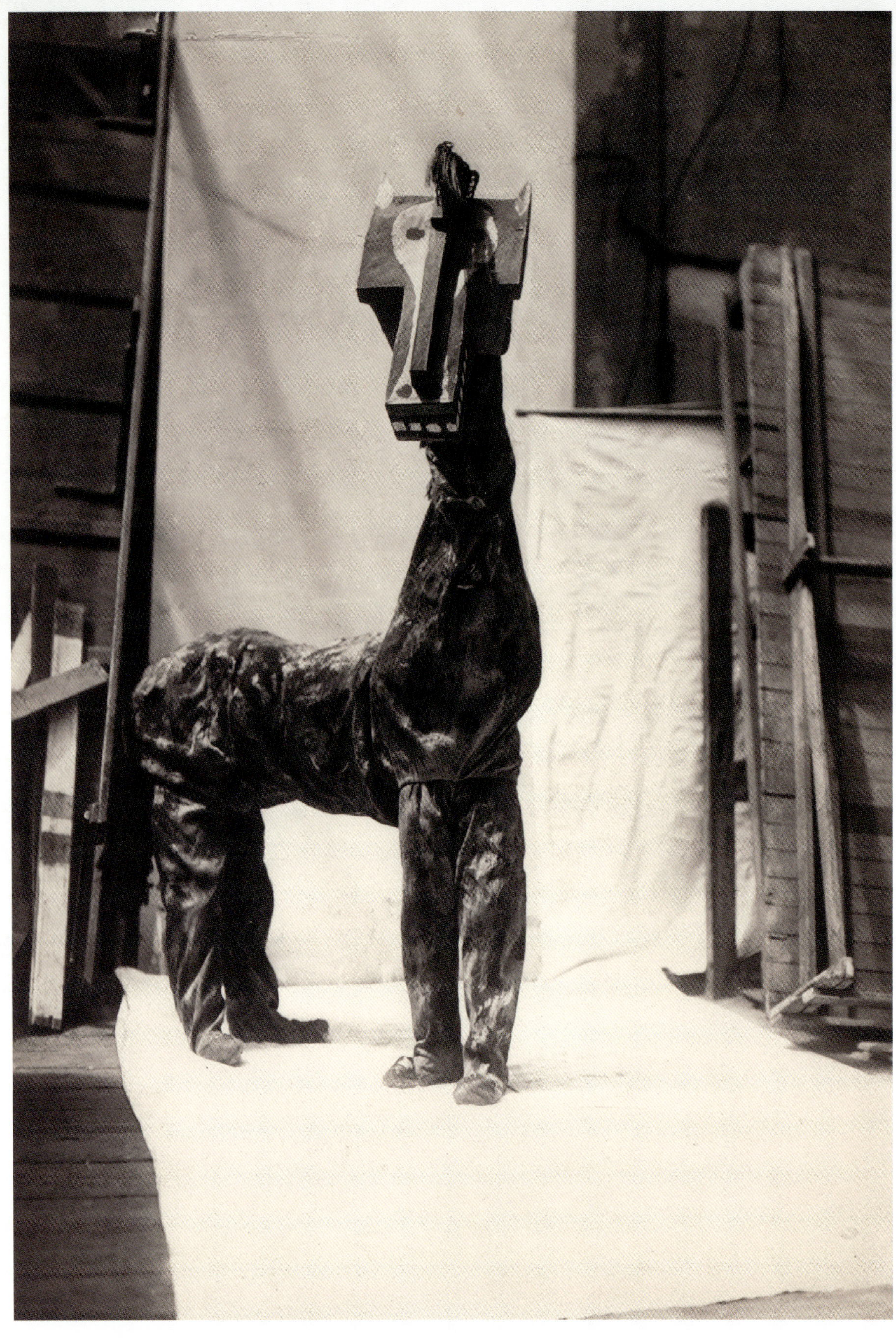

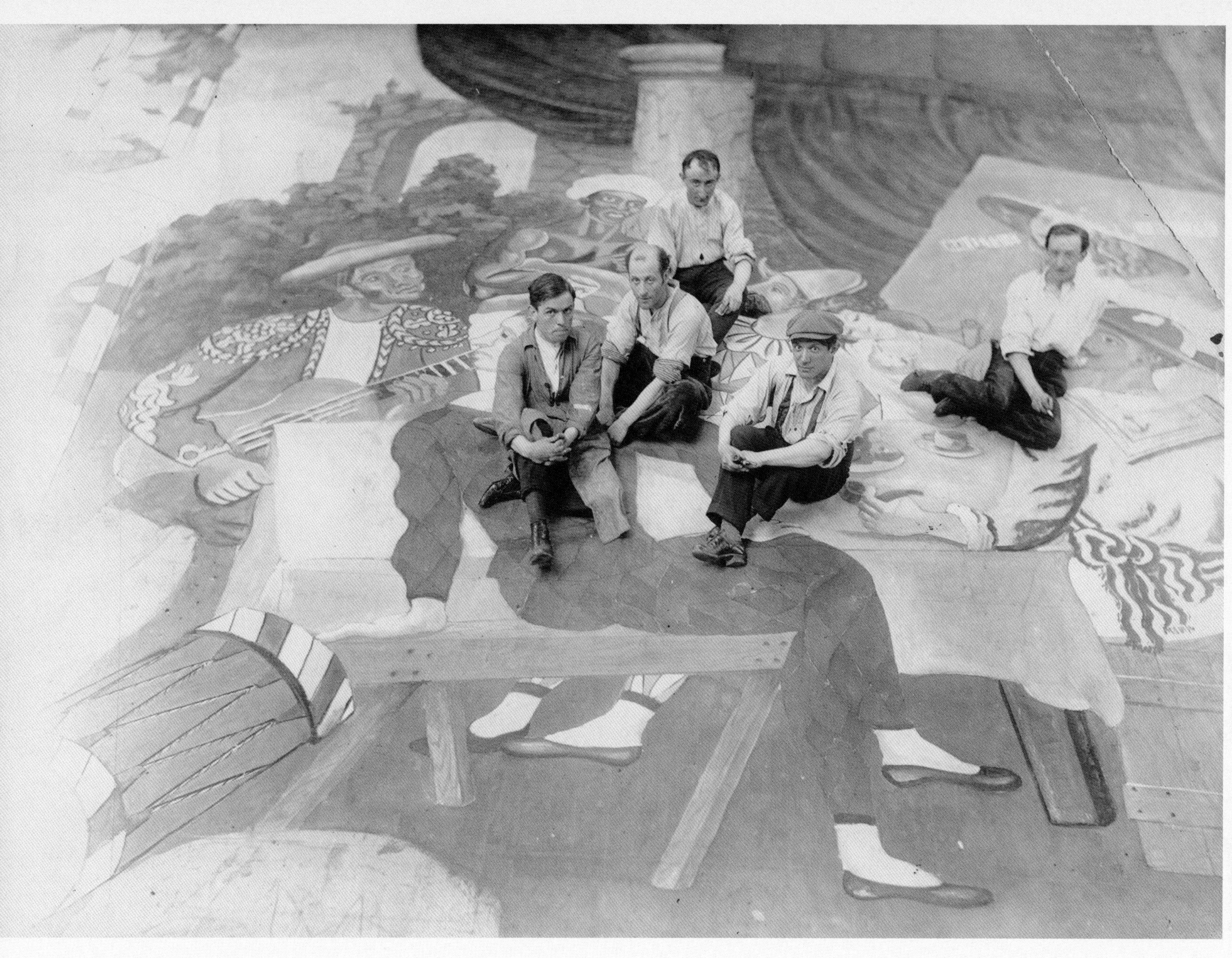

41. Harry Lachman
The Horse, 1917
Gelatin silver print, 17.5 x 12.5 cm
Paris, Bibliothèque nationale
de France, Alb.Ph.Kochno "Parade",
Bl./pl.63

42. Harry Lachman (attrib.)
Picasso and his assistants sitting
at work on the curtain of the ballet
Parade, Paris, 1917
Print from the original glass plate
negative, 18 x 24 cm
Brussels, Fundación Almine y
Bernard Ruiz-Picasso para el Arte,
inv. 107364

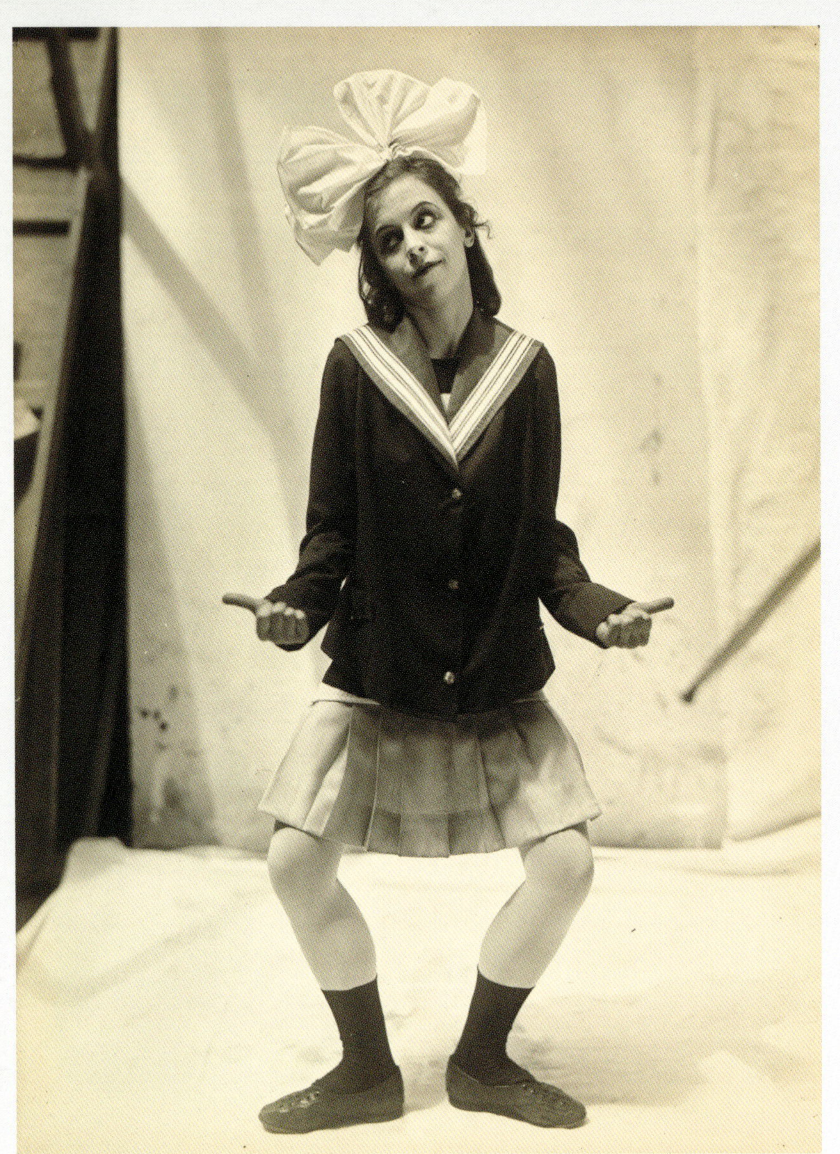

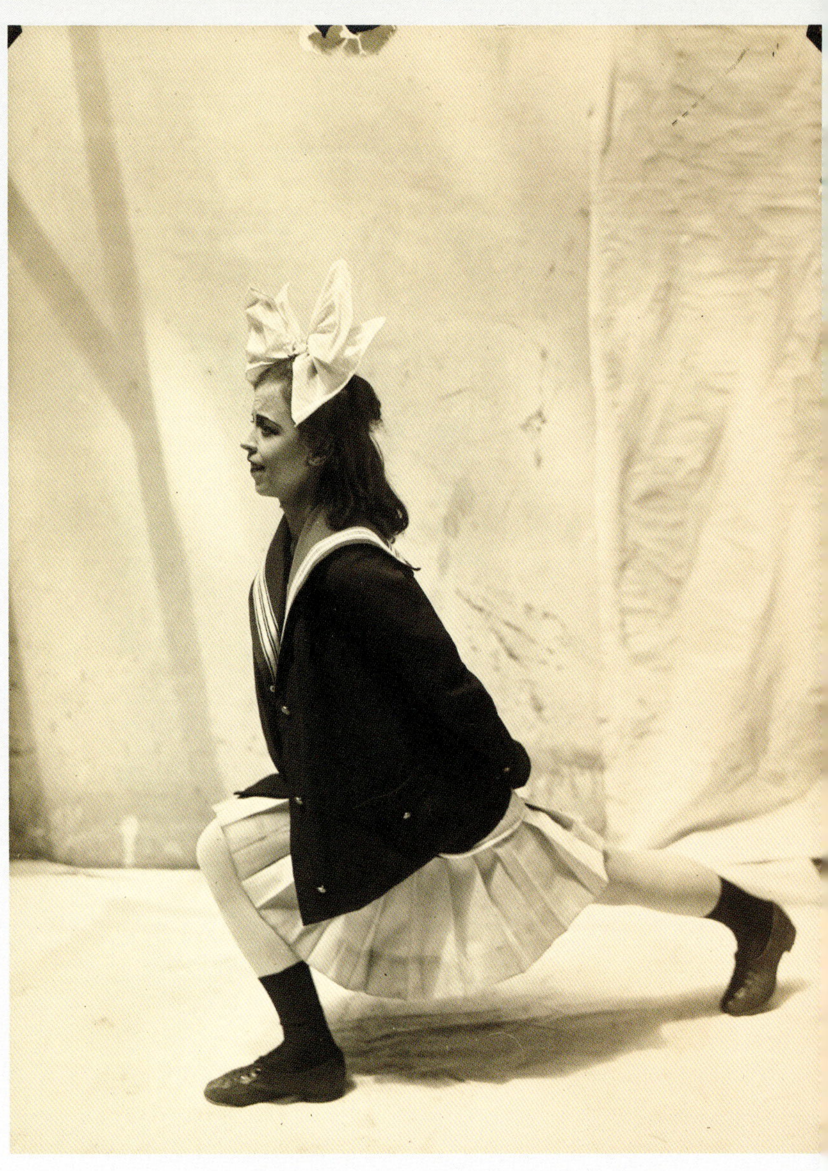

43. Harry Lachman
Marie Chabelska in the role of the Little American Girl in the ballet *Parade*, 1917
Gelatin silver print, 23.4 x 17.3 cm
Paris, Musée national Picasso-Paris, Donation of Picasso's heirs, 1992, inv. APPH4819

44. Harry Lachman
Marie Chabelska in the role of the Little American Girl in the ballet *Parade*, 1917
Gelatin silver print, 23.5 x 17.5 cm
Paris, Musée national Picasso-Paris, Donation of Picasso's heirs, 1992, inv. APPH4820

45. Pablo Picasso (attrib.)
Maquette for the set of the ballet *Parade* for the *Ballets Russes*, 1917
Gelatin silver print, 13.2 x 18.1 cm
Paris, Musée national Picasso-Paris, Donation of Picasso's heirs, 1992, inv. APPH4822

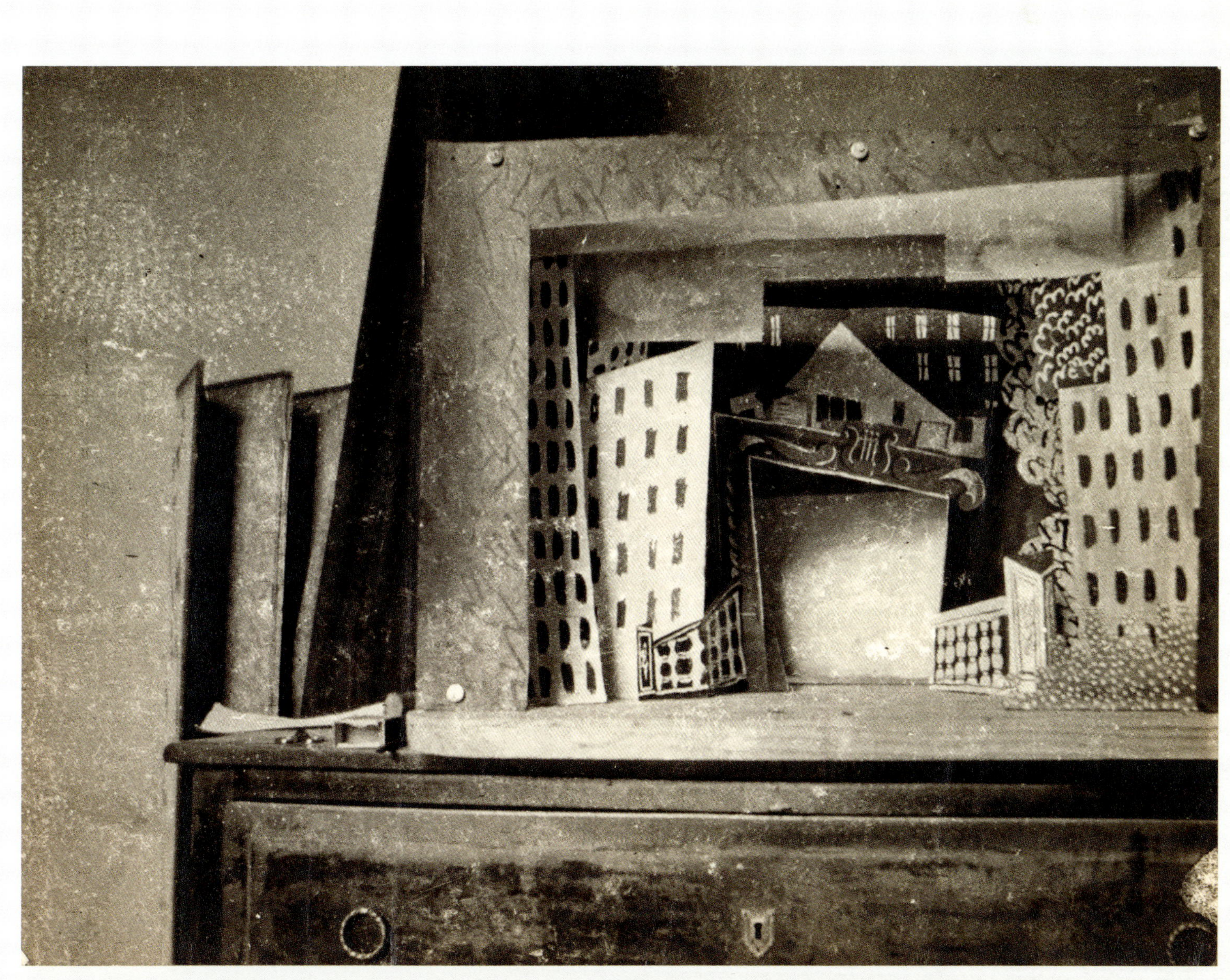

Printemps 1917

LA COLLABORATION DE " PARADE "

MON CHER AMI,

Vous me demandez quelques détails sur « *Parade* ». Les voici trop en hâte. Excusez le style et le désordre.

Chaque matin m'arrivent de nouvelles injures, quelques-unes de fort loin car des critiques s'acharnent contre nous sans avoir vu ni entendu l'œuvre; et, comme on ne comble pas des abîmes, comme il faudrait reprendre à partir d'Adam et d'Eve, j'ai trouvé plus digne de ne jamais répondre. Je consulte donc du même œil surpris l'article où on nous insulte, l'article où on nous méprise, l'article où l'indulgence le dispute au sourire, l'article où on nous félicite tout de travers.

En face de cette pile de malentendus, de myopies, d'incultures, d'insensibilités, je pense aux mois admirables où nous avons, Satie, Picasso et moi, aimé, cherché, ébauché, combiné peu à peu cette petite chose si pleine et dont la pudeur consiste justement à n'être pas agressive.

∴

L'idée m'en est venue pendant une permission d'avril 1915 (j'étais alors aux armées) en écoutant Satie jouer à quatre mains avec Viñes ses « Morceaux en forme de poire ». Le titre déroute. Une attitude d'humoriste, qui date de Montmartre, empêche le public distrait d'entendre comme il faut la musique du bon maître d'Arcueil. ~~Alors que les compositeurs de l'époque coupaient la poire en douze et affublaient chaque morceau d'un titre avantageux, promenant Mallarmé dans le « Jardin de l'Infante » (1), Satie inventait des mélodies profondes et baptisait le tout : « Morceaux en forme de poire ».~~ 19

Une sorte de télépathie nous inspira ensemble un désir de collaboration. Une semaine plus tard je rejoignais le front, laissant à Satie une liasse de notes, d'ébauches, qui devaient lui fournir le thème du Chinois, de la petite Américaine et de l'Acrobate (l'acrobate était alors seul). Ces indications n'avaient rien d'humoristique. Elles insistaient au contraire sur ~~[illegible]~~ le prolongement des personnages, sur le verso de notre baraque foraine. Le Chinois y était capable de torturer des missionnaires, la petite fille de sombrer sur le *Titanic*, l'acrobate d'être en confidence avec les astres.

Peu à peu vint au monde une partition sobre, nette, où Satie semble avoir découvert une dimension inconnue grâce à laquelle on écoute simultanément la parade et le spectacle intérieur.

Dans la première version les Managers n'existaient pas. Après chaque numéro de Music-Hall, une voix anonyme, sortant d'un trou amplificateur (imitation théâtrale du gramophone forain, masque antique à la mode moderne) chantait une phrase type, résumant les perspectives du personnage, ouvrant une brèche sur le rêve.

Lorsque Picasso nous montra ses esquisses, nous comprimes l'intérêt d'opposer

46. Jean Cocteau
Presentation of *Parade*, 1937
7 sheets (a–b)
Pen and ink, dimensions variable
Paris, Bibliothèque historique de la Ville de Paris, Fonds Jean Cocteau, inv. MF-FS-05-0343

47. Pablo Picasso
Programme of the Ballets Russes, 1920
Special issue of *La Danse* (December 1920)
Paris, Bibliothèque historique de la Ville de Paris, Fonds Jean Cocteau, inv. MS-FS-05038

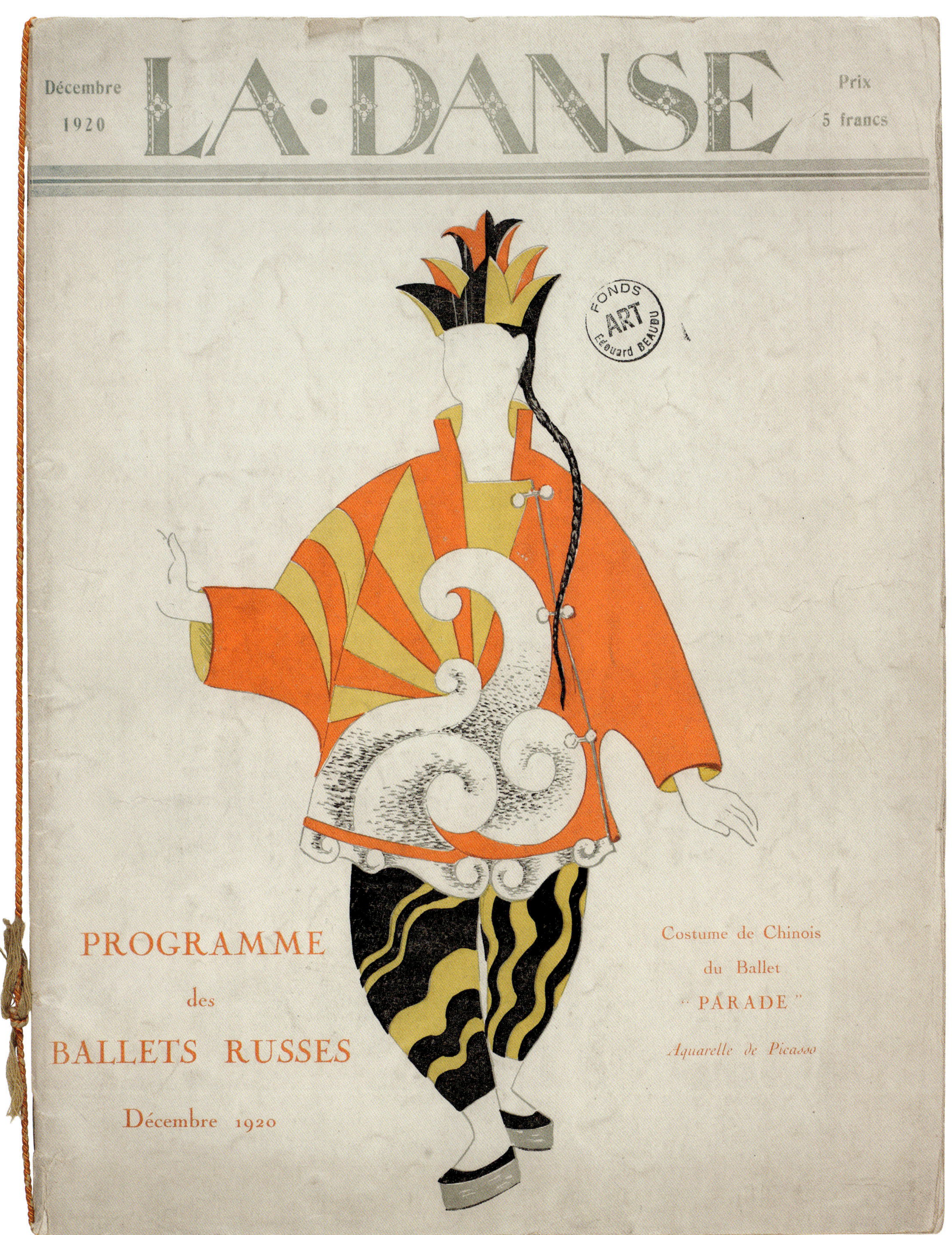
Décembre
1920
LA·DANSE
Prix
5 francs
FONDS
ART
Edouard BEAUDU
PROGRAMME
des
BALLETS RUSSES
Décembre 1920
Costume de Chinois
du Ballet
"PARADE"
Aquarelle de Picasso

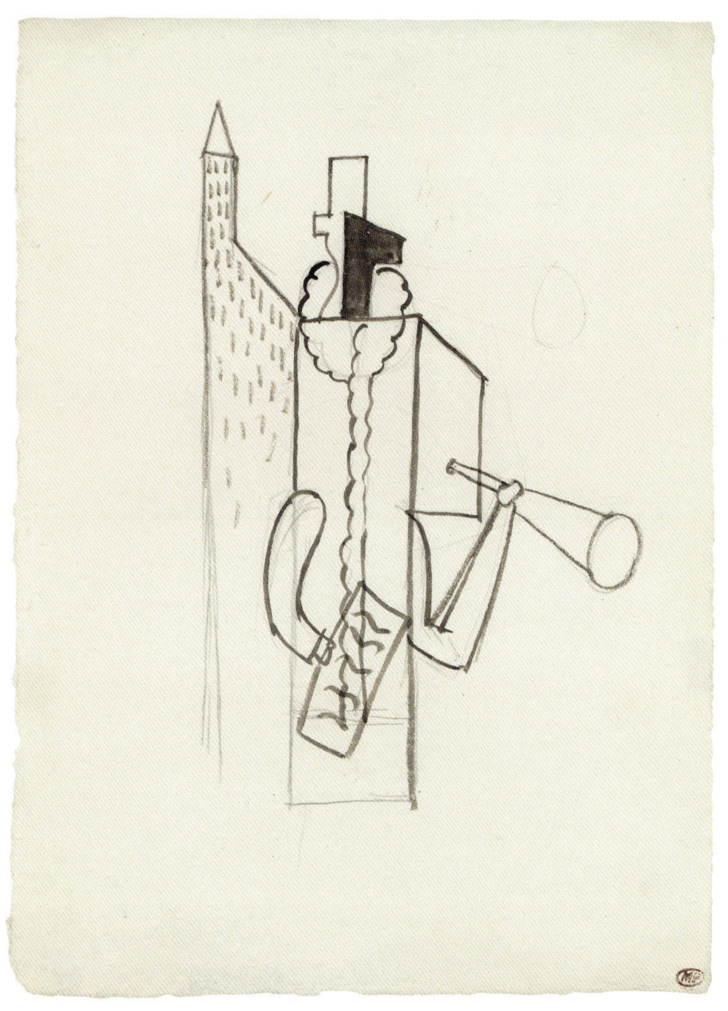

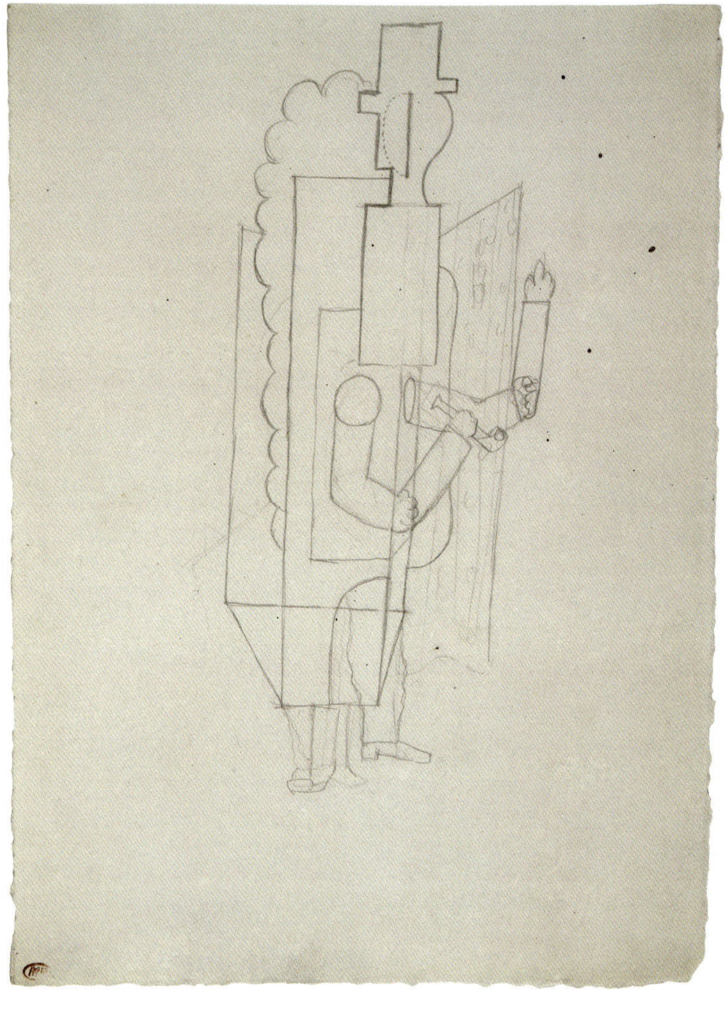

48. Pablo Picasso
Étude pour le ballet "Parade": le manager américain [Study for the American Manager in the ballet *Parade*], Paris–Rome, 1916–17
Watercolour and graphite on white vellum drawing paper, 28.1 x 20.9 cm
Paris, Musée national Picasso-Paris, Pablo Picasso Donation, 1979, inv. MP1596

49. Pablo Picasso
Étude pour le ballet "Parade": le manager français [Study for the French Manager in the ballet *Parade*], Paris–Rome, 1916–17
Pencil on drawing paper, 28.1 x 20.7 cm
Paris, Musée national Picasso-Paris, Pablo Picasso Donation, 1979, inv. MP1600

50. Pablo Picasso
Projet pour un costume d'acrobate [Sketch for an acrobat's costume (Sketch for the Acrobat in the ballet *Parade*)], Paris–Rome, 1916–17
Pencil and watercolour on paper, 28 x 20.9 cm
Paris, Musée national Picasso-Paris, Pablo Picasso Donation, 1979, inv. MP1573

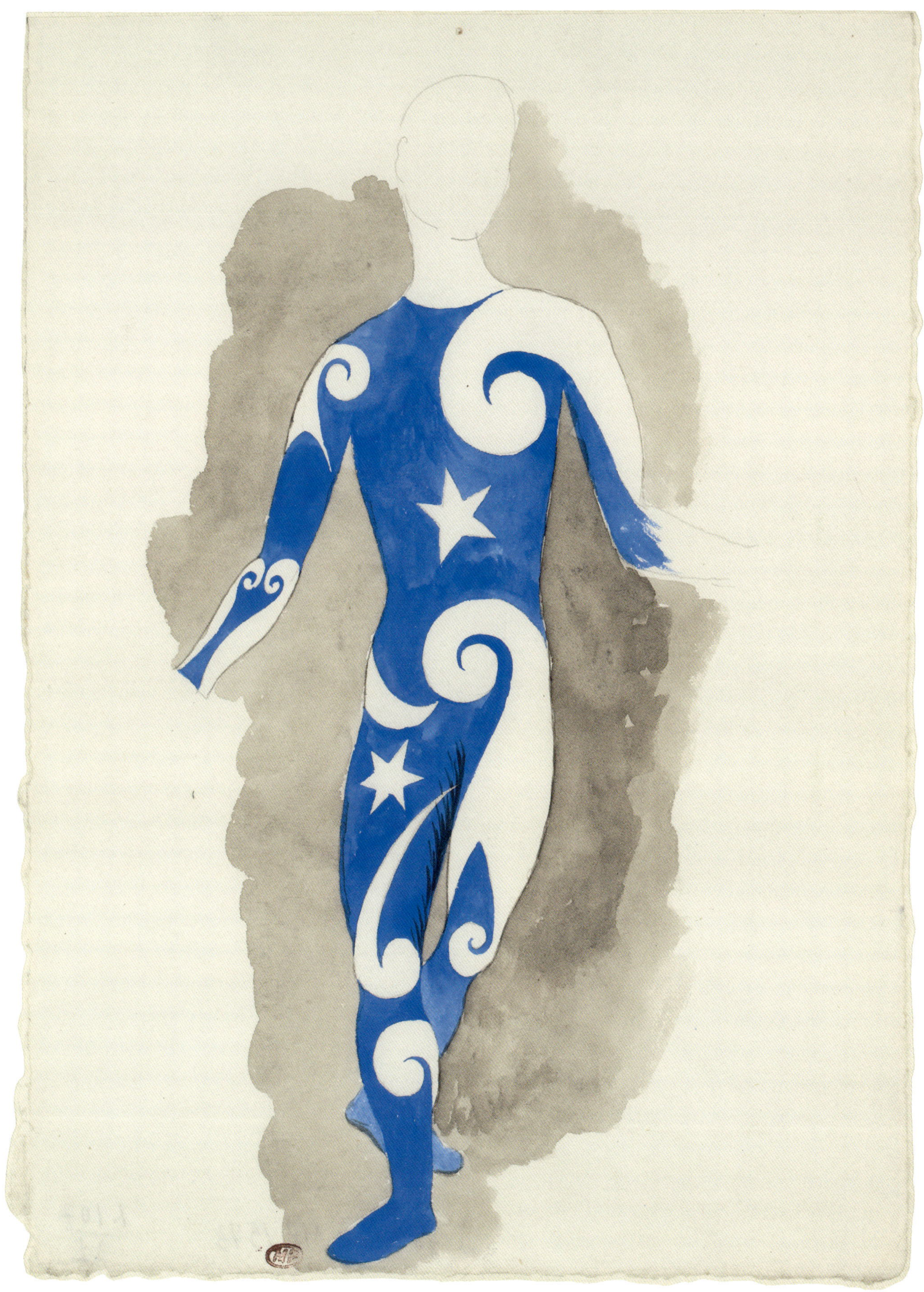

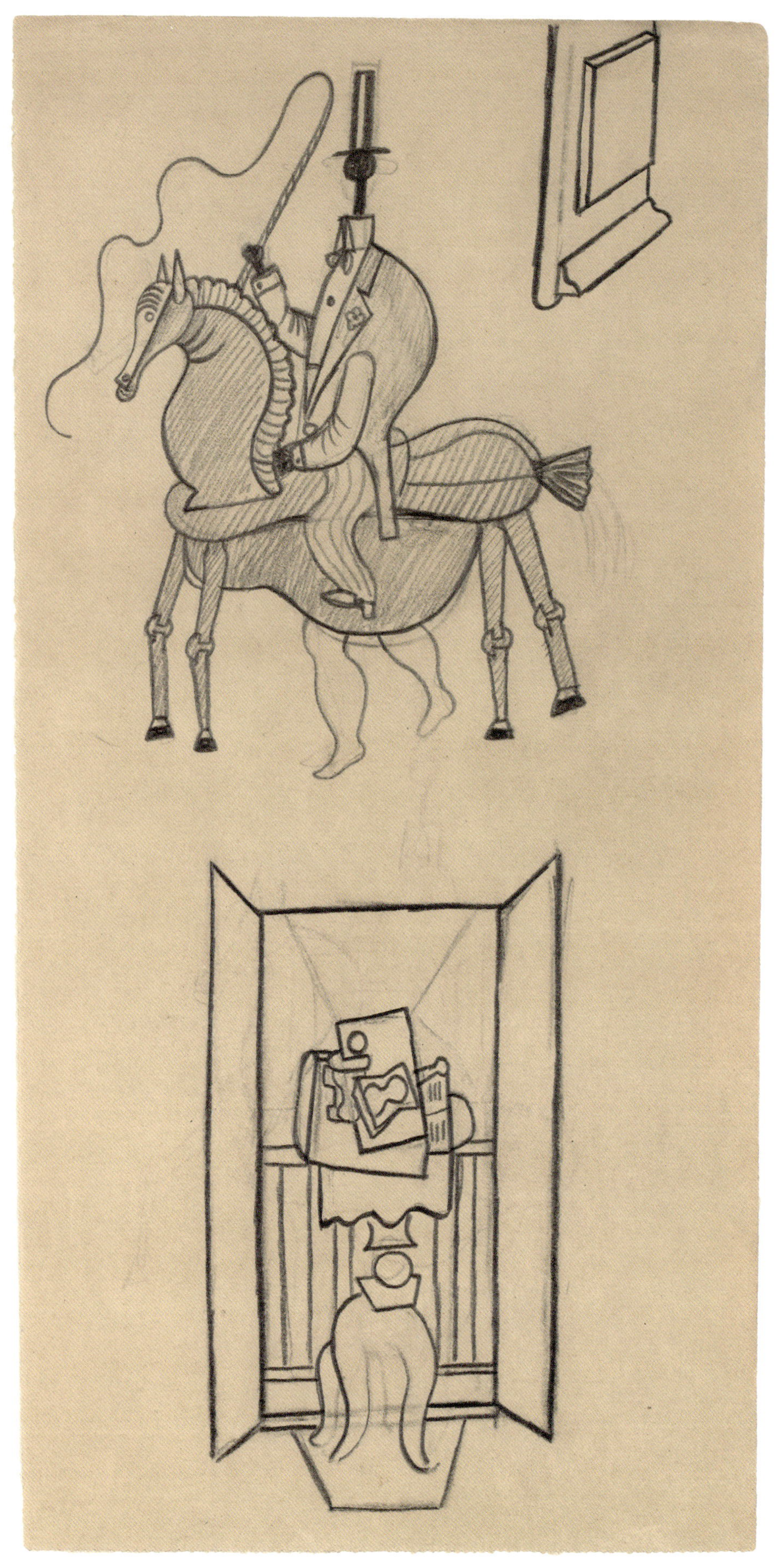

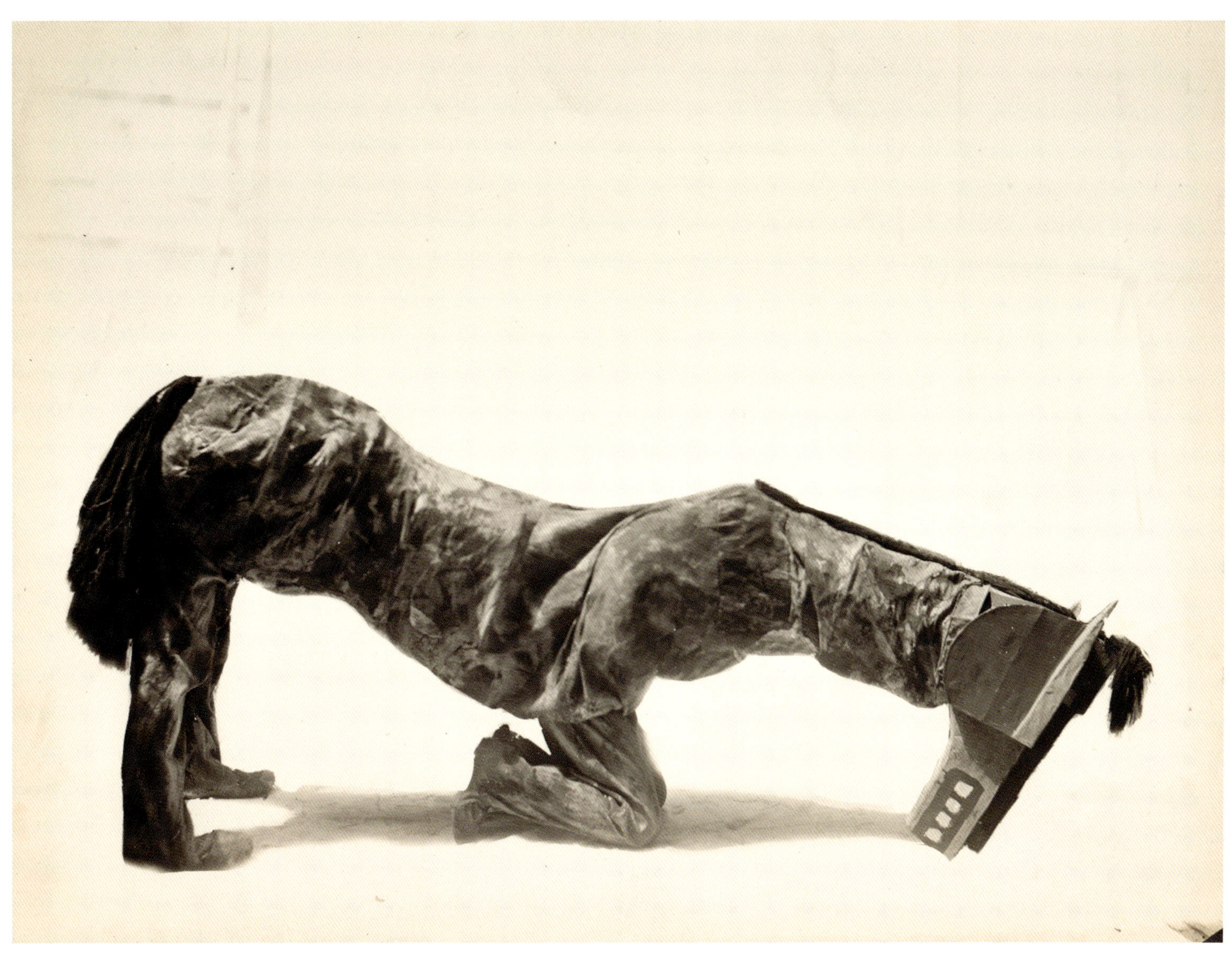

51. Pablo Picasso
Étude pour "les managers à cheval" du ballet "Parade" *et nature morte sur un guéridon devant une fenêtre ouverte* [Study for the Managers on horseback in the ballet *Parade* and still life on a table by a window], Paris–Rome, 1916–17
Pencil, watercolour and gouache on vellum drawing paper, 31 x 15.5 cm
Paris, Musée national Picasso-Paris, Pablo Picasso Donation, 1979, inv. MP1583

52. Anonymous
The Horse bowing in the ballet *Parade* with dancers Edmund Novak and George Oumansky, 1917
Gelatin silver print, 17.3 x 23.4 cm
Paris, Musée national Picasso-Paris, Pablo Picasso Donation, 1979, inv. APPH4821

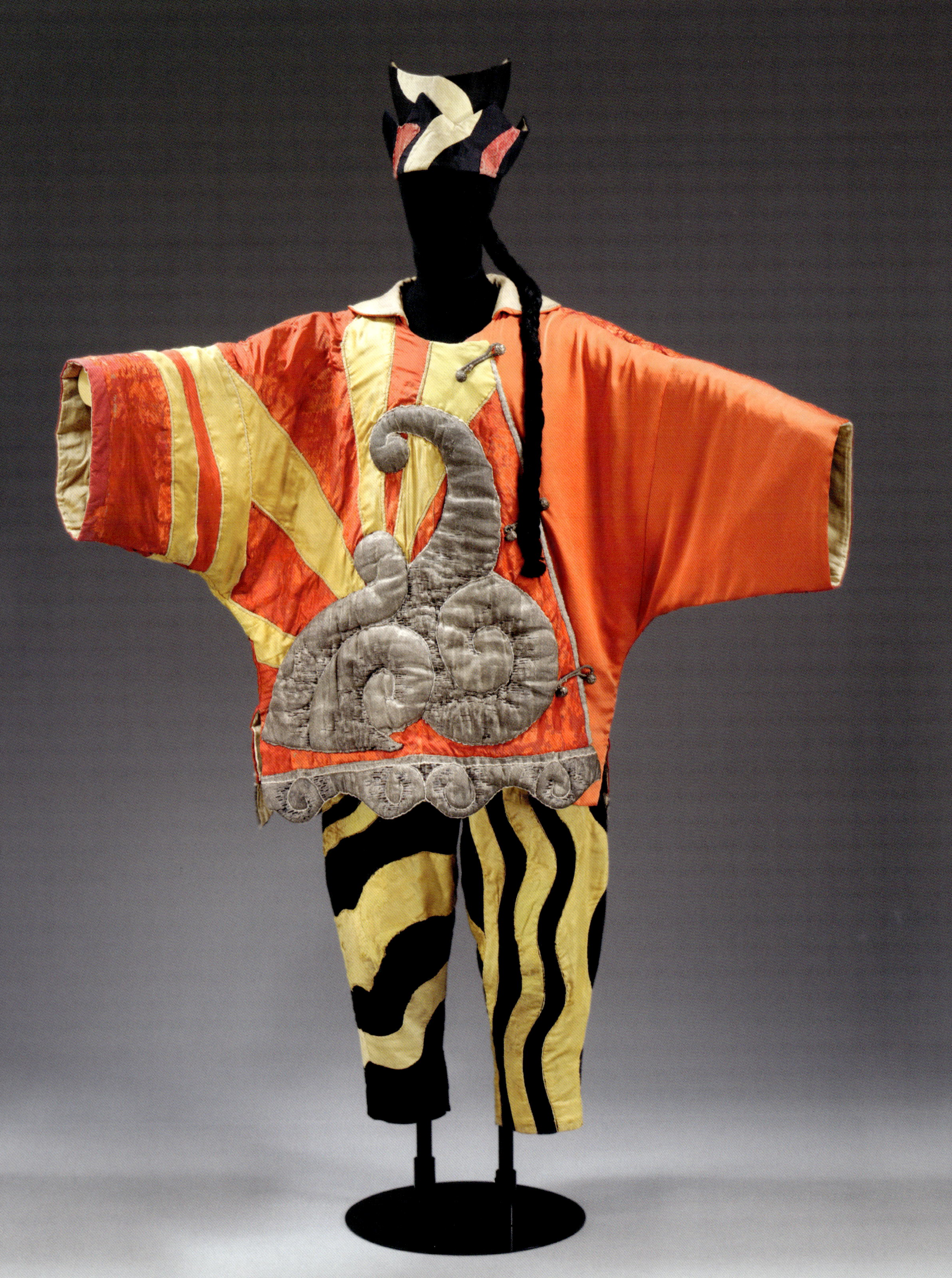

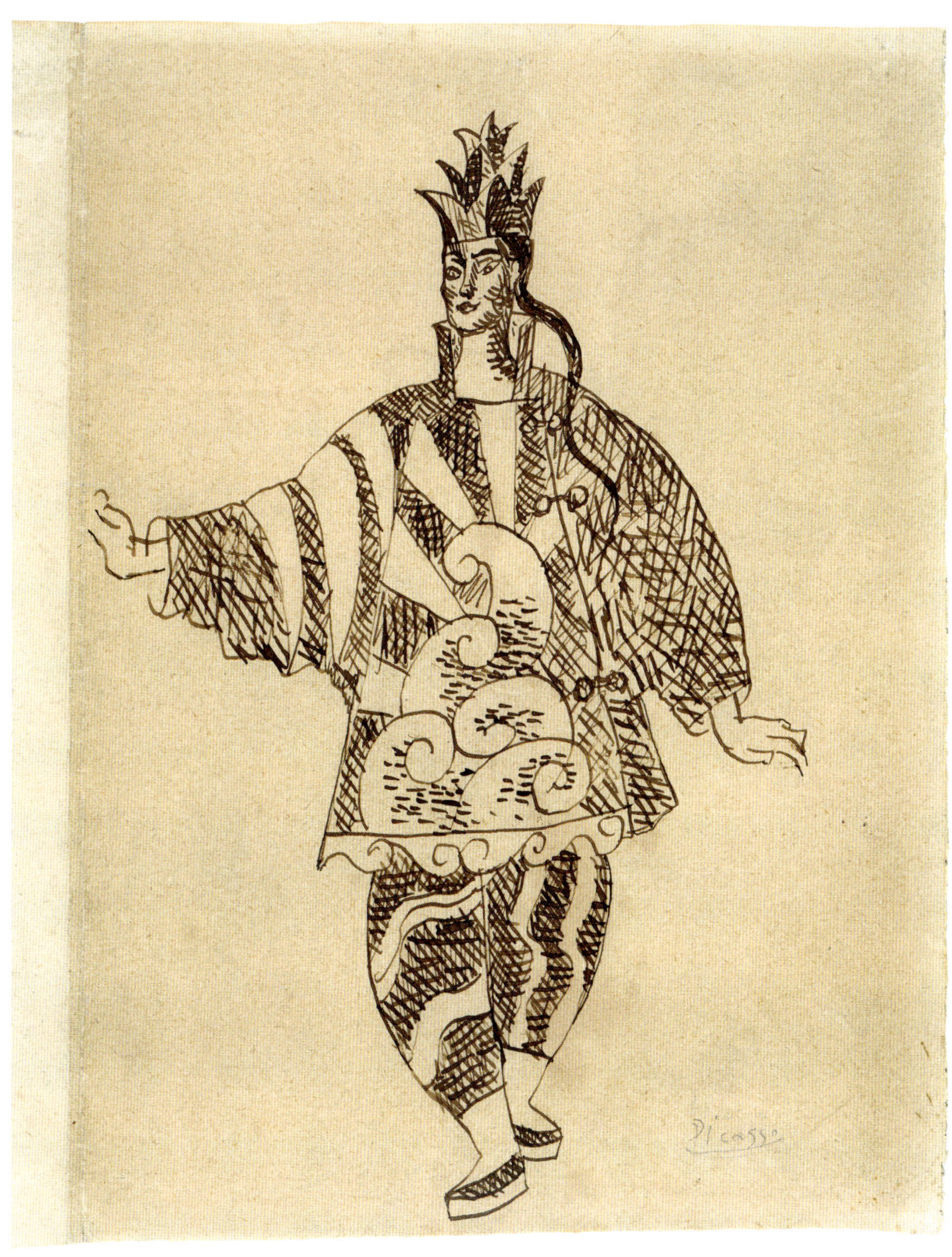

53. Costume for the Chinese Conjurer designed by Picasso for the ballet *Parade* choreographed by Massine, 1917
Hand-painted fabric with appliqué (cotton, satin and ink), 176 x 150 x 50 cm
London, Victoria and Albert Museum, Department of Theatre and Performance, inv. S.84-1985

54. Pablo Picasso
Sketch for the costume of the Chinese Conjurer in the ballet *Parade*, 1917
Ink and pen, 56.7 x 41.5 cm
London, Victoria and Albert Museum, Department of Theatre and Performance, inv. S.562&A-1983

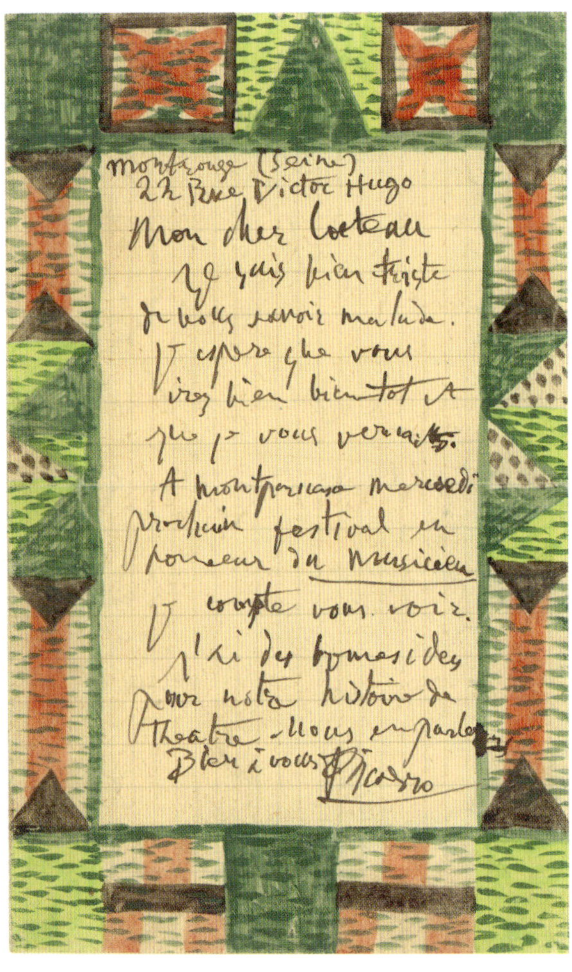

Montrouge (Seine)
22 Rue Victor Hugo
Mon cher Cocteau
Je suis bien triste
de vous savoir malade.
J'espère que vous
irez bien bientôt et
que je vous verrai.
A Montparnasse mercredi
prochain festival en
honneur du musicien
Je compte vous voir.
J'ai des [illegible]
pour notre histoire de
Theatre - nous en parlerons
Bien à vous Picasso

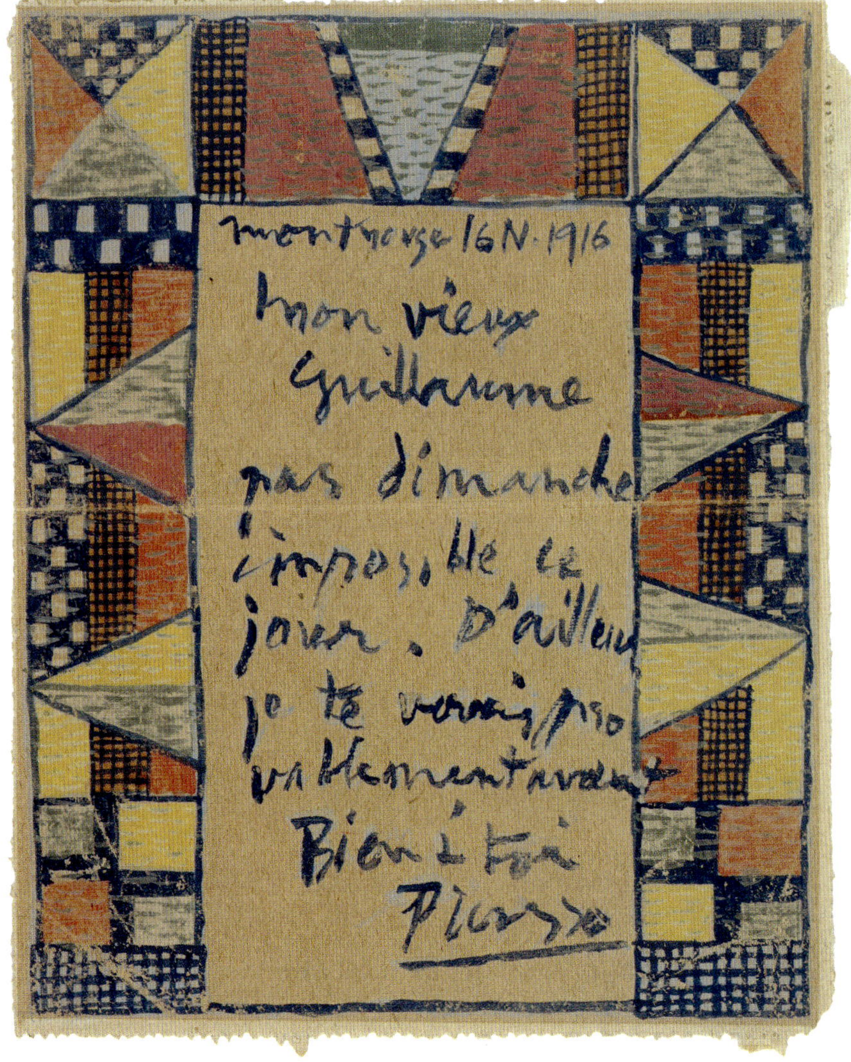

Montrouge 16 N. 1916
Mon vieux
Guillaume
pas dimanche
impossible ce
jour. D'ailleurs
je te verrai pro
bablement avant
Bien à toi
Picasso

55. Illustrated letter from Pablo Picasso to Jean Cocteau (16 November 1916)
Watercolour and ink on paper, 17.5 x 22.2 cm (open sheet)
New York, The Metropolitan Museum of Art, Thomas J. Watson Library, Bequest of William S. Lieberman, 2005, inv. 2007.49.78

56. Illustrated letter from Pablo Picasso to Guillaume Apollinaire, 16 November 1916
Ink and gouache on paper, 14 x 11.3 cm
Paris, Musée national Picasso-Paris, Achat, 1990, inv. MP 1990-2 (48)

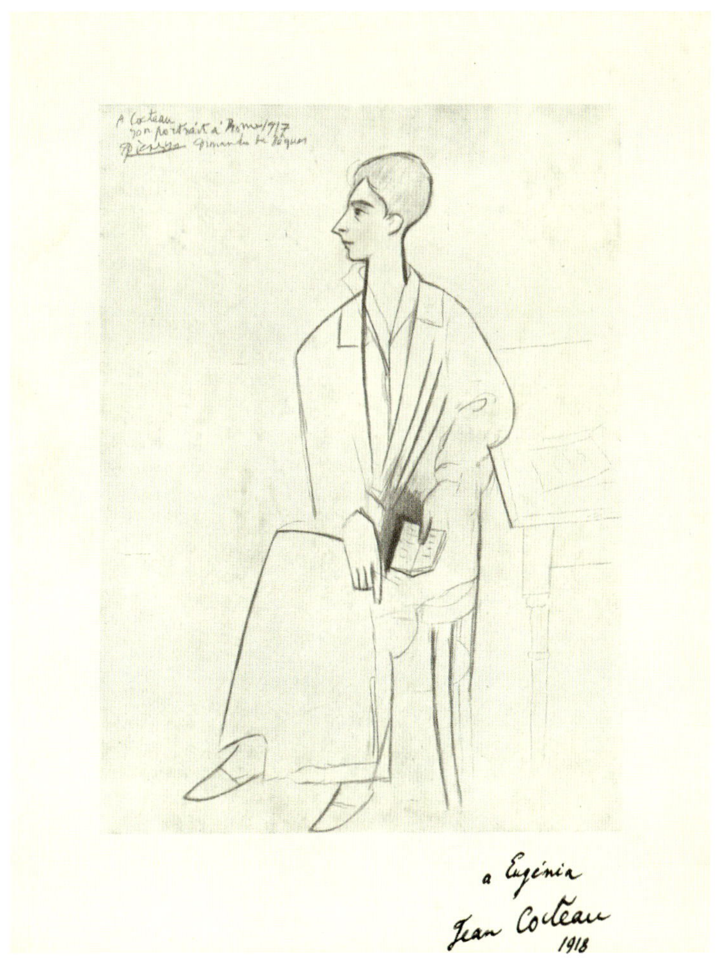

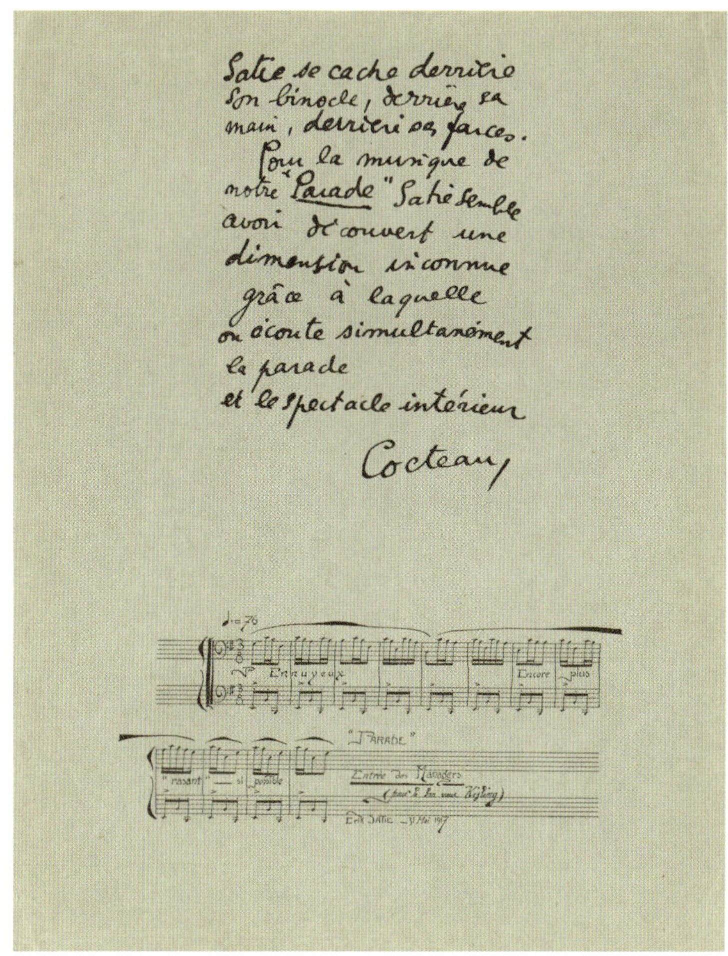

57. Anonymous
Print of a portrait of Cocteau by Picasso to Eugenia (Errázuriz), 1918
Paper, 25.7 x 29.5 cm
Paris, Musée national Picasso-Paris, Achat, 1987, inv. MP 1987-161 (3)

58. Inscription by Cocteau on a sheet of music by Satie for *Parade*, undated
Paris, Musée national Picasso Paris, Achat, 1987, inv. MP1987-161 (2)

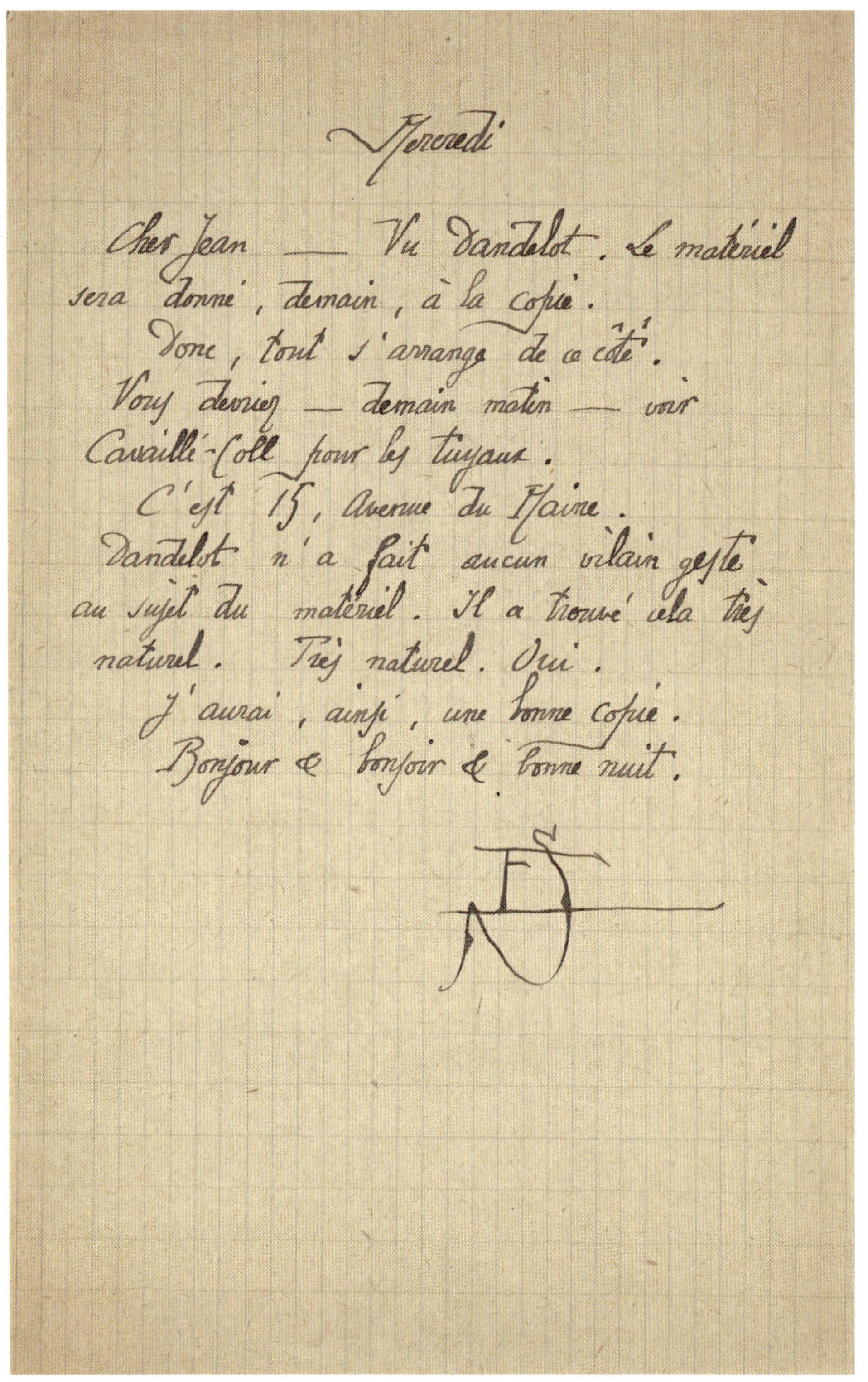

Mercredi

Cher Jean — Vu Dandelot. Le matériel sera donné, demain, à la copie.

Donc, tout s'arrange de ce côté.

Vous deviez — demain matin — voir Cavaillé-Coll pour les tuyaux.

C'est 15, Avenue du Maine.

Dandelot n'a fait aucun vilain geste au sujet du matériel. Il a trouvé cela très naturel. Très naturel. Oui.

J'aurai, ainsi, une bonne copie.

Bonjour & bonsoir & bonne nuit.

ES

59. Autograph letter of Erik Satie sent to Jean Cocteau, 1916–17
New York, The Metropolitan Museum of Art, Thomas J. Watson Library, Bequest of William S. Lieberman

60. Autograph postcard of Erik Satie sent to Jean Cocteau, 1916–17
New York, The Metropolitan Museum of Art, Thomas J. Watson Library, Bequest of William S. Lieberman

61. Autograph postcard of Erik Satie sent to Jean Cocteau, 1916
New York, The Metropolitan Museum of Art, Thomas J. Watson Library, Bequest of William S. Lieberman

Arcueil-Cachan, le 24 Mars 17

Cher Jean — J'ai froid aux doigts — même à ceux des pieds. Excusez-moi, je vous prie.

Je voudrais avoir — le plus tôt possible — la lettre de "l'Américaine" écrite à la machine. J'en ai besoin immédiatement, car j'envoie l'orchestre à la copie.

Comment vont ces bons Messieurs? — Je viens de chez Picasso: il n'y avait personne, sauf un chien qui gueulait comme un veau. Triste.

Bonjour à tour de bras de ES

P.S. Valentine Gross me dit que vous avez la frousse. Non? Quand passez-vous à Paris? J'aimerais vous voir: il y a tellement de choses à faire que j'en suis tout seul. C'est fou & faba. Chic! Bravo! Vive Cocteau!

Jeudi 18 Mai 1916

Cher Ami — N'ayez pas peur: ça marche. Quel chic sujet! Je crois que j'y suis, & bien! Veine! Où donc perchez-vous? Un mot, voulez-vous?

Votre vieux complice: ES

P.-S. Écrivez vite. Mon travail d'orchestre est suspendu.

29 Mars 1917

Cher Jean — Mais oui. Les changements me vont. Je leur reproche une chose, très grave pour la partition d'orchestre : leur (manque d') exactitude ; car je ne saisis point l'endroit précis où ils se manifestent. Songez donc, cher vieux, très précis sur ce point.

J'ai vu Mutin (Cavaillé-Coll) pour les tuyaux. Il peut — je l'ai vu — nous monter ces trucs. Il demande quinze jours pour cela — Amitiés à M. & à P.

J'écris au Bon directeur — Votre vieux :

Amitiés à Massine & à Picasso — les mêmes que plus haut. ES

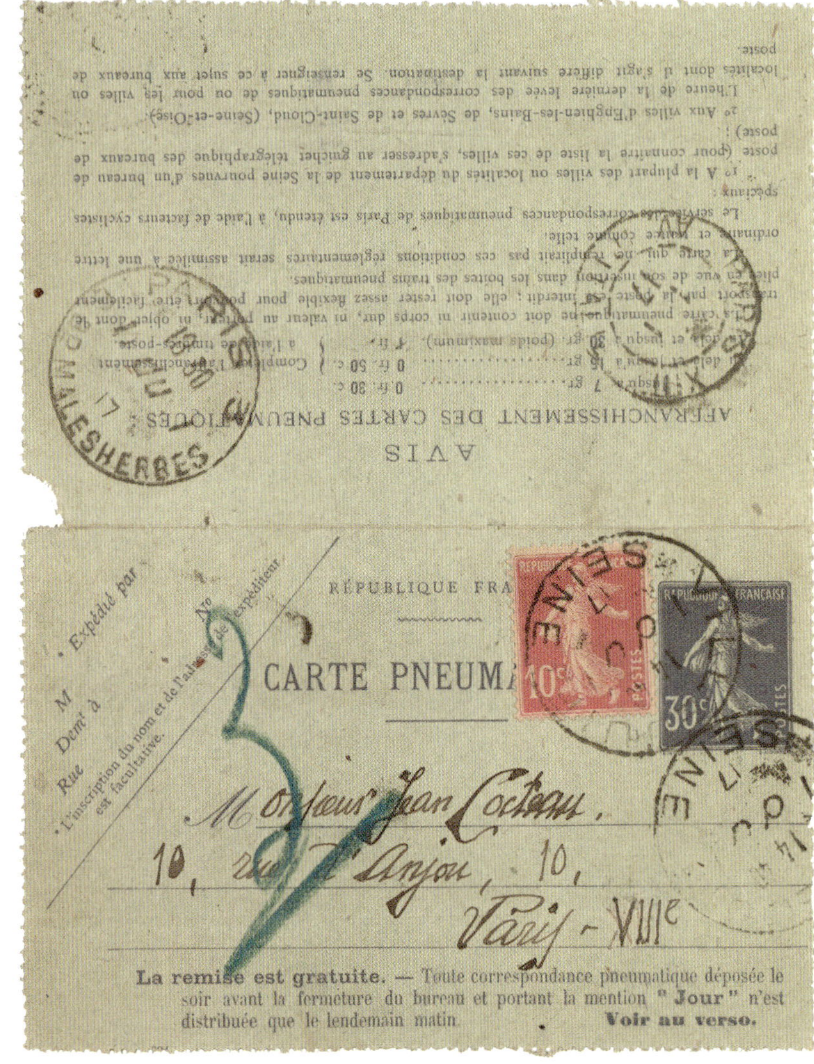

AVIS

AFFRANCHISSEMENT DES CARTES PNEUMATIQUES

Expédié par

M

Dem' à

Rue

L'inscription du nom et de l'adresse de l'expéditeur est facultative.

RÉPUBLIQUE FRA

CARTE PNEUMA

Monsieur Jean Cocteau,

10, rue d'Anjou, 10,

Paris - VIIIe

La remise est gratuite. — Toute correspondance pneumatique déposée le soir avant la fermeture du bureau et portant la mention **"Jour"** n'est distribuée que le lendemain matin. **Voir au verso.**

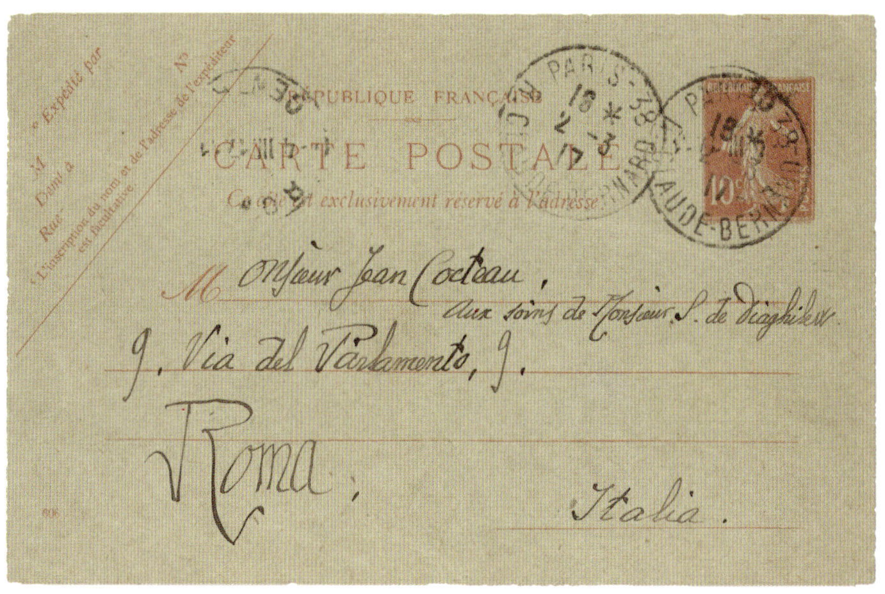

RÉPUBLIQUE FRANÇAISE

CARTE POSTALE

Ce côté est exclusivement réservé à l'adresse

Monsieur Jean Cocteau,
aux soins de Monsieur S. de Diaghilew.
9, Via del Parlamento, 9.
Roma,
Italia.

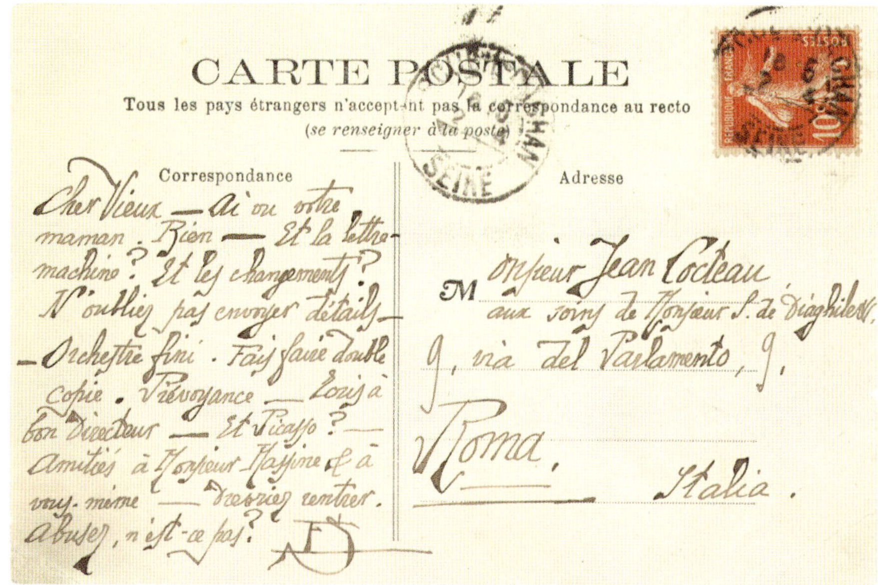

CARTE POSTALE

Tous les pays étrangers n'acceptent pas la correspondance au recto
(se renseigner à la poste)

Correspondance

Cher Vieux — Ai vu votre maman. Rien — Et la lettre-machine? Et les changements? N'oubliez pas envoyer détails — Orchestre fini. Fais faire double copie. Prévoyance — Louis à bon Directeur — Et Picasso? — Amitiés à Monsieur Massine & à vous-même — abusez, n'est-ce pas?

Adresse

Monsieur Jean Cocteau
aux soins de Monsieur S. de Diaghilew.
9, via del Parlamento, 9.
Roma,
Italia.

62. Autographed postcard of Erik Satie sent to Jean Cocteau, 1916–17
New York, The Metropolitan Museum of Art, Thomas J. Watson Library, Bequest of William S. Lieberman

63. Autographed postcard of Erik Satie sent to Jean Cocteau, 1916–17
New York, The Metropolitan Museum of Art, Thomas J. Watson Library, Bequest of William S. Lieberman

64. Autographed postcard of Erik Satie sent to Jean Cocteau, 1916–17
New York, The Metropolitan Museum of Art, Thomas J. Watson Library, Bequest of William S. Lieberman

65. Autographed postcard of Erik Satie sent to Jean Cocteau, 1916–17
New York, The Metropolitan Museum of Art, Thomas J. Watson Library, Bequest of William S. Lieberman

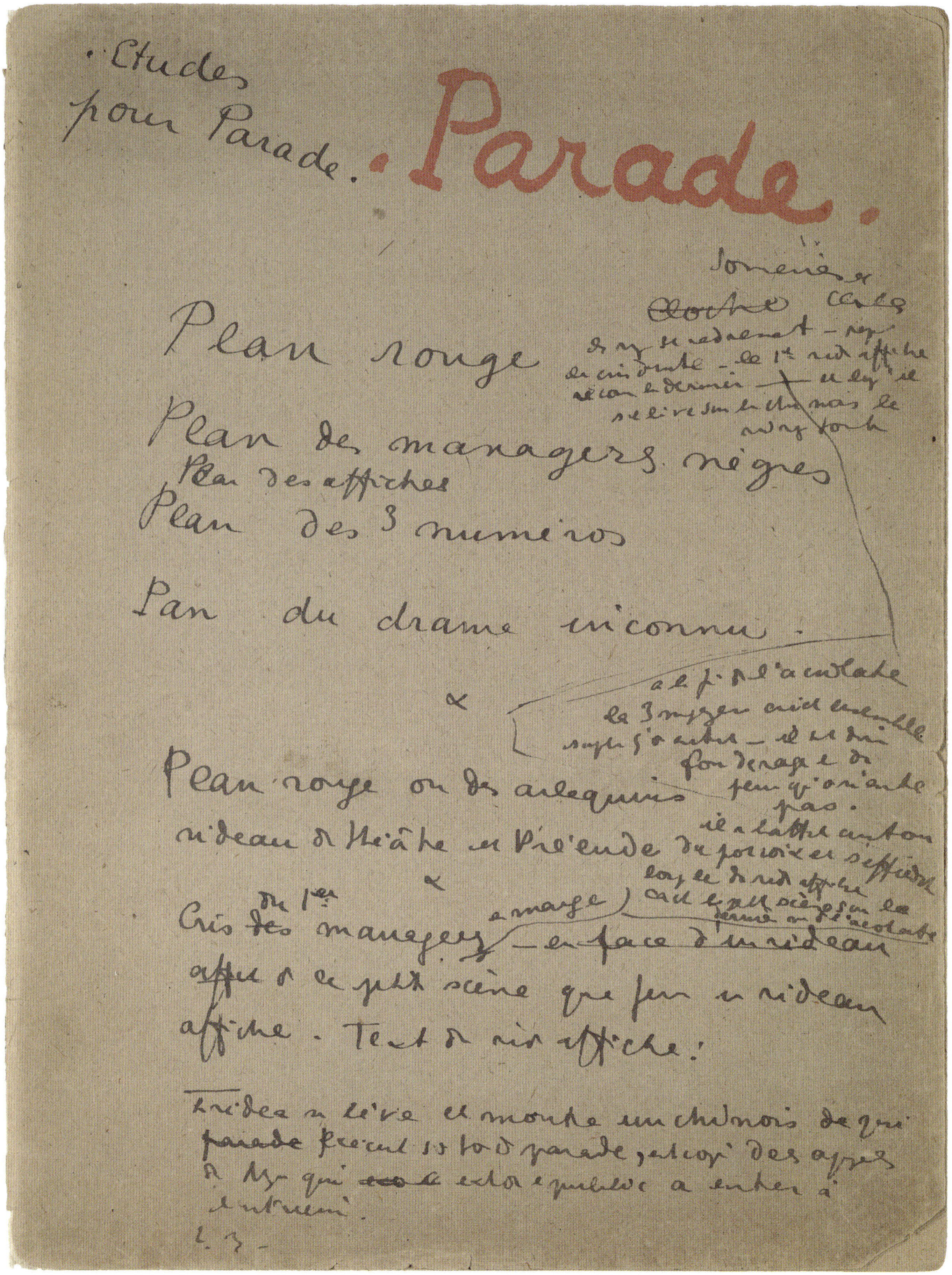

Etudes pour Parade.

Parade.

Plan rouge

Plan des managers nègres

Plan des affiches

Plan des 3 numeros

Pan du drame inconnu.

[illegible marginal notes]

x

Plan rouge ou des arlequins

rideau de théâtre et Prélude

x

Cris ~~des~~ du 1er managers – en face d'un rideau affiche de ce petit scène que fera un rideau affiche. Text de ces affiche.

Le rideau se lève et montre un chinois de qui ~~parade~~ [illegible] parade, [illegible] qui [illegible] a entrer à l'intérieur.

[illegible]

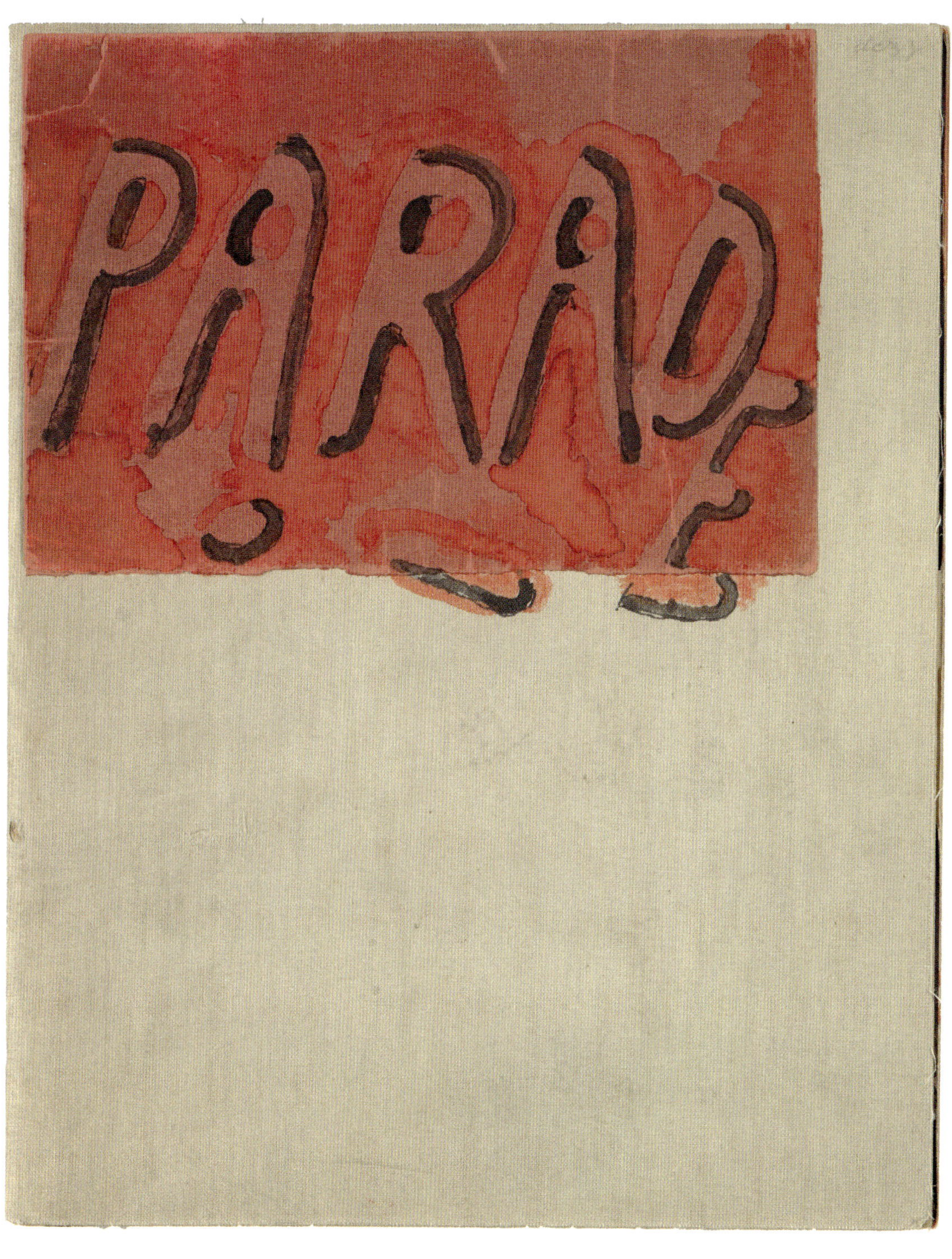

66. Notebook with Jean Cocteau's handwritten notes, 1916–17
Notebook, 32 cm
New York, The Metropolitan Museum of Art, Thomas J. Watson Library, Bequest of William S. Lieberman

67. Manuscript of Jean Cocteau for the libretto of *Parade*, 1916–17
Bound notebook, 28 cm
New York, The Metropolitan Museum of Art, Thomas J. Watson Library, Bequest of William S. Lieberman

Mon cher Satie

Voilà du travail pour bruiteurs. Je pars Samedi prochain. Dites moi d'un seul mot que l'envoi confirme notre entente. Ces trois pieds dans ce St Polycarpe multicolore avec de belles ombres bien nettes peuvent atteindre le coeur du moins compréhensif.
Votre fidèle

Jc.

68. Undated letter of Jean Cocteau to Erik Satie, 1916–17
New York, The Metropolitan Museum of Art, Thomas J. Watson Library, Bequest of William S. Lieberman

69. Undated letter of Jean Cocteau to Léonide Massine, 1916–17
New York, The Metropolitan Museum of Art, Thomas J. Watson Library, Bequest of William S. Lieberman

Mon très cher Massine

Pourquoi Diaghilew se donne-t-il tant
de mal et ne s'adresse-t-il jamais
à moi ? Je lui dirais de me
supprimer complètement [même] sur l'affiche
de Parade – mes aspirations dépassent
le journalisme, comme les rôles.
J'ai fait écrire la partition note par note
à Satie, j'ai amené Picasso contre
tous ses principes (quoi qu'il puisse en
dire) j'ai amicalement, joyeusement
et loyalement collaboré avec vous
imprimant un sens qui m'est cher
à votre travail superbe – Je ne

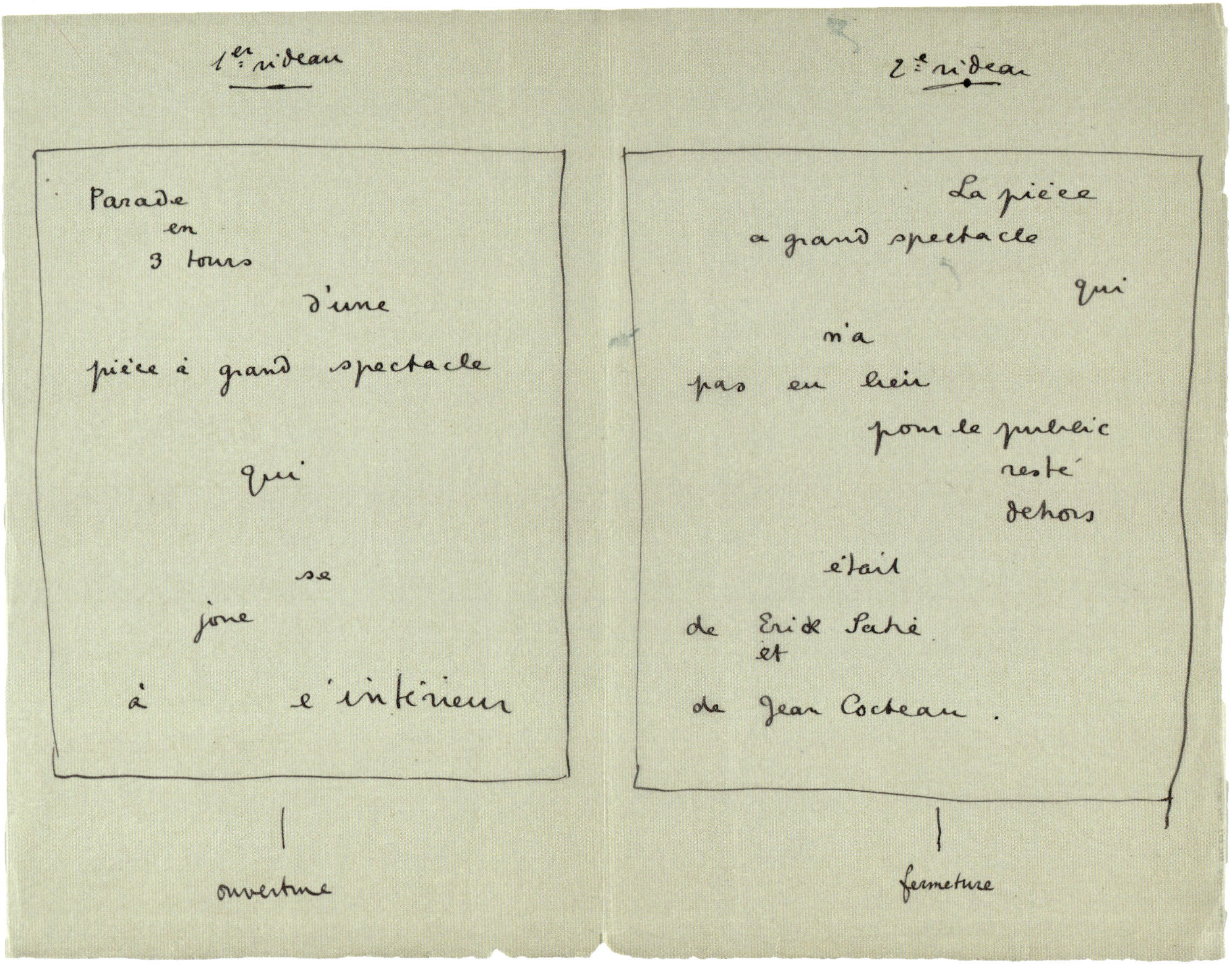

1er rideau

Parade
en
3 tours
d'une
pièce à grand spectacle

qui

se
joue

à l'intérieur

ouverture

2e rideau

La pièce
a grand spectacle
qui
n'a
pas eu lieu
pour le public
resté
dehors

était

de Erik Satie
et
de Jean Cocteau.

fermeture

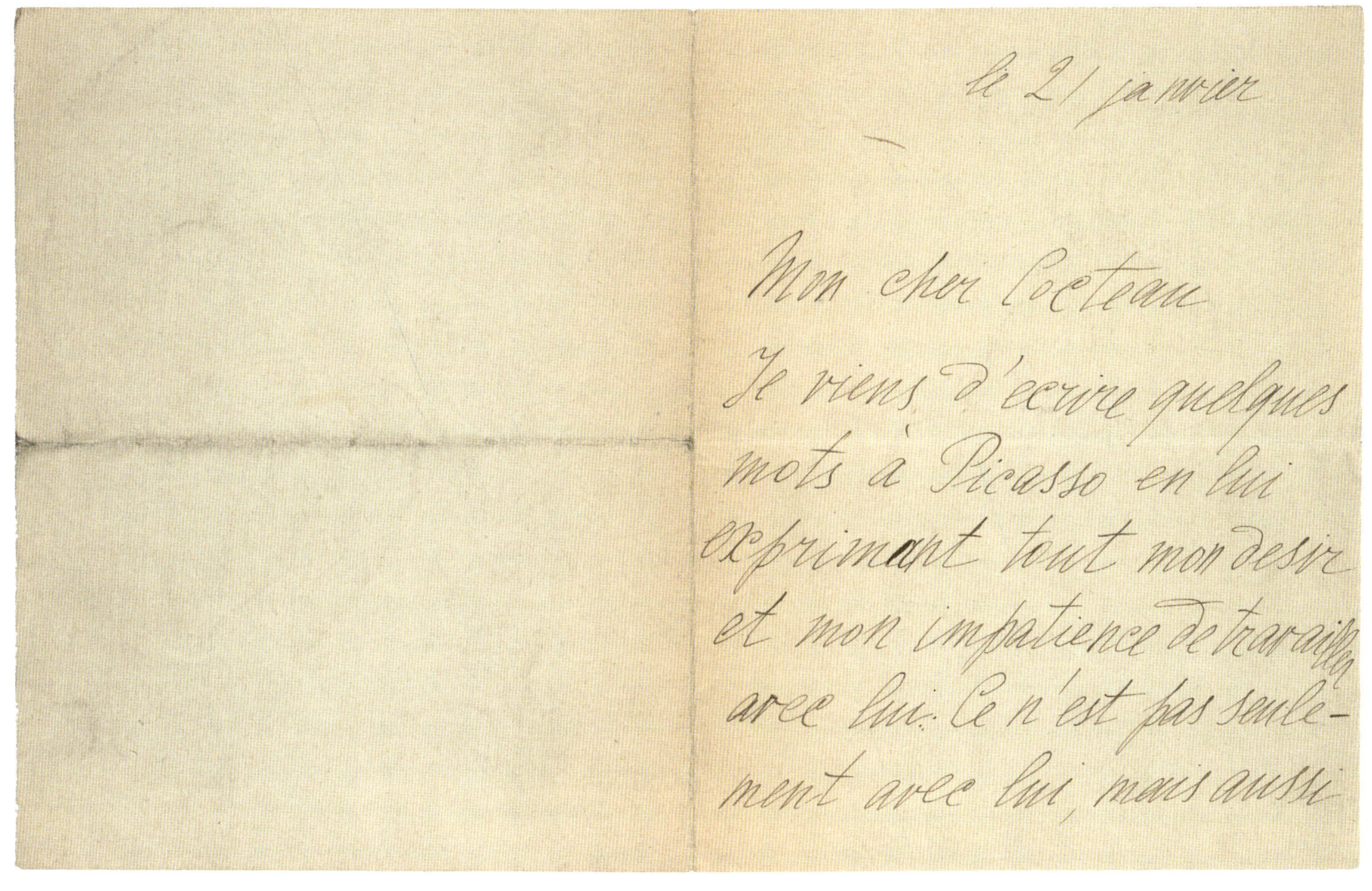

le 21 janvier

Mon cher Cocteau
Je viens d'écrire quelques
mots à Picasso en lui
exprimant tout mon désir
et mon impatience de travailler
avec lui. Ce n'est pas seule-
ment avec lui, mais aussi

70. Autograph notes of Jean Cocteau on *Parade* , 1916–17
New York, The Metropolitan Museum of Art, Thomas J. Watson Library, Bequest of William S. Lieberman

71. Autograph letter of Léonide Massine sent to Jean Cocteau, dated 21 January 1916
New York, The Metropolitan Museum of Art, Thomas J. Watson Library, Bequest of William S. Lieberman

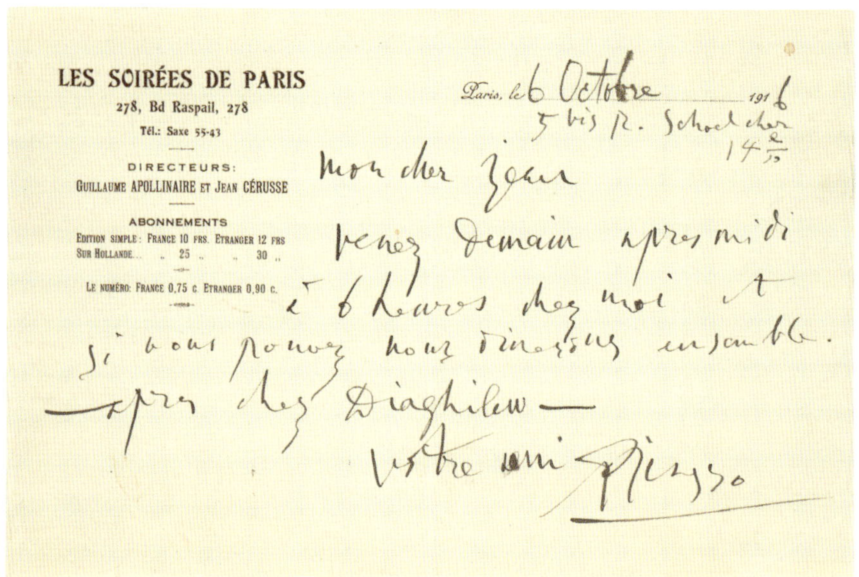

LES SOIRÉES DE PARIS
278, Bd Raspail, 278
Tél.: Saxe 55-43

DIRECTEURS:
GUILLAUME APOLLINAIRE ET JEAN CÉRUSSE

ABONNEMENTS
EDITION SIMPLE: FRANCE 10 FRS. ETRANGER 12 FRS
SUR HOLLANDE ... 25 ... 30

LE NUMÉRO: FRANCE 0,75 c. ETRANGER 0,90 c.

Paris, le 6 Octobre 1916
5 bis R. Schoelcher
14 2/5

Mon cher Jean

venez demain après midi à 6 heures chez moi et si vous pouvez nous dinerons ensemble après chez Diaghilew —

Votre ami Picasso

Samedi soir —

Cher Vieux — Merci de vos deux pneus.
Décidément, je ne viens pas ce soir.
Je serais terne, peu brillant.
Tout se passera très bien sans moi.
Vous saurez présenter justement la pénible question "avances" & obtiendrez ce qu'il faut. Cela est certain : vous me l'écrivez, du reste. J'ai confiance en vous.
Je suis très fatigué & vais me coucher.
Bonsoir, Gros Vieux. Vous avez été très gentil, hier ; & je vous en remercie.
Combien Valentine est bonne !
Picasso & vous allez parfaitement mettre "Parade" en vue, & bien !
Amitiés du pauvre

72. Manuscript letter of Pablo Picasso sent to Jean Cocteau, dated 6 October 1916
New York, The Metropolitan Museum of Art, Thomas J. Watson Library, Bequest of William S. Lieberman

73. Autographed postcard of Erik Satie sent to Jean Cocteau, 1916–17
New York, The Metropolitan Museum of Art, Thomas J. Watson Library, Bequest of William S. Lieberman

74. Manuscript letter of Pablo Picasso sent to Jean Cocteau, 1916–17
New York, The Metropolitan Museum of Art, Thomas J. Watson Library, Bequest of William S. Lieberman

75. Satie's Musical score of *Parade, Ballet réaliste*, 1916–17
New York, The Metropolitan Museum of Art, Thomas J. Watson Library, Bequest of William S. Lieberman

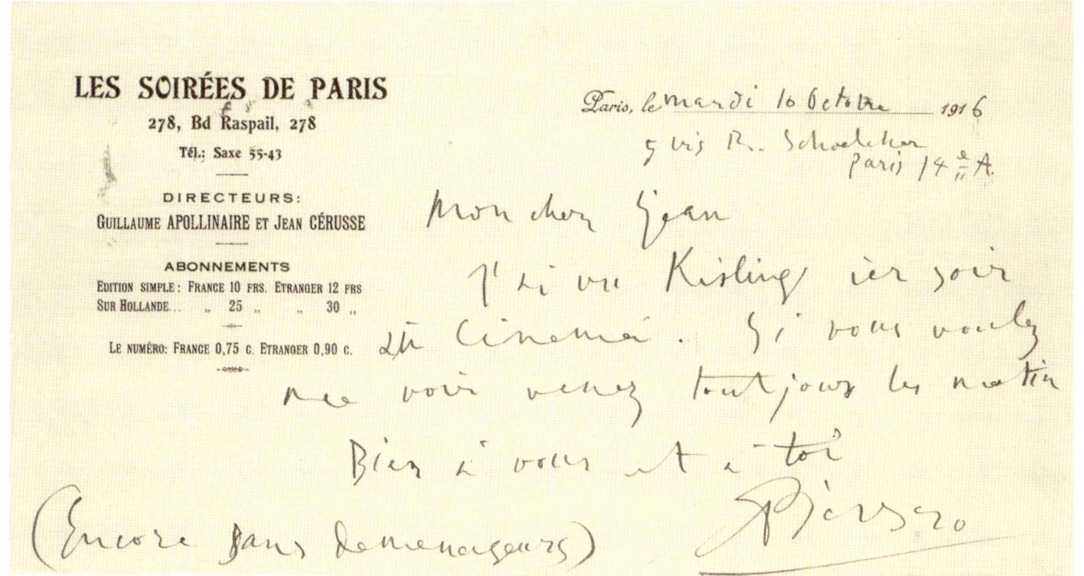

LES SOIRÉES DE PARIS
278, Bd Raspail, 278
Tél.: Saxe 55-43

DIRECTEURS:
Guillaume Apollinaire et Jean Cérusse

ABONNEMENTS
Edition simple: France 10 frs. Etranger 12 frs
Sur Hollande.. „ 25 „ „ 30 „

Le numéro: France 0,75 c. Etranger 0,90 c.

Paris, le mardi 10 octobre 1916
5 bis R. Schoelcher
Paris 14e A.

Mon cher Jean

J'ai vu Kisling hier soir au Cinema. Si vous voulez me voir venez toujours le matin

Bien à vous et à toi

Picasso

(Encore sans déménageurs)

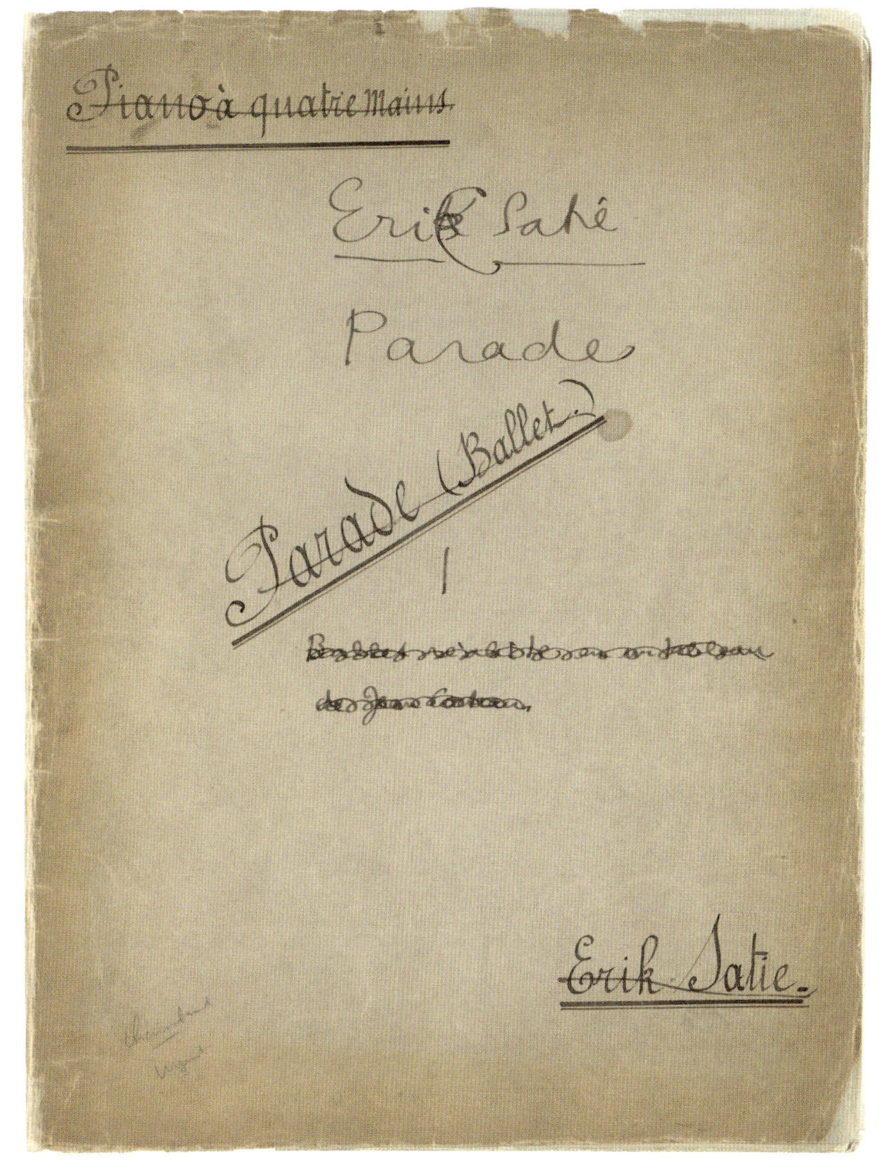

Piano à quatre mains

Erik Satie

Parade

Parade (Ballet)

I

Erik Satie.

Morges 11-VI-17

Monsieur,

J'ai envoyé une page-autographe à la revue „Sic" par mon ami Picasso (ne sachant pas l'adresse ni de la revue ni du directeur) quelques heures avant votre lettre – puisque M. Semenoff m'avait exprimé votre désir encore à Rome et je voulais bien le faire. J'espère que Picasso l'a bien reçu et le transmettra sans retard au directeur. Recevez Monsieur mes compliments distingués Igor Strawinsky

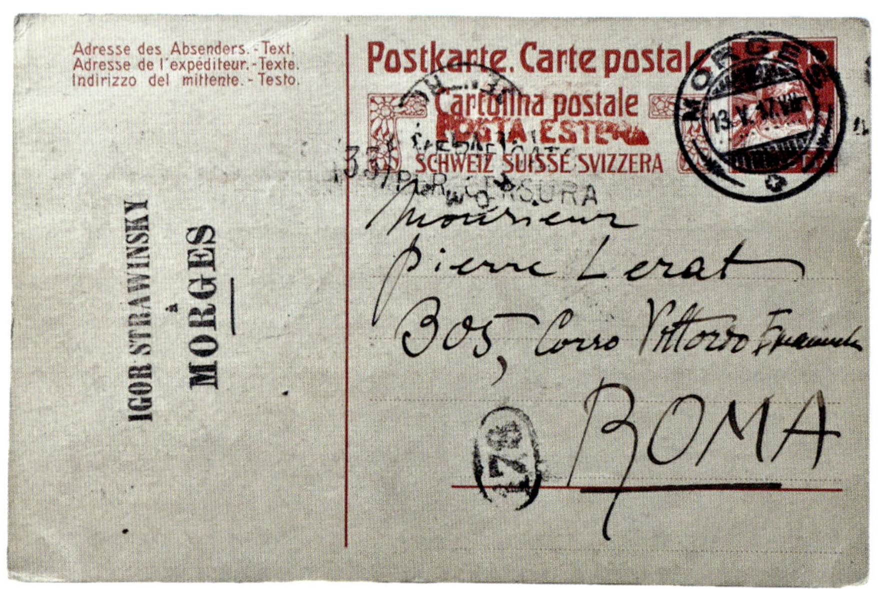

76. Postcard from Igor Stravinsky to Pierre Lerat in Rome, 13 June 1917
Ink on postcard, 9 x 14 cm
Private collection,
Courtesy of Julian Barran Ltd.

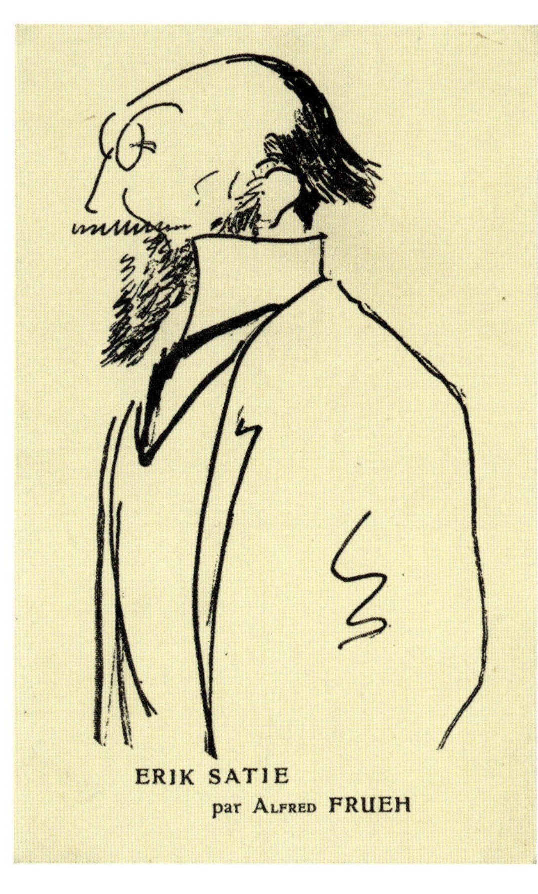

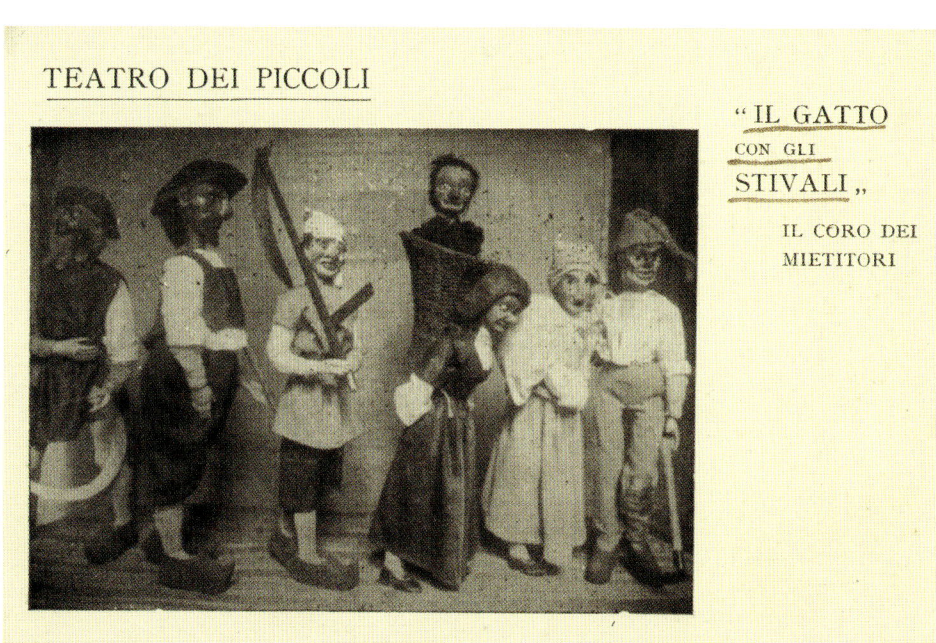

77. Autographed postcard from Pablo Picasso to Guillaume Apollinaire, 22 September 1918
Paris, Musée national Picasso-Paris, Achat, 1990, inv. MP 1990-2 (31)

78. Autographed postcard from Pablo Picasso to Apollinaire, February 1917
Paris, Musée national Picasso-Paris, Achat, 1989, inv. MP 1989-2 (24)

IV. The Ballet and the Line

79. Pablo Picasso
Portrait de Léonide Massine
[Portrait of Léonide Massine],
Rome, 1917
Pencil on paper, 67.4 x 47 cm
London, Victoria and Albert Museum,
Department of Theatre
and Performance, inv. S308-1980

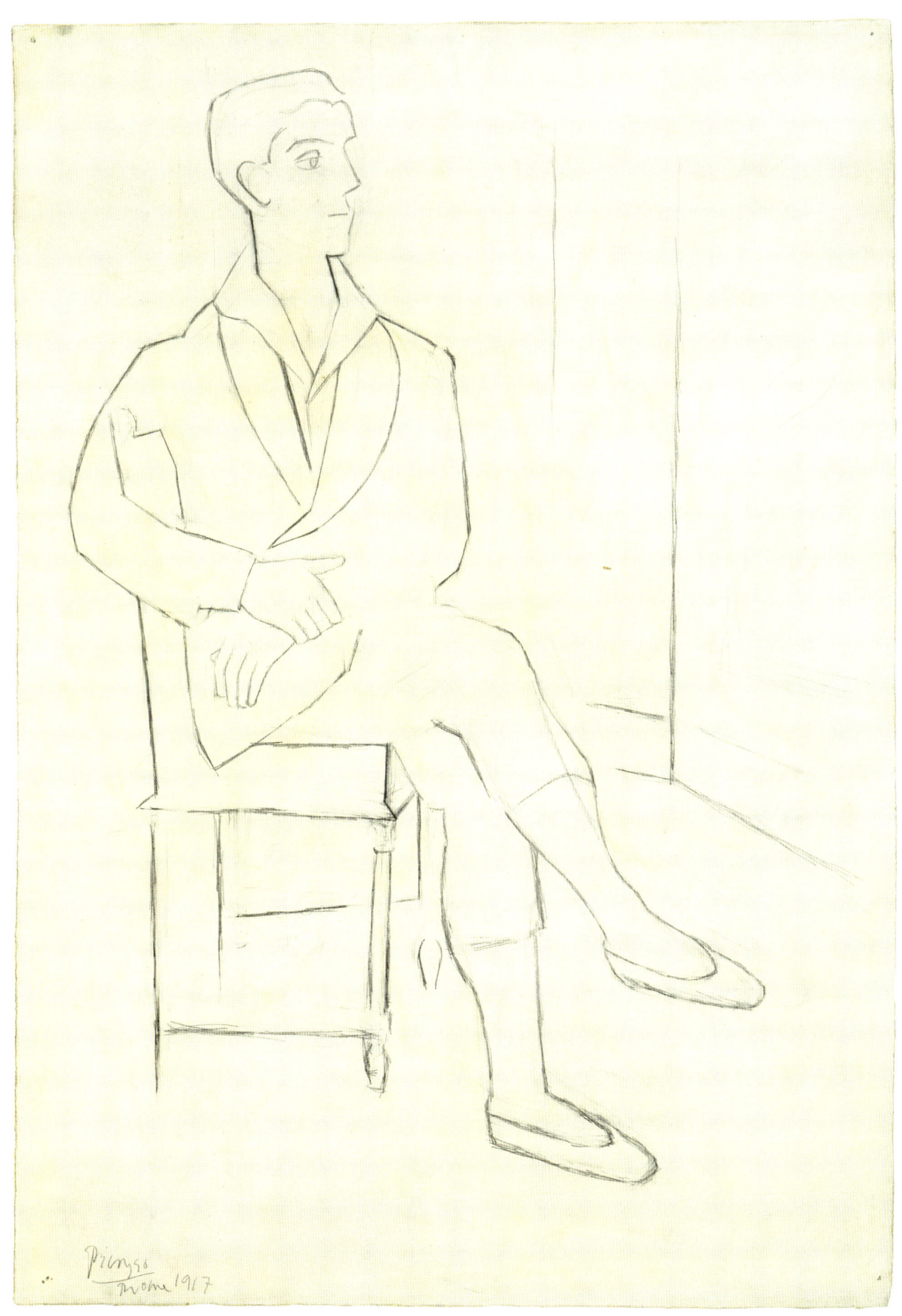
Picasso
Rome 1917

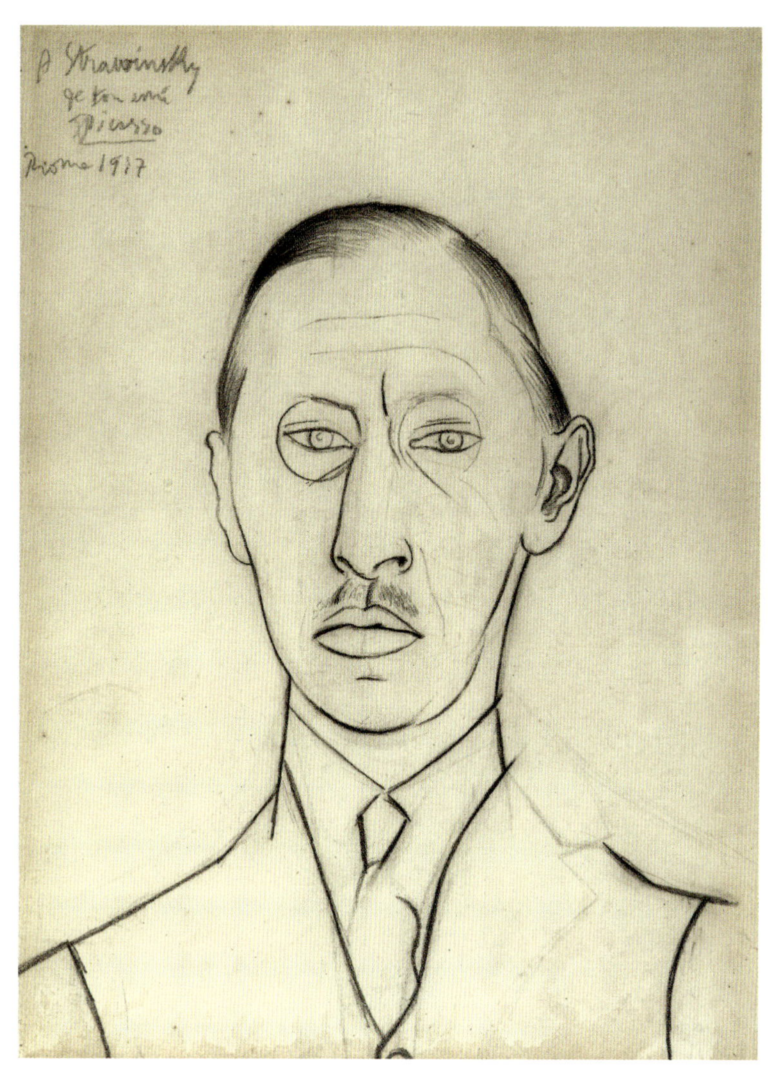

80. Pablo Picasso
Portrait d'Igor Stravinsky
[Portrait of Igor Stravinsky], 1917
Pencil on paper, 27 x 21 cm
New York, private collection

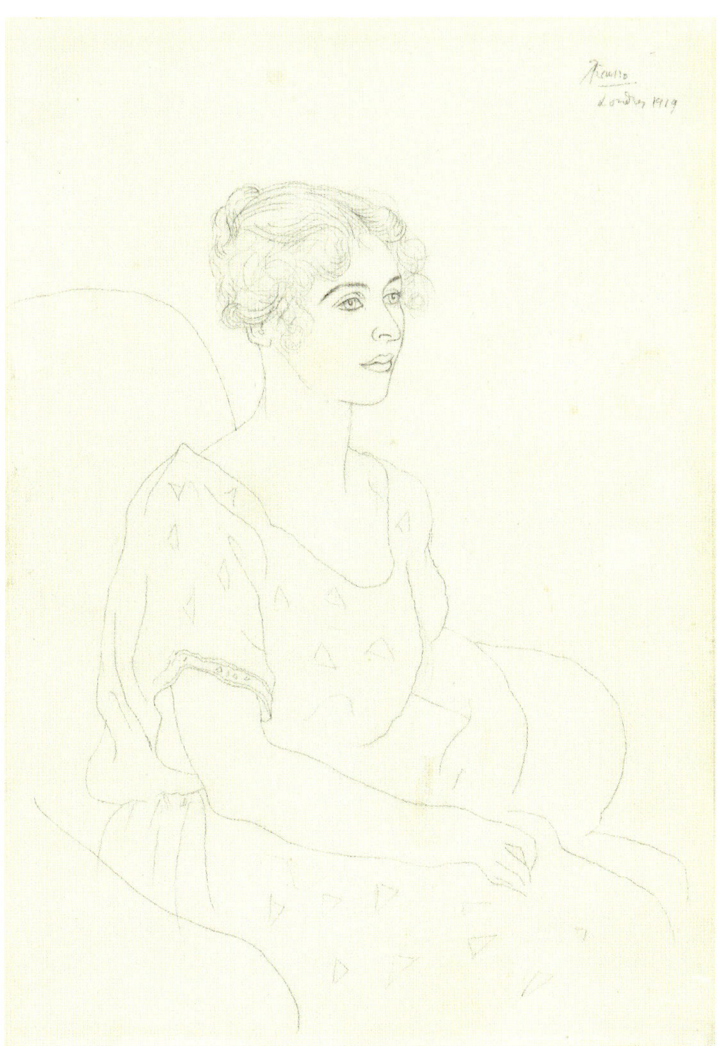

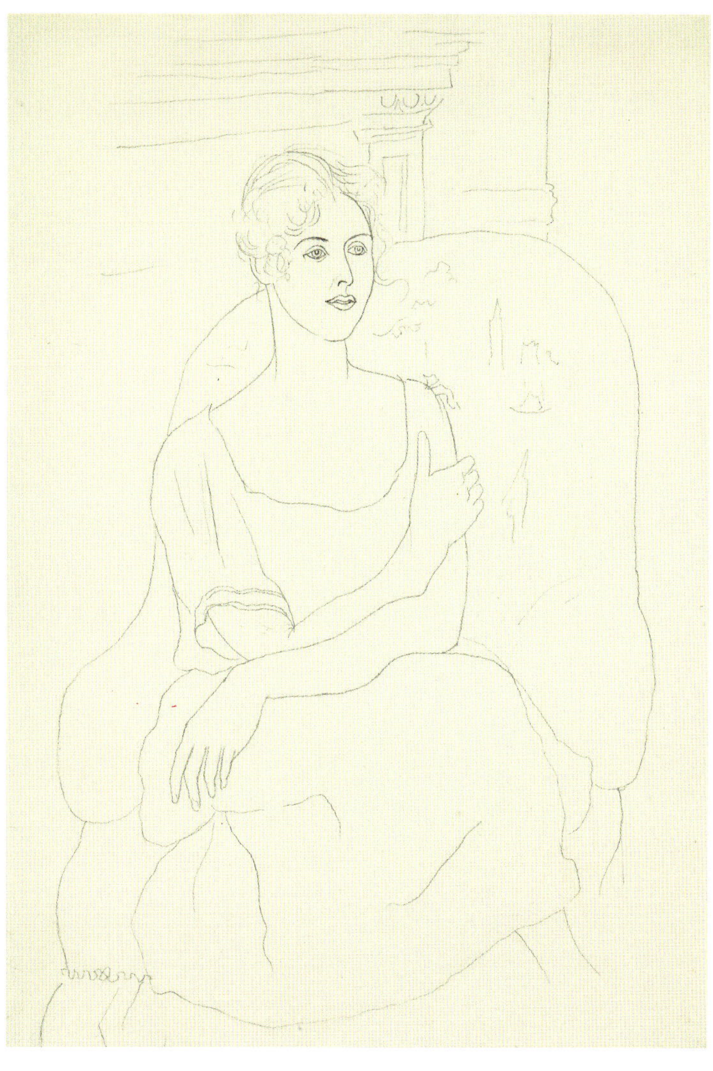

81. Pablo Picasso
Portrait de Lydia Lopokova
[Portrait of Lydia Lopokova], 1919
Pencil on paper, 37.7 x 25.5 cm
Cambridge, The Syndics of the Fitzwilliam Museum, University of Cambridge, inv. PD.6-1989

82. Pablo Picasso
Portrait de Lydia Lopokova
[Portrait of Lydia Lopokova], 1919
Pencil on paper, 35.6 x 25.4 cm
New York, The Morgan Library & Museum, Thaw Collection, inv. 2010.128

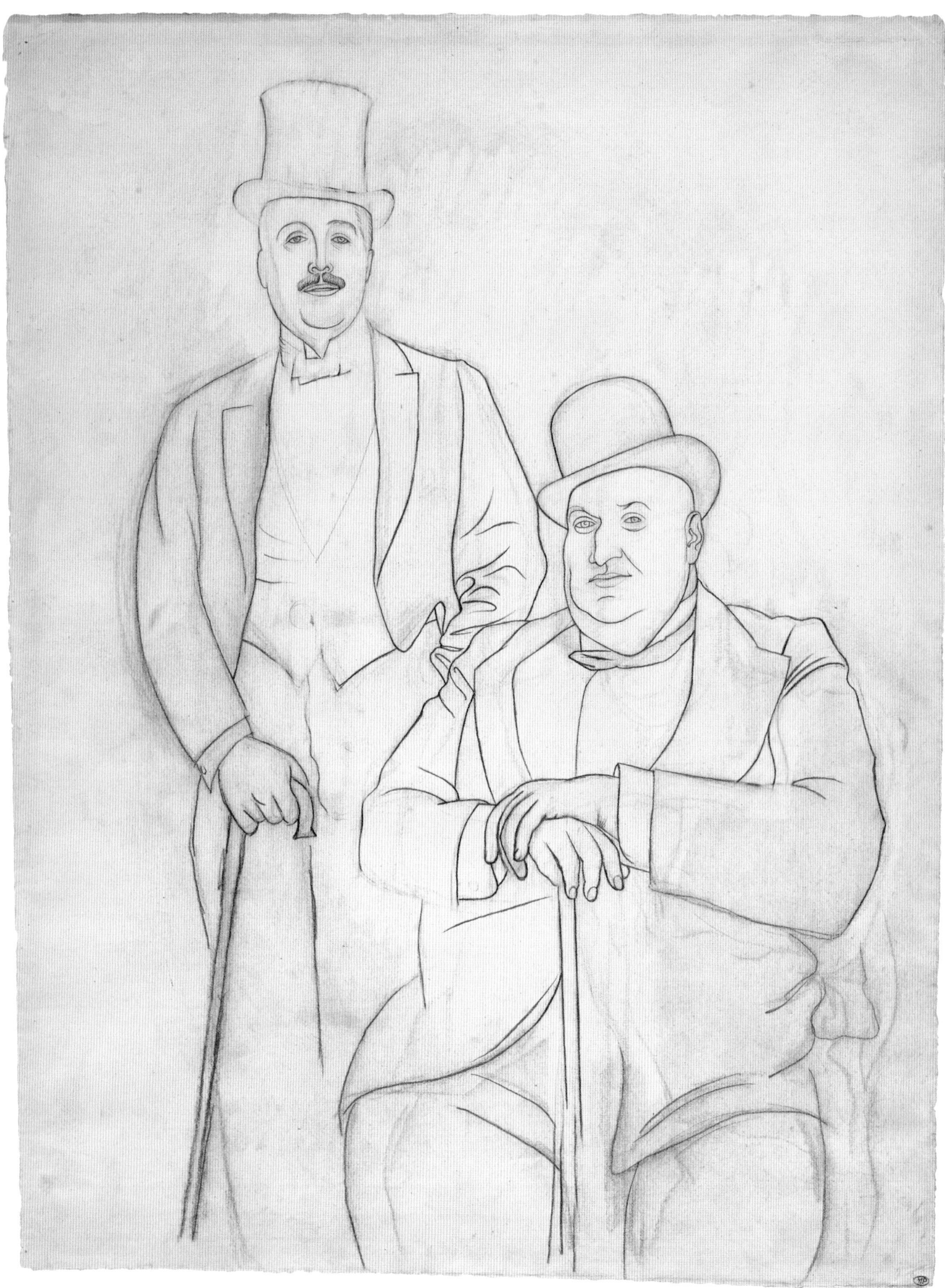

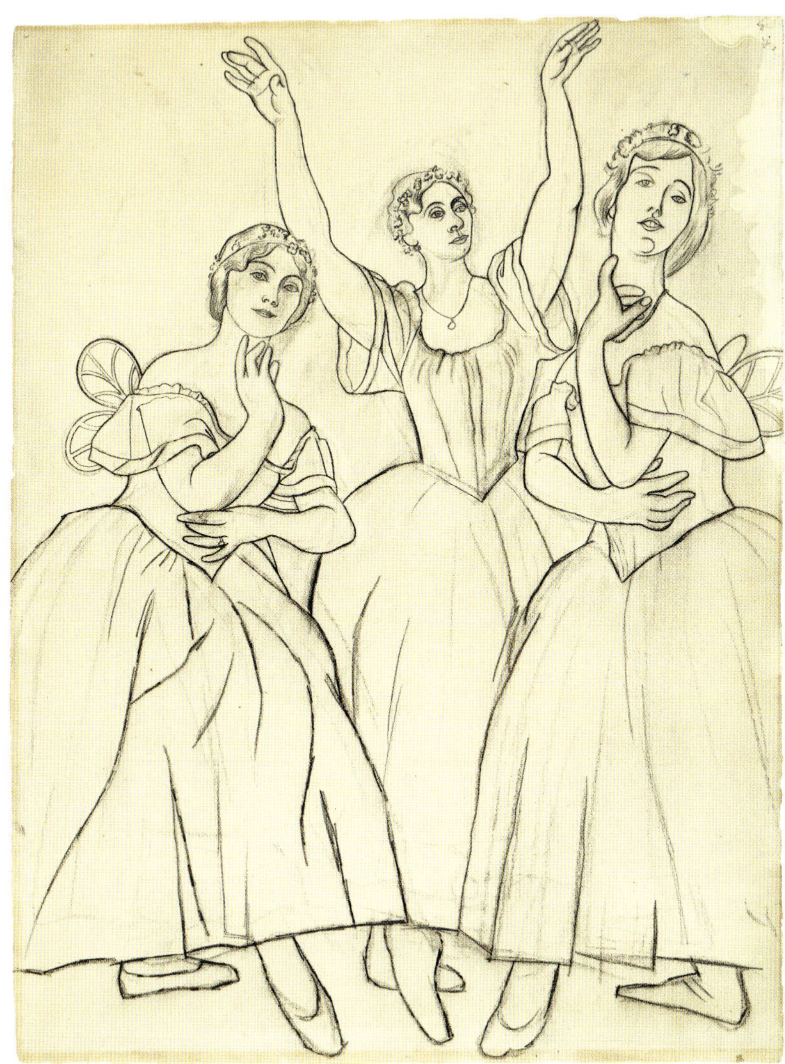

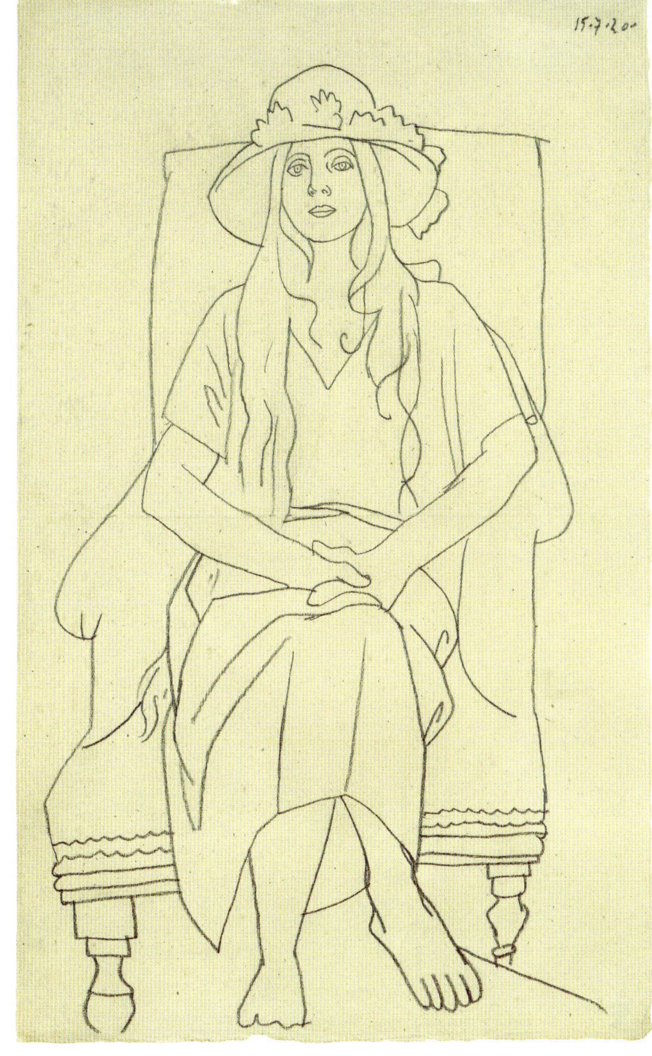

83. Pablo Picasso
Portrait de Serge Diaghilev et Alfred F. Seligsberg, d'après une photographie du comte Jean de Strelecki [Portrait of Sergei Diaghilev and Alfred F. Seligsberg, after a photograph by Count Jean de Strelecki], early 1919
Pencil and charcoal on drawing paper, 65.4 x 48 cm
Paris, Musée national Picasso-Paris, Pablo Picasso Donation, 1979, inv. MP839

84. Pablo Picasso
Trois danseuses: Olga Khokhlova, Lydia Lopokova et Ljubov Chernicheva, d'après une photographie [Three Ballerinas: Olga Khokhlova, Lydia Lopokova and Lubov Tchernicheva, after a photograph], early 1919
Pencil and charcoal on paper, 62.5 x 47.5 cm
Paris, Musée national Picasso-Paris, Pablo Picasso Donation, 1979, inv. MP834

85. Pablo Picasso
Femme au chapeau, assise dans un fauteuil [Woman with a Hat in an Armchair], Juan-les-Pins, 15 July 1920
Pastel on paper, 43 x 27 cm
Brussels, Fundación Almine y Bernard Ruiz-Picasso para el Arte, inv. 02713

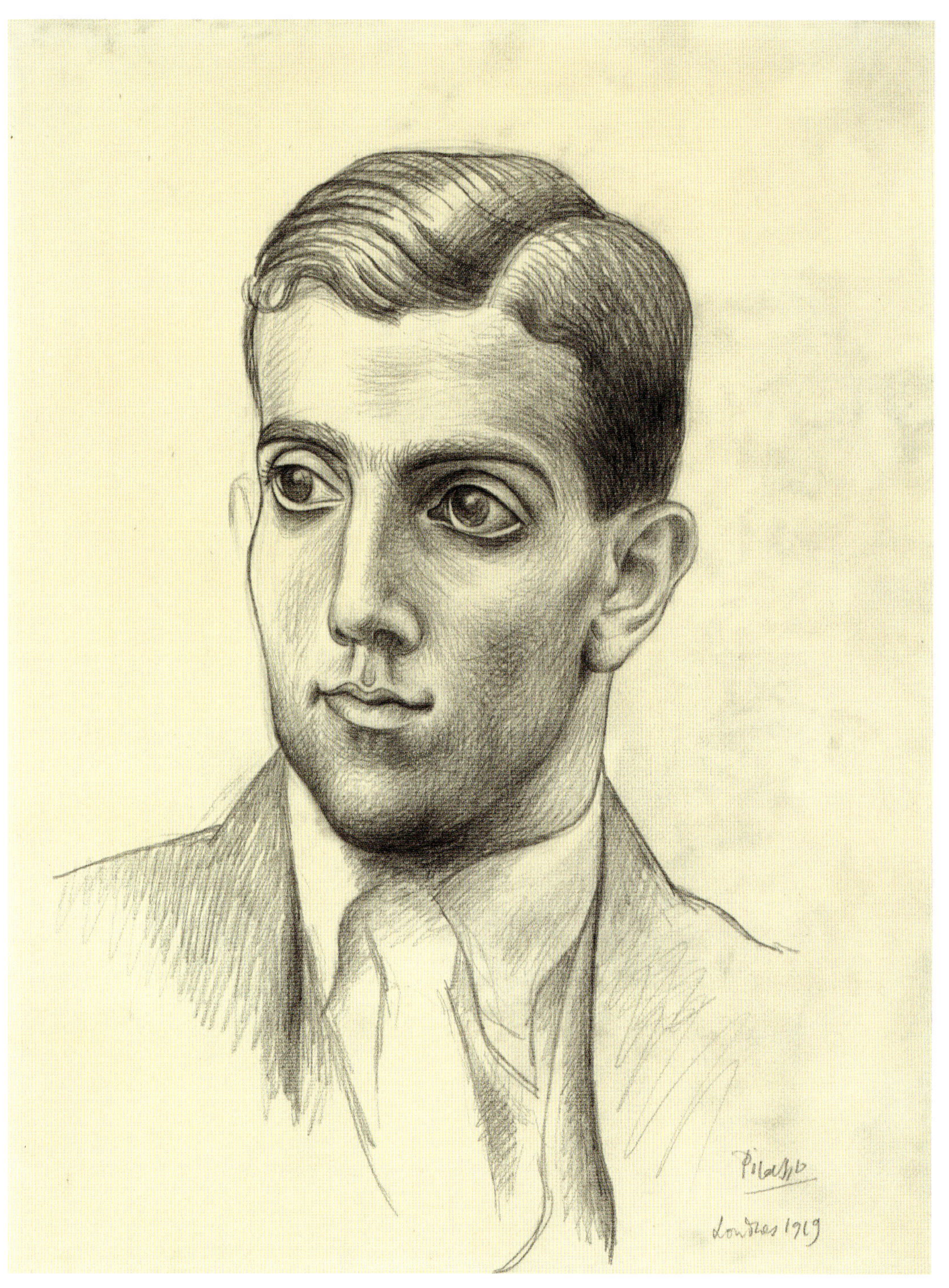

86. Pablo Picasso
Léonide Massine, 1919
Pencil on paper, 39.9 x 31.3 cm
Chicago, Art Institute of Chicago,
Margaret Day Blake Collection,
inv. 1972.970

87. Pablo Picasso
Portrait d'Igor Stravinsky
[Portrait of Igor Stravinsky],
Paris, 24 May 1920
Pencil and charcoal on paper,
62.4 x 48.5 cm
Paris, Musée national Picasso-Paris,
Pablo Picasso Donation, 1979,
inv. MP911

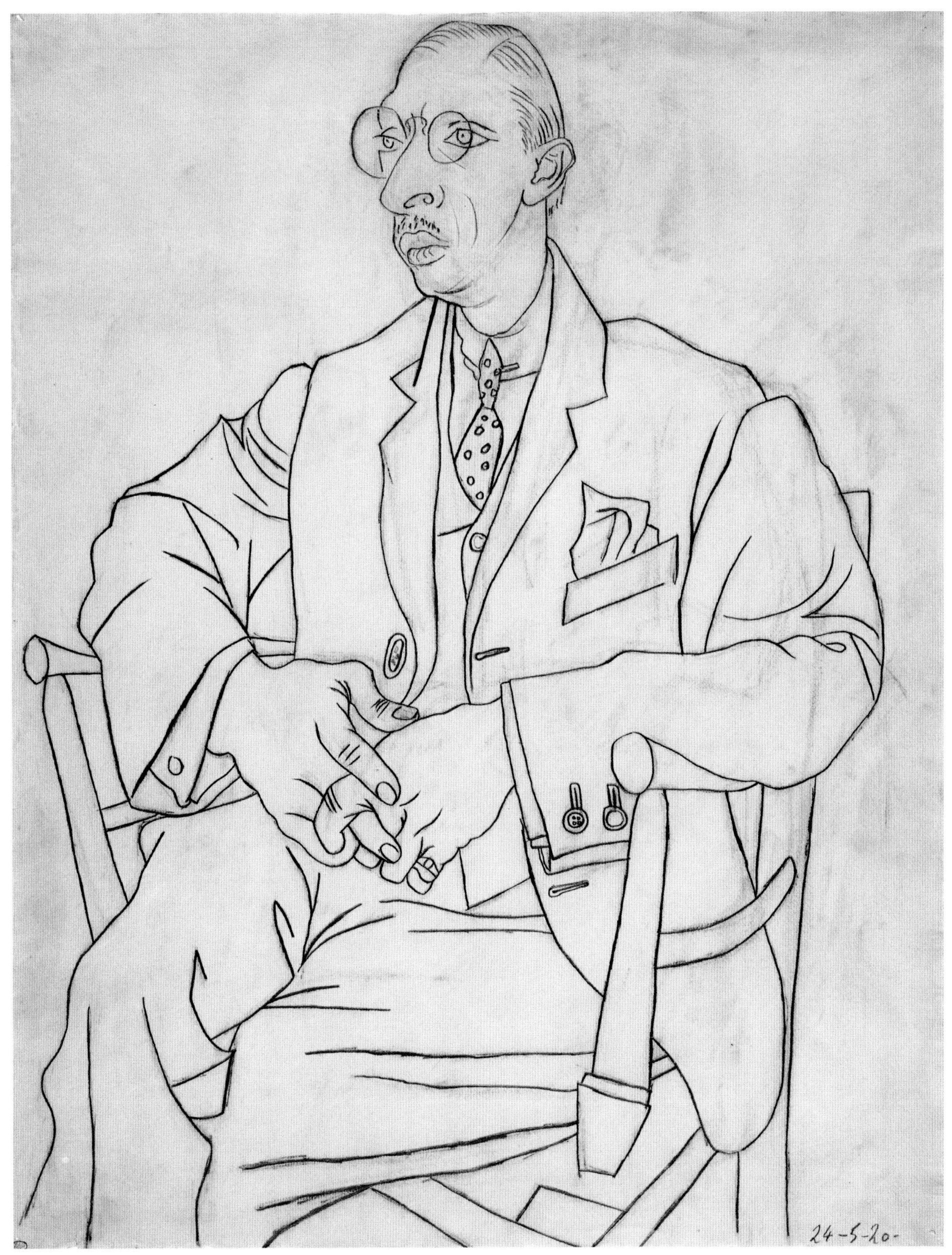
24-5-20-

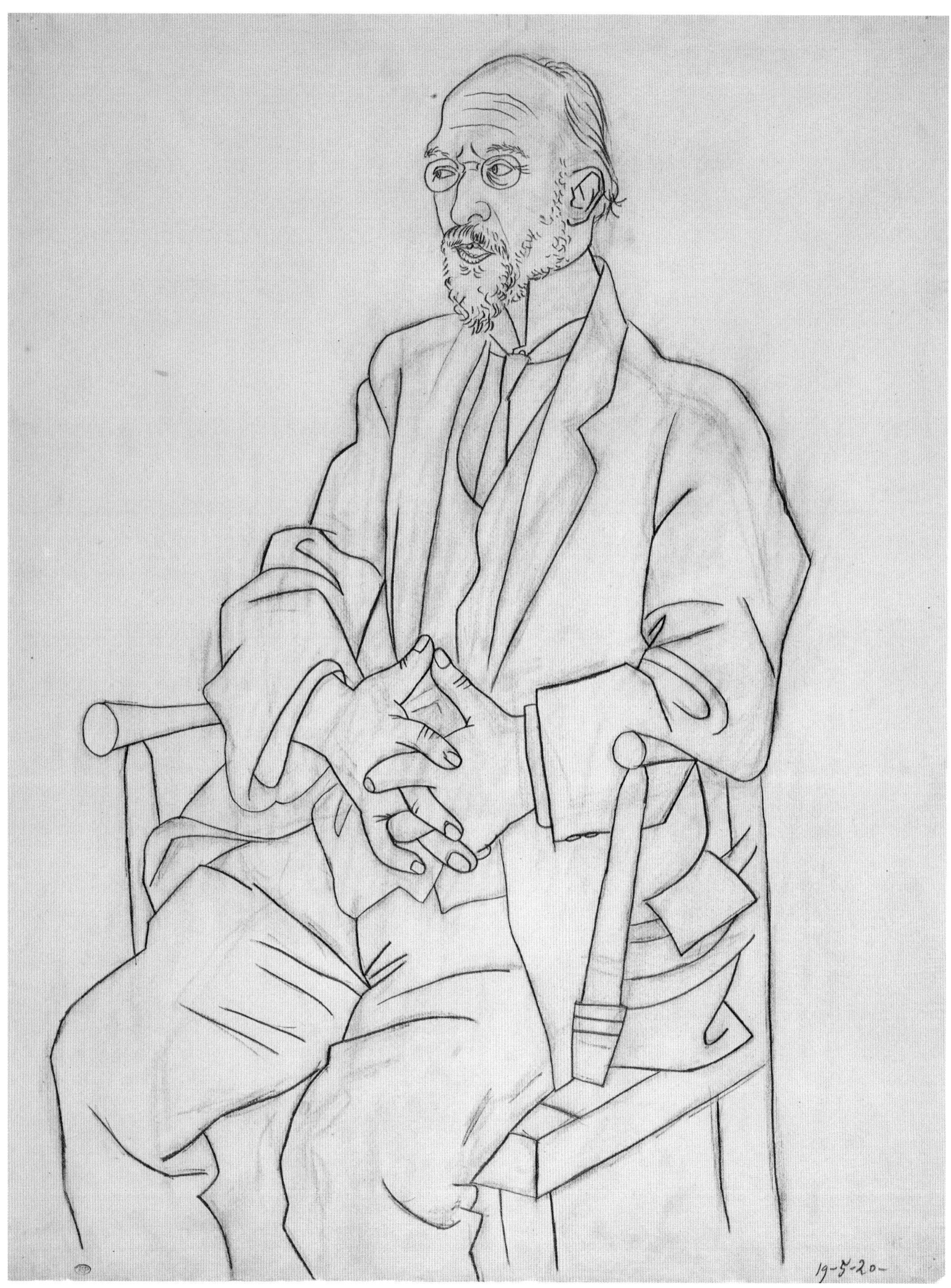
19-5-20

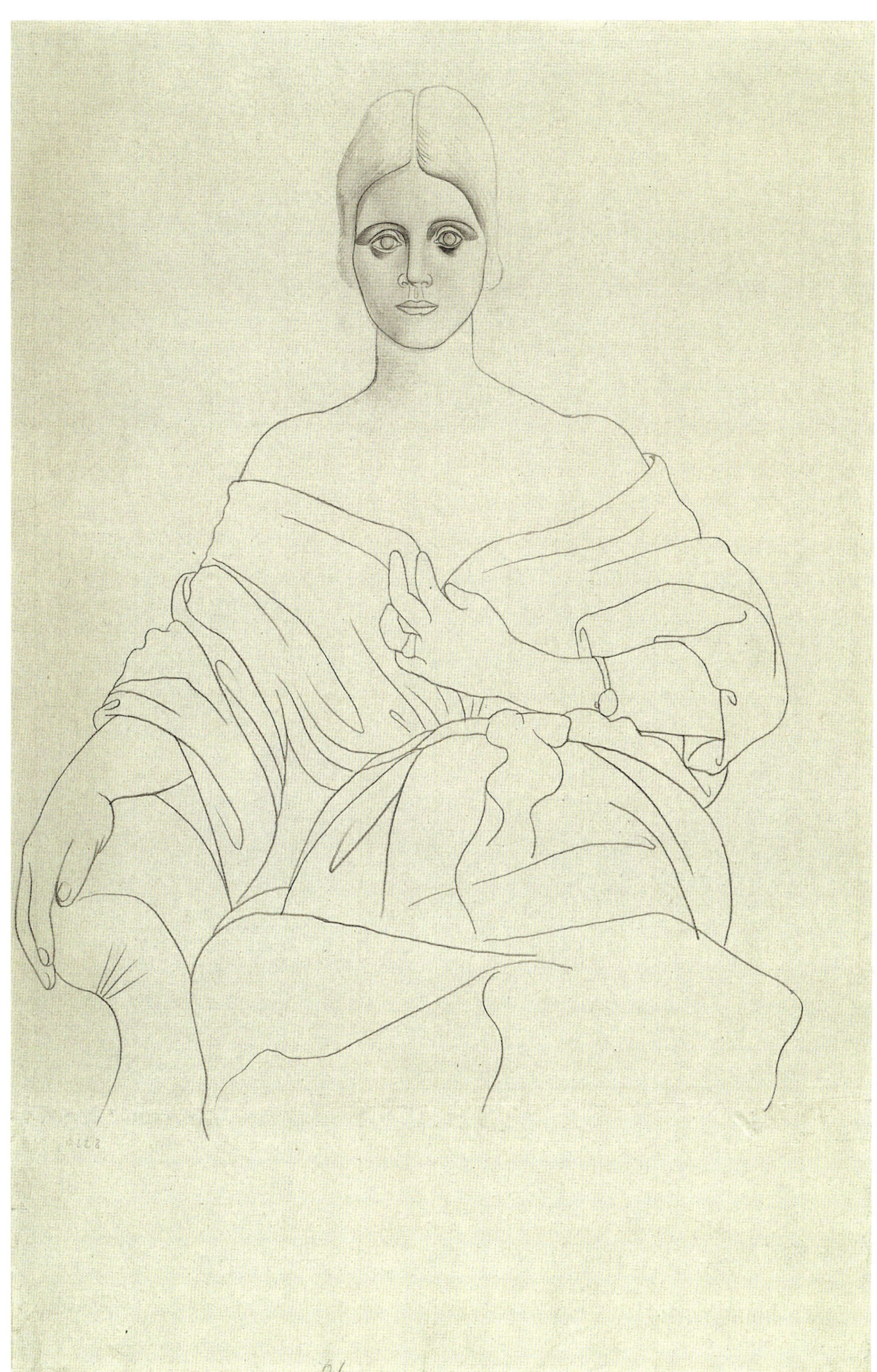

88. Pablo Picasso
Portrait d'Erik Satie
[Portrait of Erik Satie],
Paris, 19 May 1920
Pencil and charcoal on drawing paper, 62 x 48 cm
Paris, Musée national Picasso-Paris, Pablo Picasso Donation, 1979, inv. MP910

89. Pablo Picasso
Portrait d'Olga [Portrait of Olga], c. 1920
Pencil on paper, 48.5 x 32 cm
Private collection, on loan to Staatliche Museen zu Berlin, Nationalgalerie, Museum Berggruen

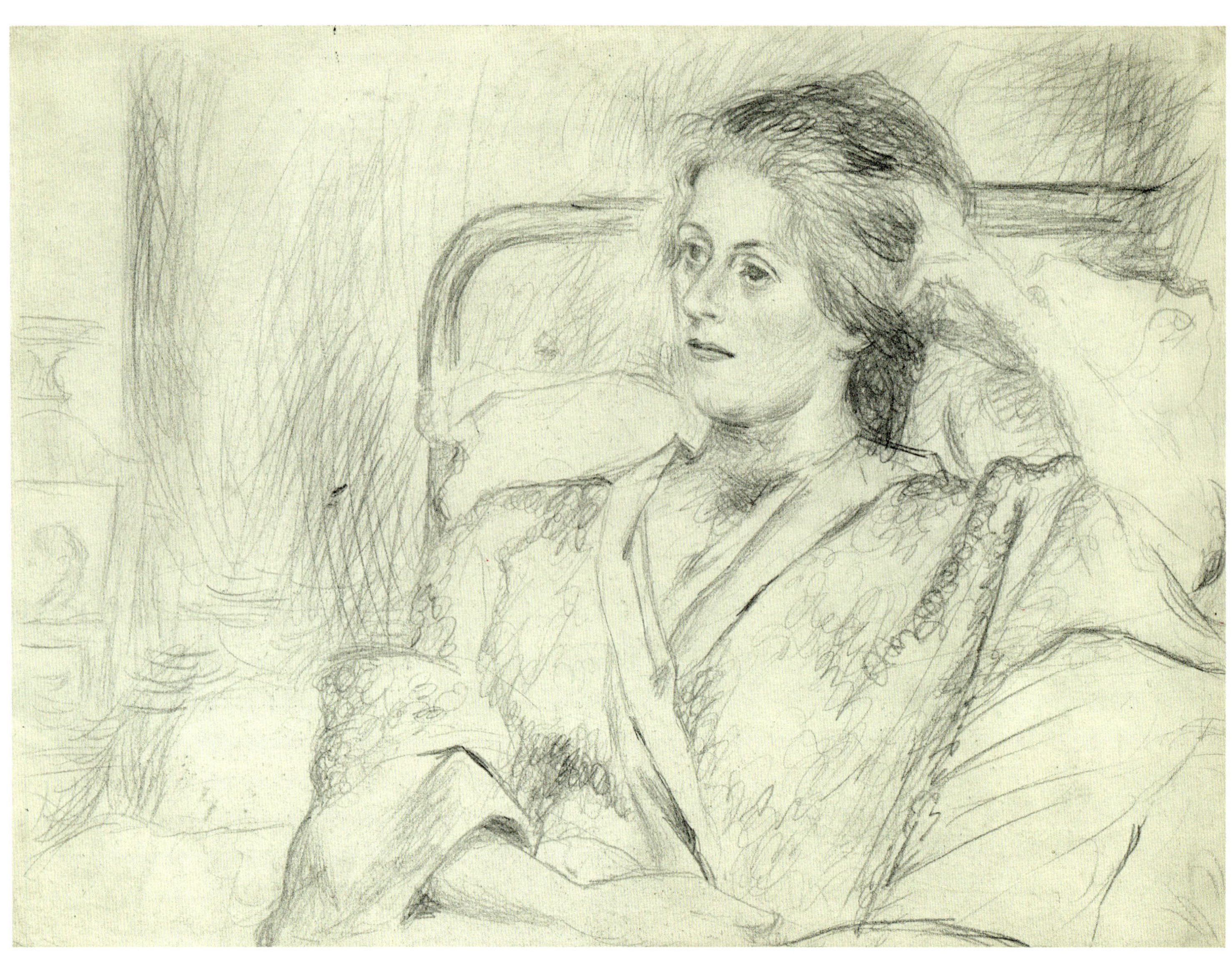

90. Pablo Picasso
Olga alitée [Bed-ridden Olga],
Paris, February 1921
Pastel on paper, 25 x 34 cm
Brussels, Fundación Almine y
Bernard Ruiz-Picasso para el Arte,
inv. 02678

91. Pablo Picasso
Deux danseurs [Two Dancers],
April 1925
Pen and ink on paper, 35.2 x 25.2 cm
Courtesy of Richard and Mary
L. Gray, Trustees of Gray Collection
Trust

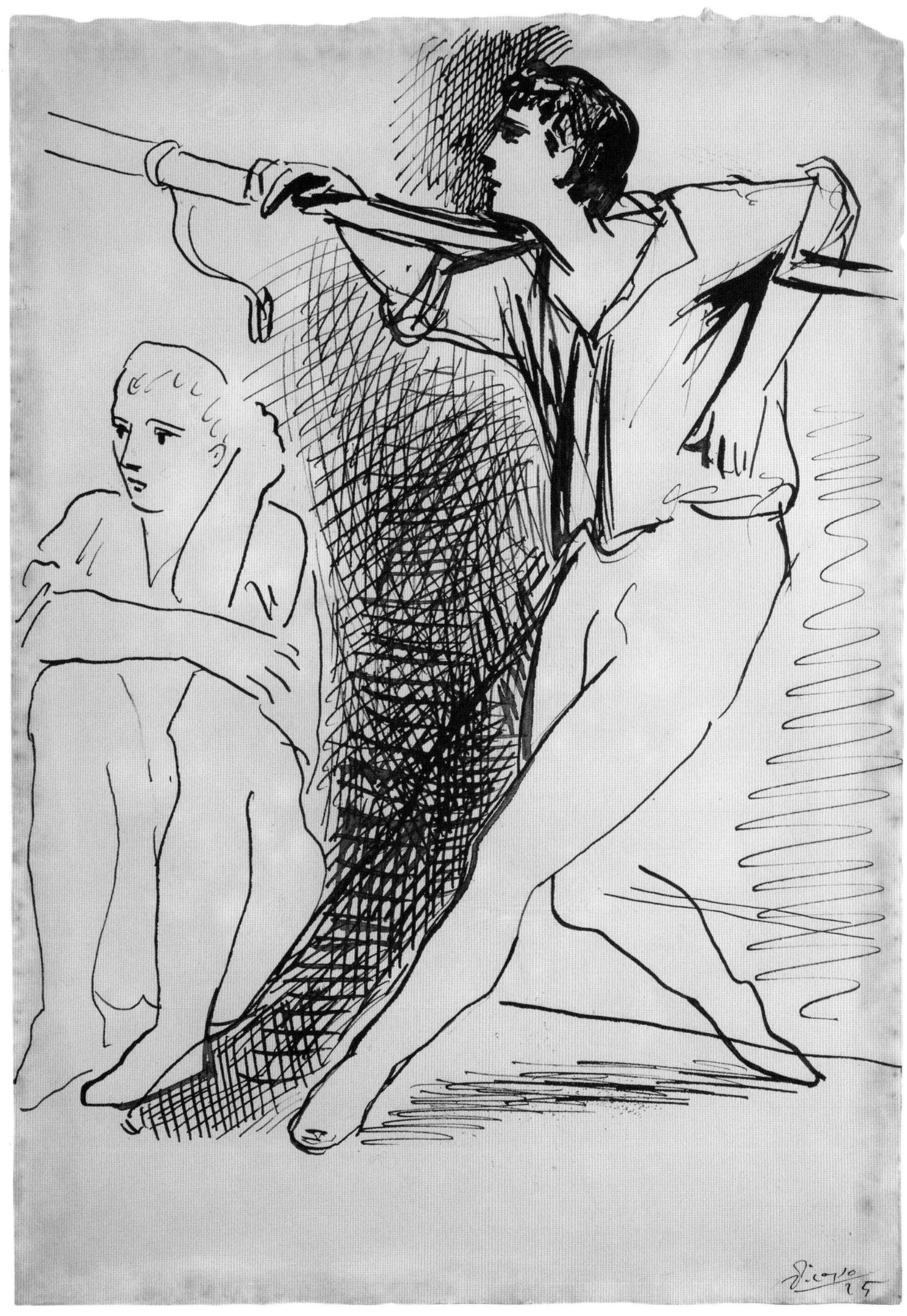

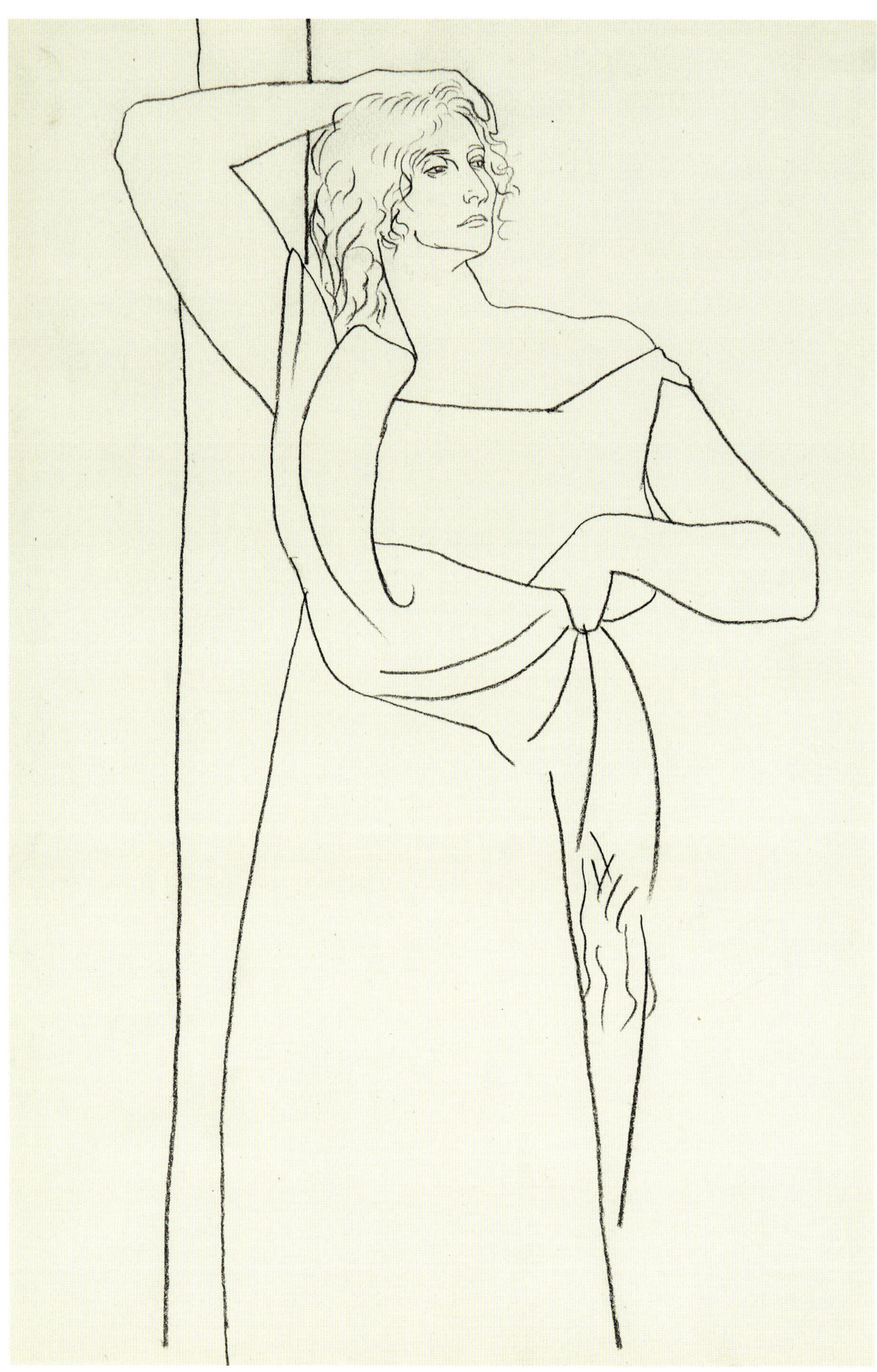

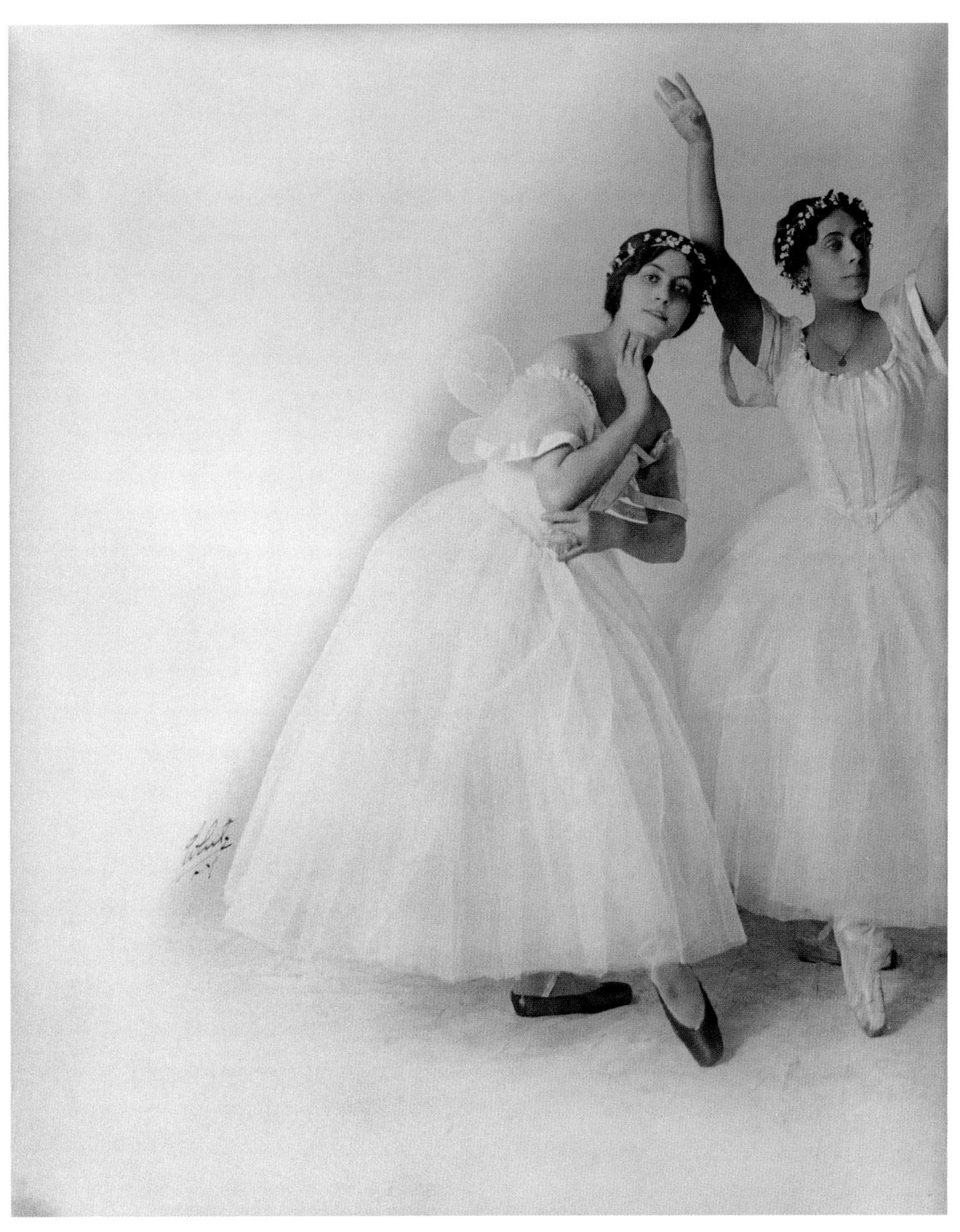

92. Pablo Picasso
Femme drapée (Olga Picasso)
[Draped Woman (Olga Picasso)],
1922
Pencil on paper, 33.5 x 22.5 cm
Private collection

93. Clarence H. White
Olga Khokhlova and Lydia Lopokova,
Les Sylphides, New York,
January 1916
Modern print from the original
negative, 15 x 13 cm
Brussels, Fundación Almine y
Bernard Ruiz-Picasso para el Arte,
inv. 102909

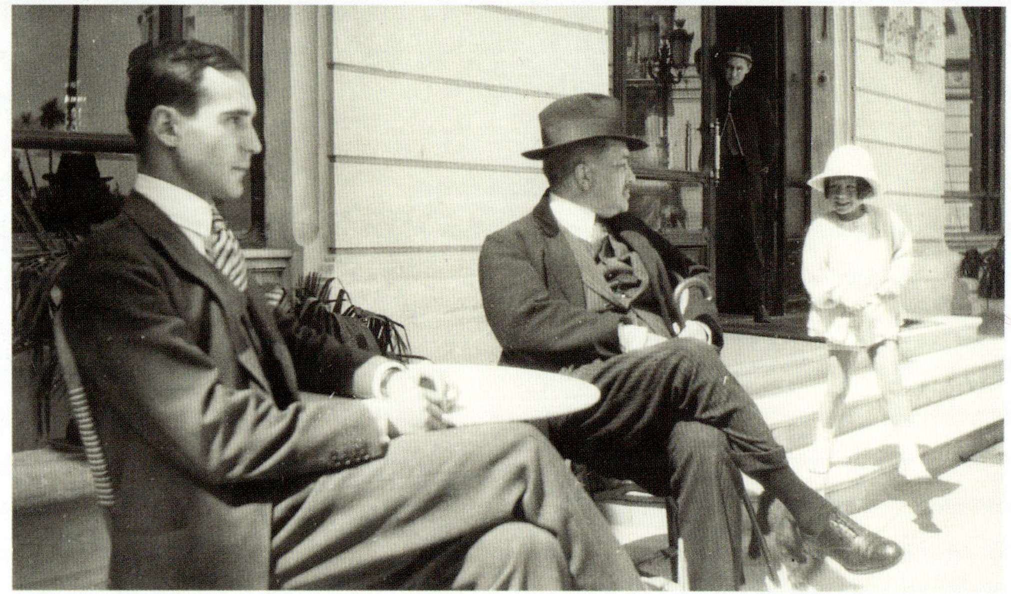

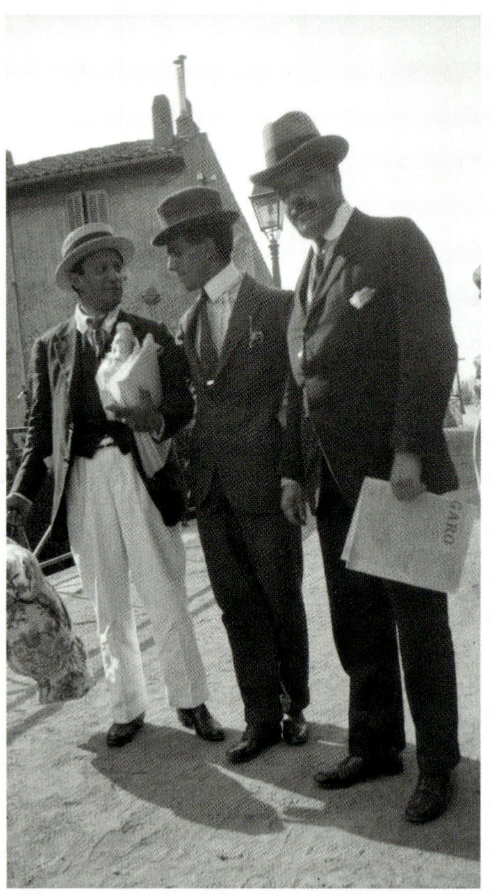

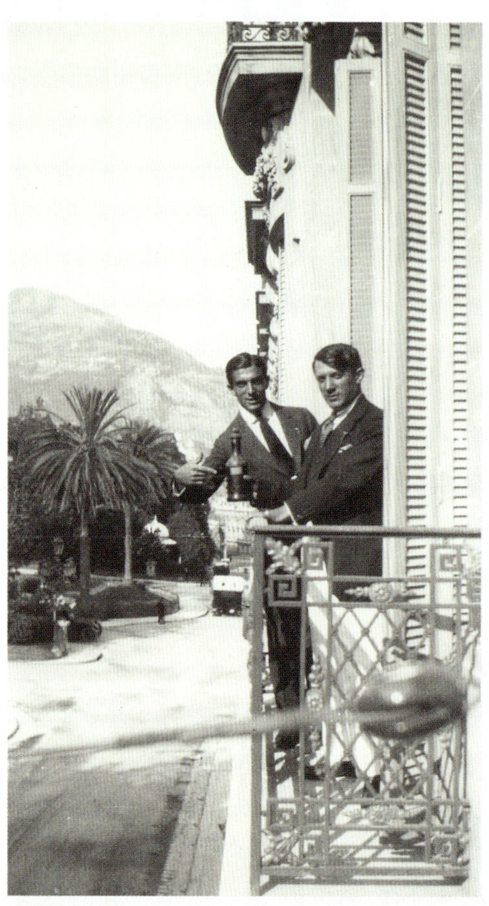

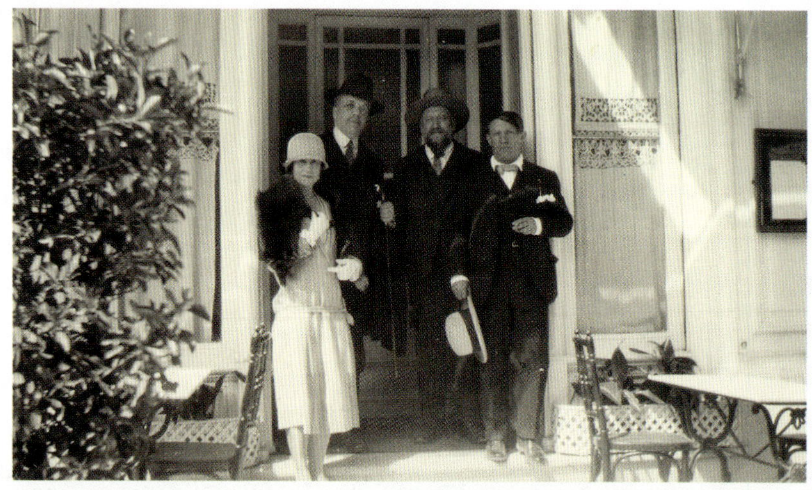

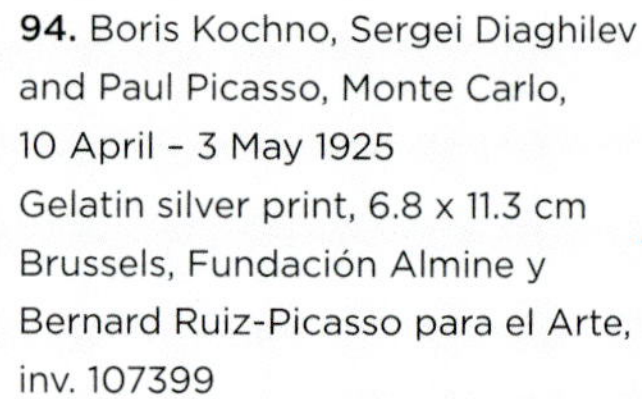

94. Boris Kochno, Sergei Diaghilev and Paul Picasso, Monte Carlo, 10 April – 3 May 1925
Gelatin silver print, 6.8 x 11.3 cm
Brussels, Fundación Almine y Bernard Ruiz-Picasso para el Arte, inv. 107399

95. Pablo Picasso, Léonide Massine and Sergei Diaghilev, Monte Carlo, 1920
Gelatin silver print, 12.1 x 6.9 cm
Brussels, Fundación Almine y Bernard Ruiz-Picasso para el Arte, inv. 100760

96. Léonide Massine and Pablo Picasso, Hôtel de Paris, Monte Carlo, 1920
Modern print from the original glass plate negative, 11.3 x 7 cm
Brussels, Fundación Almine y Bernard Ruiz-Picasso para el Arte, inv. 103214

97. Olga Picasso, Sergei Diaghilev, Edwin Evans and Pablo Picasso, Monte Carlo, 10 April – 3 May 1925
Gelatin silver print, 6.5 x 10.9 cm
Brussels, Fundación Almine y Bernard Ruiz-Picasso para el Arte, inv. 103816

98. Olga Picasso, Juan-Les-Pins, Villa Belle Rose, Summer 1925
Contact print from the original negative, 12.1 x 6.9 cm
Brussels, Fundación Almine y Bernard Ruiz-Picasso para el Arte, inv. 102599

99. Olga Khokhlova as one of the Sultan's wives in *Scheherazade*, 1916
Modern print from the original glass plate negative, 11.5 x 7.5 cm
Brussels, Fundación Almine y Bernard Ruiz-Picasso para el Arte, inv. 102911

100. Olga Khokhlova as a nymph in *L'Après-midi d'un faune*, 1916
Modern print from the original glass plate negative, 11.9 x 7.4 cm
Brussels, Fundación Almine y Bernard Ruiz-Picasso para el Arte, inv. 102907

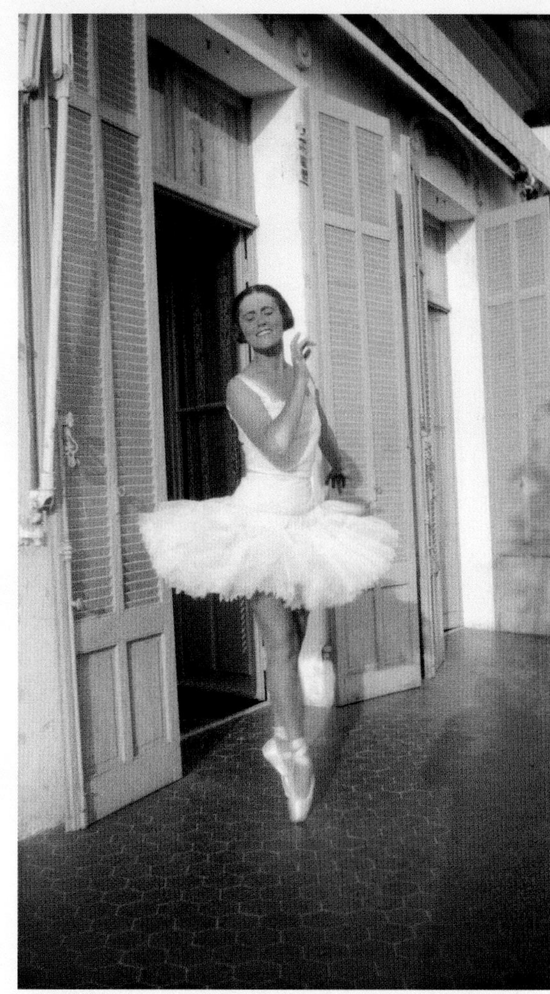

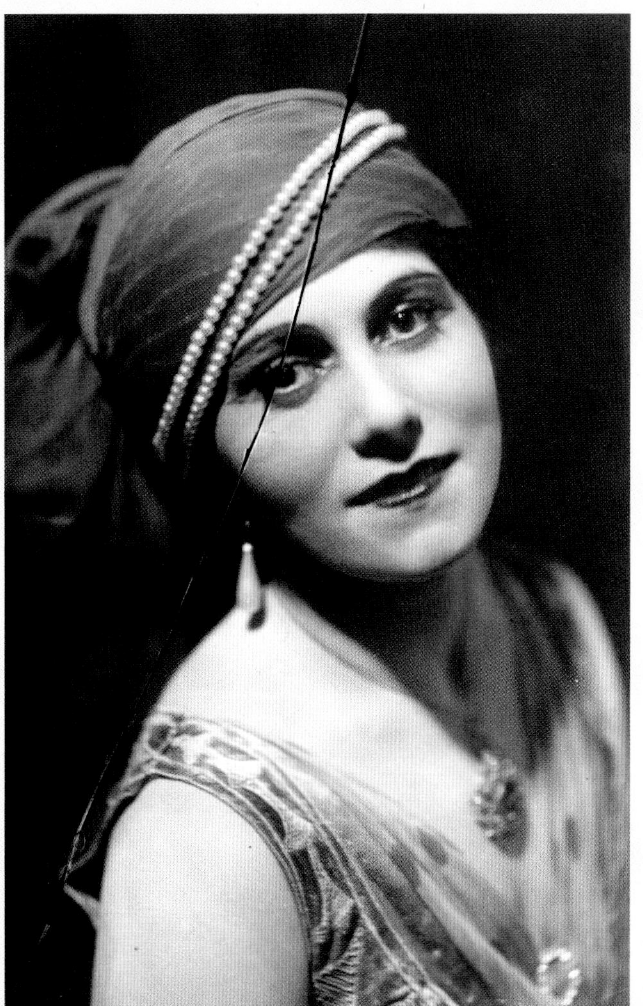

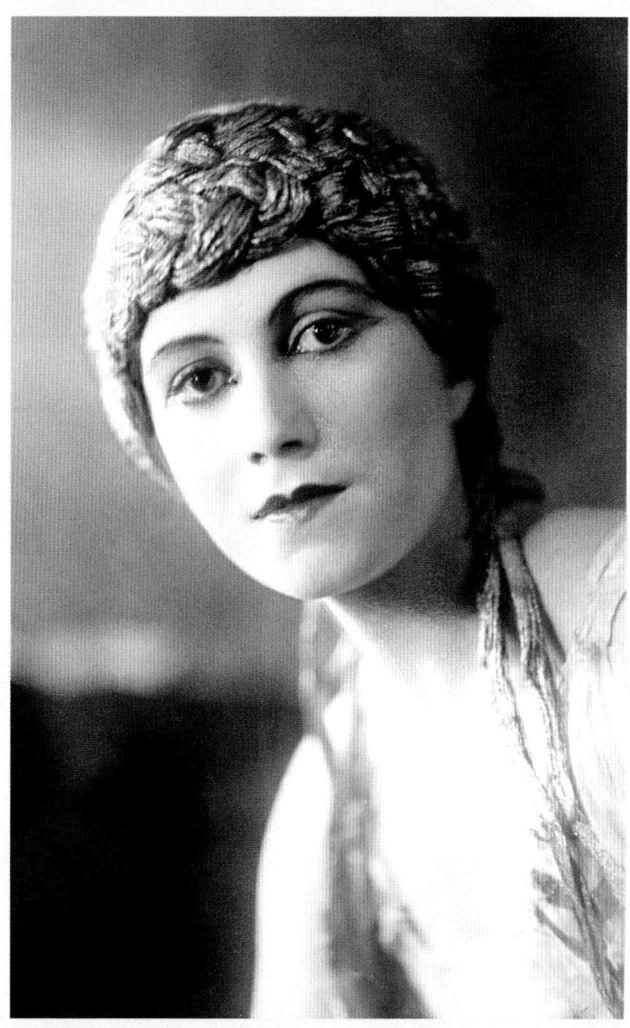

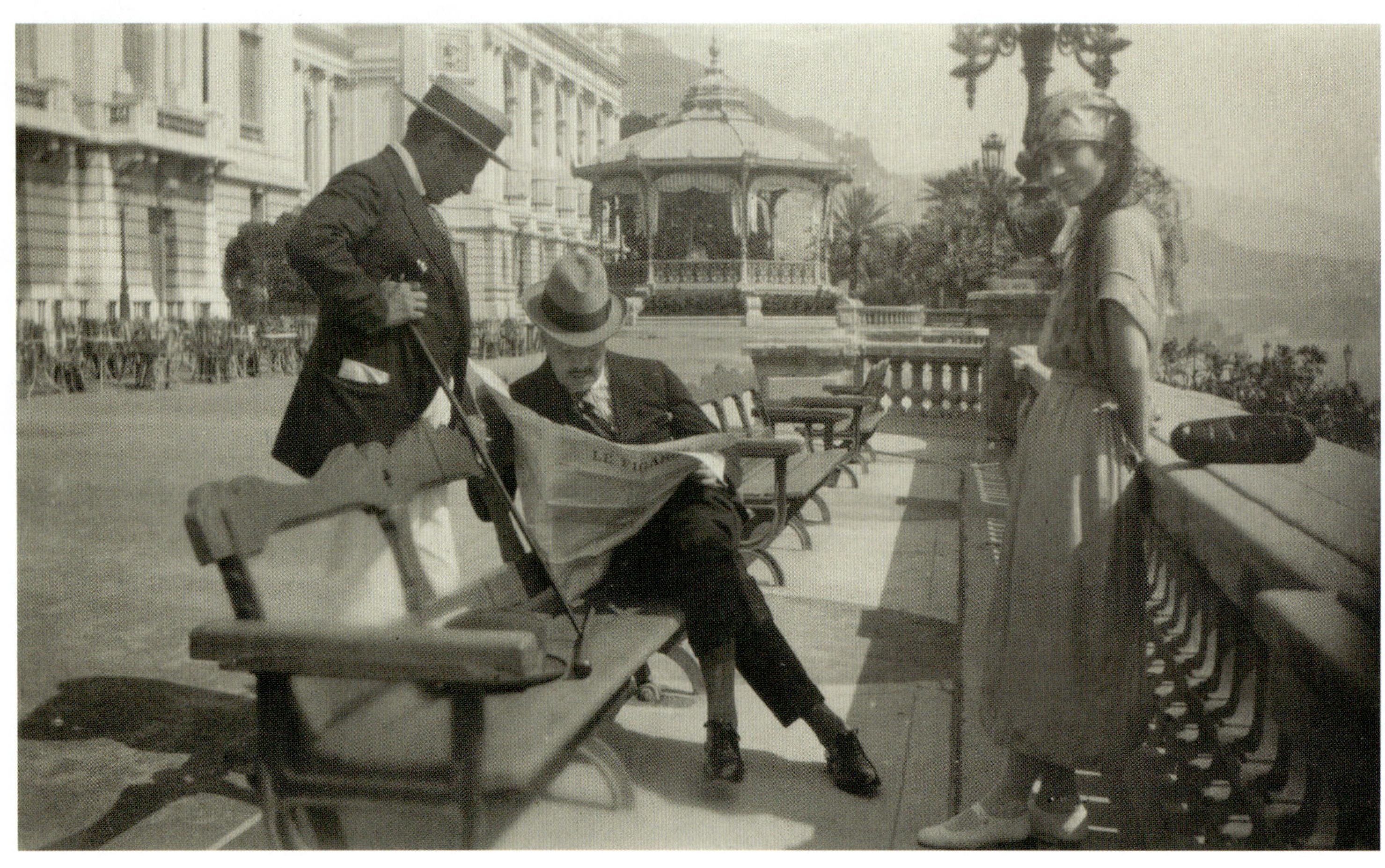

101. Pablo Picasso, Sergei Diaghilev, Olga Picasso, Monte Carlo, 1920
Gelatin silver print, 6.9 x 11.4 cm
Brussels, Fundación Almine y Bernard Ruiz-Picasso para el Arte, inv. 106969

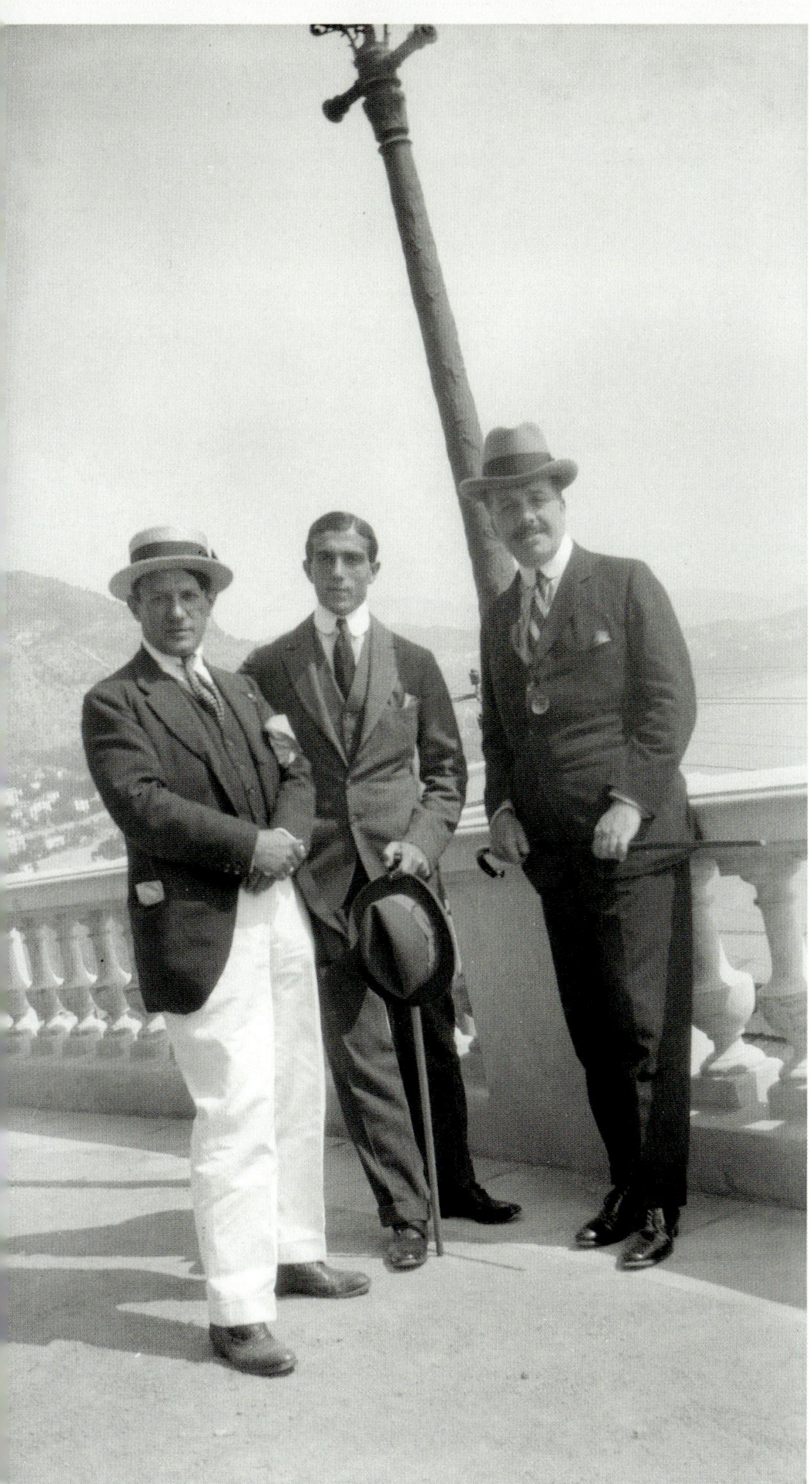

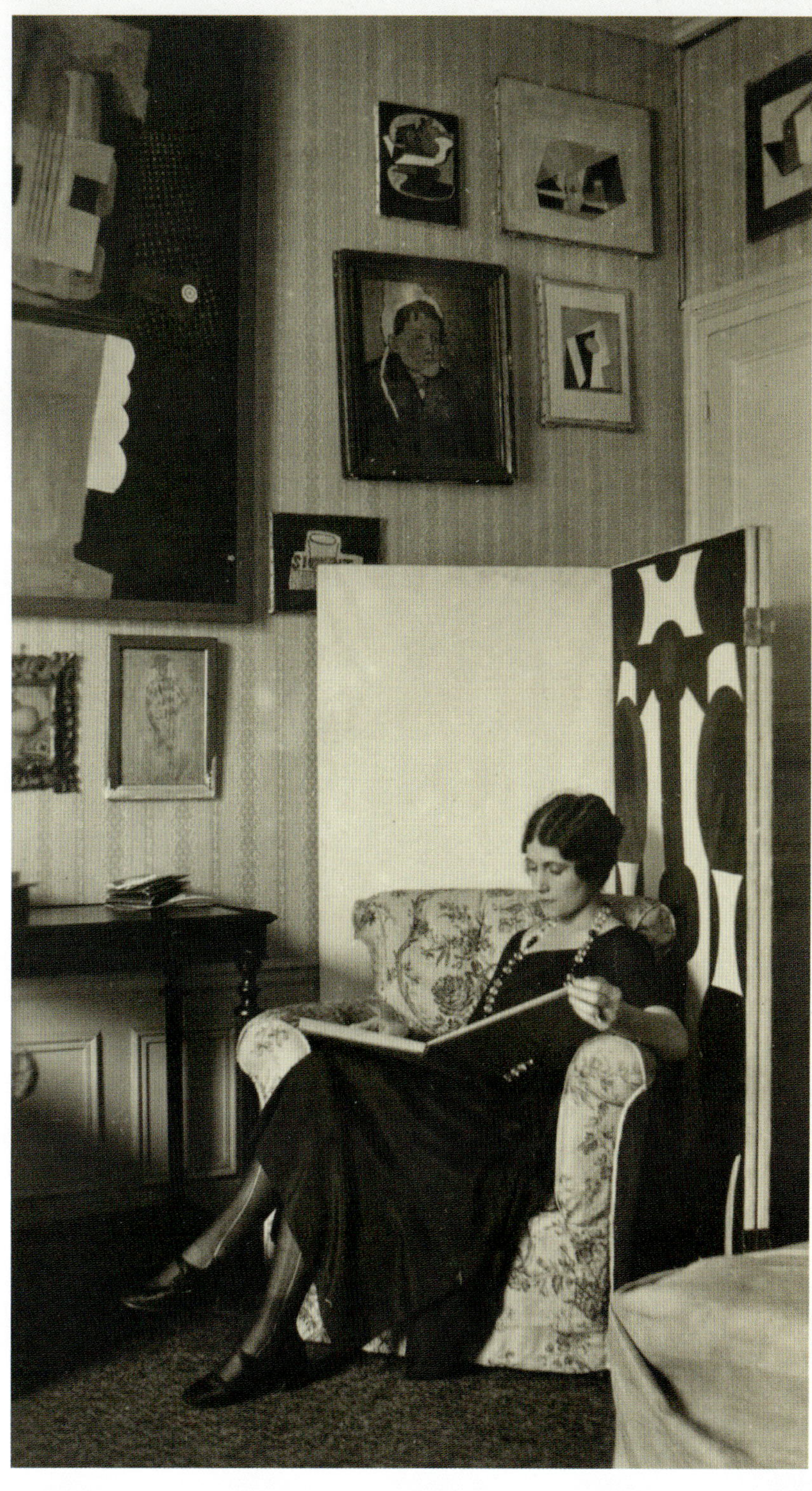

102. Picasso, Léonide Massine and Sergei Diaghilev, Monte Carlo, 1920
Print from the original glass plate negative, 12.4 x 6.9 cm
Brussels, Fundación Almine y Bernard Ruiz-Picasso para el Arte, inv. 100768

103. Pablo Picasso
Olga Picasso reading in the sitting room, 23 rue La Boétie, Paris, 1920
Gelatin silver print, 14 x 8.8 cm
Brussels, Fundación Almine y Bernard Ruiz-Picasso para el Arte, inv. 103251

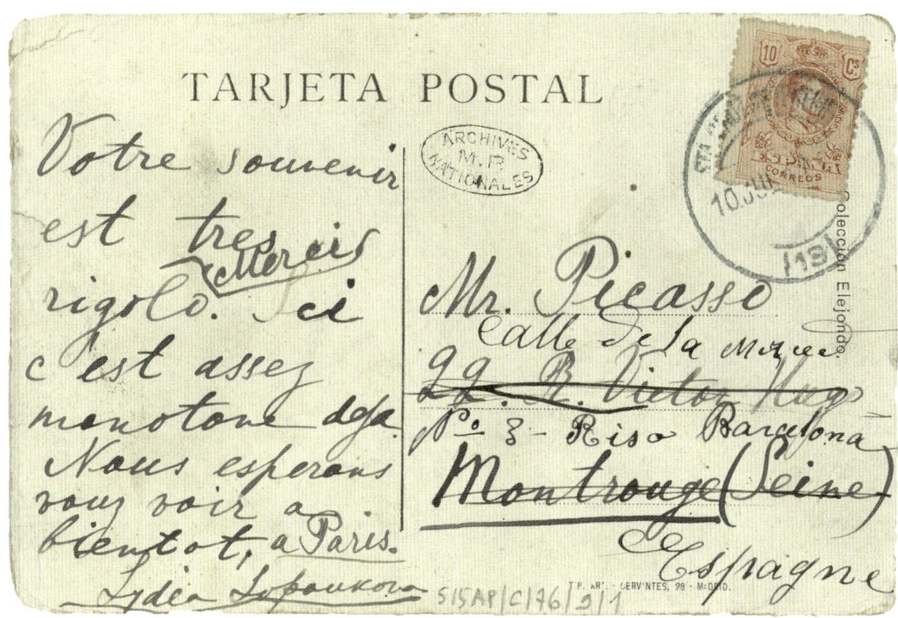
TARJETA POSTAL

Votre souvenir est tres merci rigolo. Ici c'est assez monotone deja. Nous esperons vous voir a bientot, a Paris.
Lydia Lopoukova

ARCHIVES M.P. NATIONALES

Mr. Picasso
Calle de la Merced
~~22. R. Victor Hugo~~
No. 3 - Piso Barcelona
~~Montrouge (Seine)~~
Espagne

Colección Elejondo

515AP/C/76/9/1

P. ART. CERVANTES, 28 - MADRID.

104. Postcard from Lydia Lopokova to Pablo Picasso, [10 July 1917?]
Postcard, 9 x 14 cm
Paris, Musée national Picasso-Paris, Donation of Picasso's heirs, 1992, inv. 515AP/C/76/9/1

105. Exhibition catalogue of Léonide Massine's paintings collection, Rome, 1917
Dépliant, 22 x 16 cm
Julian Barran, England

106. Illustrated program for the 1917 season of the *Ballets Russes* at the Théâtre du Châtelet (cover by Picasso), 1917
24.8 x 31.7 x 0.8 cm
London, Victoria and Albert Museum, Department of Theatre and Performance, inv. THM/DIS/2016/BR/1

107. Illustrated program for the 1921 season of the *Ballets Russes* at the Théâtre de la Gaité-Lyrique (cover by Picasso), 1921
31.8 x 24.6 cm
London, Victoria and Albert Museum, Department of Theatre and Performance, inv. THM/DIS/2016/BR/2

108. Illustrated program for the 1924 season of the *Ballets Russes* at the Théâtre des Champs-Élysées (cover by Picasso), May–June 1924
27 x 21.5 x 0.7 cm
London, Victoria and Albert Museum, Department of Theatre and Performance, inv. THM/DIS/2016/BR/3

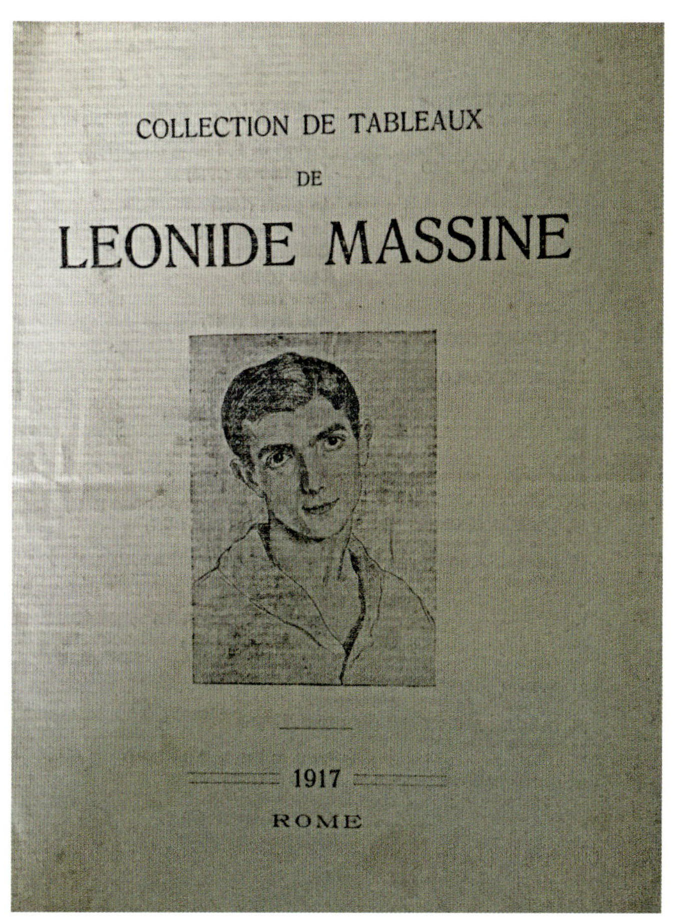
COLLECTION DE TABLEAUX
DE
LEONIDE MASSINE
1917
ROME

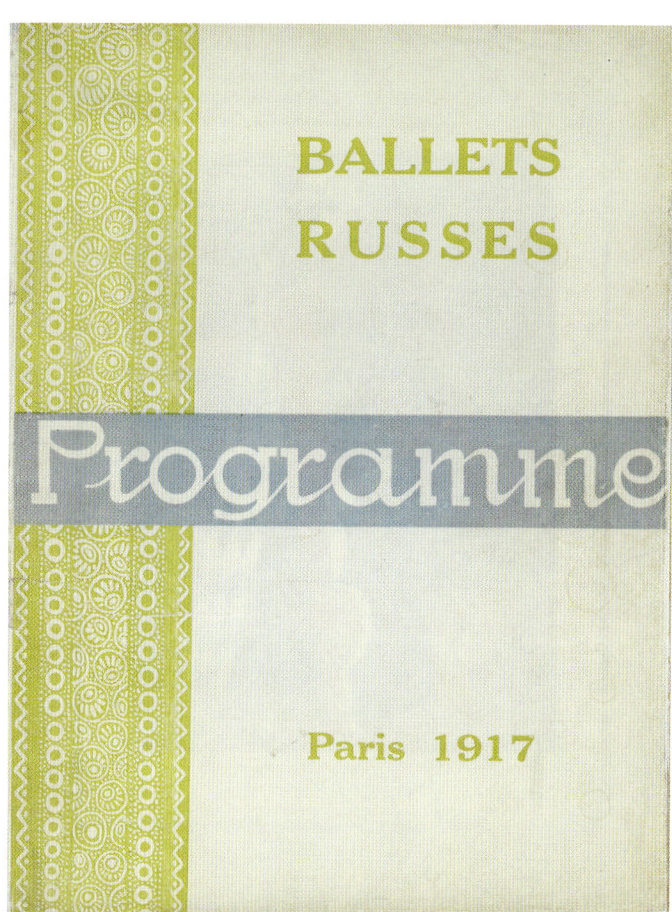
BALLETS
RUSSES
Programme
Paris 1917

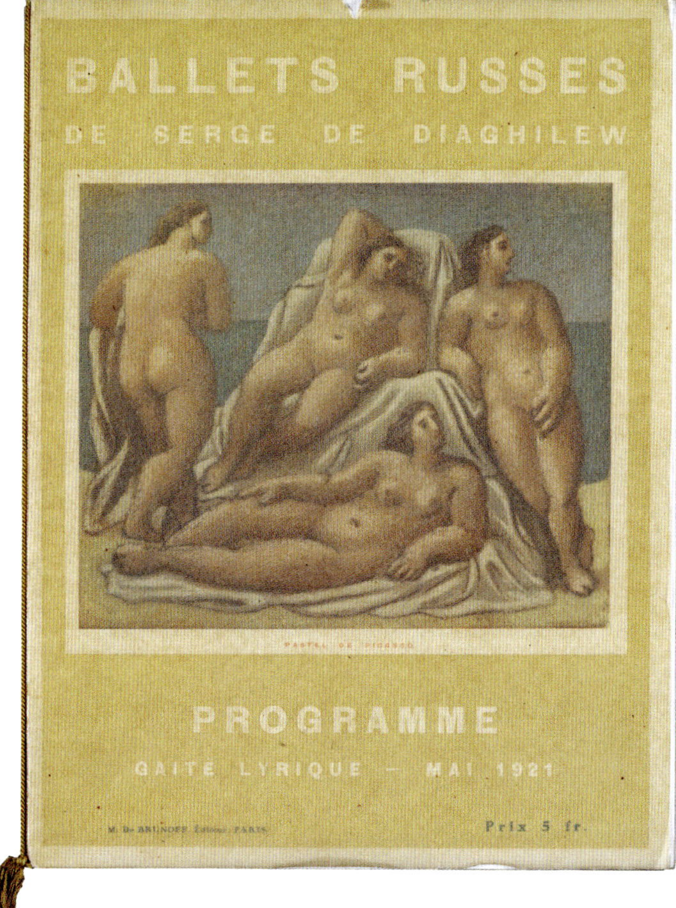
BALLETS RUSSES
DE SERGE DE DIAGHILEW
PROGRAMME
GAITÉ LYRIQUE – MAI 1921
Prix 5 fr.

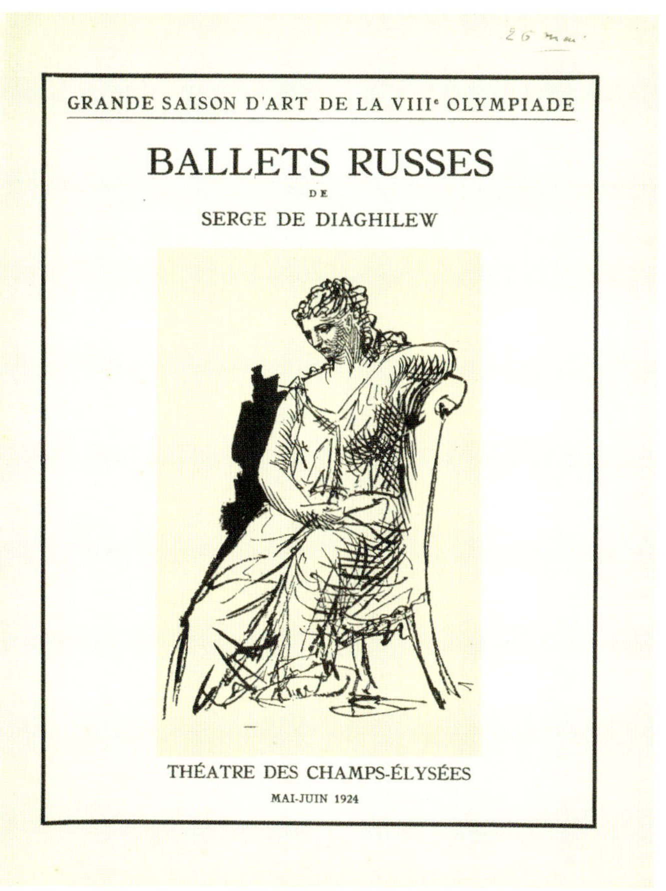
GRANDE SAISON D'ART DE LA VIIIe OLYMPIADE
BALLETS RUSSES
DE
SERGE DE DIAGHILEW
THÉATRE DES CHAMPS-ÉLYSÉES
MAI-JUIN 1924

Roma 11 - Aprile 917

Cher Picasso

Vous devait moi excuser se ecrit-
parçeque au concert d'hier j'ai entendu
dir que vôtre „decor„ serait exécutés par
le peintre Carlo Socrate, qui a exécutés le
„decor„ par Bakst. Je suis ~~plu~~ tre-deplaisant.
j'esperét e croirét de faire quelque chose
aussi moi pour vôtre „decor„ parçeque
je croit que un peintre futuriste aurait
plus faculté de interpretation les
discipline cubiste, que un passeiste
j'esper bientôt d'avoir une vôtre visite
au mon atelier commen ~~vo~~ m'avait
vous dit autrefois.
J'attende un lieu de rendez vous et
je vous donne beaucoup de salutation
vôtre Enrico Prampolini
peintre
Via Tanaro 89.
CITTÀ

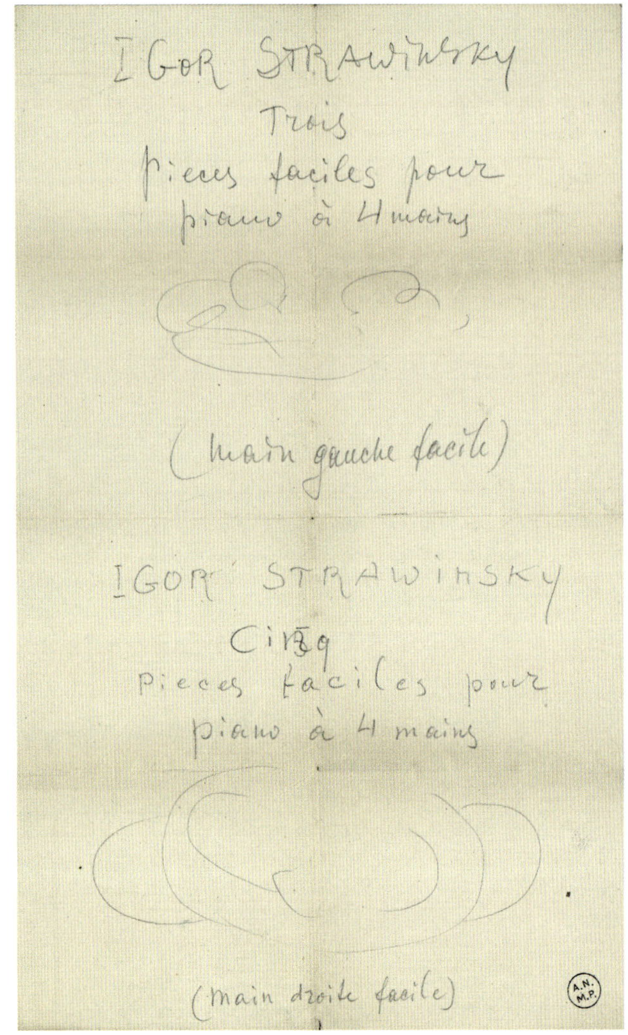

IGOR STRAWINSKY
Trois
pieces faciles pour
piano à 4 mains

(main gauche facile)

IGOR STRAWINSKY
Cinq
pieces faciles pour
piano à 4 mains

(main droite facile)

109. Letter from Enrico Prampolini to Pablo Picasso, 11 April 1917
27 x 21 cm
Paris, Musée national Picasso-Paris, Donation of Picasso's heirs, 1992, inv. 515AP/C/130/18/1

110. Message from Igor Stravinsky: "Igor Stravinsky, three pieces for piano four hands...", undated
Paris, Musée national Picasso-Paris, Donation of Picasso's heirs, 1992, inv. 515AP/C/165/26/2

Voici mon cher Guillaume
ces vers que les danseuses
du ballet ont fait pour
moi.

Tu serais bien gentil
si tu me écrivais.

Je te enverrai un de
ces jours un souvenir
de Pompei (as tu reçu
la feuille de laurier que je
t'ai envoyé de là bas)

Amitiés embrasse les
mains de Ruby.

La main très amie
de Picasso

Rome 1917 Hôtel de Russie

Поэтическое Морсо.
Сочинить совсем не трудно
В честь красотки Пикассо
Полюбивши безрассудно
Был нескучный бы союз
Балерина с футуристом
И для Вас я брачных уз?
По желанию вреали Истомин
Мой лирический морсо
Посвящен любви новой
Будет жданой, чтобы Пикассо
Объяснялся бы с Хохловой?

111. Autograph letter from Pablo Picasso to Guillaume Apollinaire, March 1917
15.9 x 11.2 cm
Paris, Musée national Picasso-Paris, Achat, 1990, inv. MP 1990-2 (53)

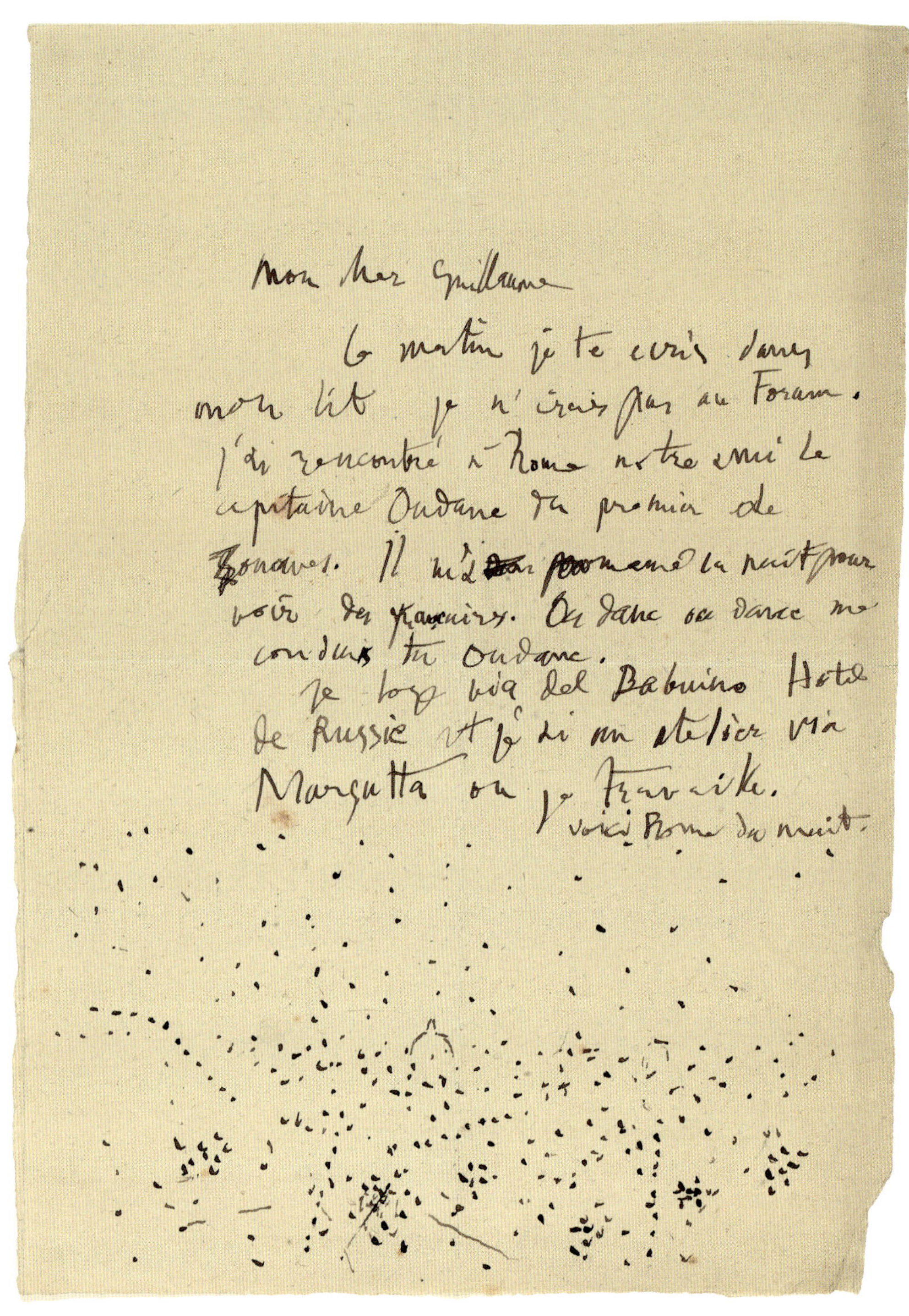

Mon cher Guillaume

Ce matin je te écris dans mon lit je n'écris pas au Forum. J'ai rencontré à Rome notre ami le capitaine Oudane du premier de Zouaves. Il m'a promené la nuit pour voir des [illegible]. Ou dane ou danse me conduis tu Oudane.

Je loge via del Babuino Hotel de Russie et j'ai un atelier via Margutta où je travaille.

Voici Rome de nuit.

112. Autograph letter from Pablo Picasso to Guillaume Apollinaire, March 1917
15.9 x 11.2 cm
Paris, Musée national Picasso-Paris, Achat, 1990, inv. MP 1990-2 (53)

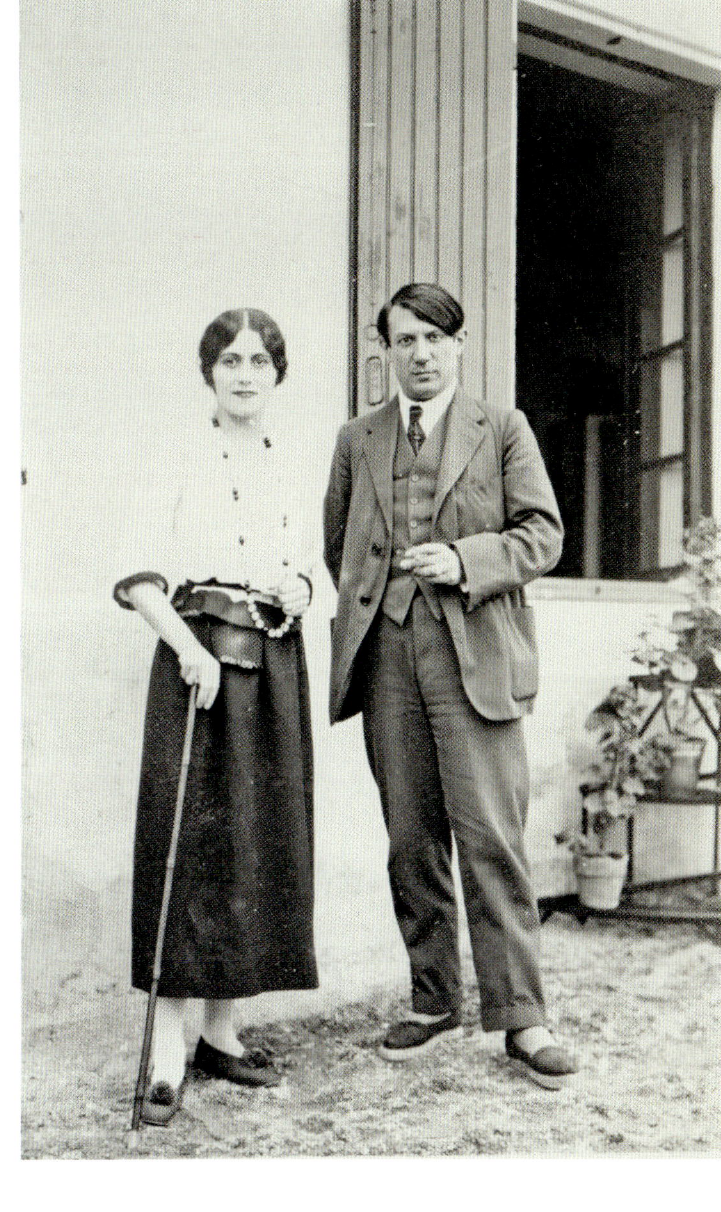

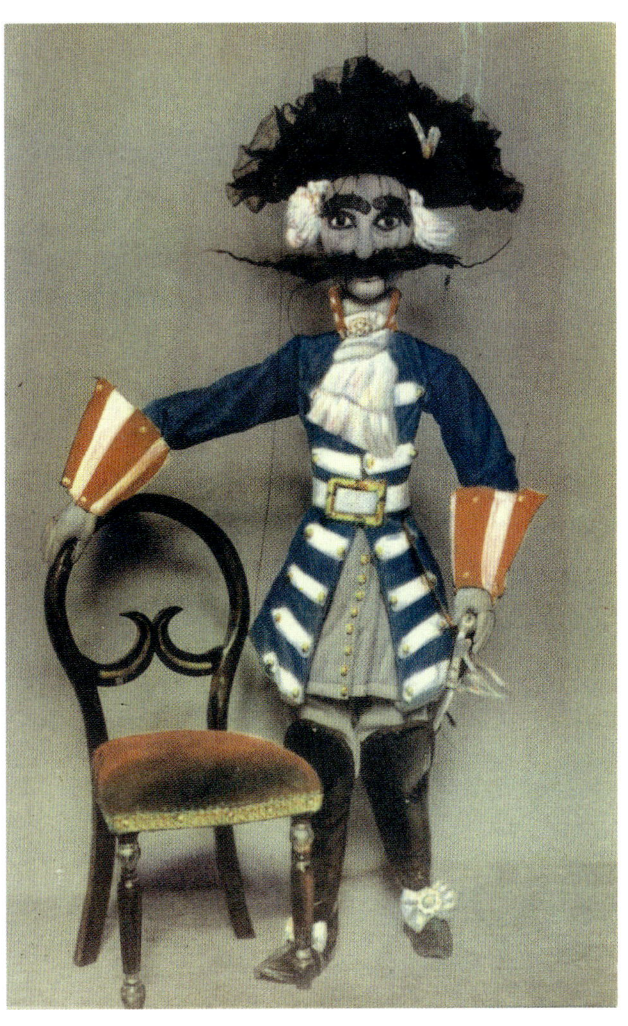

113. Postcard to Jacqueline and Guillaume Apollinaire with Picasso and Olga in Biarritz in 1918, Biarritz, 1918
Ink on postcard, 14 x 9 cm
Paris, Musée national Picasso-Paris, Achat, 1990, inv. MP2001-2

114. Handwritten postcard to Guillaume Apollinaire, February 1917
Ink on postcard, 9.8 x 13.8 cm
Paris, Musée national Picasso-Paris, Achat, 1989, inv. MP1989-2 (25)

V. Stylistic Fluidity

115. Pablo Picasso
Études [Studies], Paris, 1920
Oil on canvas, 100 x 81 cm
Paris, Musée national Picasso-Paris,
inv. MP65

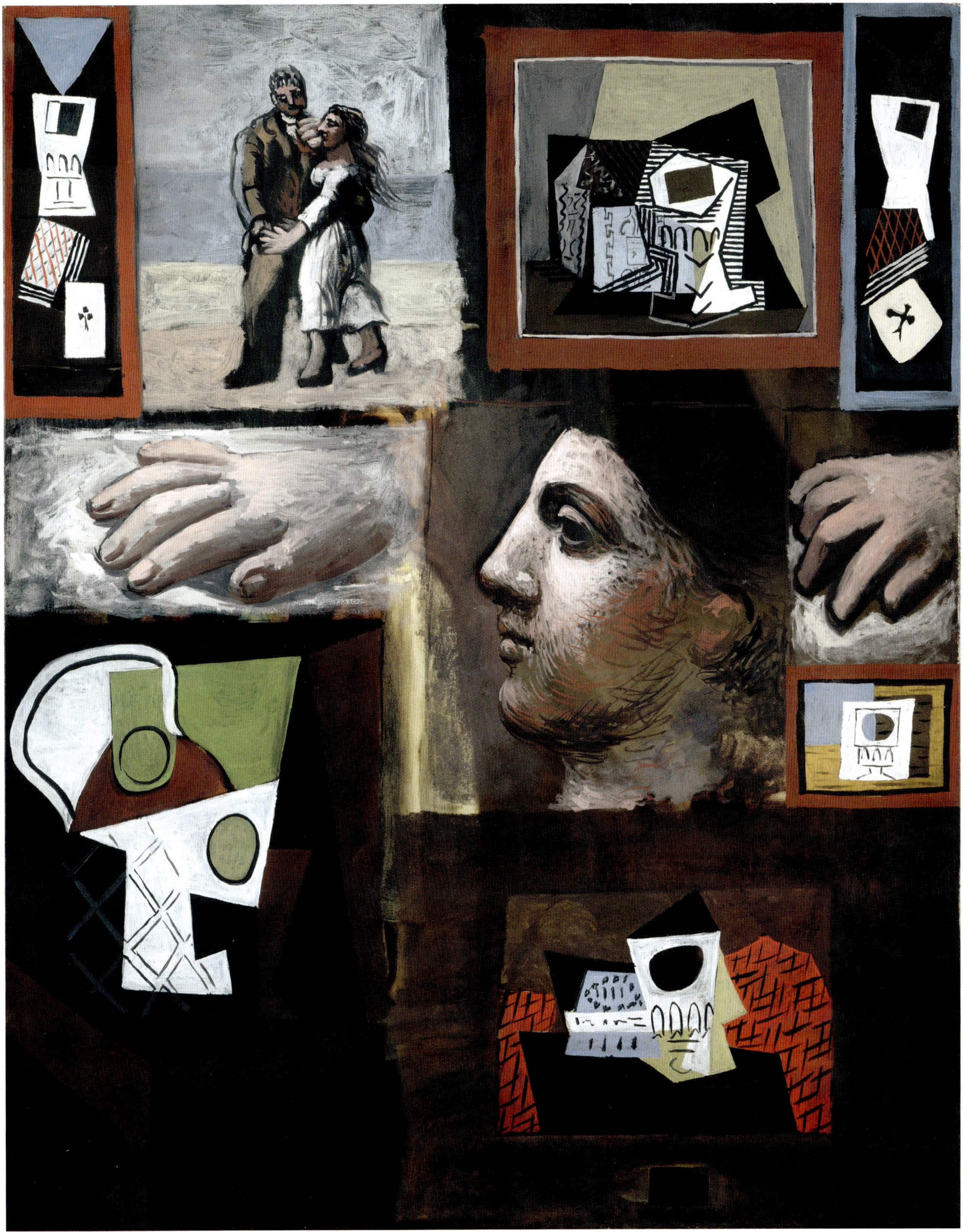

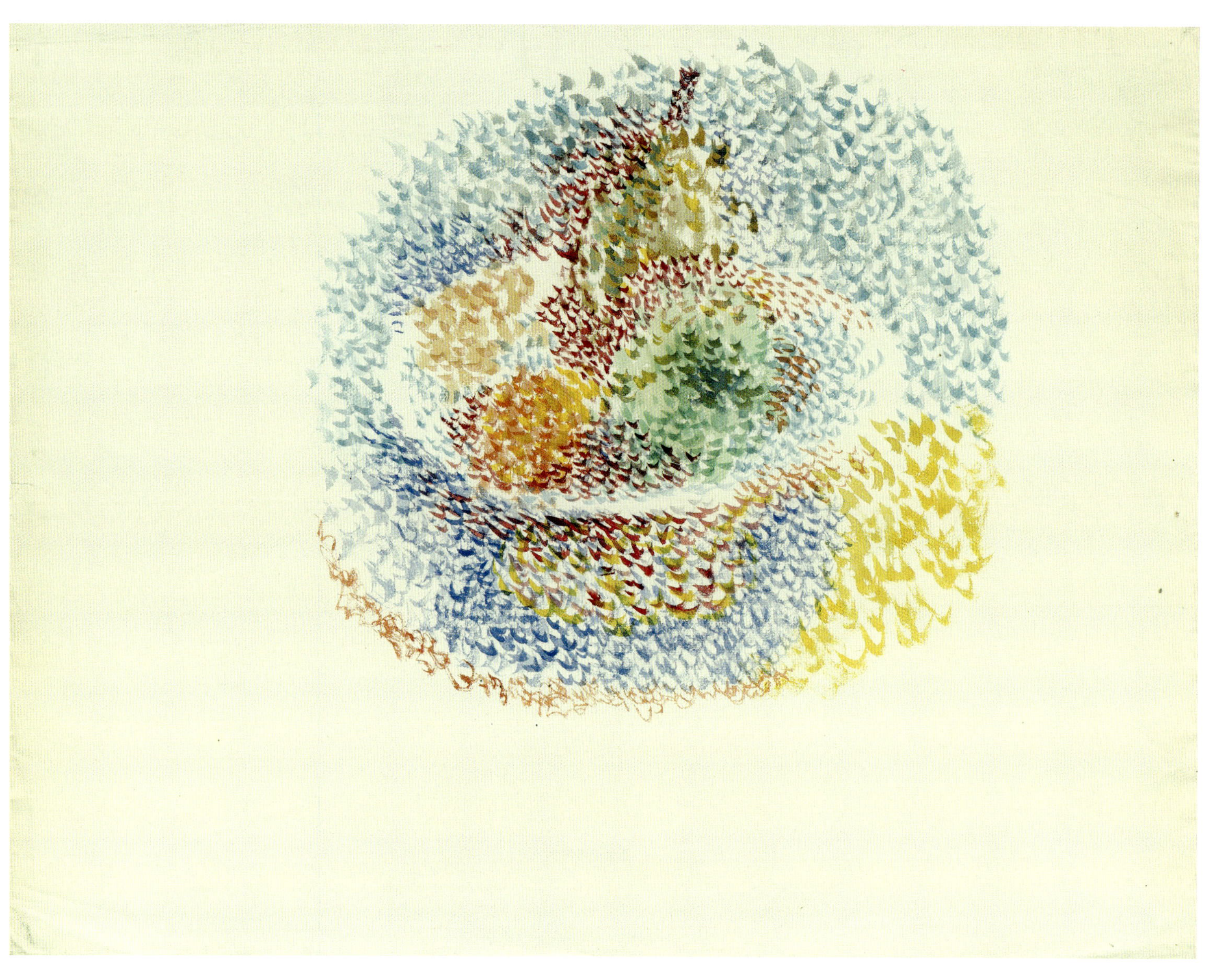

116. Pablo Picasso
Compotier avec fruits [Fruit Bowl],
Montrouge, late 1917
Watercolour on paper, 47.8 x 62 cm
Brussels, Fundación Almine y
Bernard Ruiz-Picasso para el Arte,
inv. 02873

117. Pablo Picasso
Le retour du baptême,
d'après Le Nain [Return
from the Baptism, after Le Nain],
Montrouge, Autumn 1917
Oil on canvas, 164 x 118 cm
Paris, Musée national Picasso-Paris,
Pablo Picasso Donation, 1979,
inv. MP56

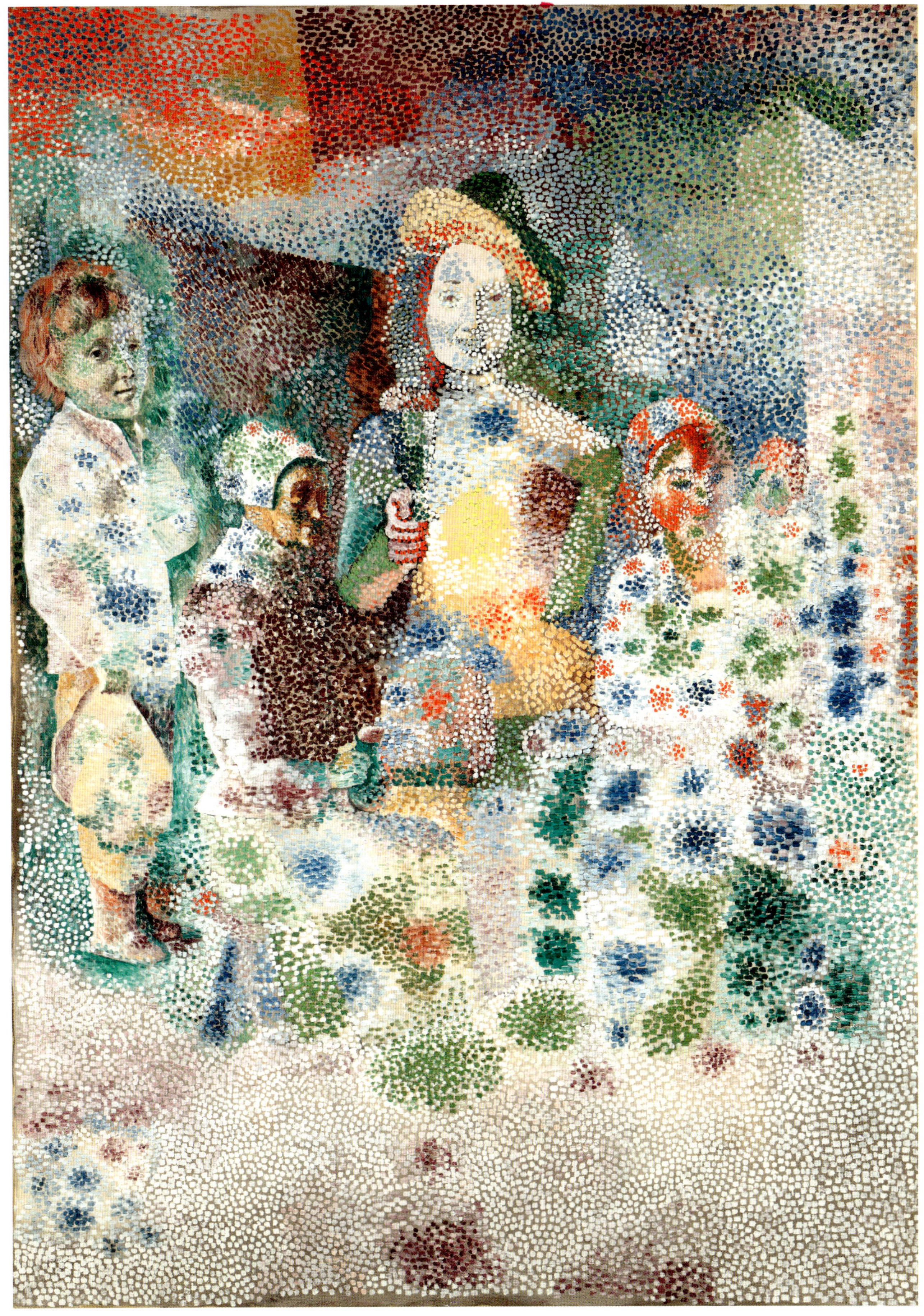

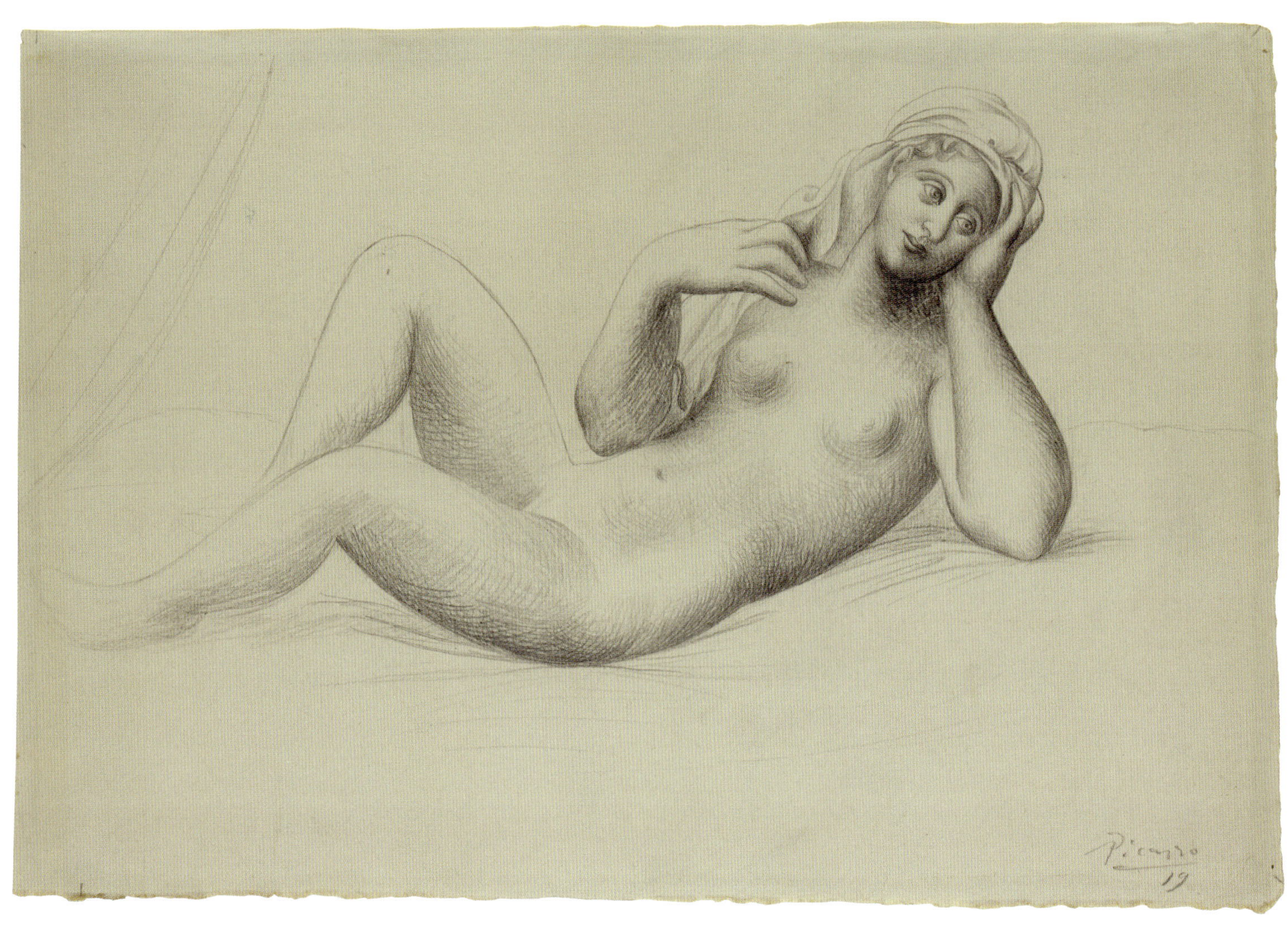

118. Pablo Picasso
Nu allongé au turban [Reclining Nude with Turban], Paris, 1919
Pencil on paper, 21.5 x 31.5 cm
Private collection

119. Pablo Picasso
Femme à la cruche
[Woman with Jug], 1919
Pencil and charcoal on paper, 65.5 x 48.6 cm
Santa Barbara, Museum of Art, Gift of Wright S. Ludington, inv. 1946.10.1

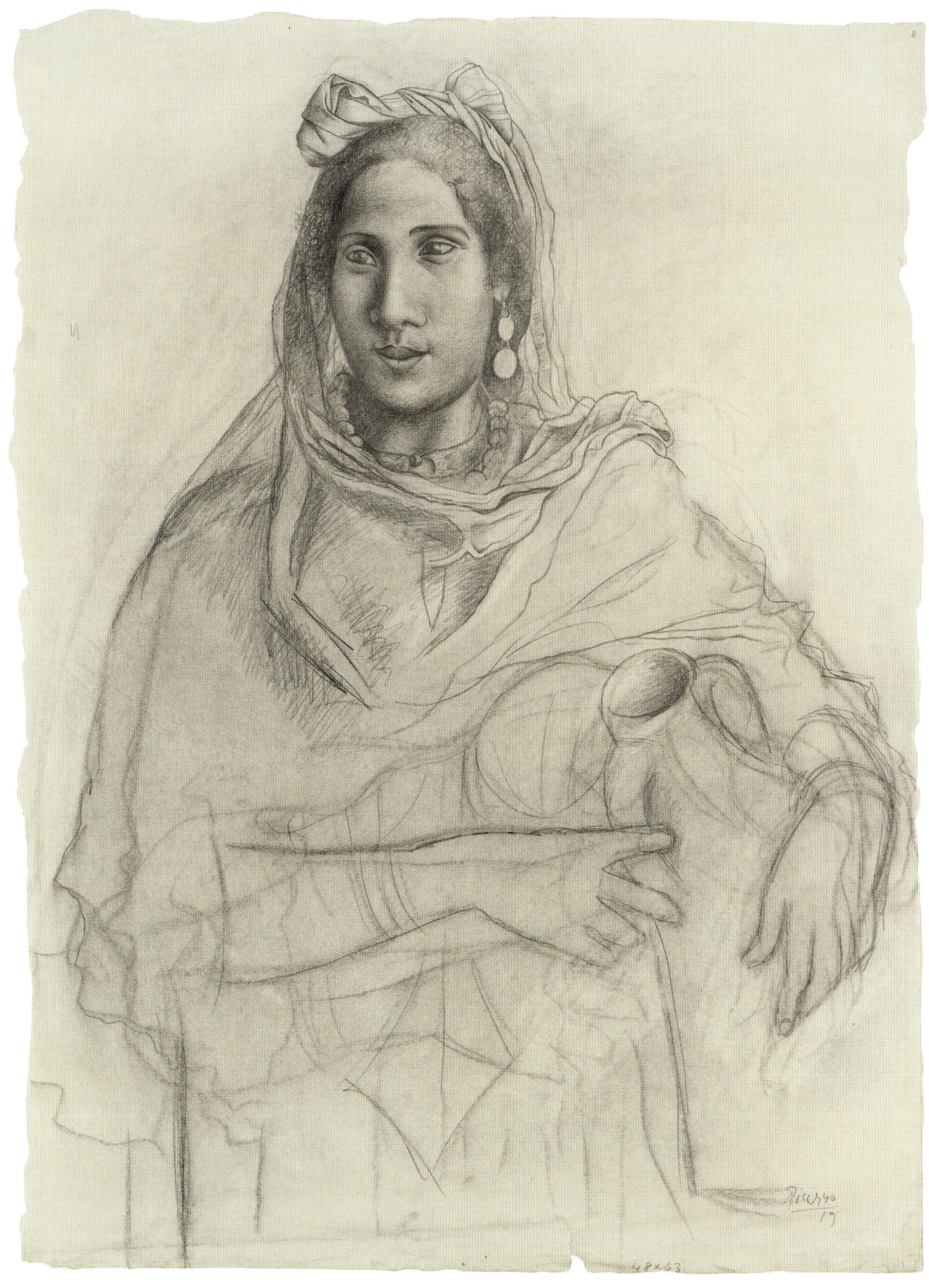

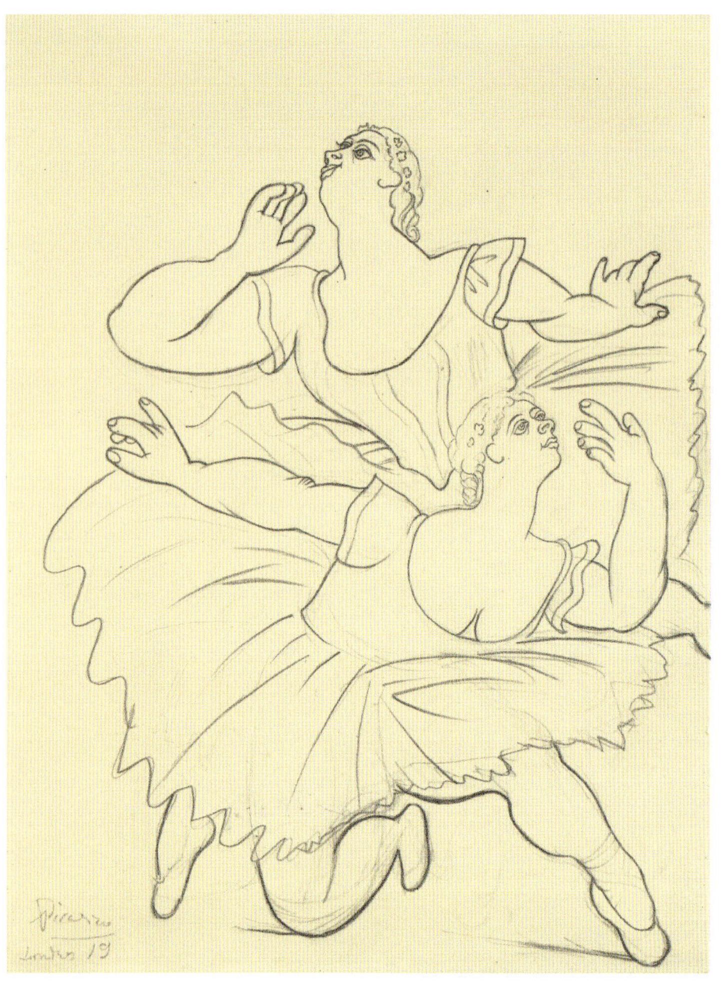

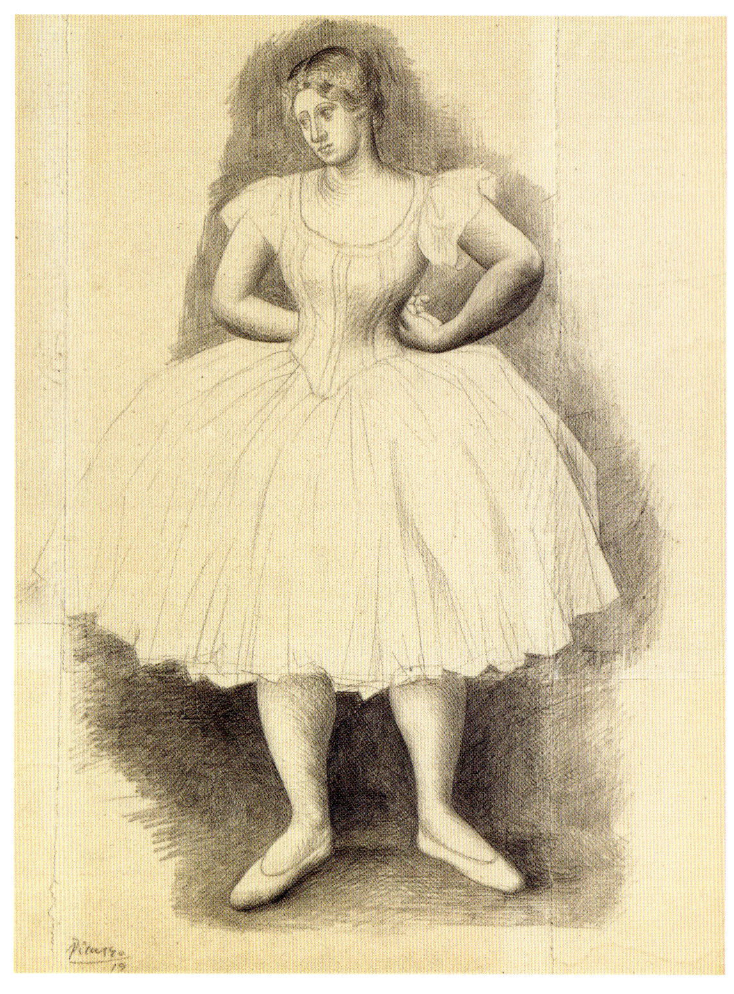

120. Pablo Picasso
Deux Danseuses [Two Ballerinas], 1919
Pencil on paper, 31 x 23.9 cm
New York, Museum of Modern Art, The John S. Newberry Collection, inv. 178.1963

121. Pablo Picasso
Danseuse [Ballerina], 1919
Pencil on paper, 39.2 x 29.8 cm
Private collection

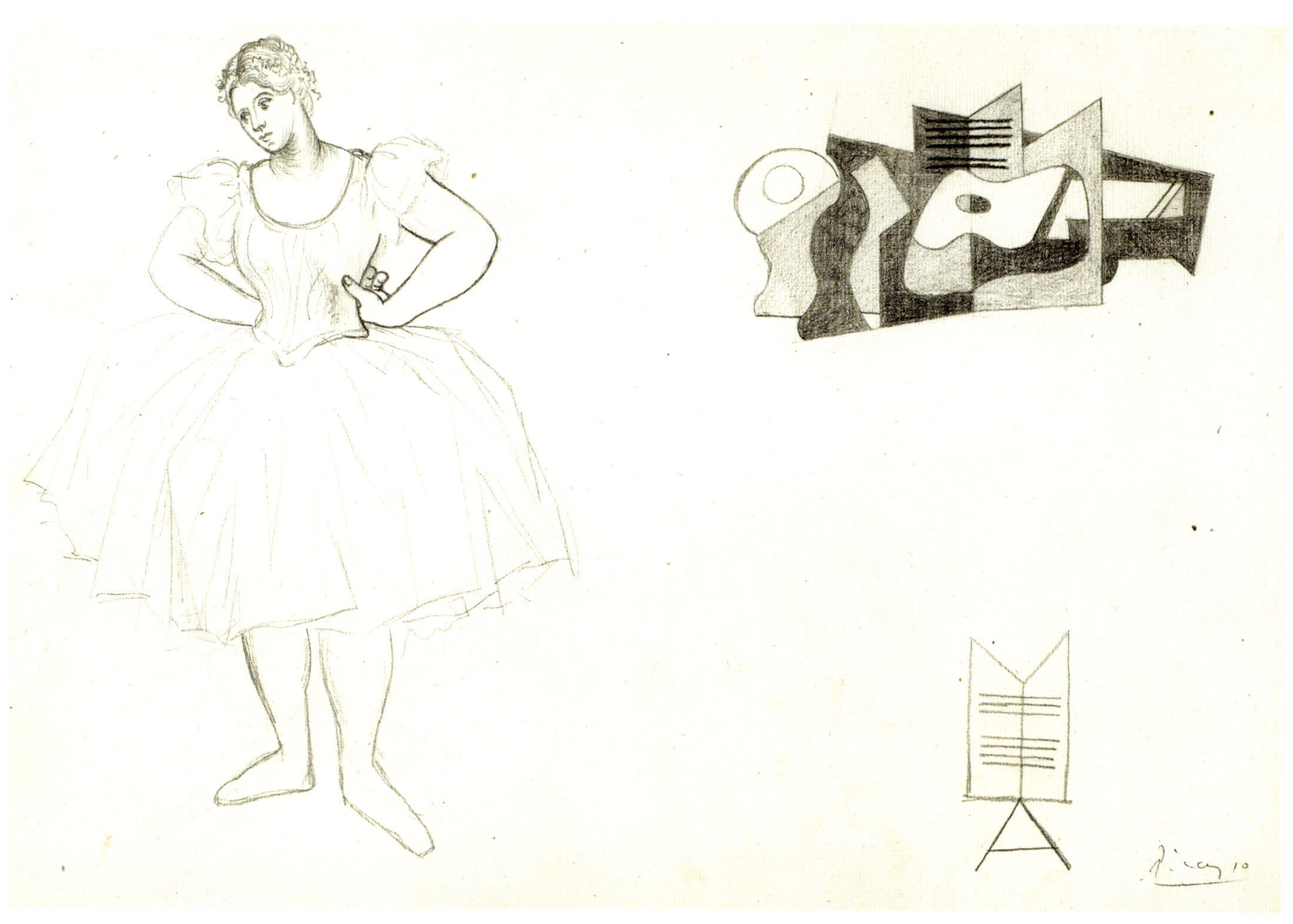

122. Pablo Picasso
Danseuse et Composition Cubiste
[Ballerina and Cubist Composition],
1919
Pencil on paper, 21.8 x 31.5 cm
Private collection, on loan to
Staatliche Museen zu Berlin,
Nationalgalerie, Museum Berggruen

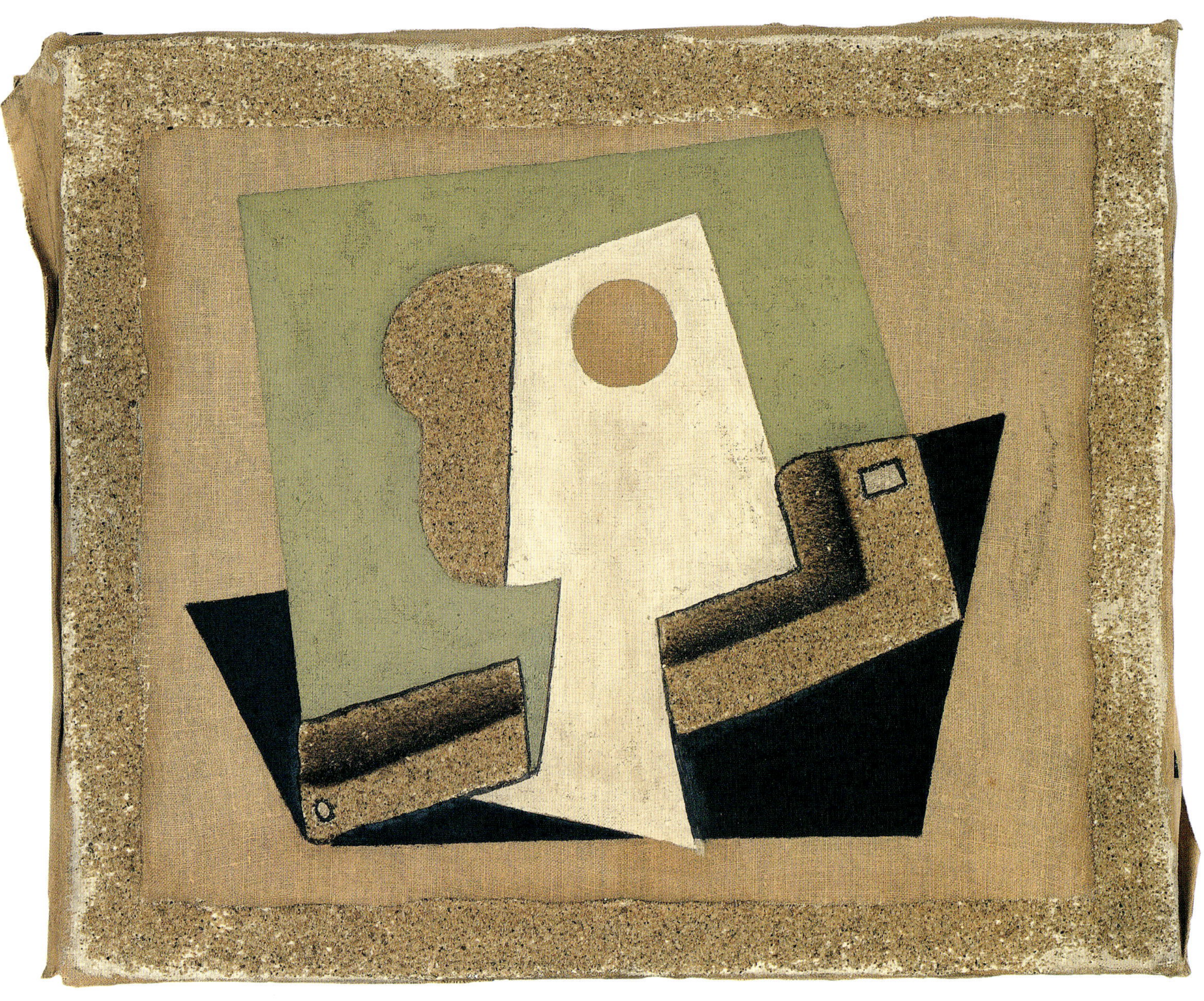

123. Pablo Picasso
Composition au verre et à la pipe
[Composition with Glass and Pipe],
Montrouge, 1917
Oil and sand on canvas, 22 x 27 cm
Brusselles, Fundación Almine y
Bernard Ruiz-Picasso para el Arte,
inv. 12174

124. Pablo Picasso
Nature morte à la guitare devant une fenêtre [Still Life with Guitar
by a Window], Saint-Raphaël,
Summer 1919
Pastel and watercolour on paper,
34 x 23.5 cm
Brussels, Fundación Almine y
Bernard Ruiz-Picasso para el Arte,
inv. 02549

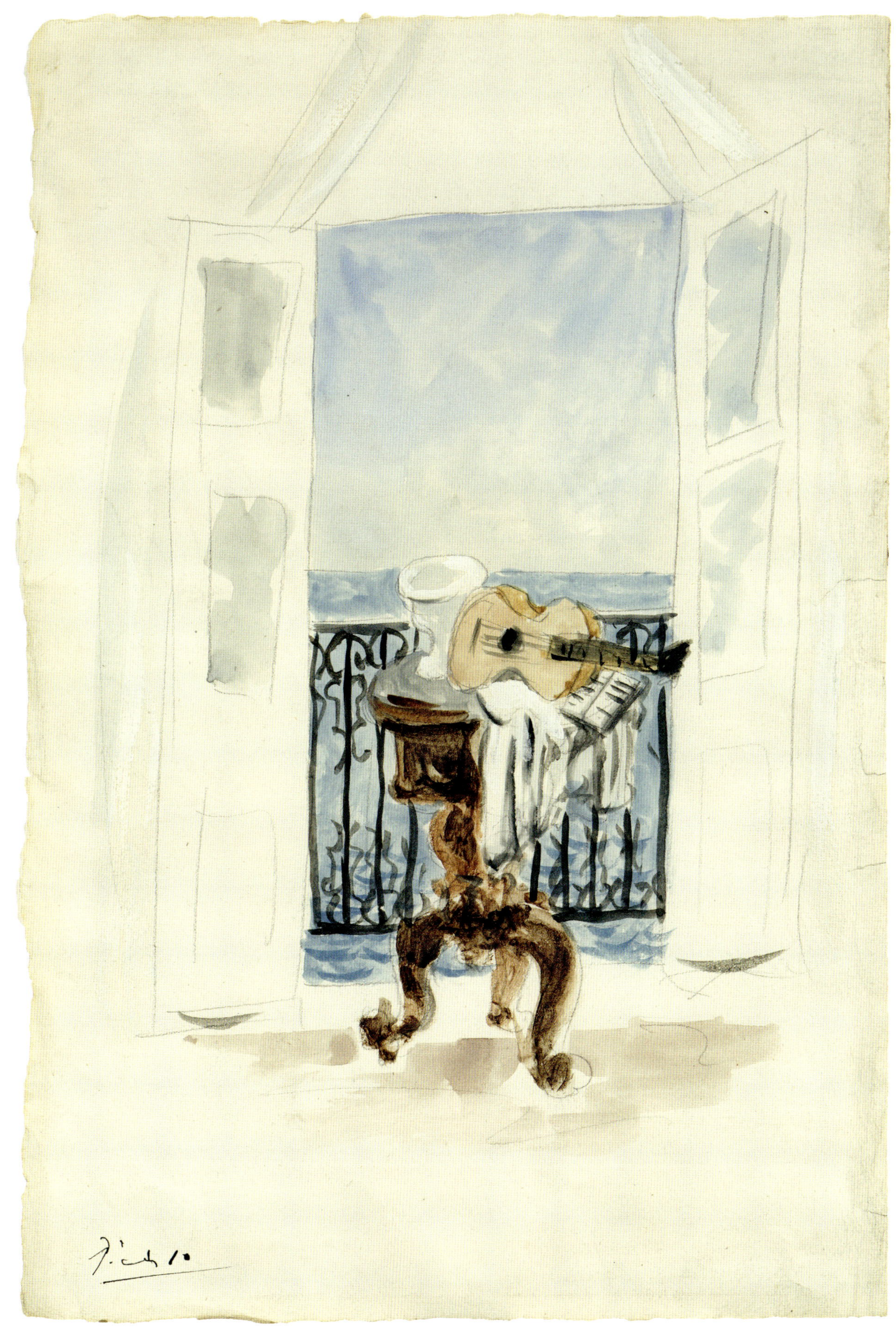

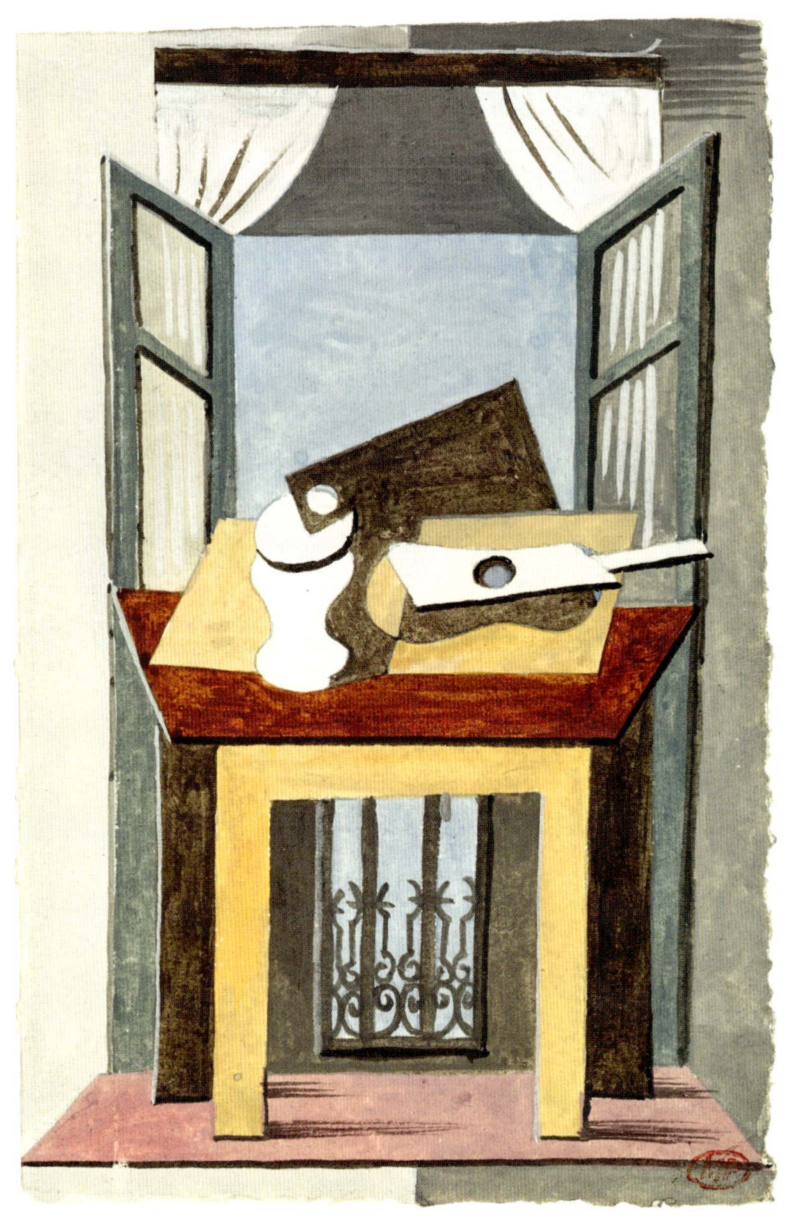

125. Pablo Picasso
Nature morte sur une table devant une fenêtre ouverte [Still Life on a Table by an Open Window], Paris, 26 October 1919
Gouache on drawing paper, 15.7 x 10.6 cm
Paris, Musée national Picasso-Paris, Pablo Picasso Donation, 1979, inv. MP859

126. Pablo Picasso
Nature morte devant une fenêtre [Still Life by a Window], Saint-Raphaël, 1919
Gouache and pencil on paper, 35.5 x 25 cm
Berlin, Staatliche Museen zu Berlin, Nationalgalerie, Museum Berggruen, inv. NG MB 31/2000

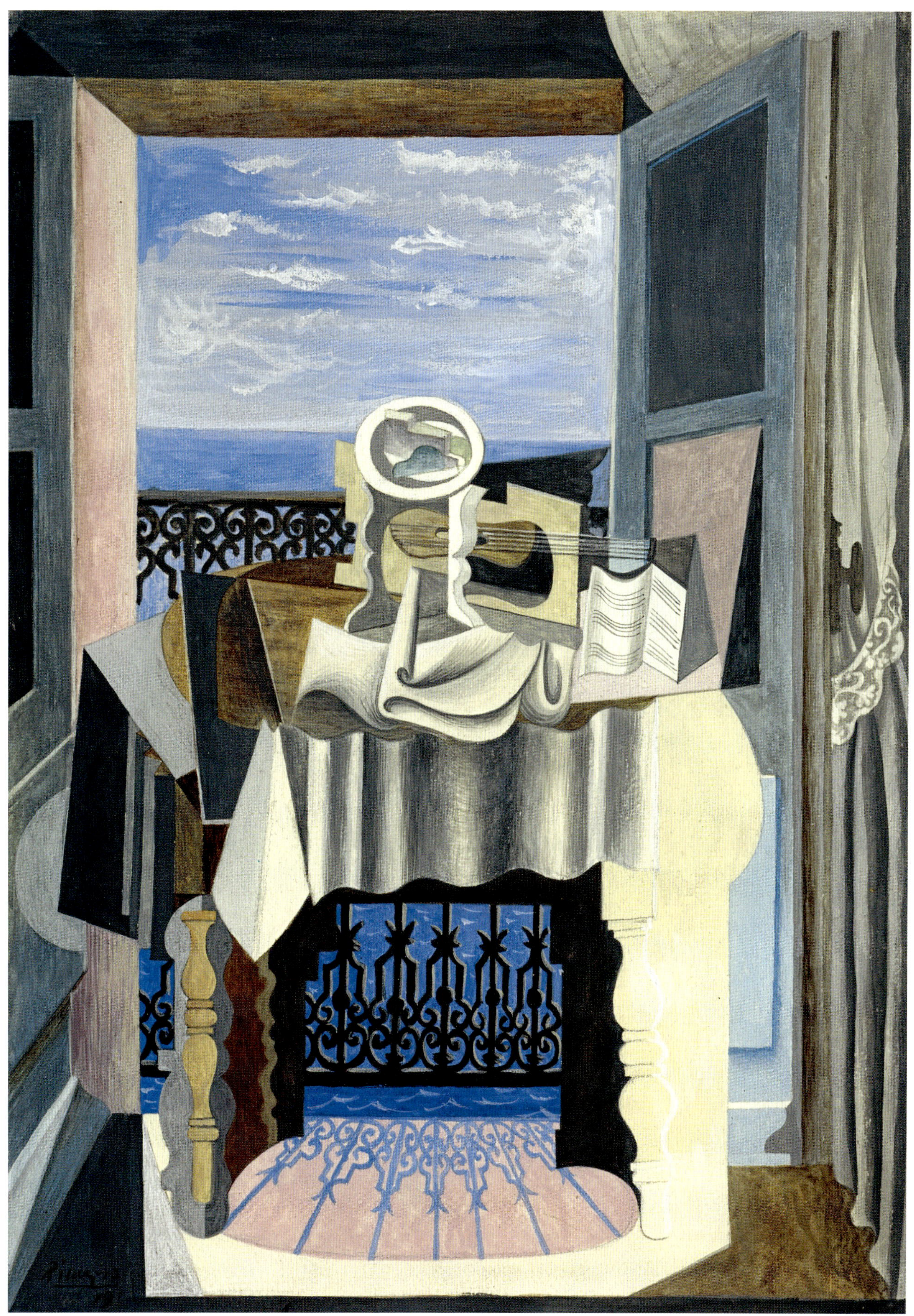

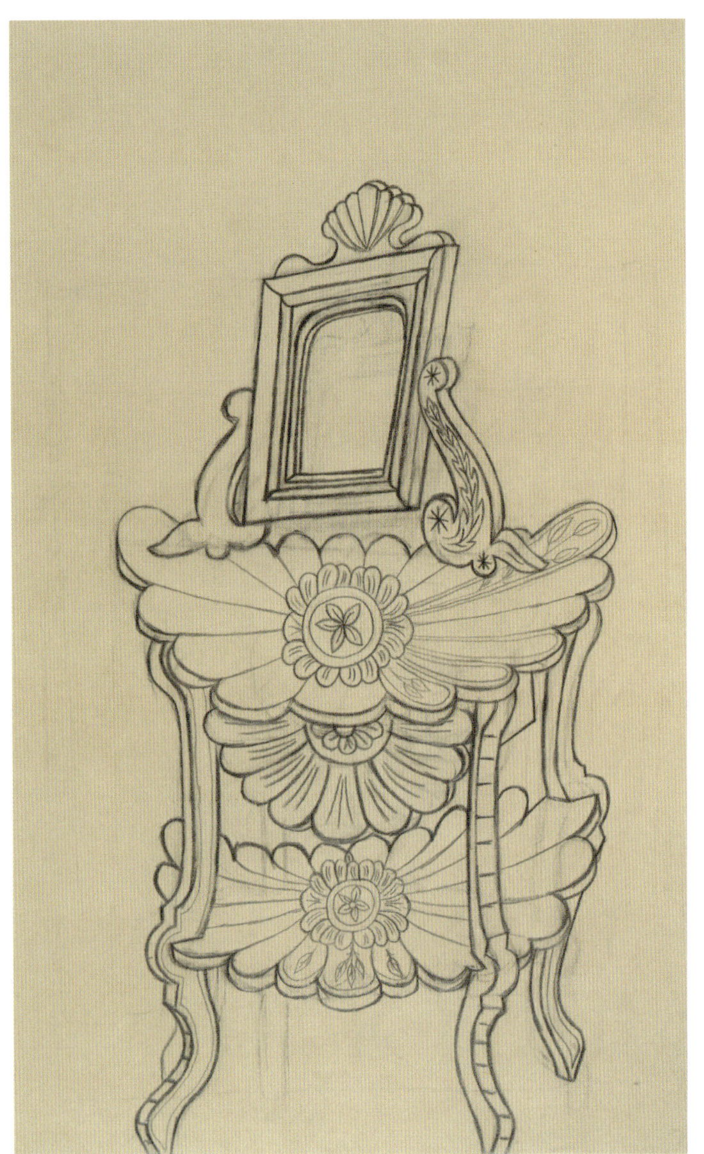

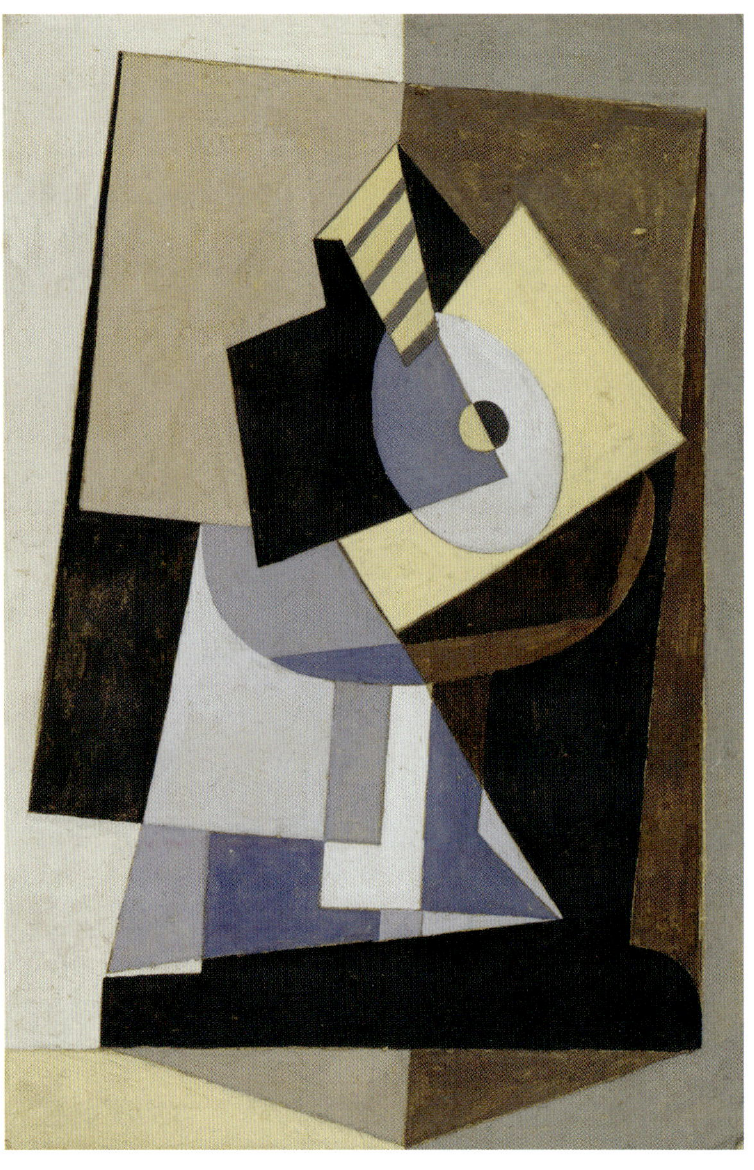

127. Pablo Picasso
La coiffeuse [Dressing Table], 1921
Pencil on paper
Private collection

128. Pablo Picasso
Mandoline sur un guéridon [Mandolin on a Table], Paris, 11 February 1920
Gouache on pasteboard, 30 x 20 cm
Paris, Musée national Picasso-Paris, Pablo Picasso Donation, 1979, inv. MP876

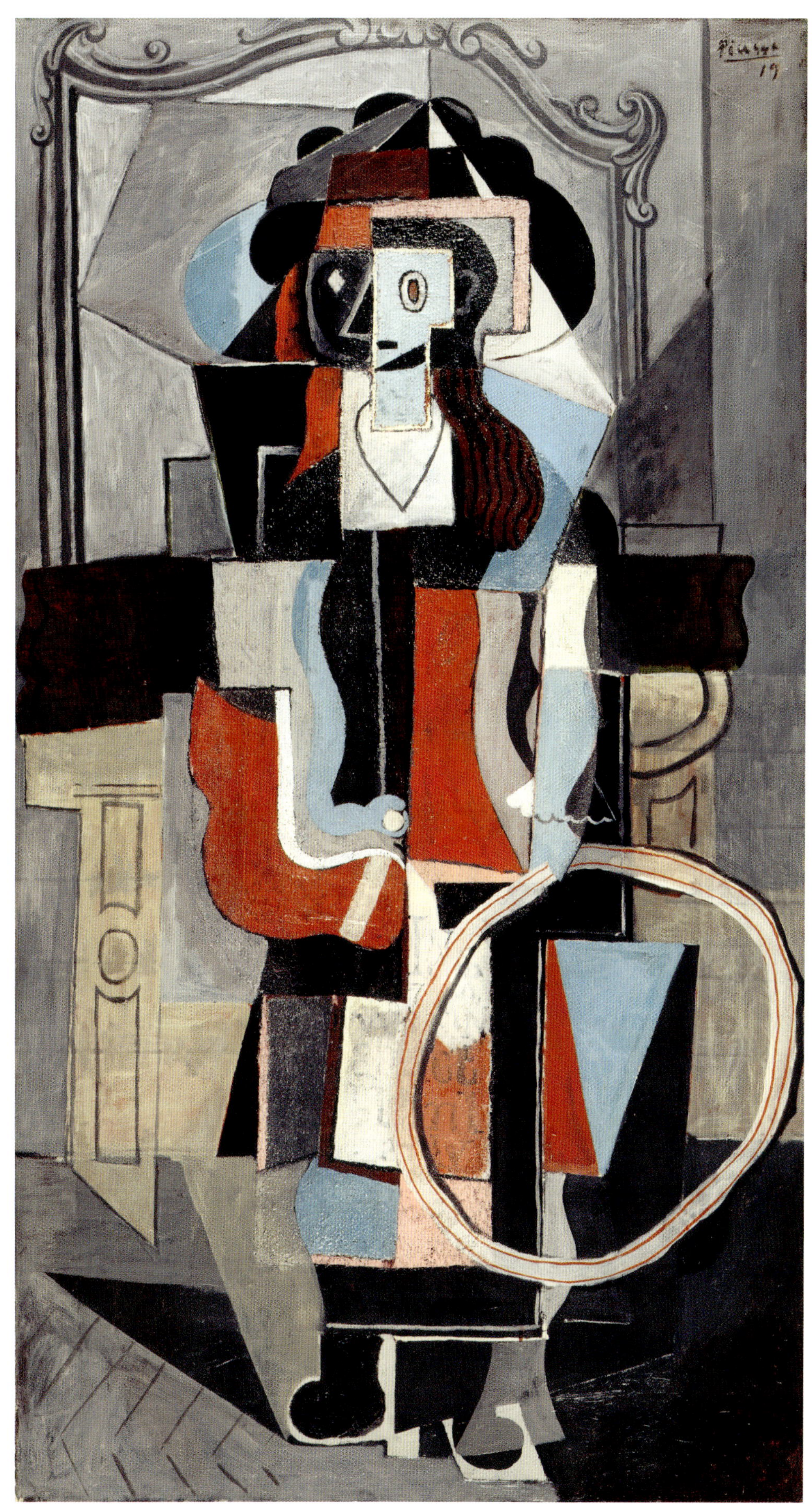

129. Pablo Picasso
Fillette au cerceau
[Girls with a Hoop], 1919
Oil and sand on canvas,
142.5 x 79 cm
Paris, Centre Georges Pompidou,
Musée National d'Art Moderne /
Centre de création industrielle,
inv. AM 4312 P

VI. The Harlequin and the Muse

130. Pablo Picasso
Arlequin (Léonide Massine)
[Harlequin (Léonide Massine)], 1917
Oil on canvas, 117 x 89.5 cm
Barcelona, Museu Picasso,
Given by the Barcelona City Council,
1963, inv. MPB 10.941

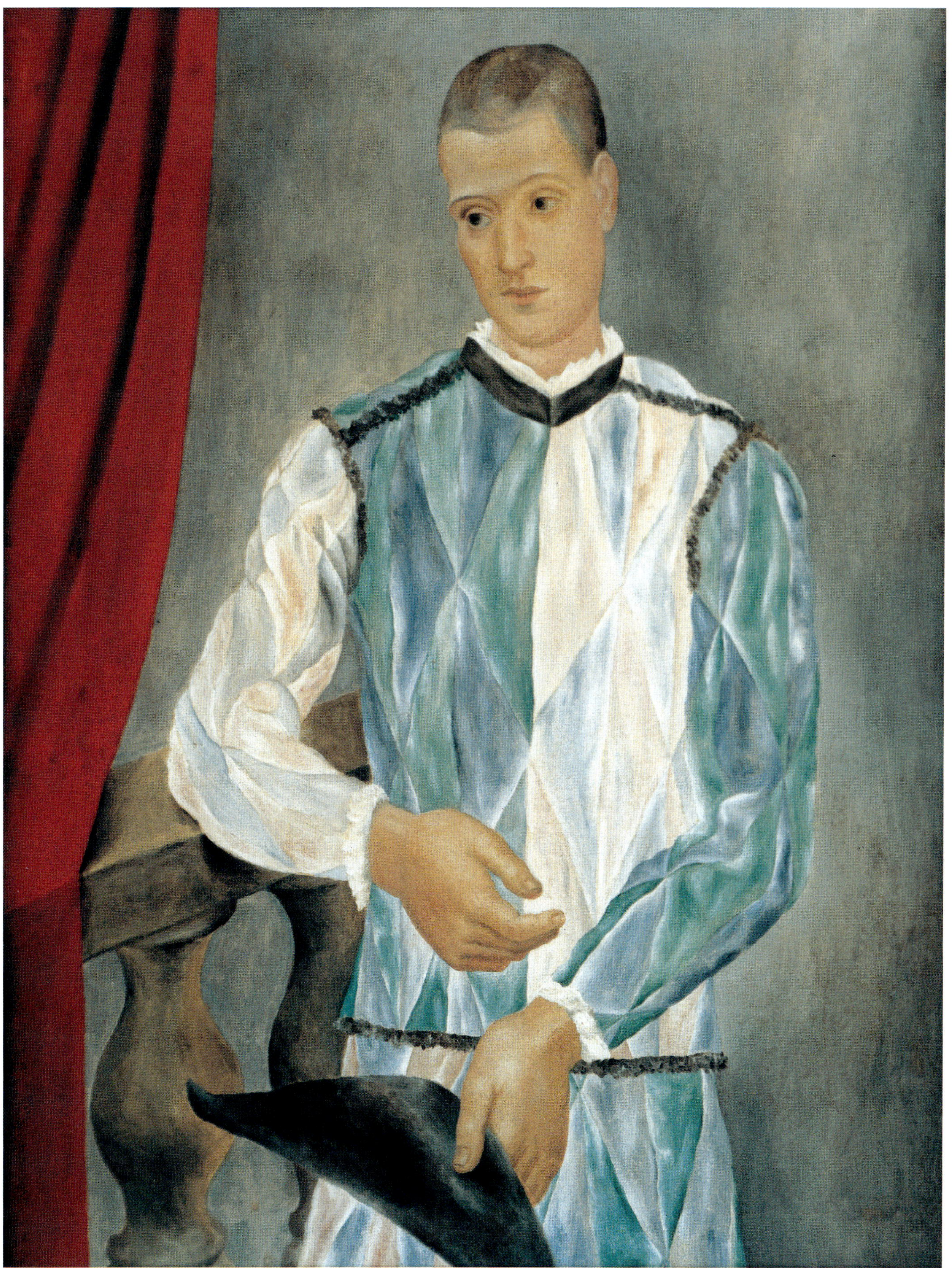

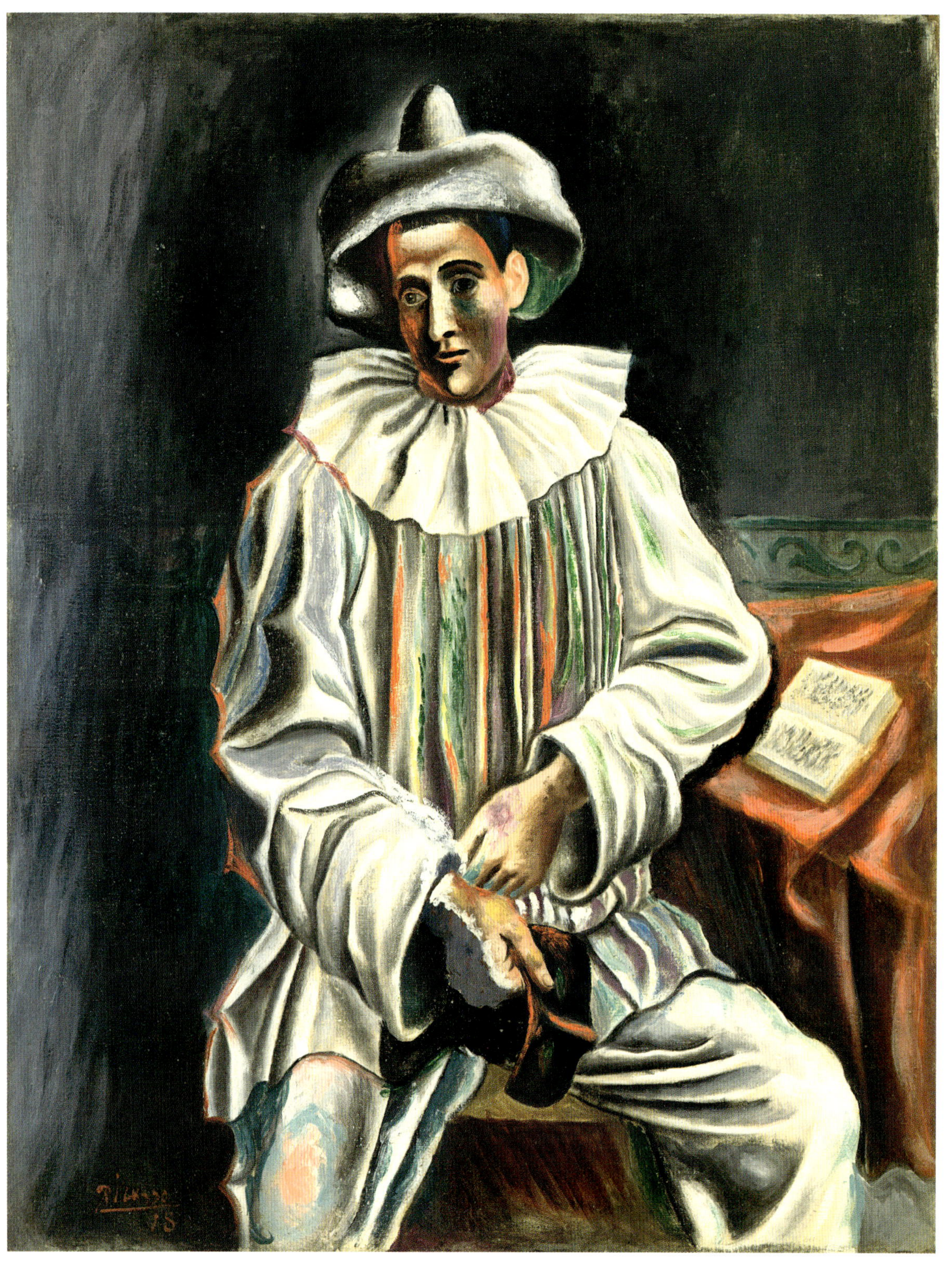

131. Pablo Picasso
Pierrot, 1918
Oil on canvas, 92.7 x 73 cm
New York, The Museum of Modern Art, Sam A. Lewisohn Bequest, 1952, inv. 121952

132. Pablo Picasso
Portrait d'Olga dans un fauteuil
[Portrait of Olga in an Armchair], Montrouge, Spring 1918
Oil on canvas, 130 x 88.8 cm
Paris, Musée national Picasso-Paris, Pablo Picasso Donation, 1979, inv. MP55

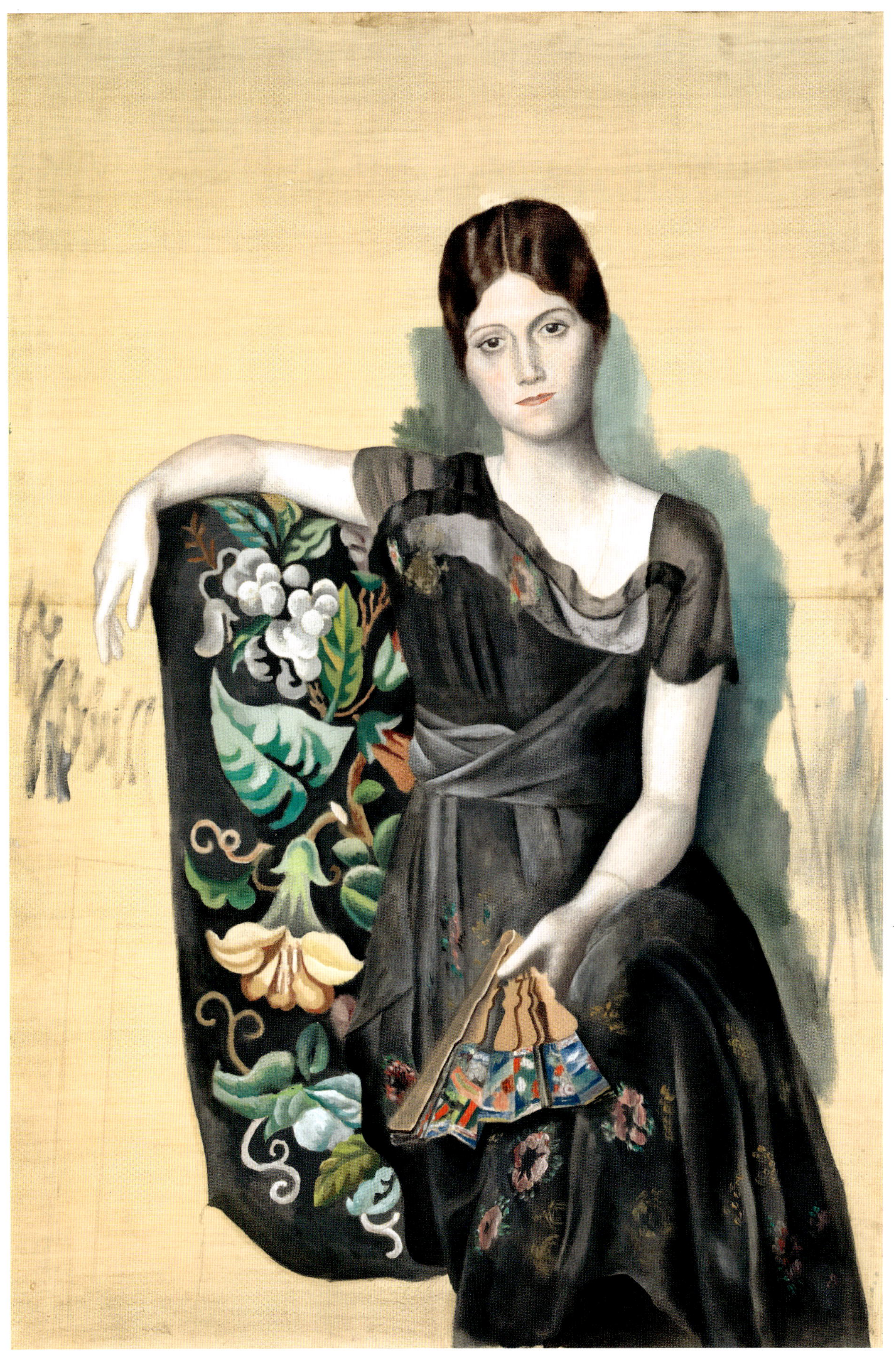

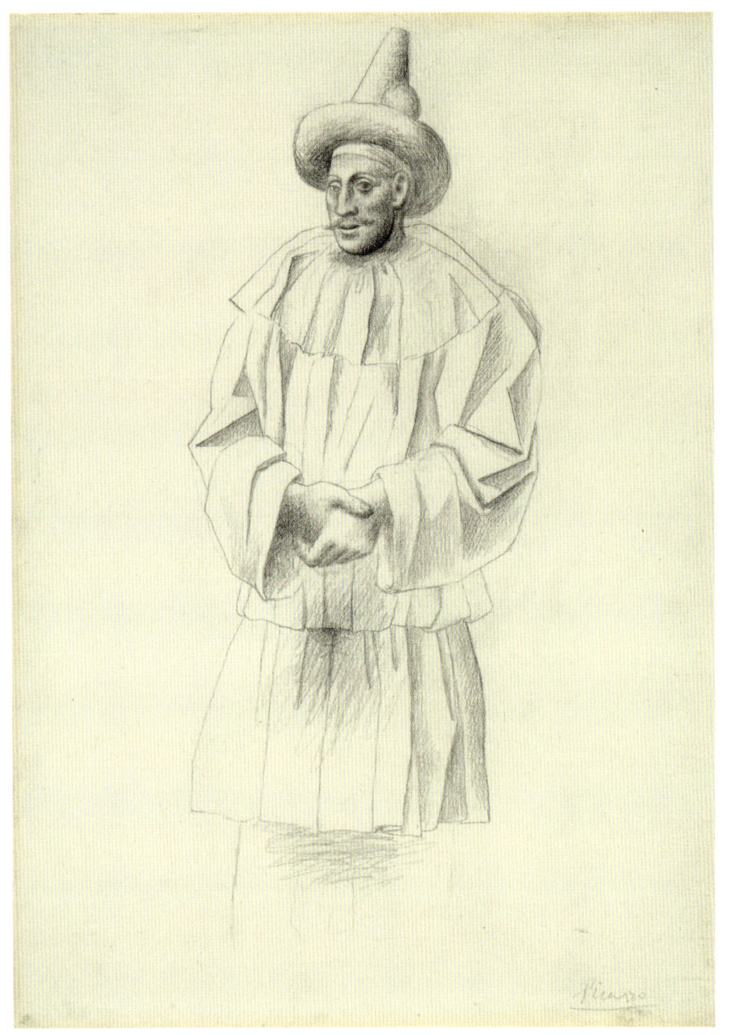

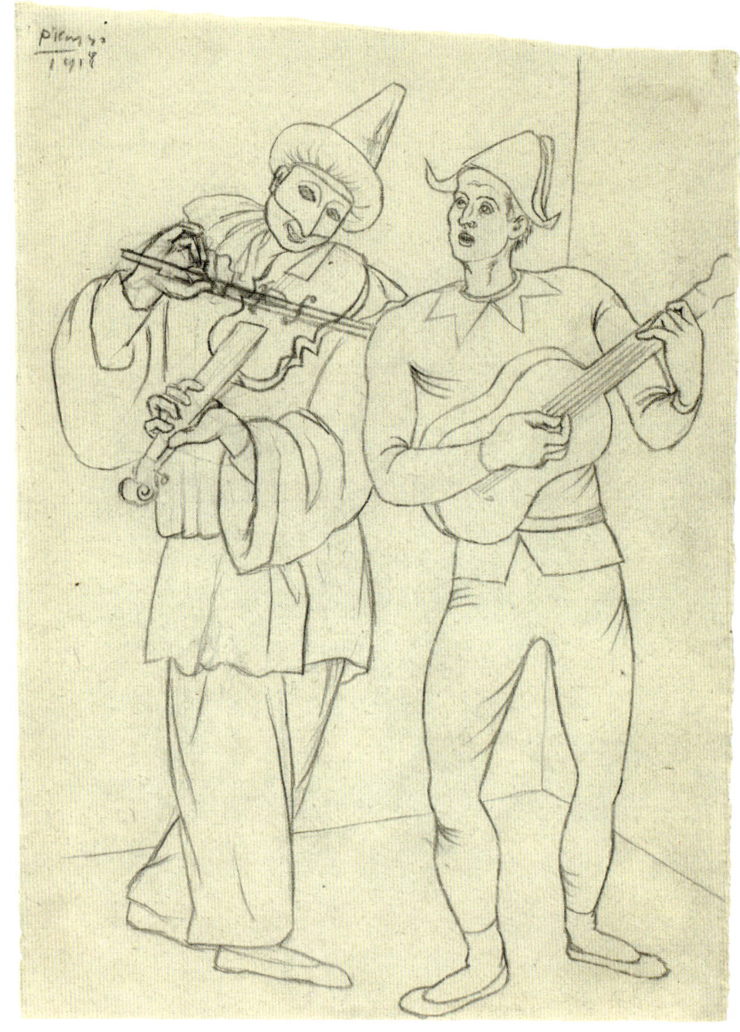

133. Pablo Picasso
Pierrot, 1918
Pencil on paper, 34.1 x 25 cm
Chicago, Art Institute of Chicago,
Gift of Dorothy Braude Edinburg
to the Harry B. and Bessie K. Braude
Memorial Collection, inv. 1998.718

134. Pablo Picasso
Pierrot et Arlequin
[Pierrot and Harlequin], 1918
Pencil on paper, 26.5 x 19.5 cm
Chicago, Art Institute of Chicago,
Given in memory of Charles Barnett
Goodspeed by Mrs. Charles
B. Goodspeed, inv. 1947.875

135. Pablo Picasso
Arlequin avec guitare
[Harlequin with Guitar], 1918
Oil on panel, 35x 27 cm
Berlin, Staatliche Museen zu Berlin,
Nationalgalerie, Museum Berggruen,
inv. NG MB 30/2000

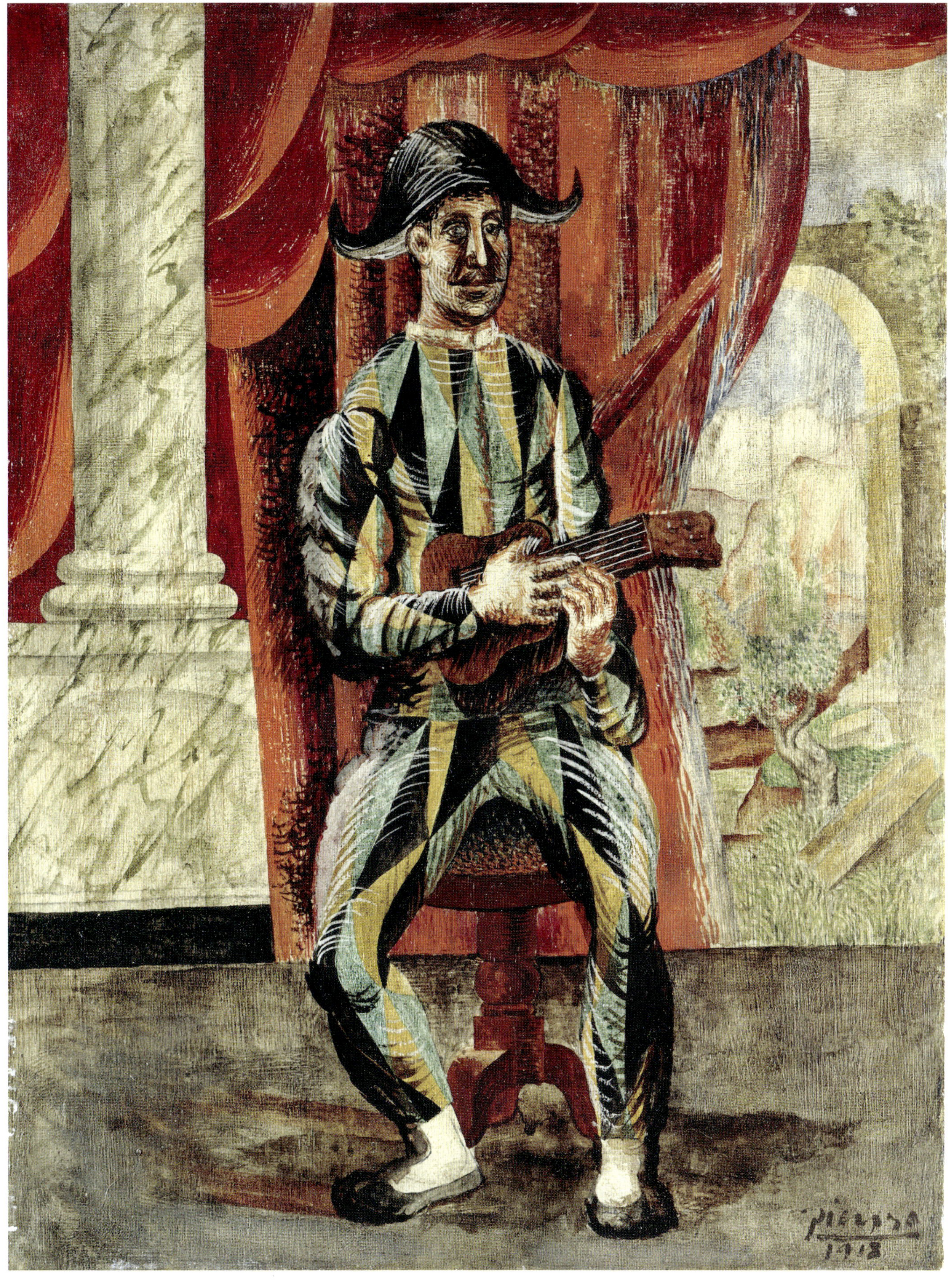

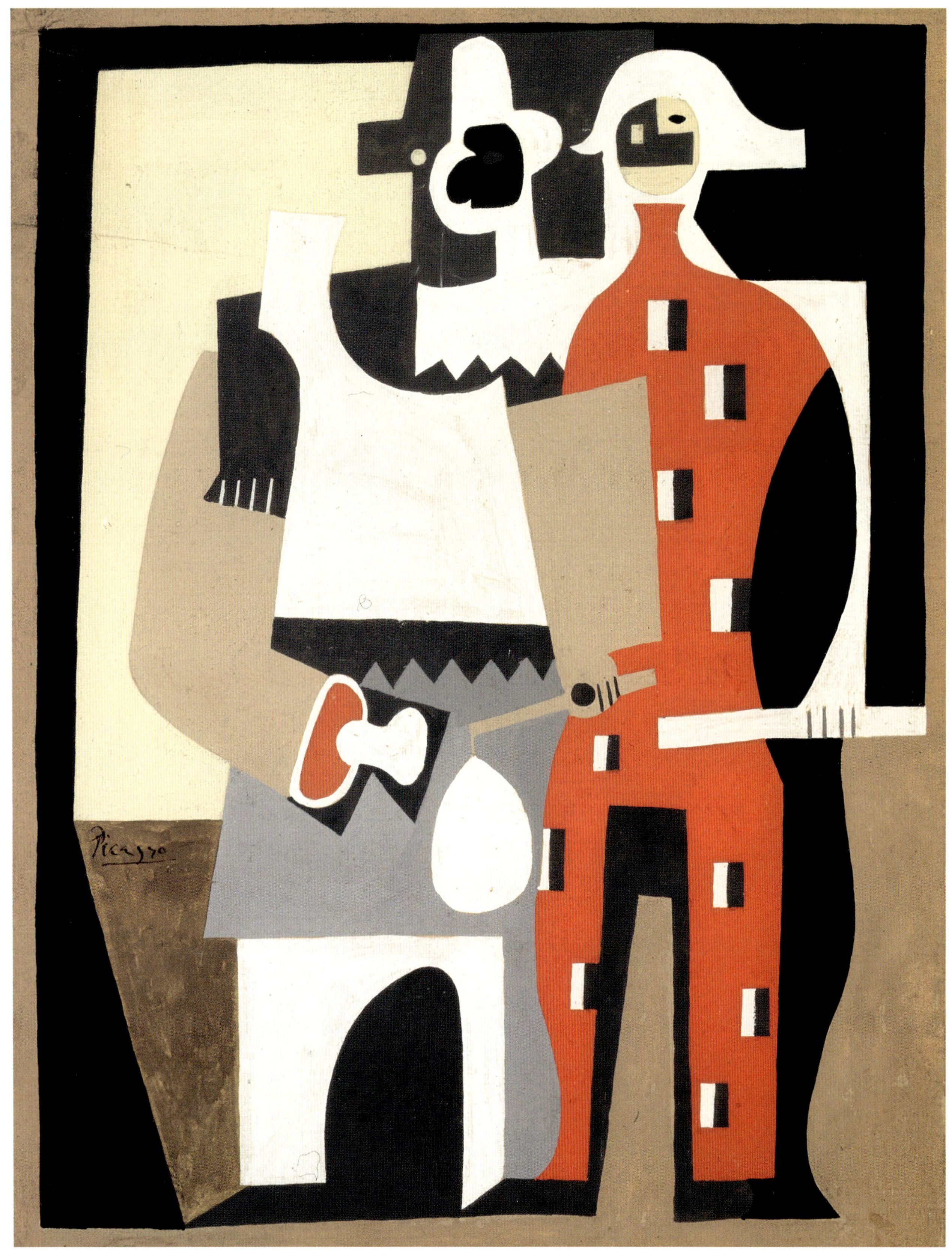
Picasso

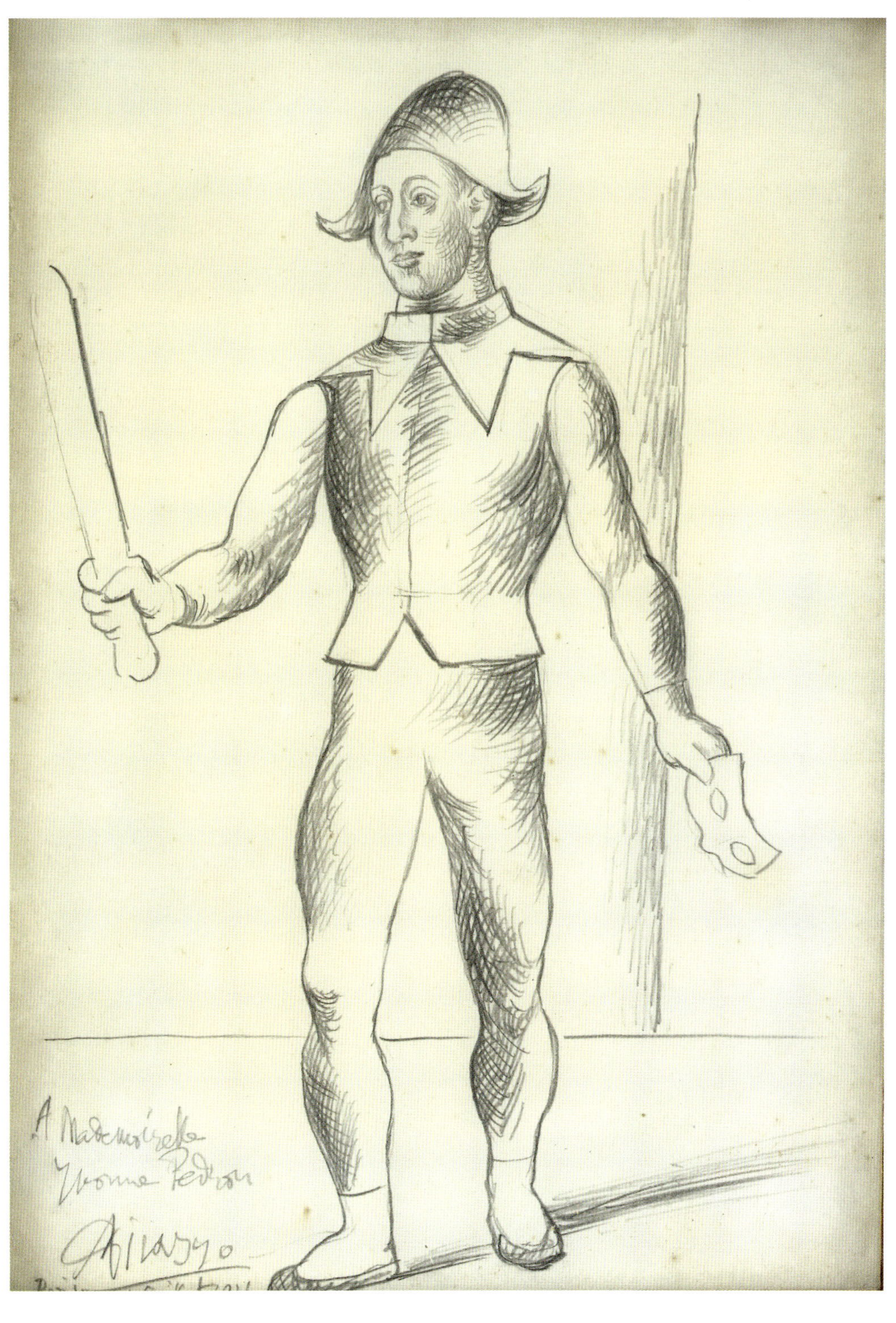

136. Pablo Picasso
Pierrot et Arlequin
[Pierrot and Harlequin], 1920
Watercolour on paper, 26.6 x 21 cm
New York, private collection

137. Pablo Picasso
Arlequin [Harlequin], 1916
Pencil on paper, 20 x 14.5 cm
Nicolas Berggruen Charitable Foundation

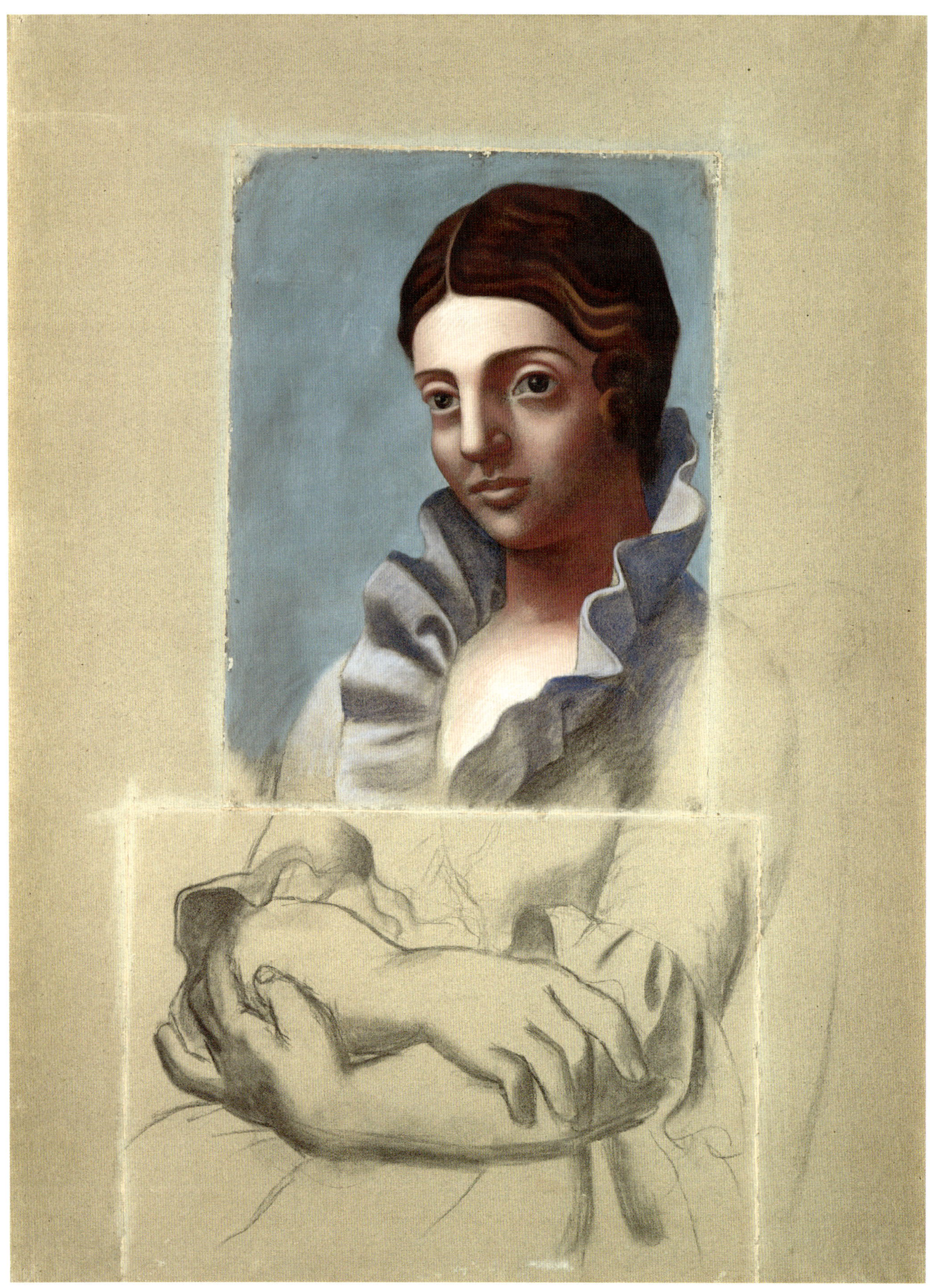

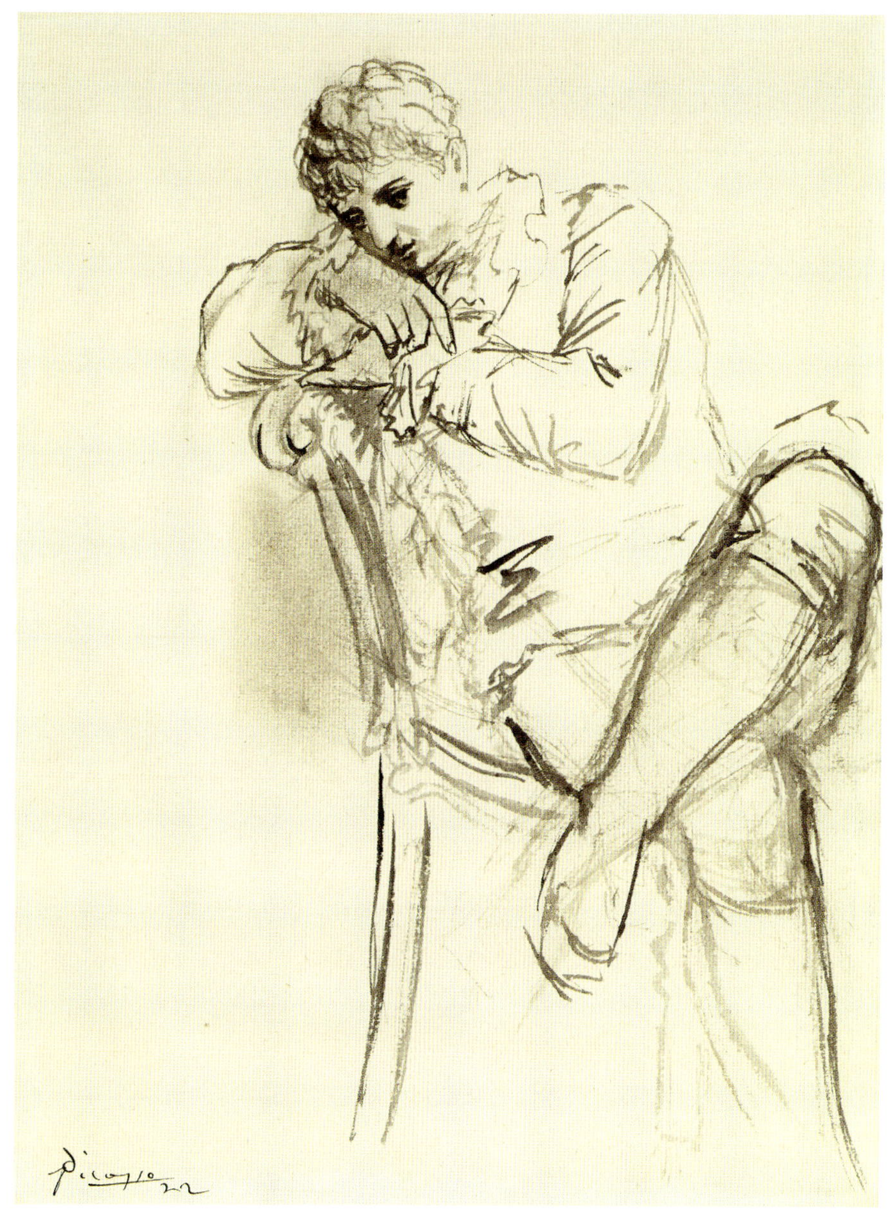

138. Pablo Picasso
Portrait d'Olga [Portrait of Olga],
1921
Pastel and charcoal on paper glued to canvas, 127 x 96.5 cm
Paris, Musée national Picasso-Paris, Jacqueline Picasso Donation, 1990, inv. MP 1990-70
(work not exhibited)

139. Pablo Picasso
Saltimbanque accoudé sur une chaise [Acrobat Sitting on a Chair],
1922
Pencil on paper, 29.2 x 22.7 cm
Zurich, private collection

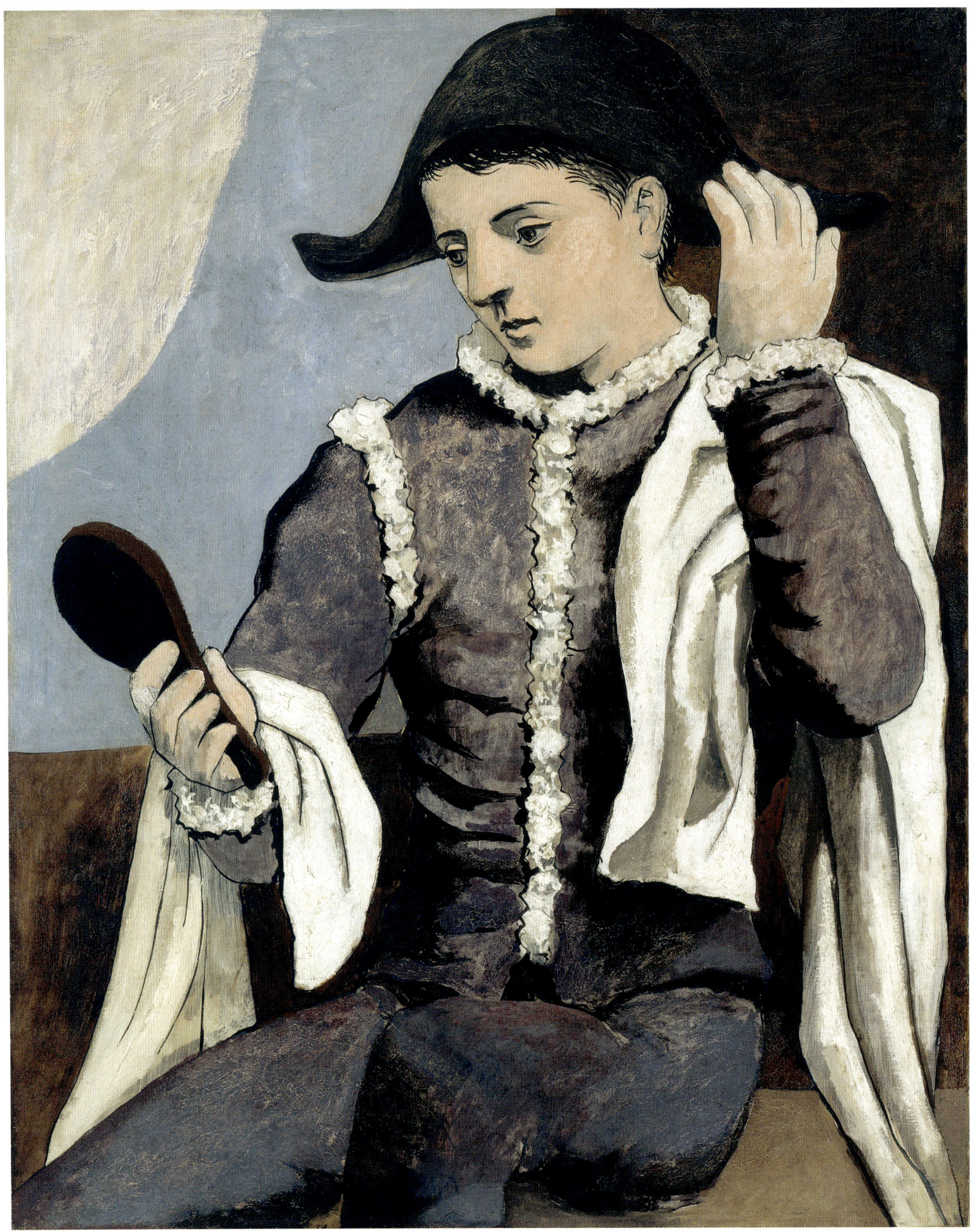

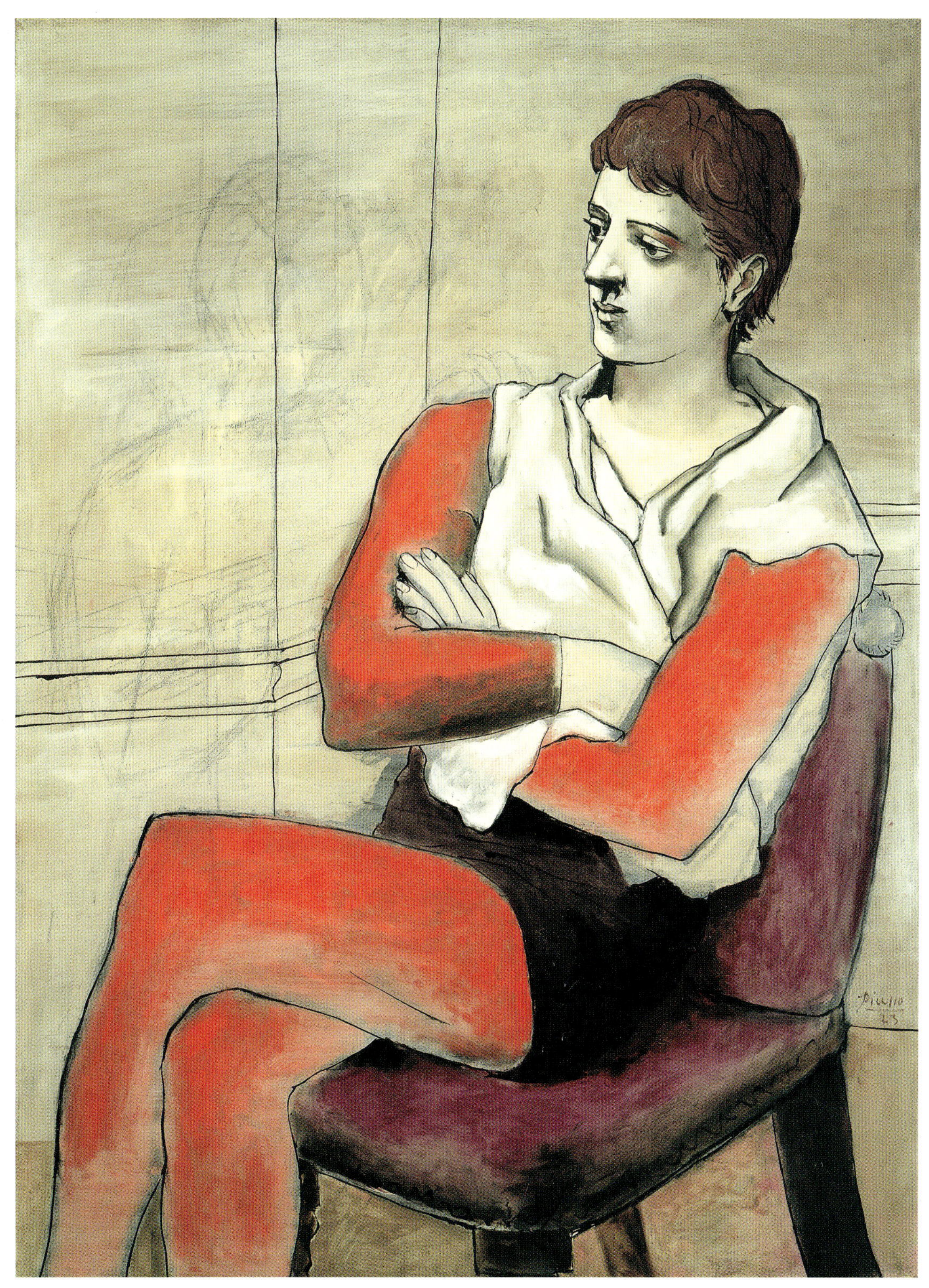

140. Pablo Picasso
Arlequin au miroir
[Harlequin with a mirror], 1923
Oil on canvas, 100 x 81 cm
Madrid, Museo Thyssen-Bornemisza, inv. 709 (1979.87)

141. Pablo Picasso
Saltimbanque assis, les bras croisés
[Seated Acrobat with Folded Arms], Paris, 1923
Oil on canvas, 130.5 x 97 cm
Tokyo, Bridgestone Museum of Art, Ishibashi Foundation

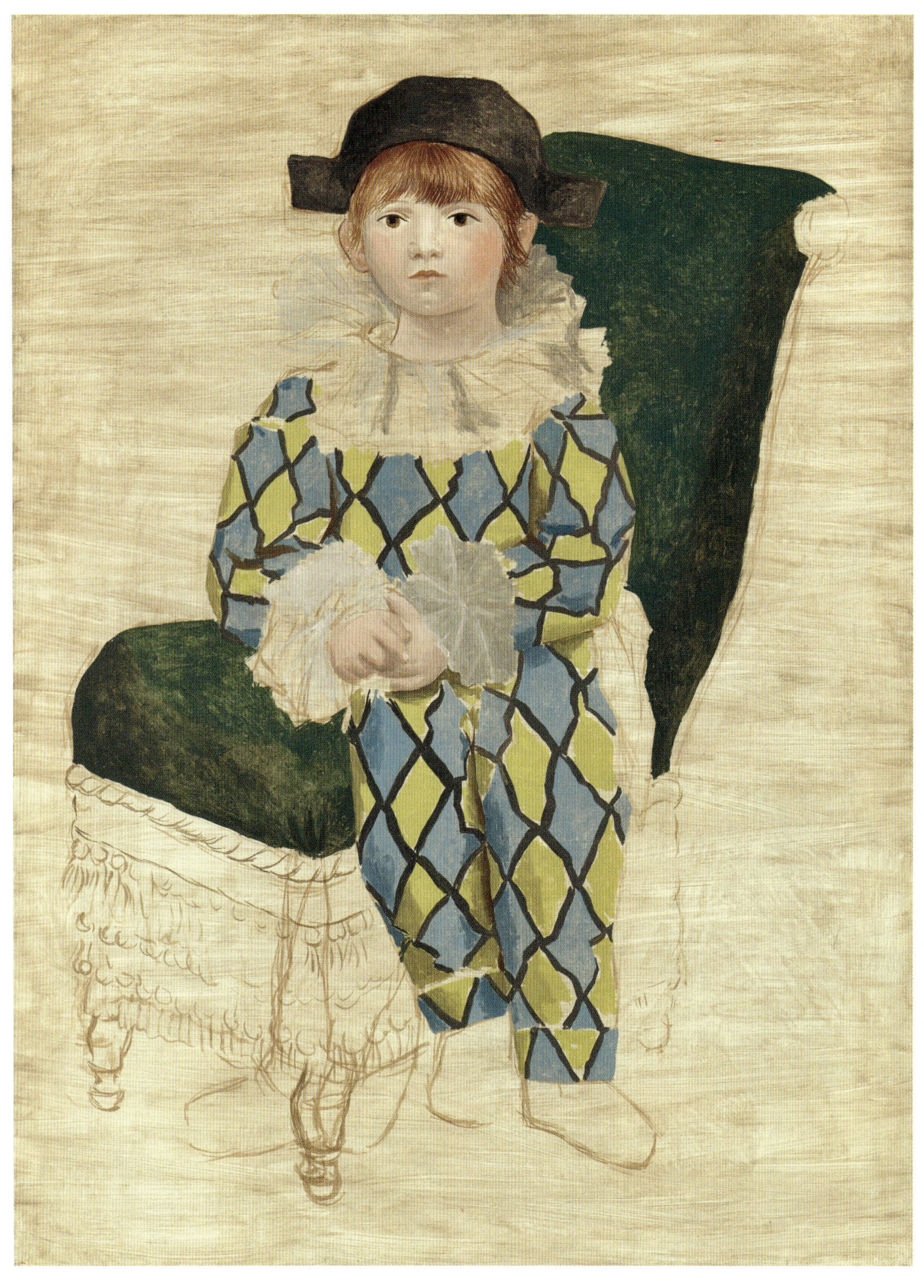

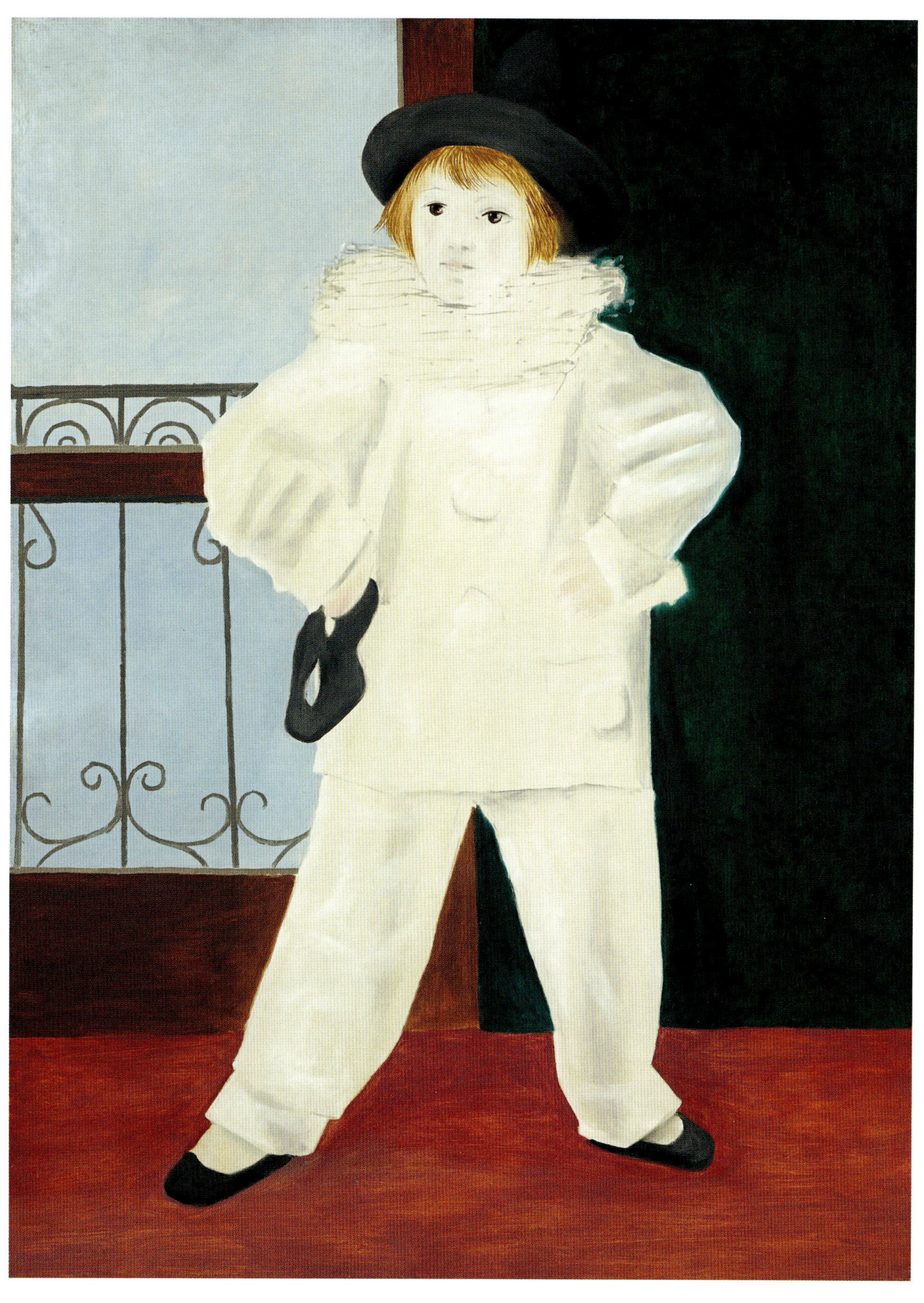

142. Pablo Picasso
Paul en Arlequin [Paul Dressed as Harlequin], Paris, 1924
Oil on canvas, 130 x 97.5 cm
Paris, Musée national Picasso-Paris, Pablo Picasso Donation, 1979, inv. MP83

143. Pablo Picasso
Paul en Pierrot [Paul Dressed as Pierrot], Paris, 28 February 1925
Oil on canvas, 130 x 97 cm
Paris, Musée national Picasso-Paris, Pablo Picasso Donation, 1979, inv. MP84

VII. Commedia dell'arte

144. Pablo Picasso
Projet de costume pour le ballet "Le Tricorne": la dame avec l'Aragonais [Study for the costume of a lady with a mantilla for the ballet *Le Tricorne*], London, 1919
Gouache, watercolour and pencil on vellum drawing paper, 26.6 x 20 cm
Paris, Musée national Picasso-Paris, Pablo Picasso Donation, 1979, inv. MP1708

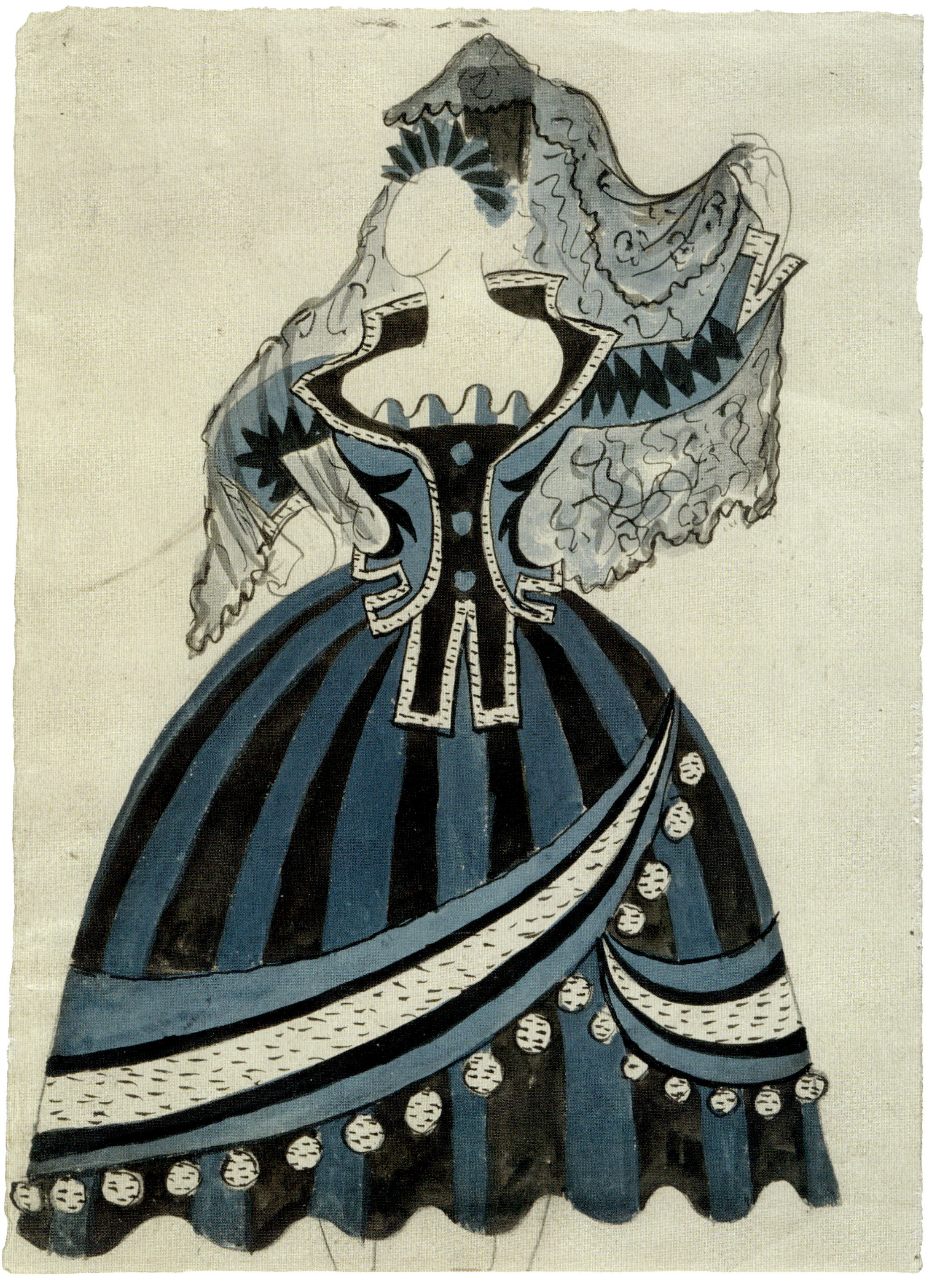

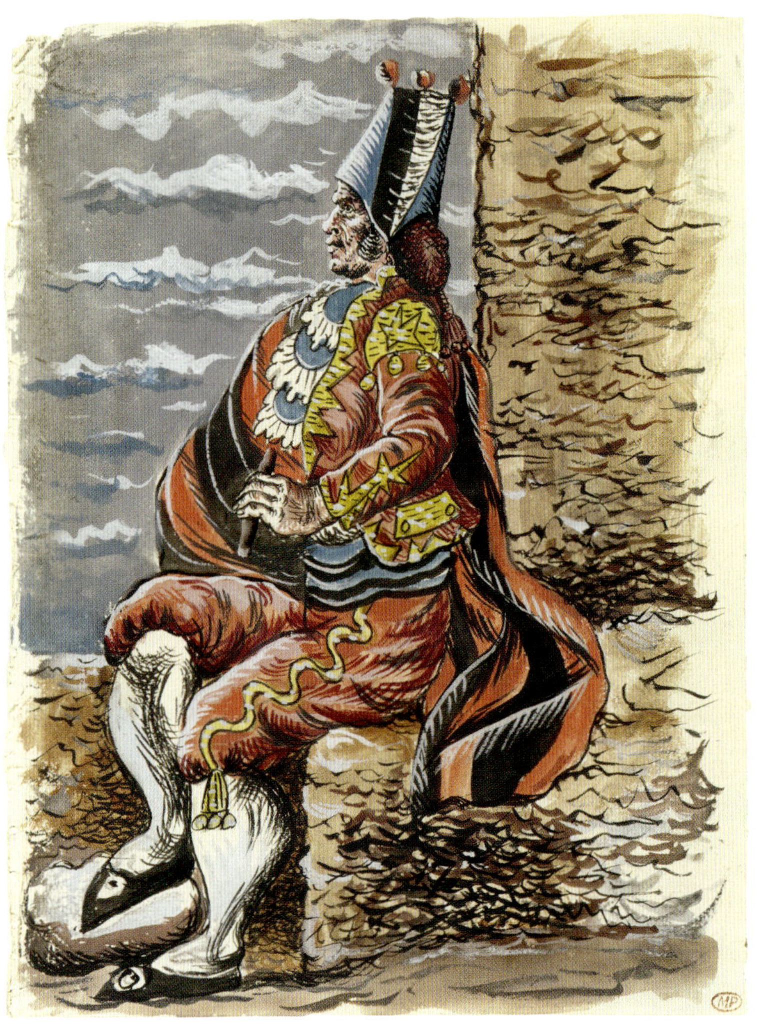

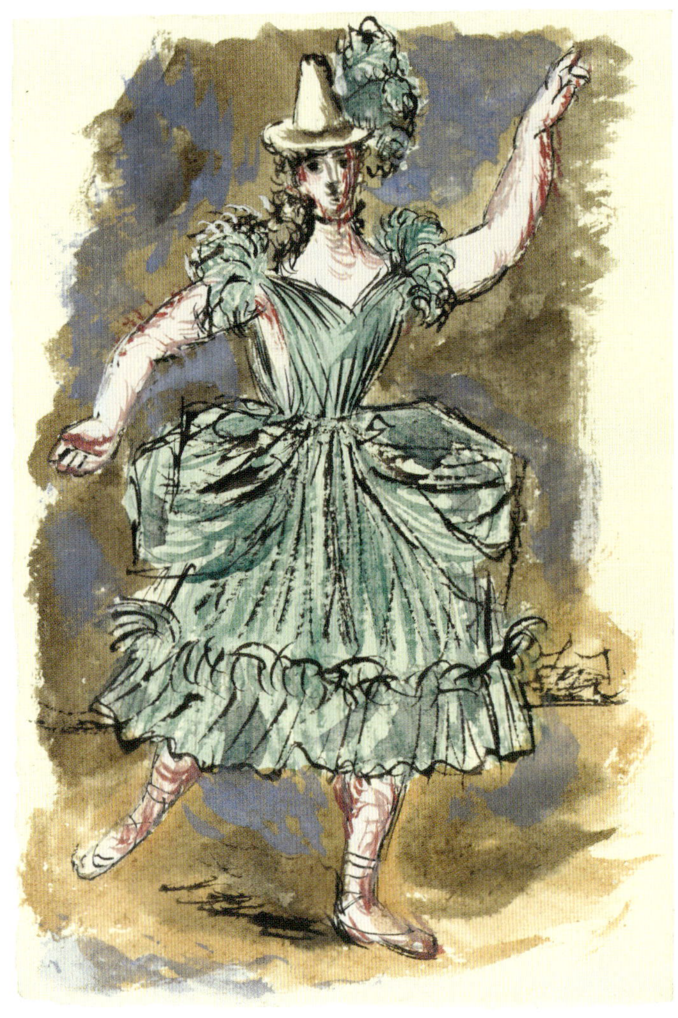

145. Pablo Picasso
Projet de costume pour le ballet "Le Tricorne": le torero [Study for the costume of the Bullfighter in the ballet *Le Tricorne*], London, 1919
Gouache, watercolour, pen and India ink on vellum drawing paper, 26 x 20 cm
Paris, Musée national Picasso-Paris, Pablo Picasso Donation, 1979, inv. MP1676

146. Pablo Picasso
Étude de costume pour le ballet "Pulcinella": Prudenza [Study for the costume of Prudenza in the ballet *Pulcinella*], Paris, 1920
Gouache, watercolour and India ink on drawing paper, 15.8 x 10.7 cm
Parigi, Musée national Picasso-Paris, Pablo Picasso Donation, 1979, inv. MP1809

147. Pablo Picasso
Projet de décor pour le ballet "Le Tricorne" [Study for the scenery of the ballet *Le Tricorne*], London, 1919
Gouache and pencil on vellum drawing paper, 10.7 x 13 cm
Paris, Musée national Picasso-Paris, Pablo Picasso Donation, 1979, inv. MP1640

148. Pablo Picasso
Étude de décor pour le ballet "Pulcinella" [Study for the scenery of the ballet *Pulcinella*], Paris, 1920
Gouache, watercolour and India ink on drawing paper, 26.5 x 34 cm
Paris, Musée national Picasso-Paris, Pablo Picasso Donation, 1979, inv. MP1750(r)

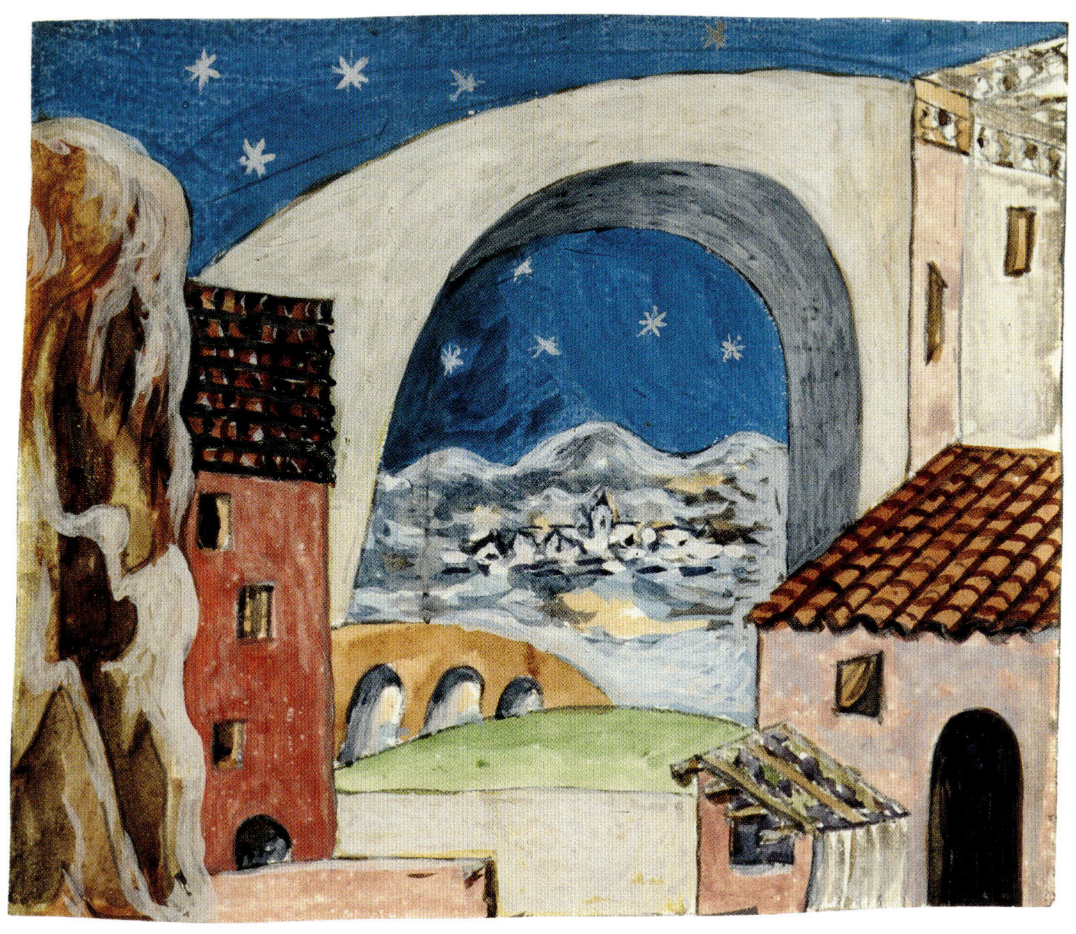

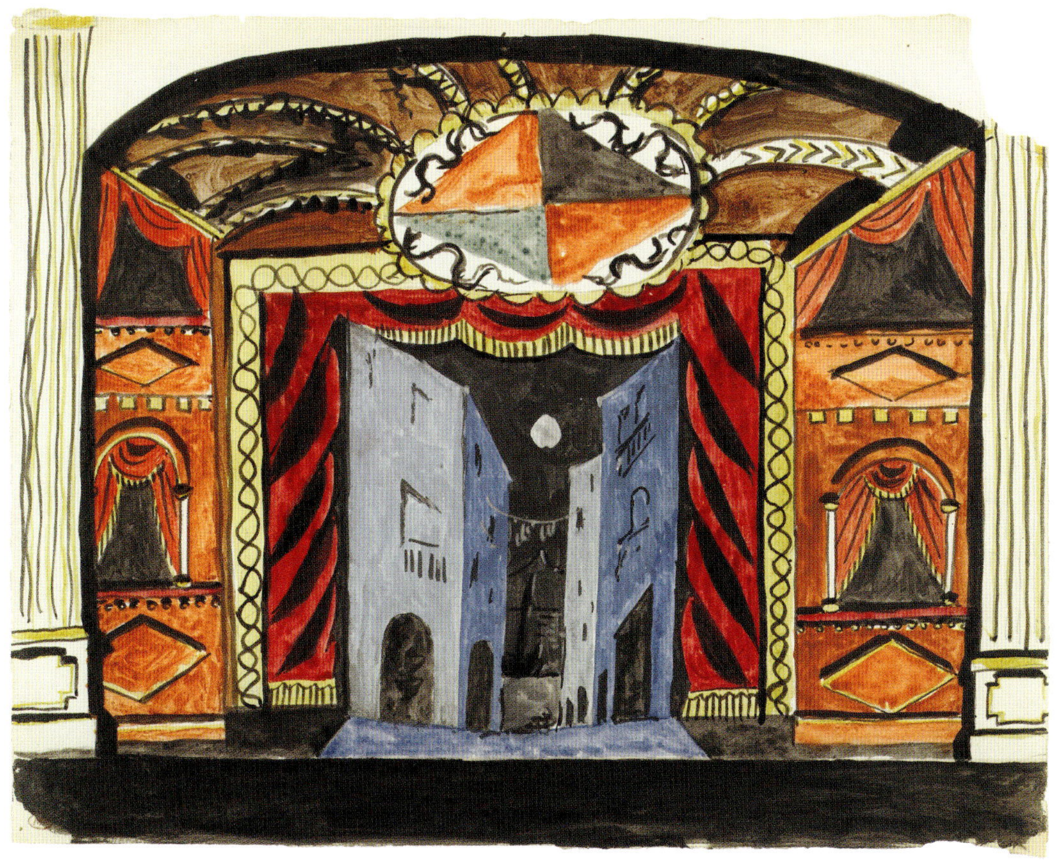

149. Anthony Gordon
Léonide Massine as the miller
in the ballet *Le Tricorne*, 1919
Gelatin silver print, 30 x 25 cm
Paris, Bibliothèque nationale de
France, Alb. Kochno "Tricorne" 28

150. Pablo Picasso
Pulcinella mask, 1920
Wood, paper and painted fabric,
17 x 14 x 21.5 cm
Paris, Musée national Picasso-Paris,
Pablo Picasso Donation, 1979,
inv. MP1790

151. Pablo Picasso
Projet de costume pour le ballet "Pulcinella": Pulcinella, Parigi
[Study for the costume of Pulcinella
in the ballet *Pulcinella*], Paris, 1920
Gouache, watercolour and pencil
on paper, 34 x 23.9 cm
Paris, Musée national Picasso-Paris,
Pablo Picasso Donation, 1979,
inv. MP1791

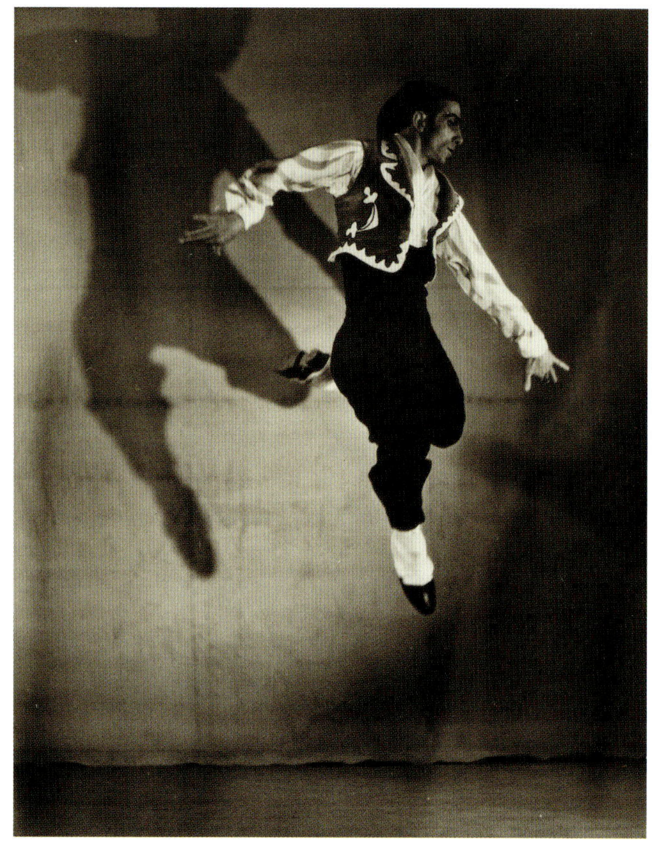

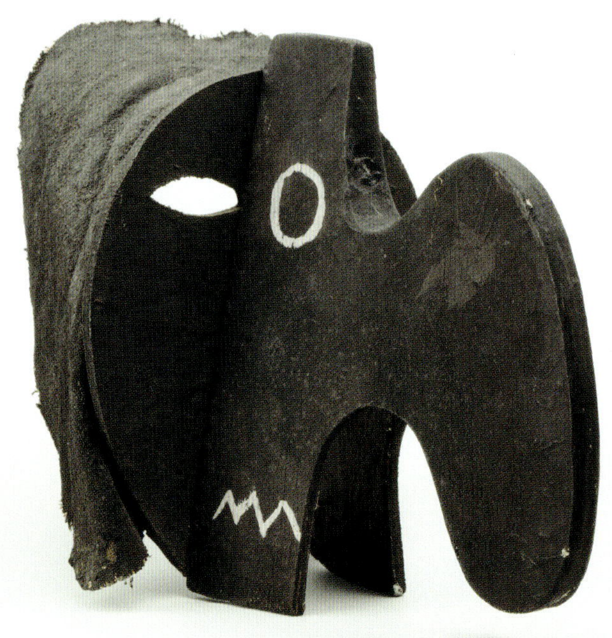

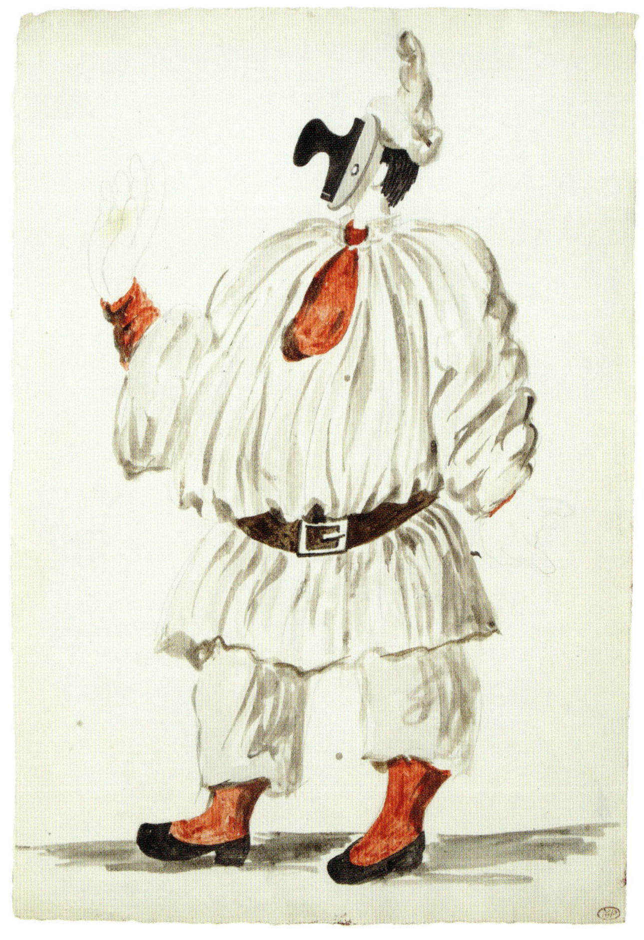

152. Pablo Picasso
Projet de décor pour le ballet “Cuadro flamenco” [Study for the scenery of the ballet *Cuadro flamenco*], 1921
Gouache and pencil on cut and glued paper, 23.5 x 34 cm
Paris, Musée national Picasso-Paris, Pablo Picasso Donation, 1979, inv. MP1824

153. Joseph Enrietti
Léonide Massine in the role of Pulcinella, 1920
Gelatin silver print, 16 x 8.5 cm
Paris, Bibliothèque nationale de France, Alb. Ph. Kochno “Pulcinella” pl.05

154. Leonide Massine
Pulcinella, 1919–20
Manuscript with annotations by Igor Stravinsky, October 1919
20 x 20.8 cm
Basel, Paul Sacher Foundation, Igor Stravinsky Collection

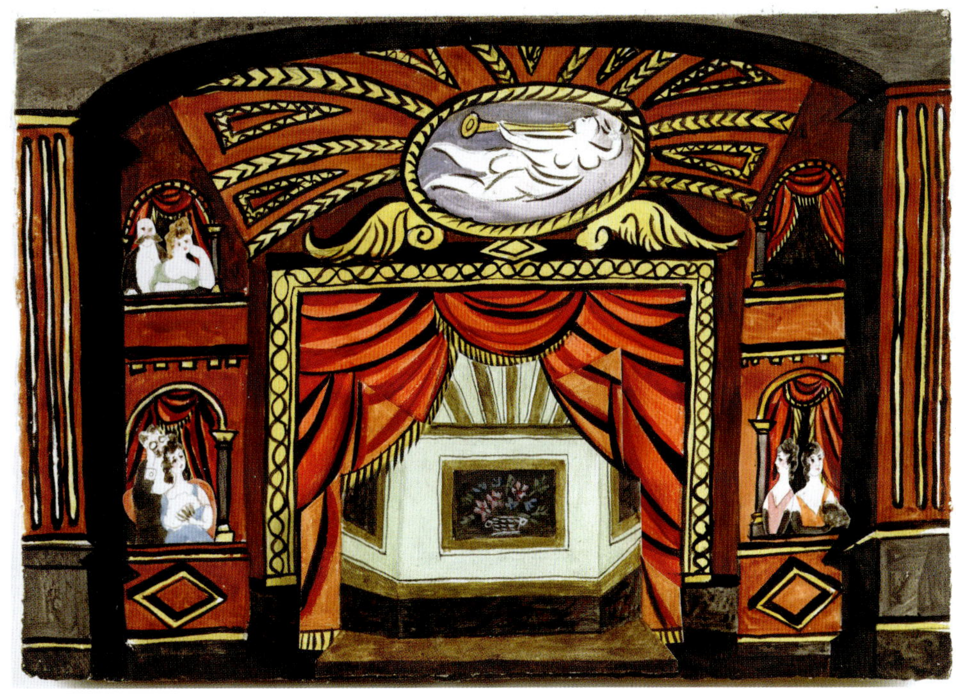

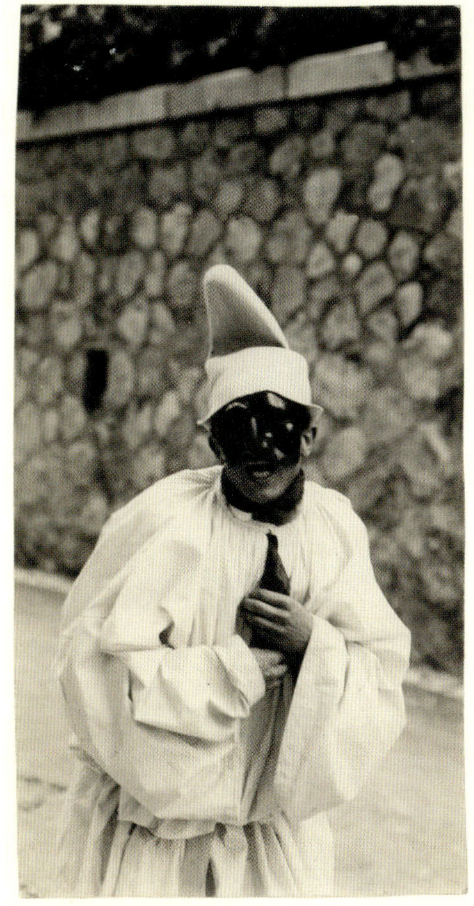

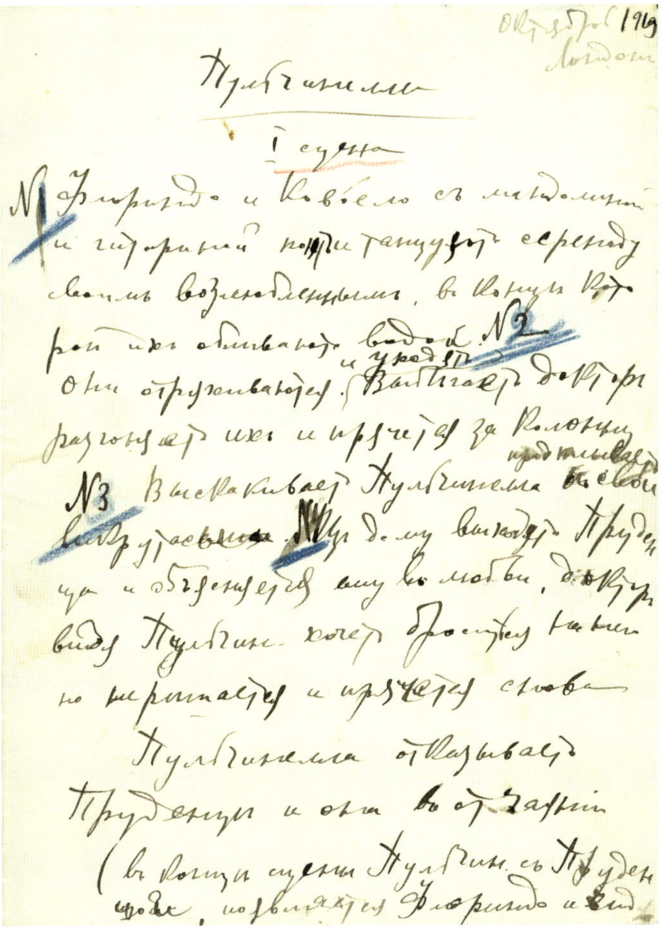

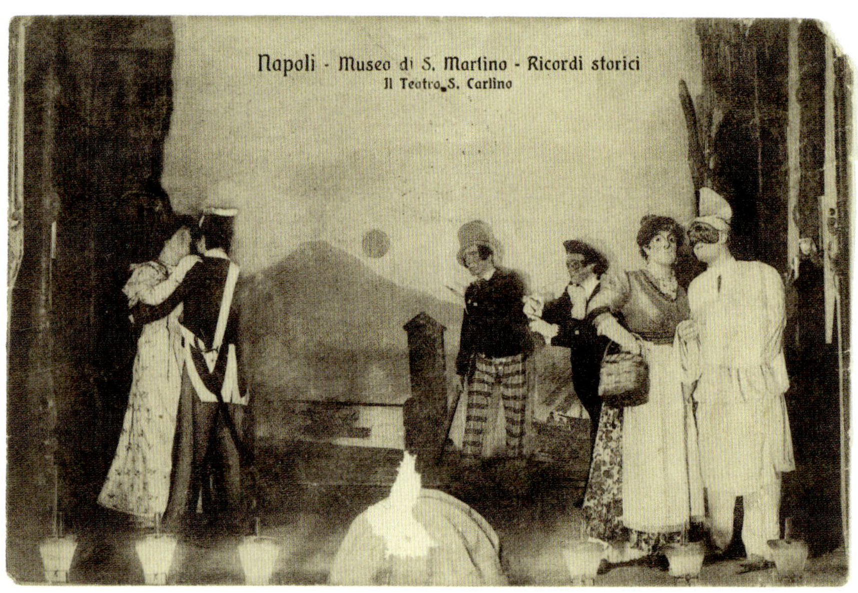

155a-b. Postcard of the Teatro di Pulcinella in the Museo di San Martino, Naples, with a drawing by Olga on the back sent to Jean Cocteau
9 x 13.5 cm
Paris, Bibliothèque historique de la Ville de Paris, Fonds Jean Cocteau, inv. MS-FS-05-6394

156. Igor Stravinsky
Pulcinella (sheet from the musical score), 1919–20
Manuscript, 37.5 x 27.9 cm
Basel, Paul Sacher Foundation, Igor Stravinsky Collection

157. Joseph Enrietti
Pulcinella. Dormant group, 1920
Gelatin silver print, 13 x 18 cm
Paris, Bibliothèque nationale de France, Alb. Kochno Pulcinella 07

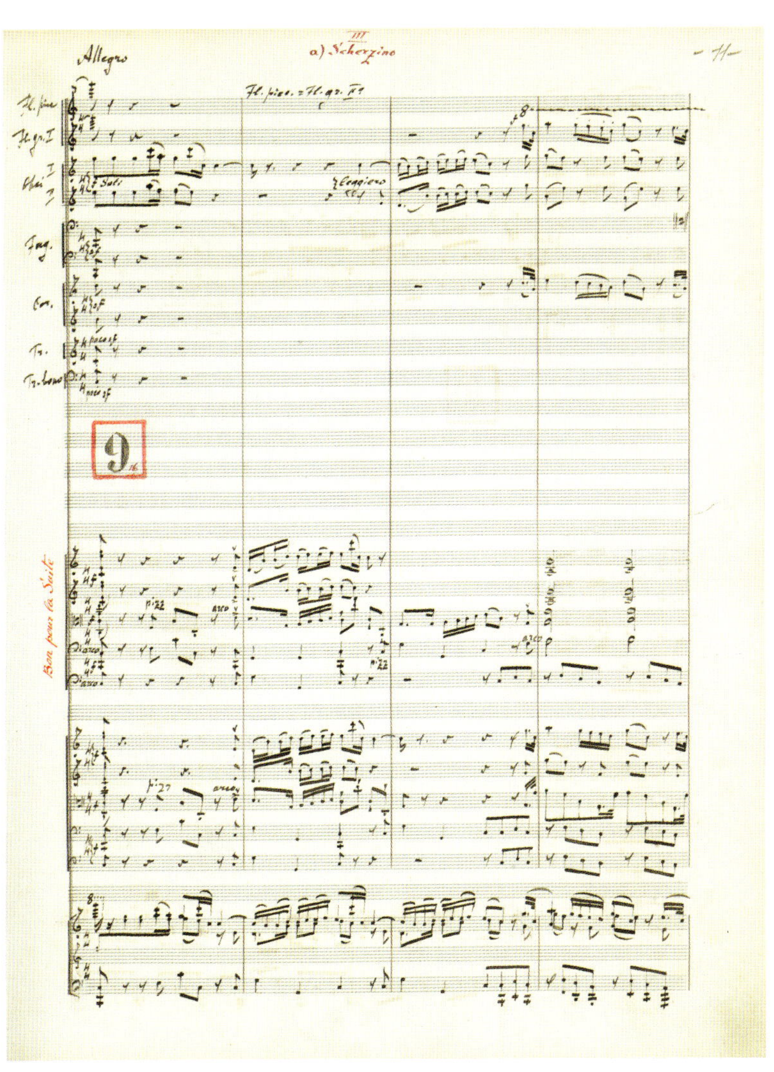
Allegro
III
a) Scherzino
- 11 -
Bon pour la Suite

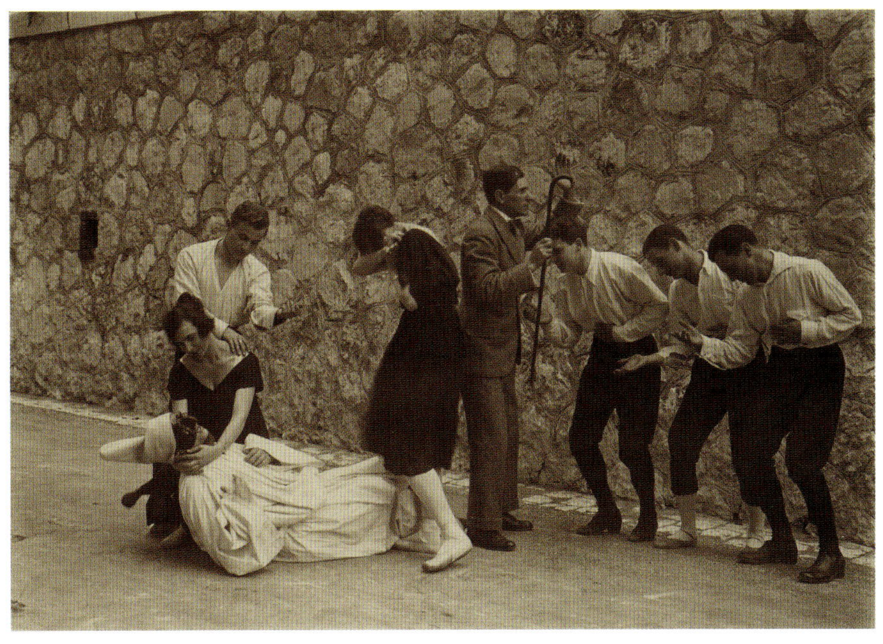

VIII. Reinventing the Classical

158. Pablo Picasso
Deux Baigneuses [Two Bathers],
Paris, 24 October 1920
Gouache, pastel, red chalk
and Conté pencil on drawing paper,
107.8 x 75.2 cm
Paris, Musée national Picasso-Paris,
Pablo Picasso Donation, 1979,
inv. MP944

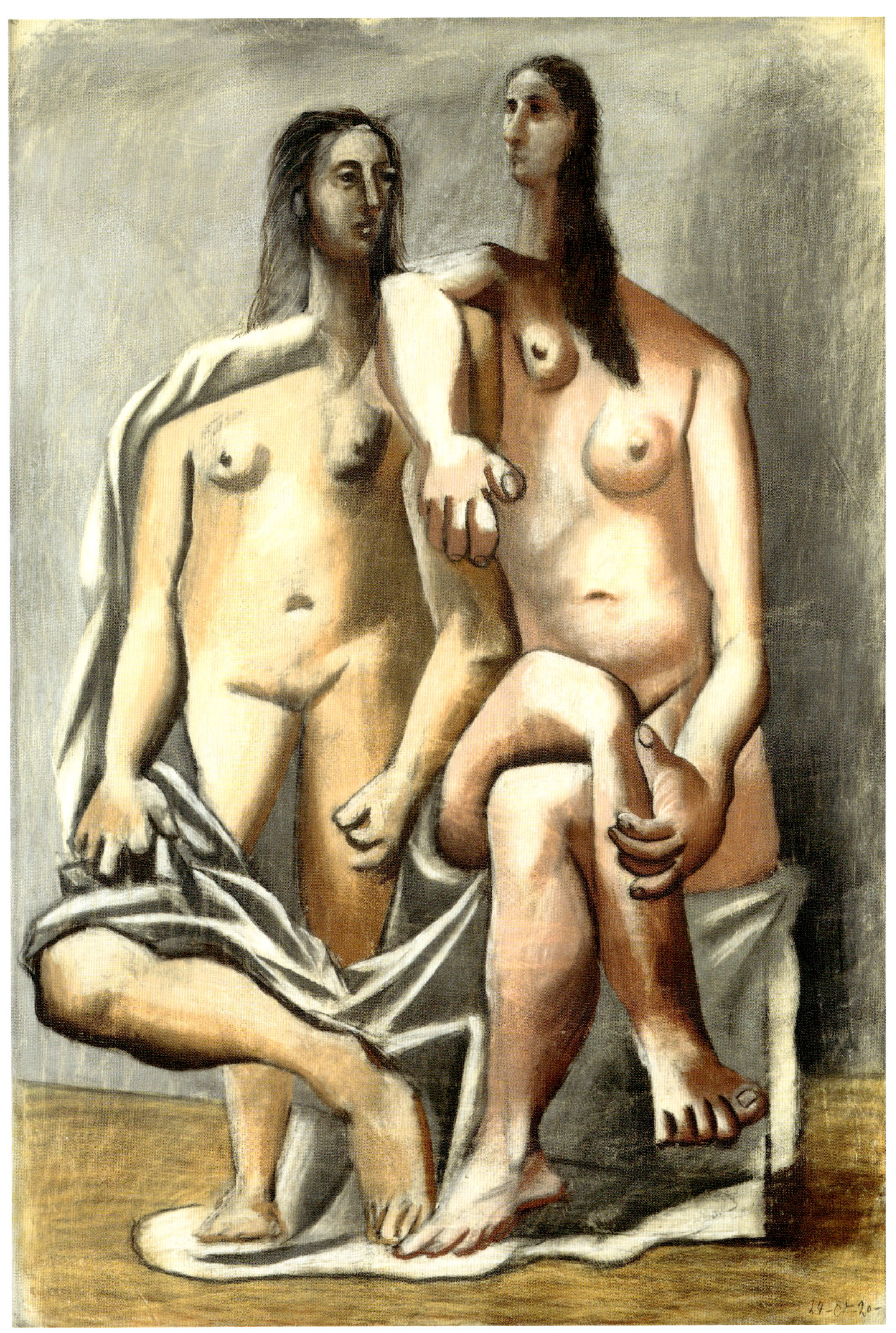

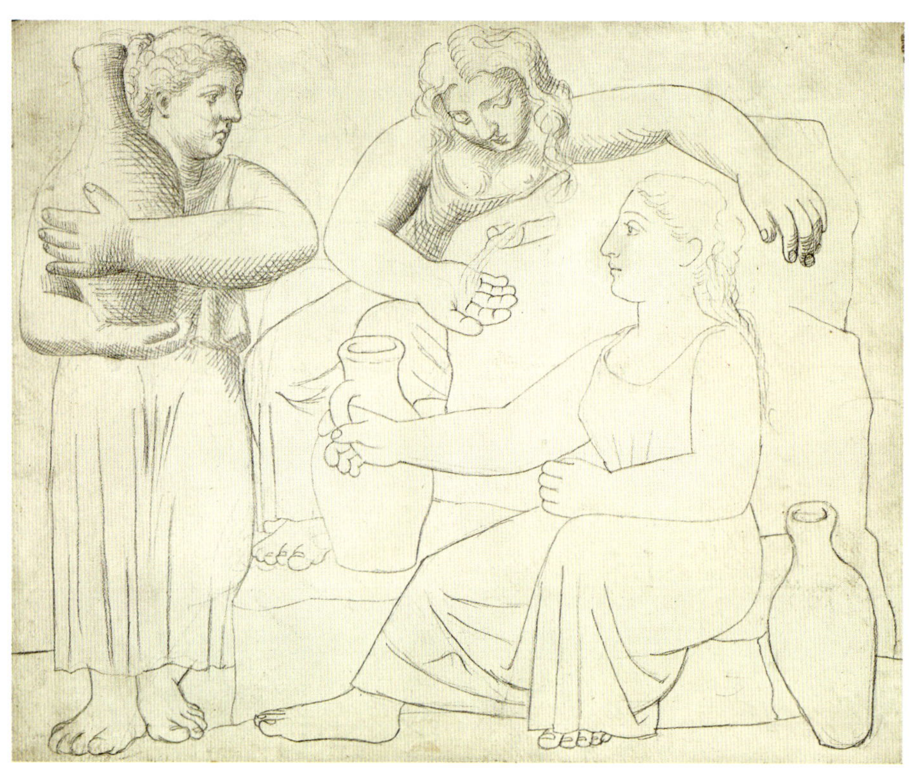

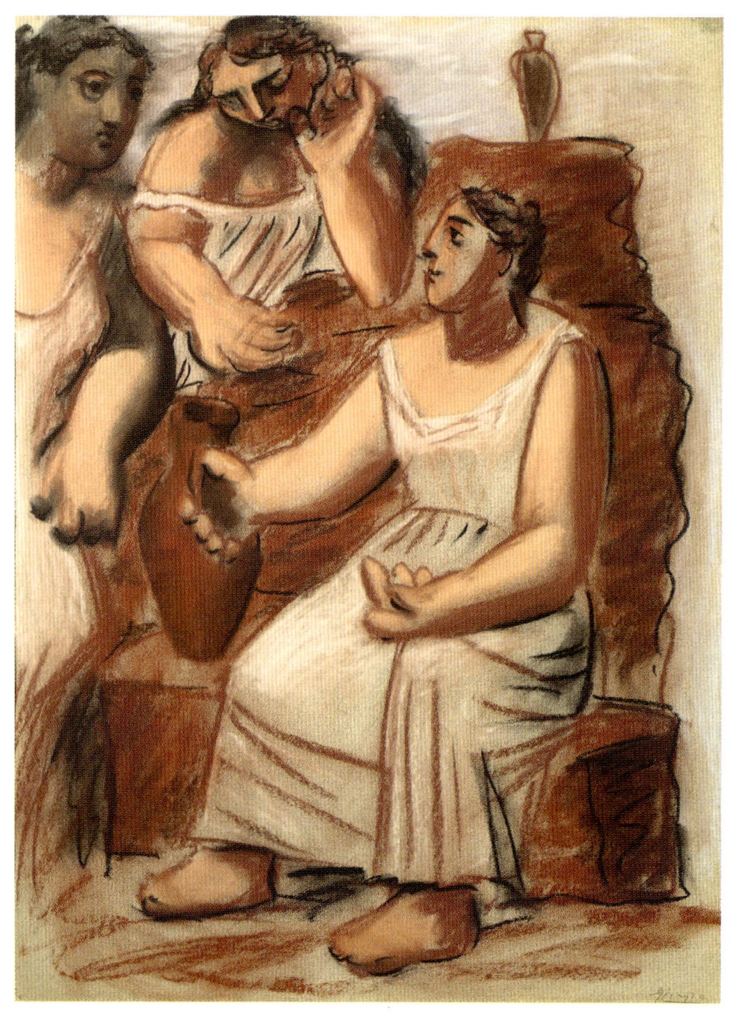

159. Pablo Picasso
Étude pour "Trois femmes à la fontaine" [Study for *Three Women by a Fountain*], Fontainebleau, 1921
Pastel and oil on wood, 21.5 x 27 cm
Paris, Musée national Picasso-Paris, Pablo Picasso Donation, 1979, inv. MP965

160. Pablo Picasso
Femmes à la fontaine
[Women by a Fountain], 1921
Pastel on paper, 66 x 50.8 cm
Marlborough International Fine Art

161. Pablo Picasso
Trois femmes à la fontaine
[Three Women by a Fountain], Fontainebleau, Summer 1921
Red chalk on canvas, 200 x 161 cm
Paris, Musée national Picasso-Paris, inv. MP74

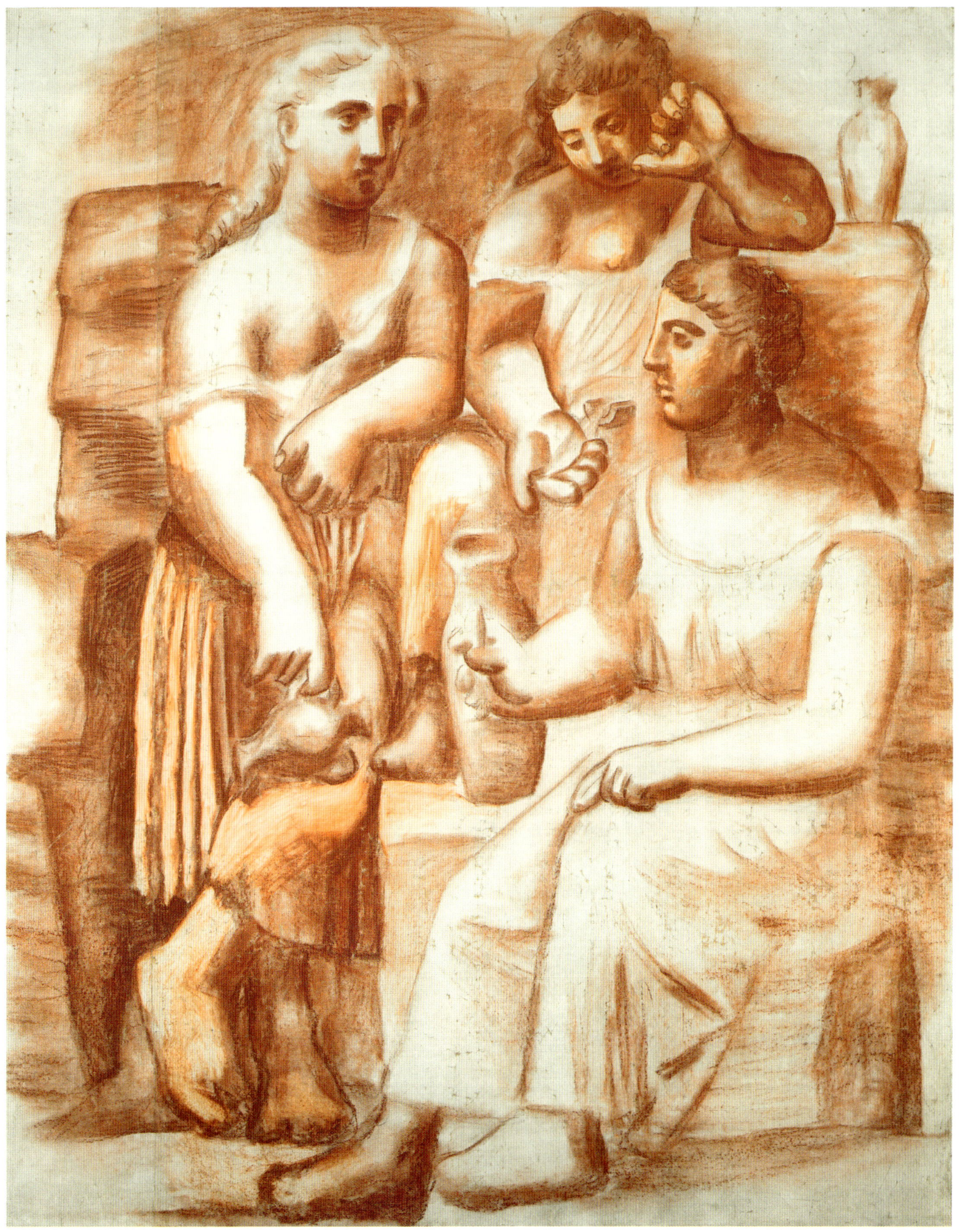

162. Pablo Picasso
Tête de femme [Head of a Woman],
Fontainebleau, Summer 1921
Pastel on paper, 63.5 x 49 cm
Basel, Fondation Beyeler, Beyeler
Collection, inv. 89.7

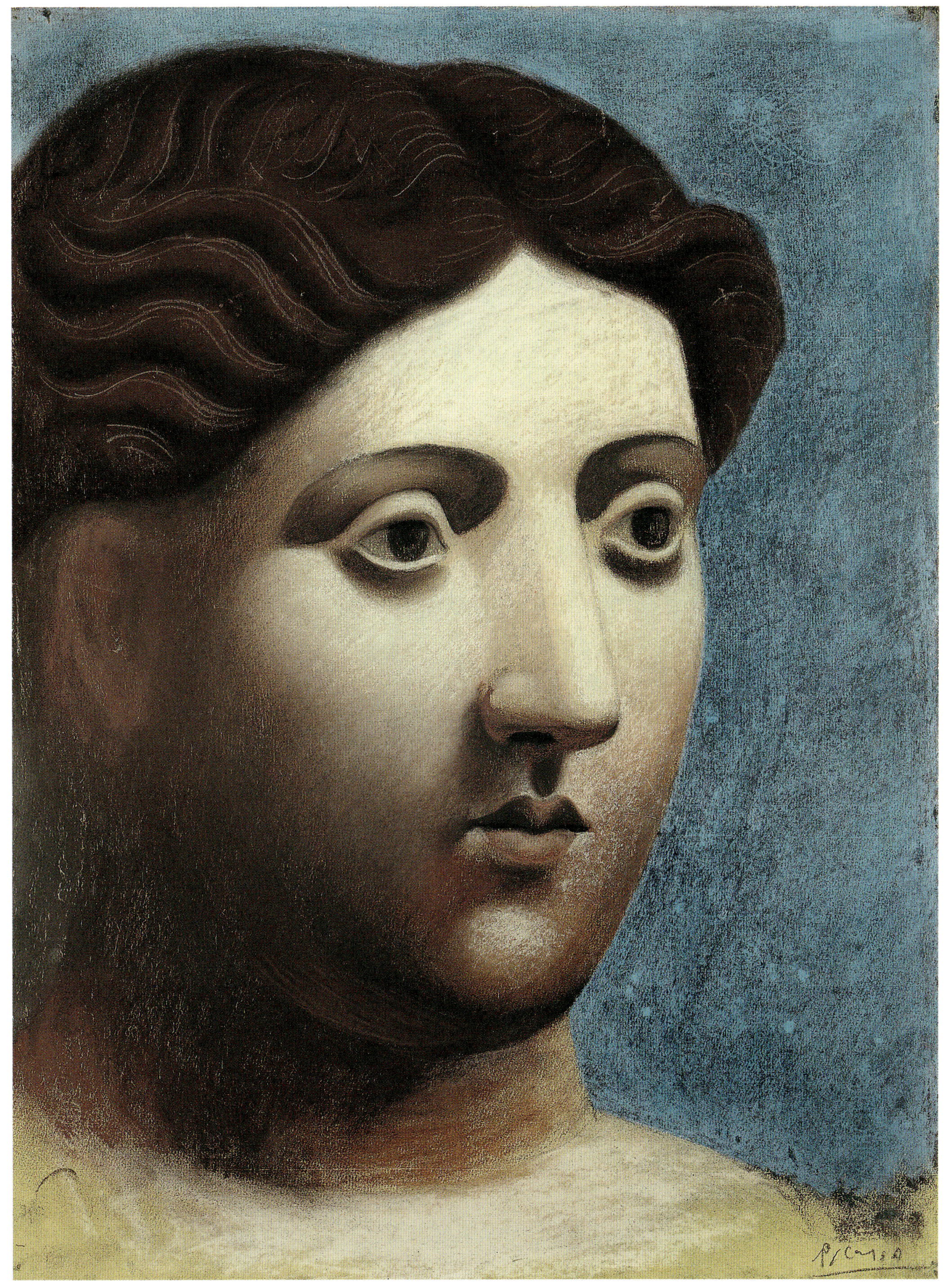

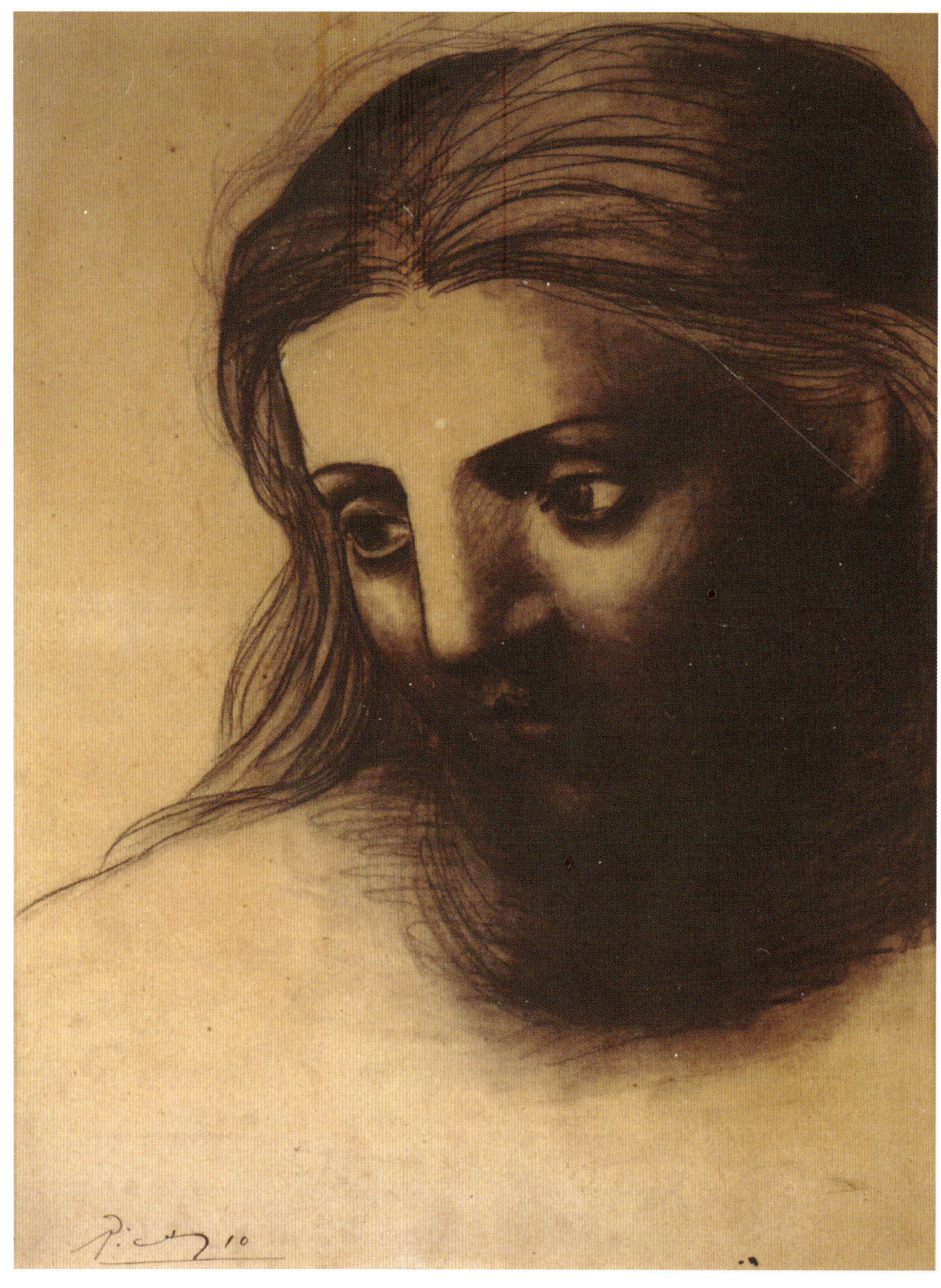

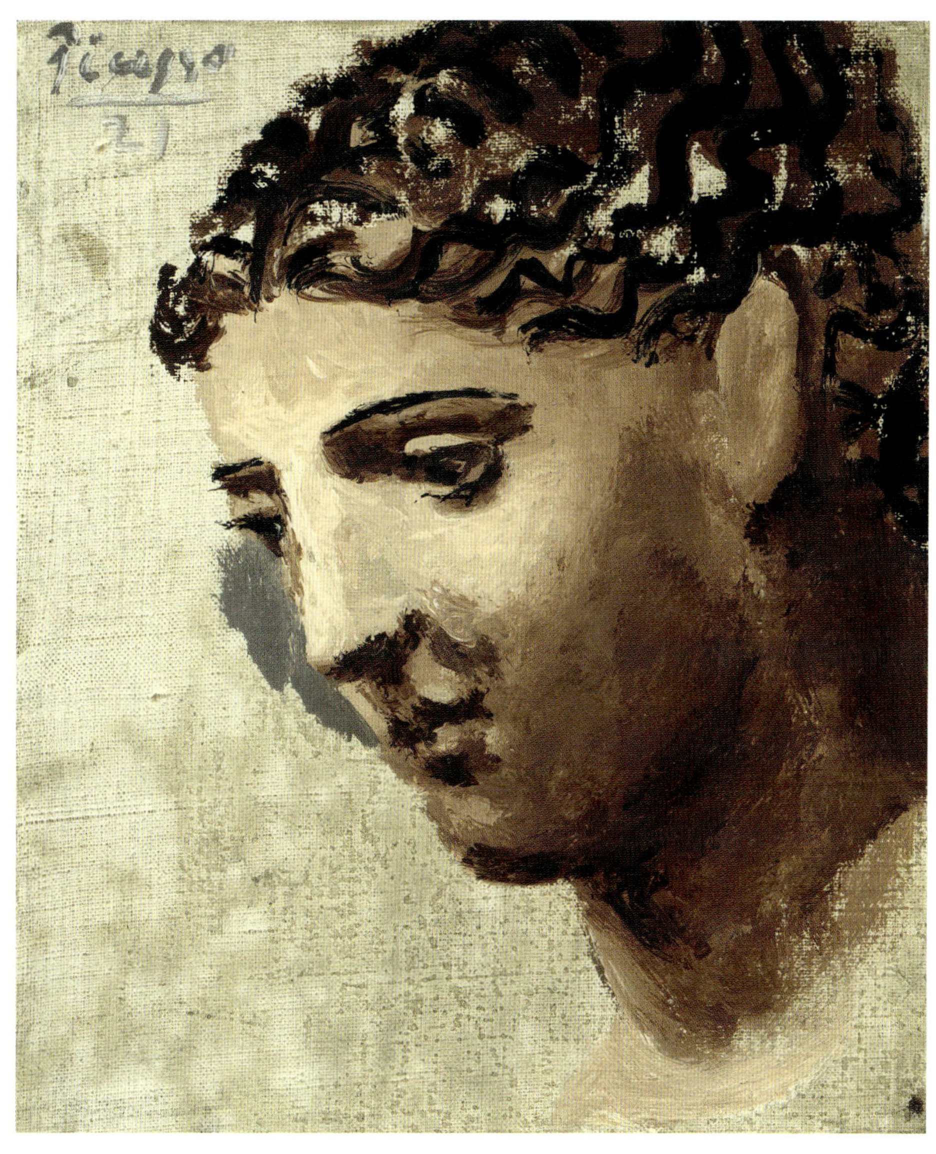

163. Pablo Picasso
Tête de femme
[Head of woman], 1921
Charcoal on paper, 61 x 47 cm
New York, private collection

164. Pablo Picasso
Tête de femme
[Head of a woman], 1921
Oil on canvas, 18.5 x 16 cm
Private collection, on loan to
Staatliche Museen zu Berlin,
Nationalgalerie, Museum Berggruen

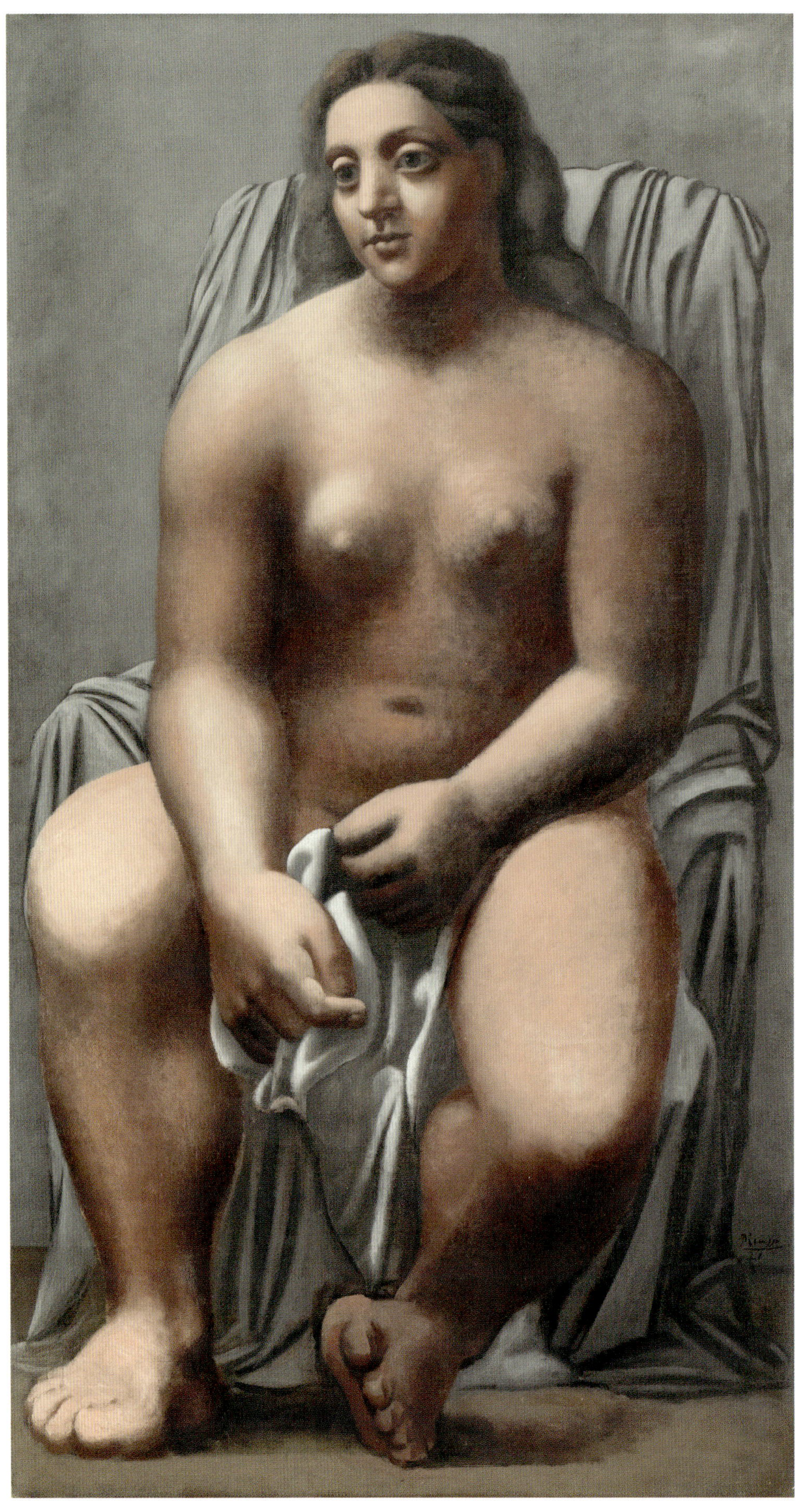

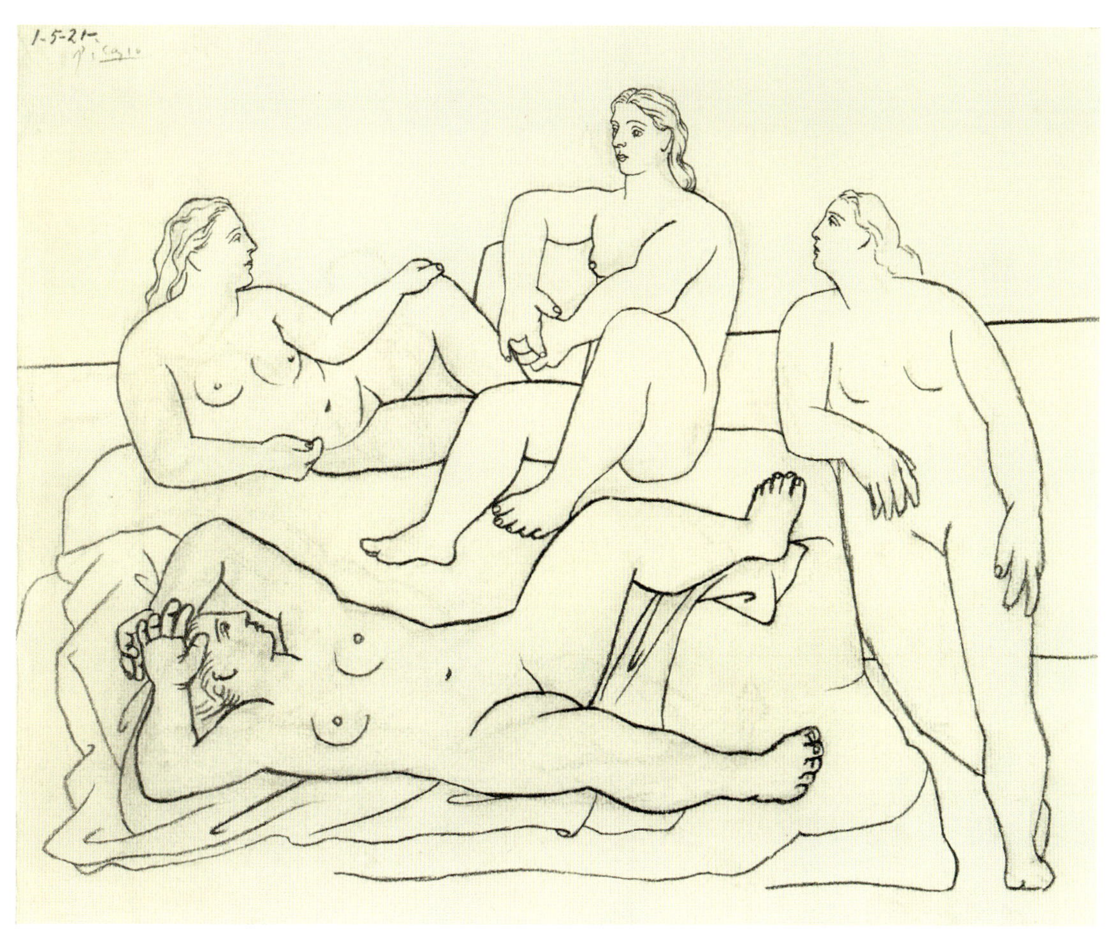

165. Pablo Picasso
Grande baigneuse
[Large Bather], 1921
Oil on canvas, 182 x 101 cm
Paris, Musée de l'Orangerie, collection Jean Walter et Paul Guillaume, inv. RF 1963-77

166. Pablo Picasso
Groupe de quatre baigneuses
[Group of Four Bathers], 1921
Pencil on paper, 24.7 x 30.3 cm
Private collection, on loan to Staatliche Museen zu Berlin, Nationalgalerie, Museum Berggruen

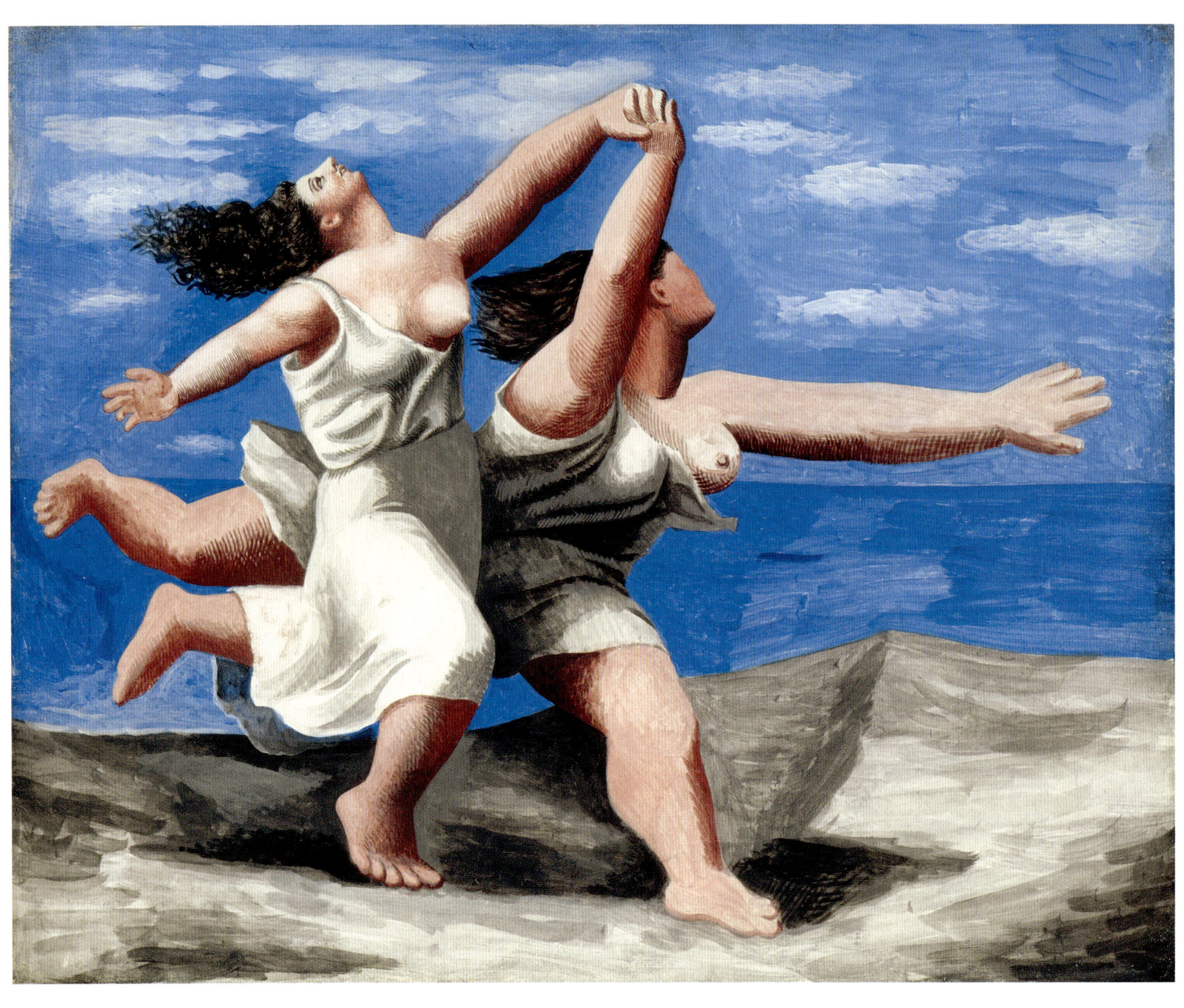

167. Pablo Picasso
Deux femmes courant sur la plage (La course) [Two Women Running on the Beach (The Race)], Dinard, Summer 1922
Gouache on panel, 32.5 x 41.1 cm
Paris, Musée national Picasso-Paris, Pablo Picasso Donation, 1979, inv. MP78

168. Pablo Picasso
Nu debout [Standing Nude], 1922
Pencil on paper, 41.9 x 29.2 cm
New York, The Metropolitan Museum of Art, Bequest of Gregoire Tarnopol, 1979 and Gift of Alexander Tarnopol, 1980, inv. 1980.21.22

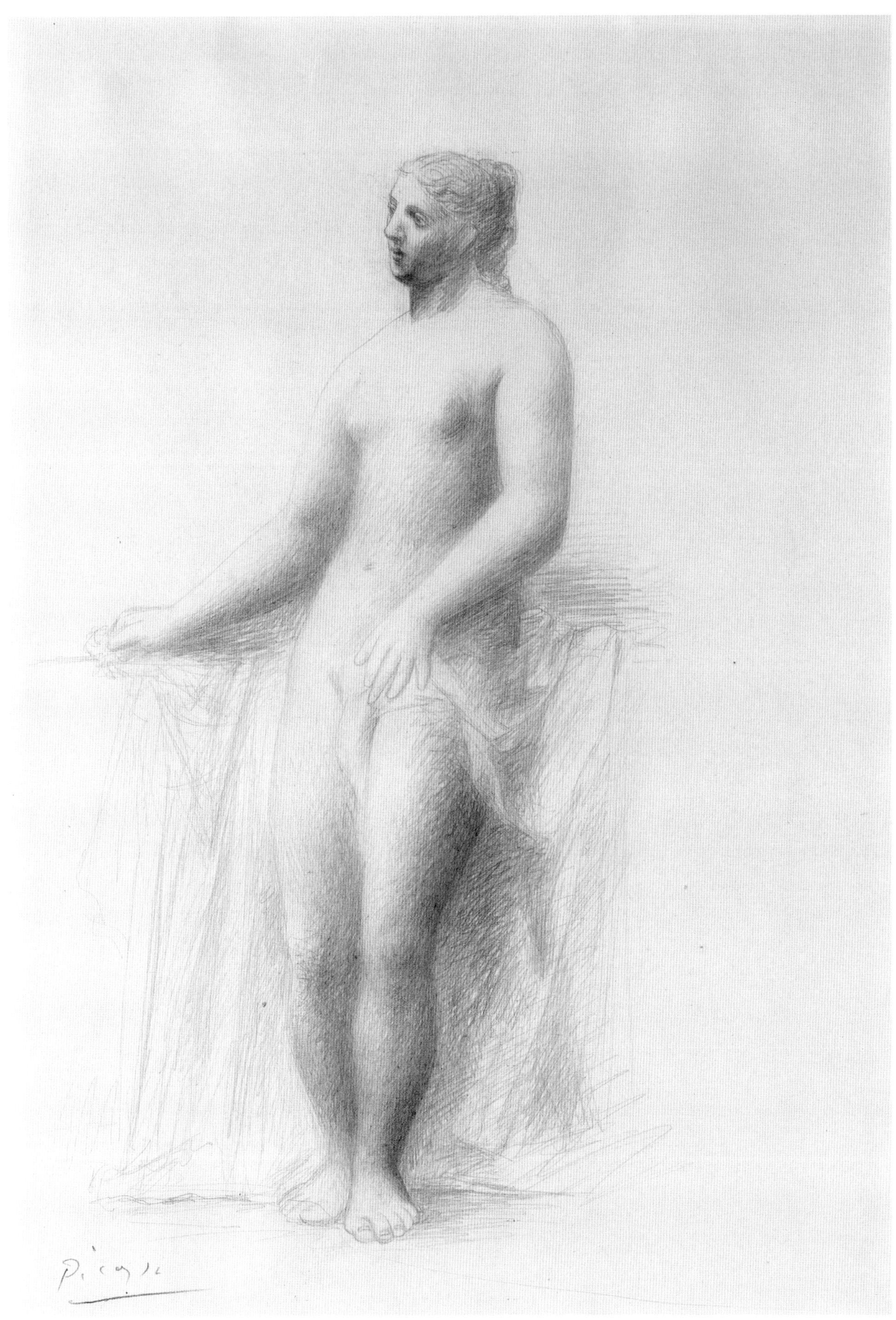

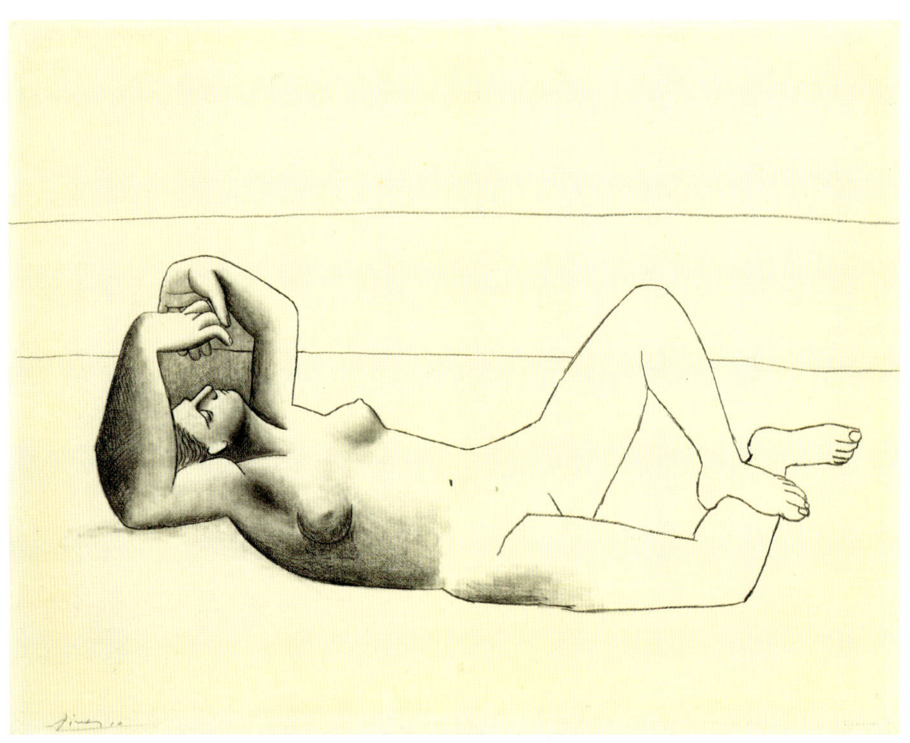

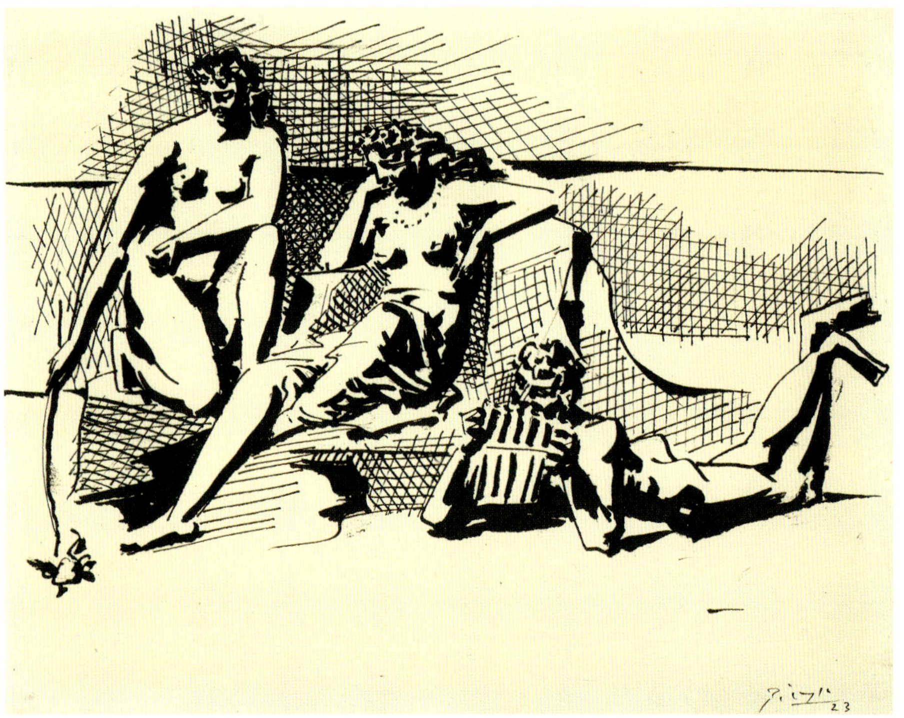

169. Pablo Picasso
Baigneuse allongée
[Reclining Bather], c. 1923
Pencil on paper, 49 x 63.5 cm
Paris, Bibliothèque nationale de France, inv. RC-A-63480

170. Pablo Picasso
Deux nus et joueur de flûte de Pan
[Two Nudes with Pan-flute Player], 1923
India ink on paper, 24 x 31.2 cm
Berlin, Staatliche Museen zu Berlin, Nationalgalerie, Museum Berggruen, inv. MB 44/2000

171. Pablo Picasso
Femme assise en chemise
[Seated Woman in a Chemise], 1923
Oil on canvas, 92.1 x 73 cm
Tate, Bequeathed by C. Frank Stoop 1933, inv. N04719

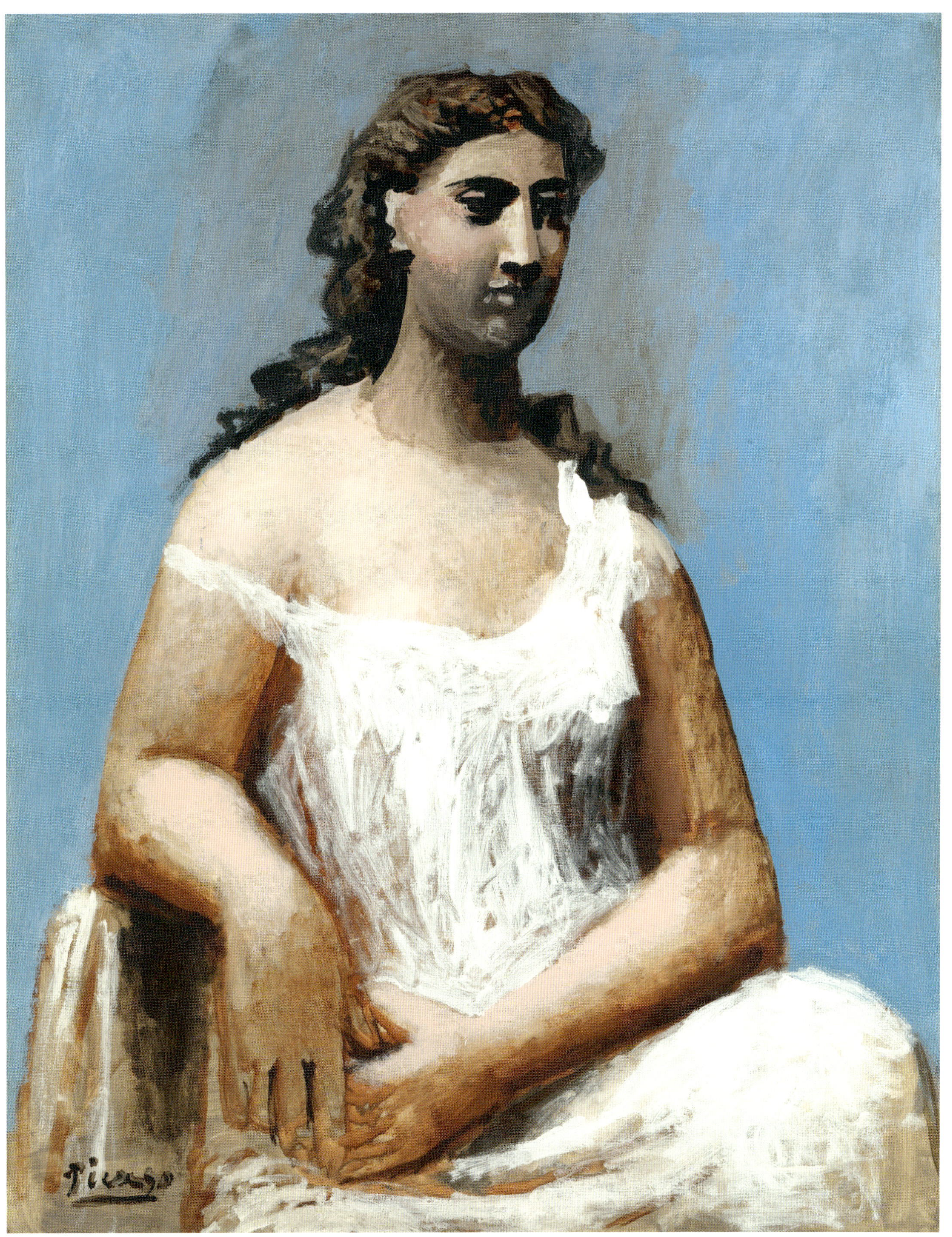
Picasso

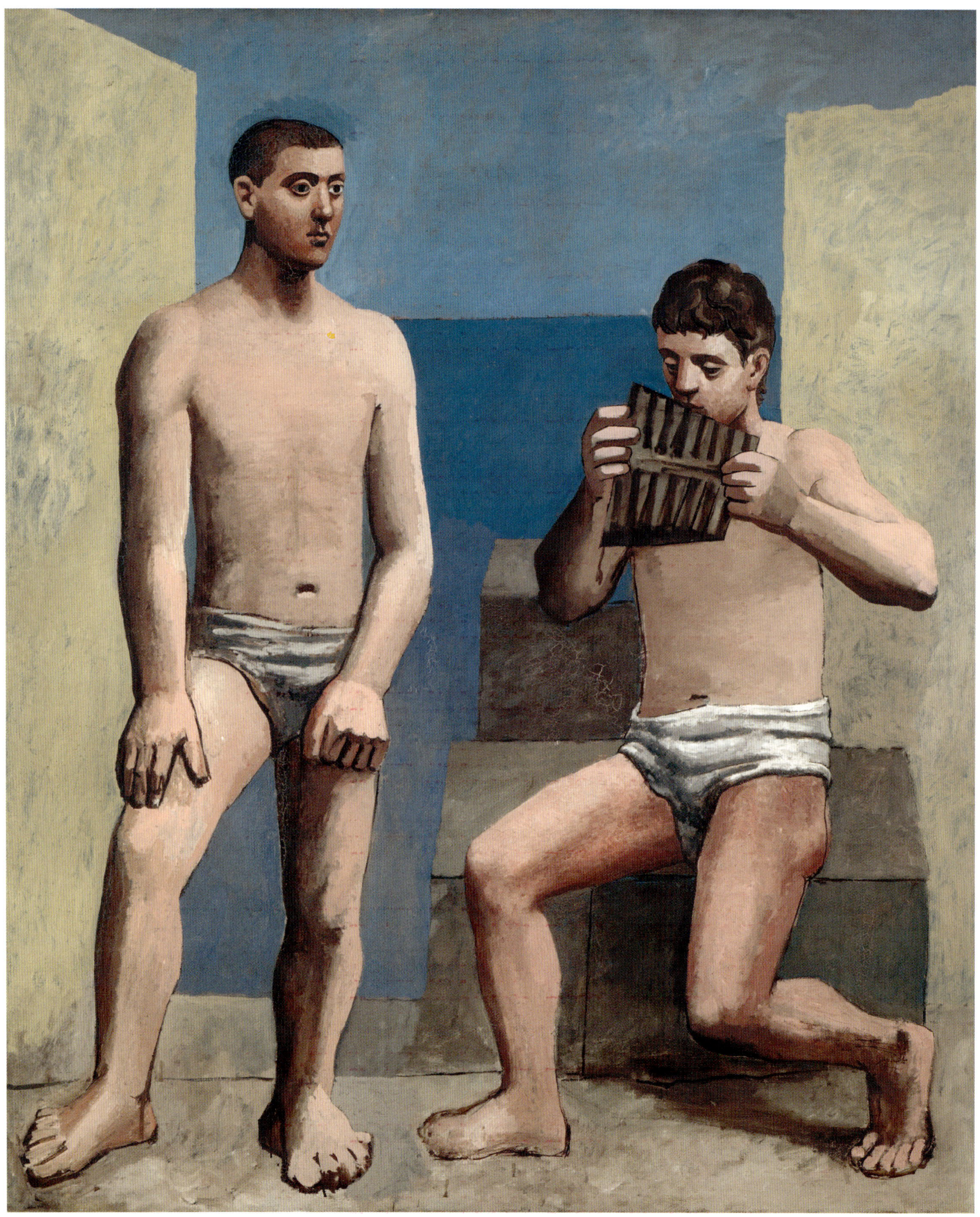

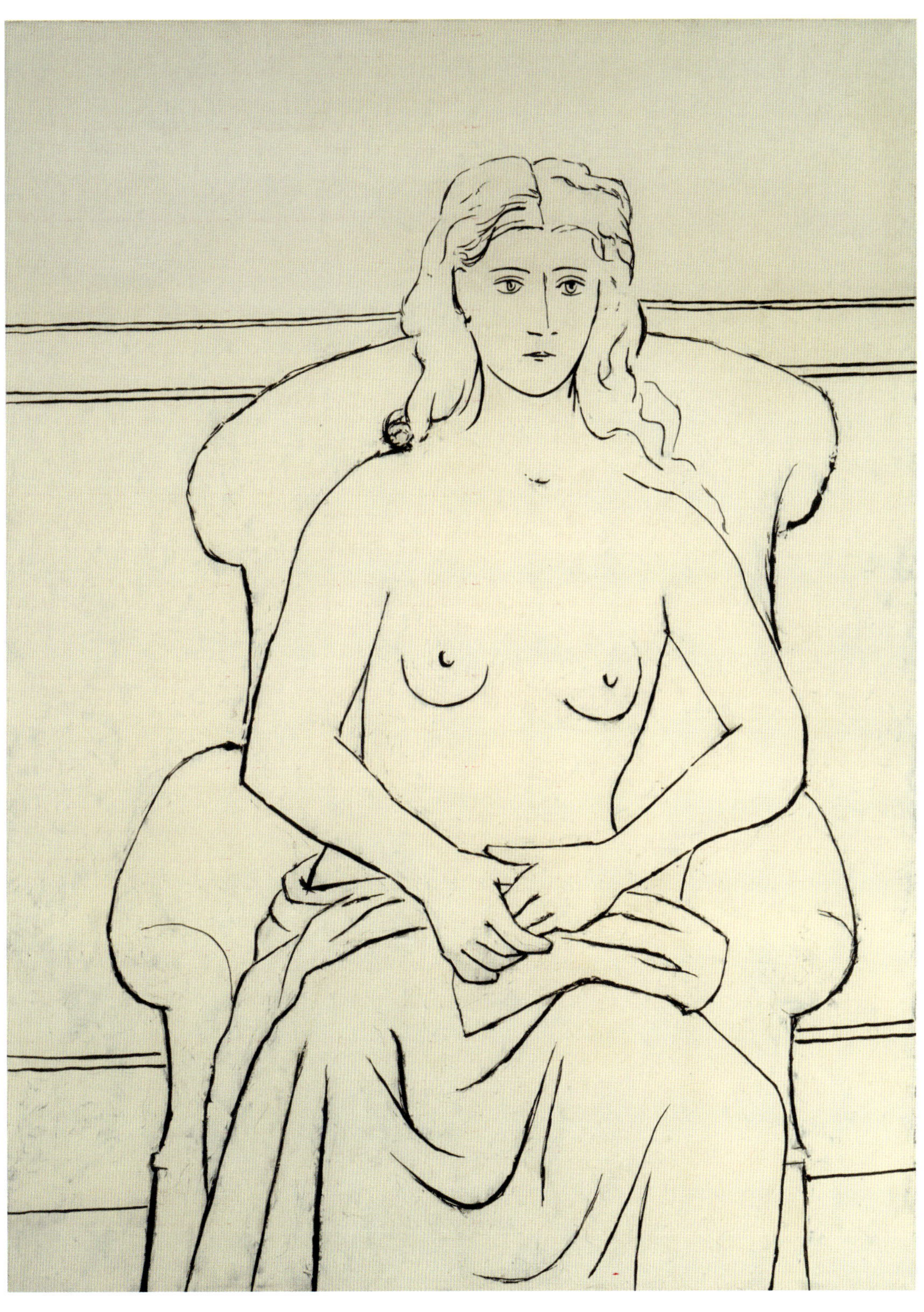

172. Pablo Picasso
La Flûte de Pan [The Pipes of Pan],
Antibes, Summer 1923
Oil on canvas, 205 x 174 cm
Paris, Musée national Picasso-Paris,
Pablo Picasso Donation, 1979,
inv. MP79

173. Pablo Picasso
Nu drapé assis dans un fauteuil
[Nude with Drapery in an Armchair],
1923
Oil on canvas, 130 x 97 cm
Private collection

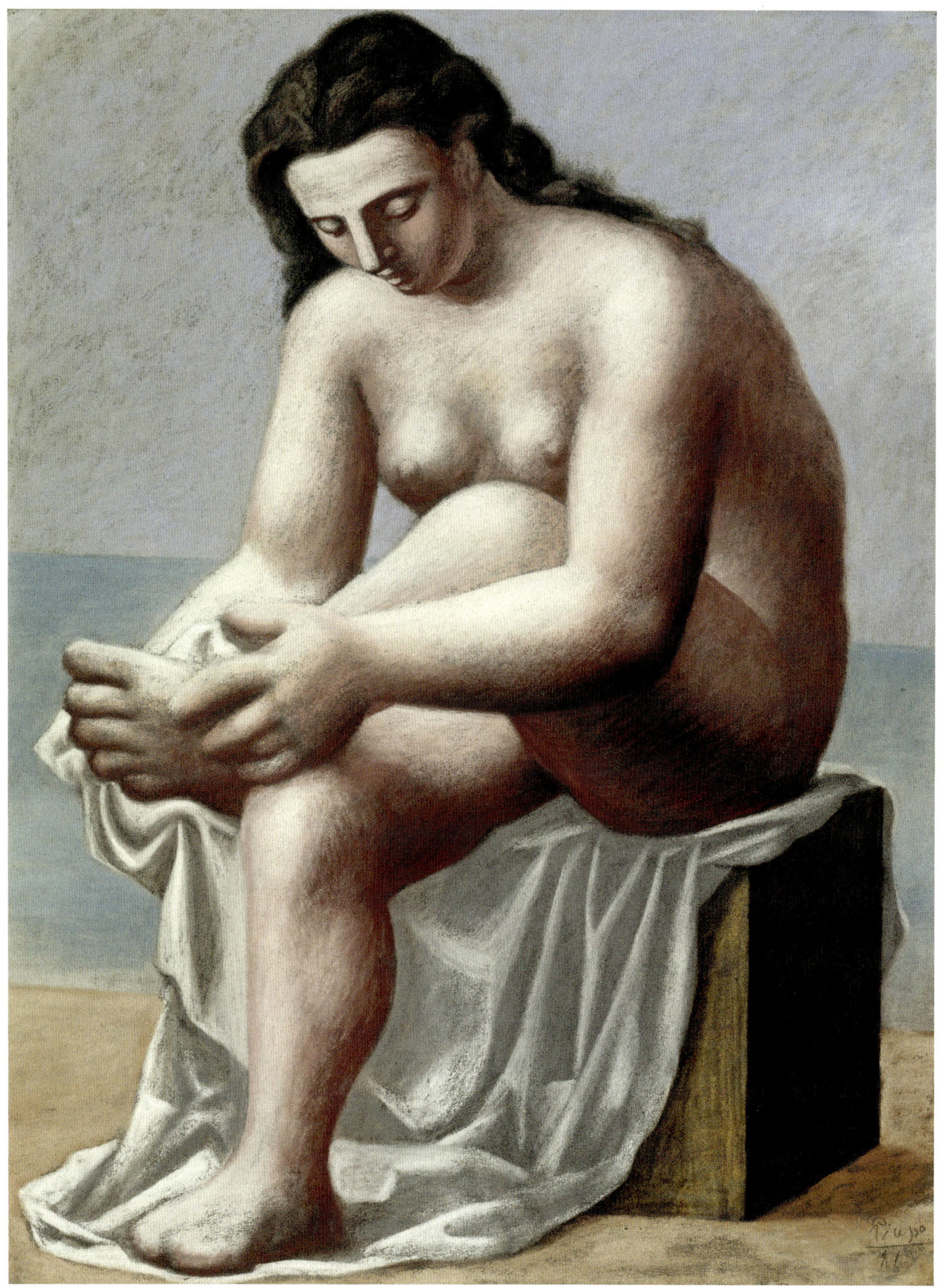

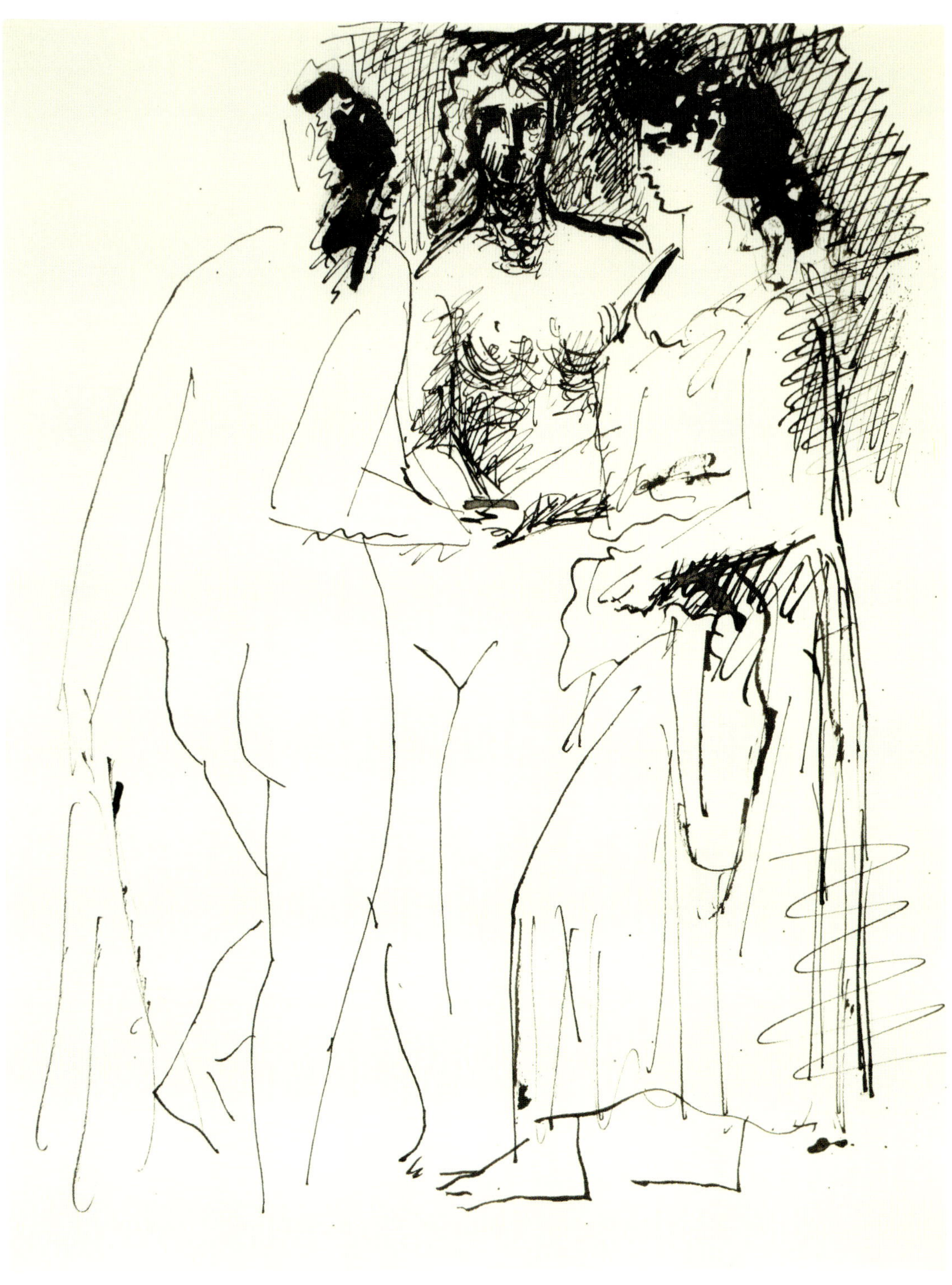

174. Pablo Picasso
Nu assis s'essuyant le pied
[Seated Nude Drying Her Feet], 1921
Pastel on paper, 60 x 50.8 cm
Berlin, Staatliche Museen zu Berlin, Nationalgalerie, Museum Berggruen,
inv. NG MB 38/2000

175. Pablo Picasso
Trois nus [Three Nudes],
Antibes, Summer 1923
Pen and India ink on paper,
28.9 x 22.4 cm
Paris, Musée national Picasso-Paris,
Pablo Picasso Donation, 1979,
inv. MP990

IX. Farewell to the Theatre

176. Pablo Picasso
Guitare sur une table
[Guitar on a Table], Juan-Les-Pins, Summer 1924
Pencil and watercolour on paper, 15 x 18 cm
Private collection

177. Pablo Picasso
Guitare sur une table
[Guitar on a Table], Juan-Les-Pins, Summer 1924
Pencil and watercolour on paper, 15.5 x 20 cm
Private collection

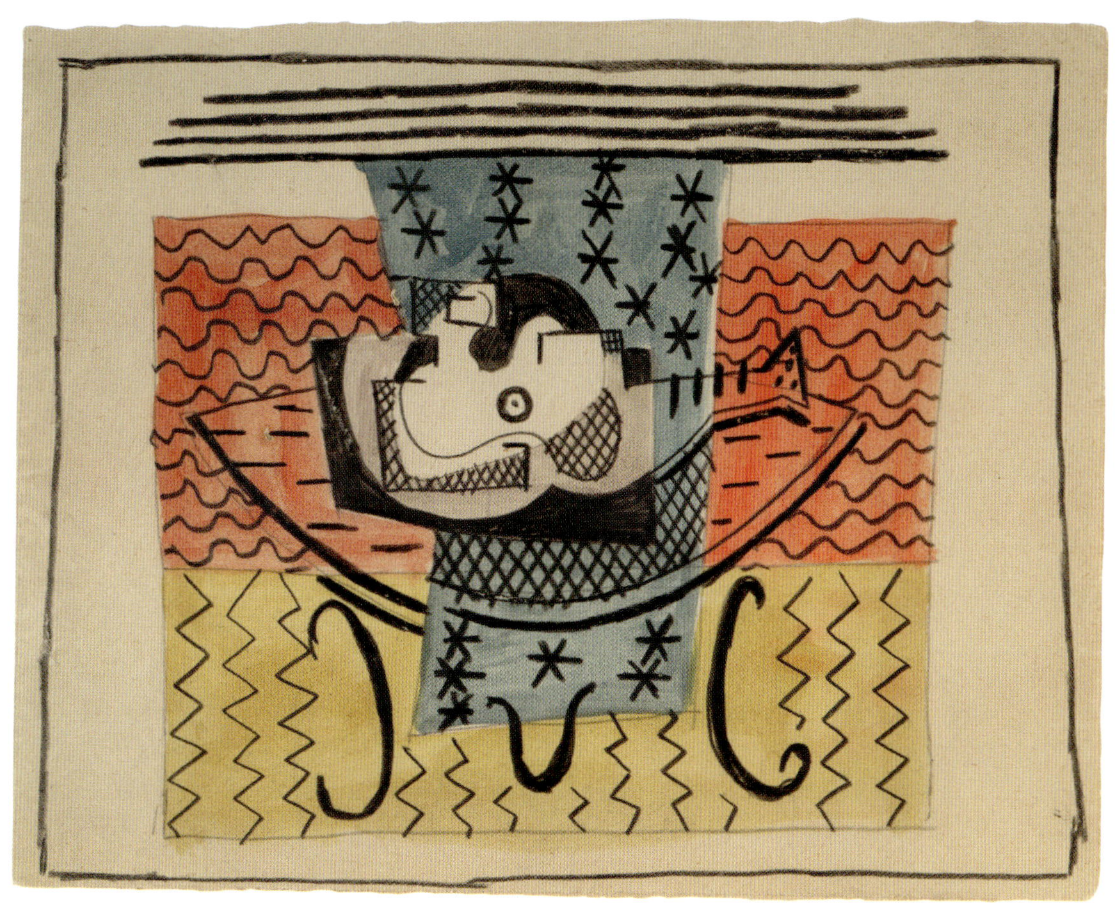

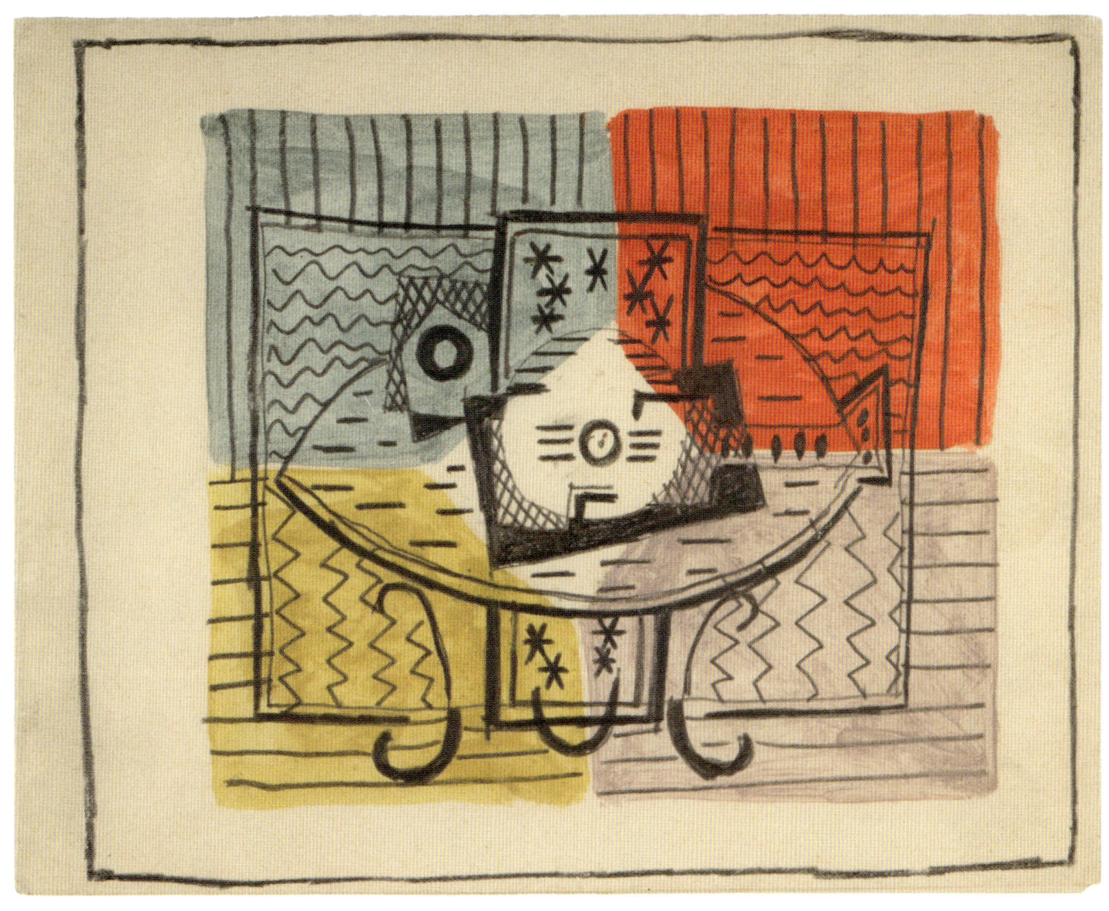

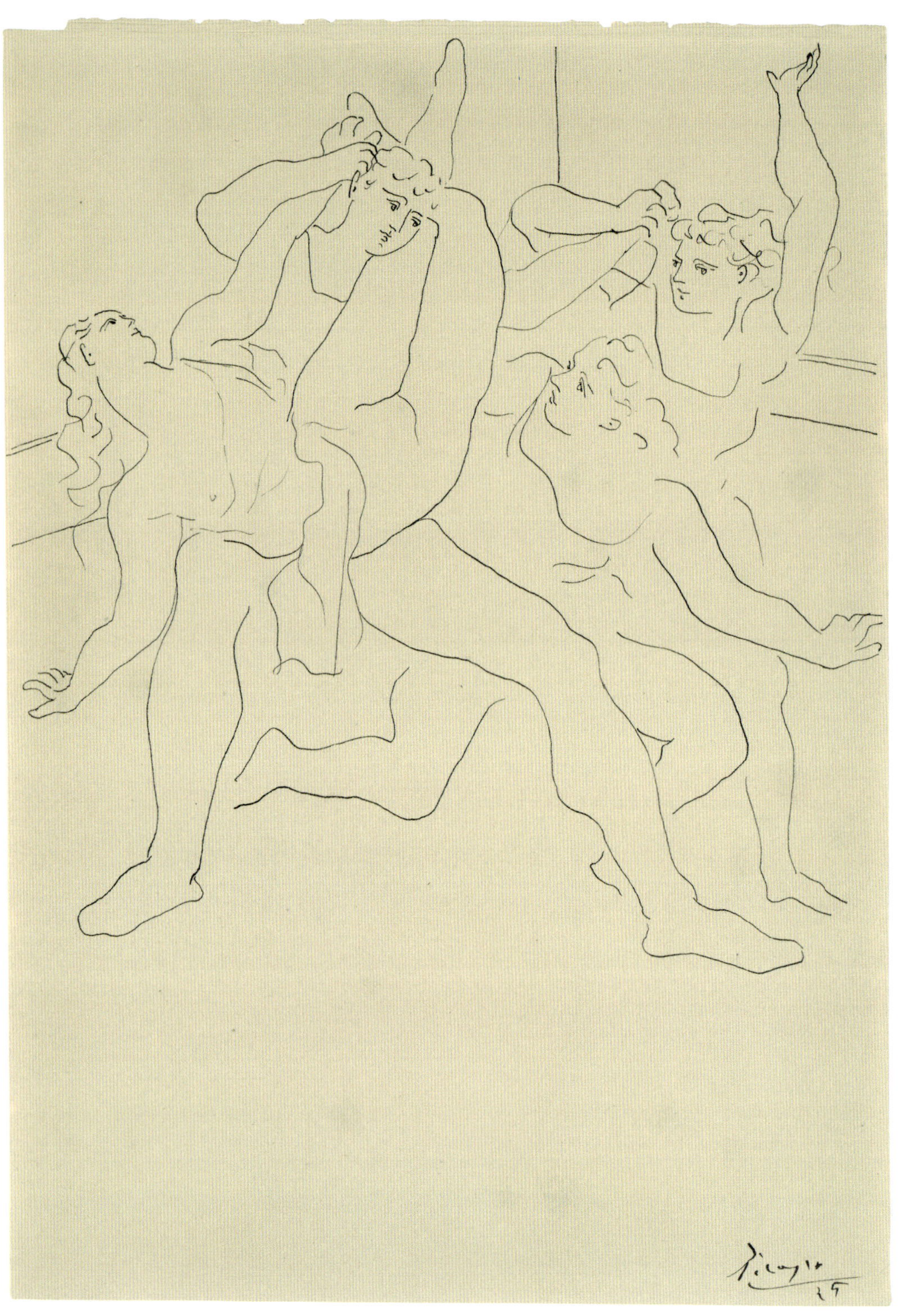

178. Pablo Picasso
Quatre danseurs
[Four Dancers], 1925
India ink on paper, 35.2 x 25.4 cm
New York, The Museum of Modern Art, Gift of Abby Aldrich Rockefeller, inv. 128.1935

179. Pablo Picasso
Deux femmes conversant, en pied, fond bicolore bleu et beige
[Standing Women in Conversation on a Blue and Beige Background], Juan-Les-Pins, Summer 1924
Oil on canvas, 34.5 x 25.5 cm
Private collection

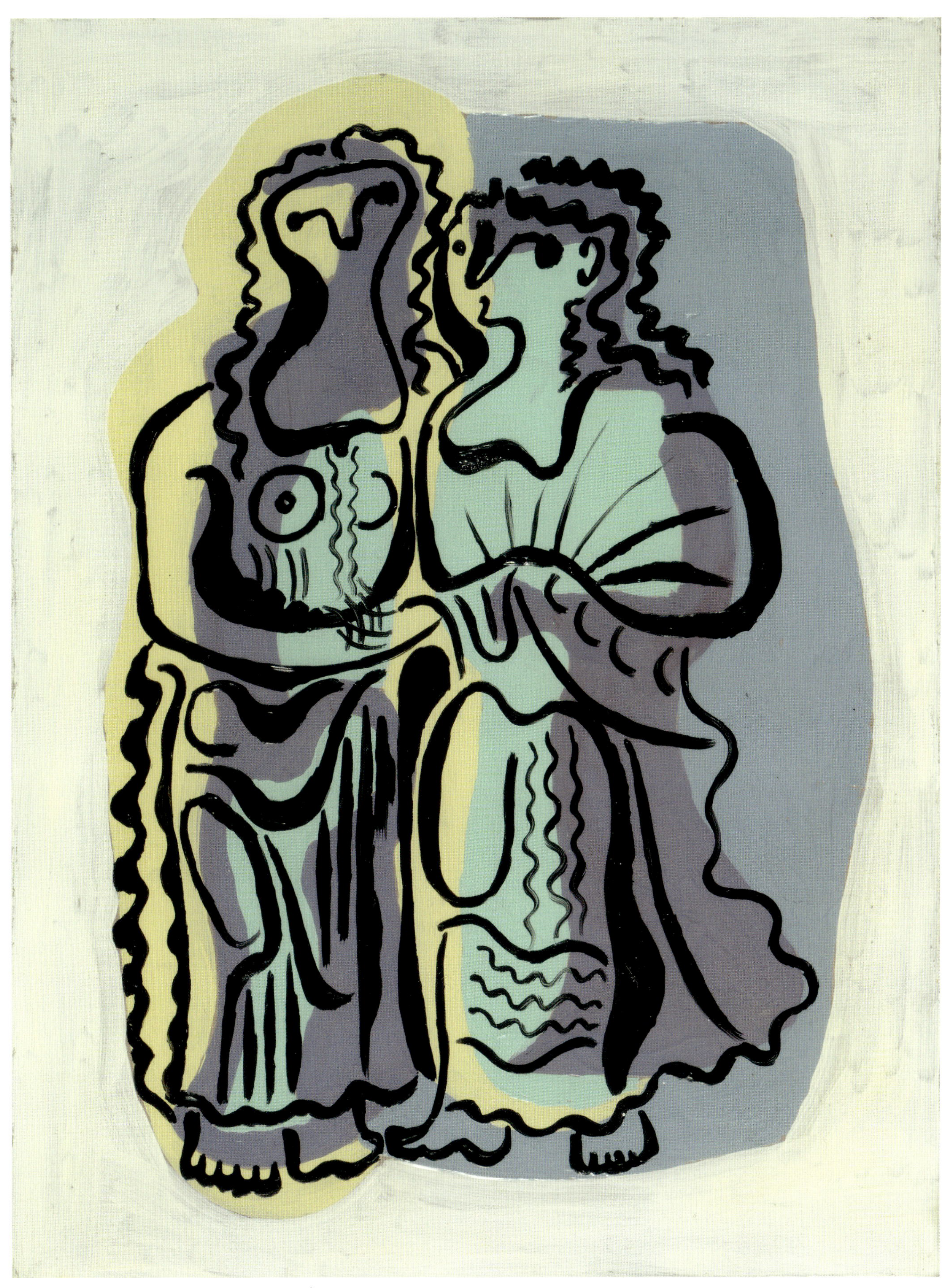

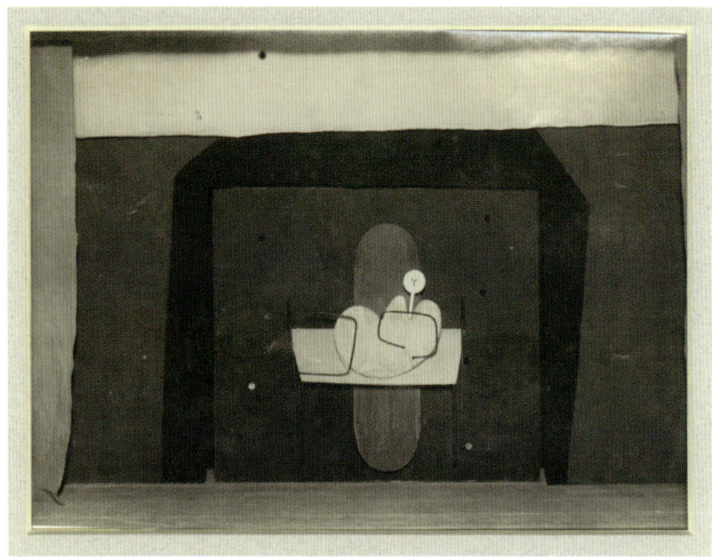

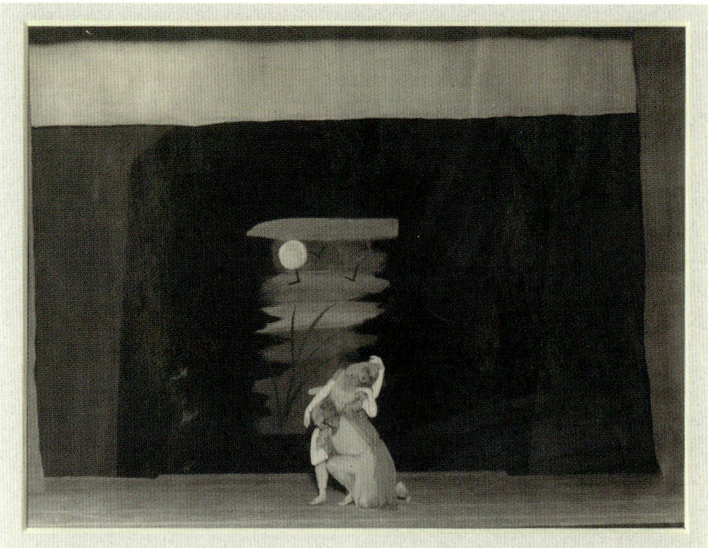

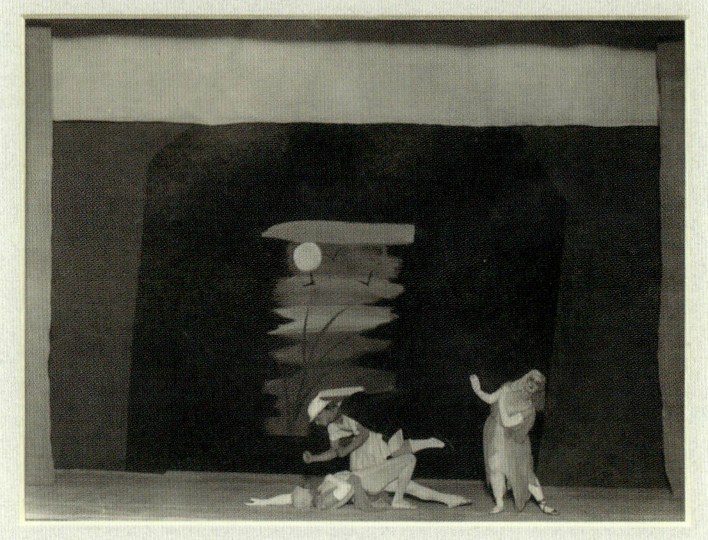

180. *Mercure*, Night, Summer 1924
Photographic print, 17 x 22 cm
Saint-Germain la Blanche-Herbe, Fonds Erik Satie – Archives de France / Archives IMEC, 165SAT/153/0

181. *Mercure*, Apollo and Venus: the Dance of Tenderness, Spring 1924
Photographic print, 17 x 22 cm
Saint-Germain la Blanche-Herbe, Fonds Erik Satie – Archives de France / Archives IMEC, 165SAT/153/0

182. *Mercure*, Signs of the Zodiac, Spring 1924
Photographic print, 17 x 22 cm
Saint-Germain la Blanche-Herbe, Fonds Erik Satie – Archives de France / Archives IMEC, 165SAT/153/0

183. *Mercure*, Mercury kills Apollo and revives him, Spring 1924
Photographic print, 17 x 22 cm
Saint-Germain la Blanche-Herbe, Fonds Erik Satie – Archives de France / Archives IMEC, 165SAT/153/0

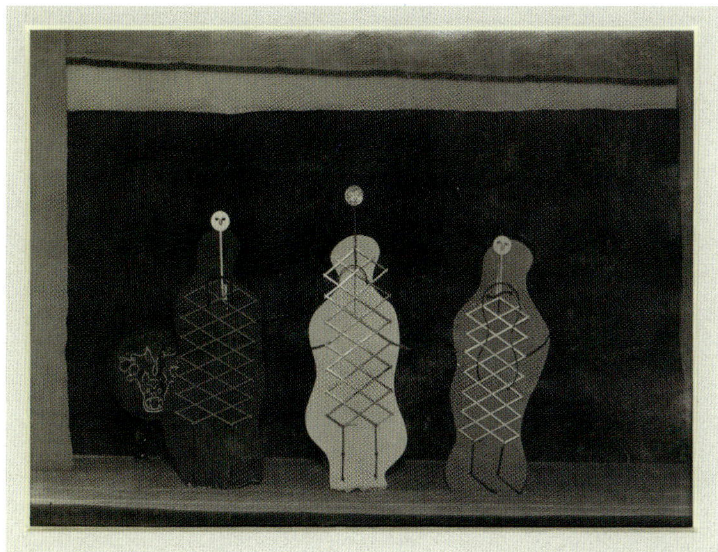

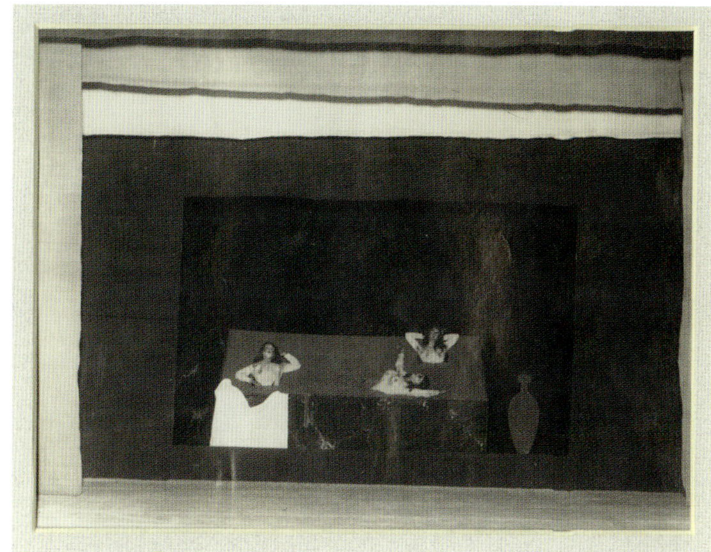

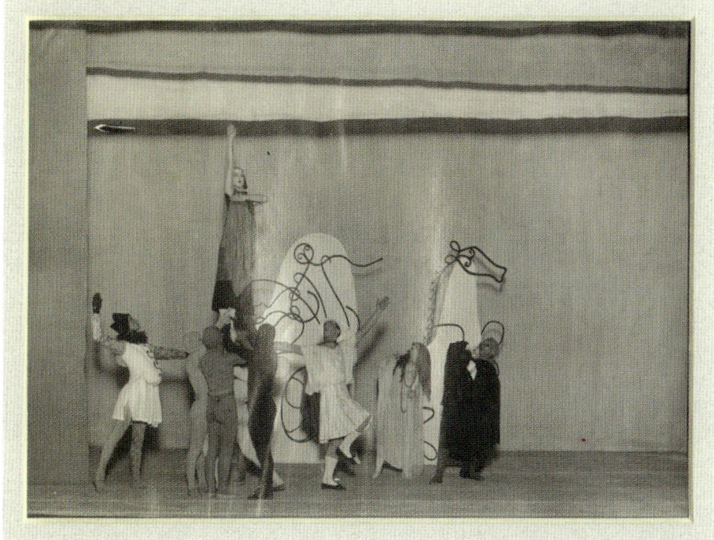

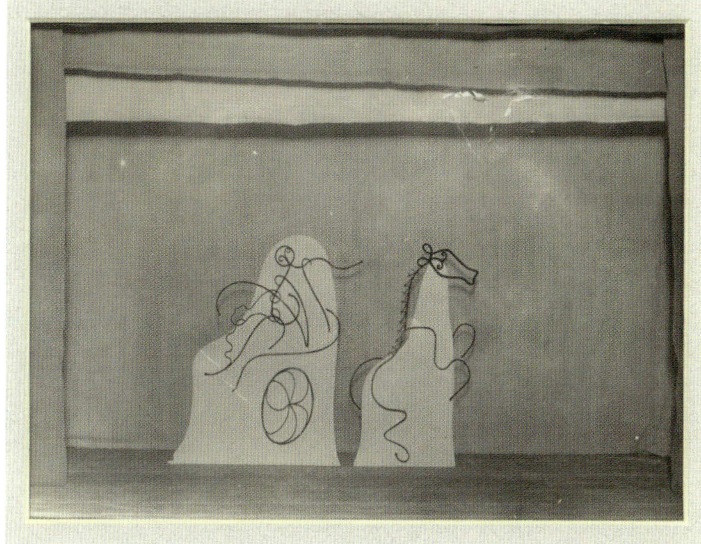

184. *Mercure*, The Fury of Cerberus, Spring 1924
Photographic print, 17 x 22 cm
Saint-Germain la Blanche-Herbe, Fonds Erik Satie - Archives de France / Archives IMEC, 165SAT/153/0

185. *Mercure*, The Three Graces Bathing, Spring 1924
Photographic print, 17 x 22 cm
Saint-Germain la Blanche-Herbe, Fonds Erik Satie - Archives de France / Archives IMEC, 165SAT/153/0

186. *Mercure*, Feast in the home of Bacchus, Spring 1924
Photographic print, 17 x 22 cm
Saint-Germain la Blanche-Herbe, Fonds Erik Satie - Archives de France / Archives IMEC, 165SAT/153/0

187. *Mercure*, Rape of Proserpine, Spring 1924
Photographic print, 17 x 22 cm
Saint-Germain la Blanche-Herbe, Fonds Erik Satie - Archives de France / Archives IMEC, 165SAT/153/0

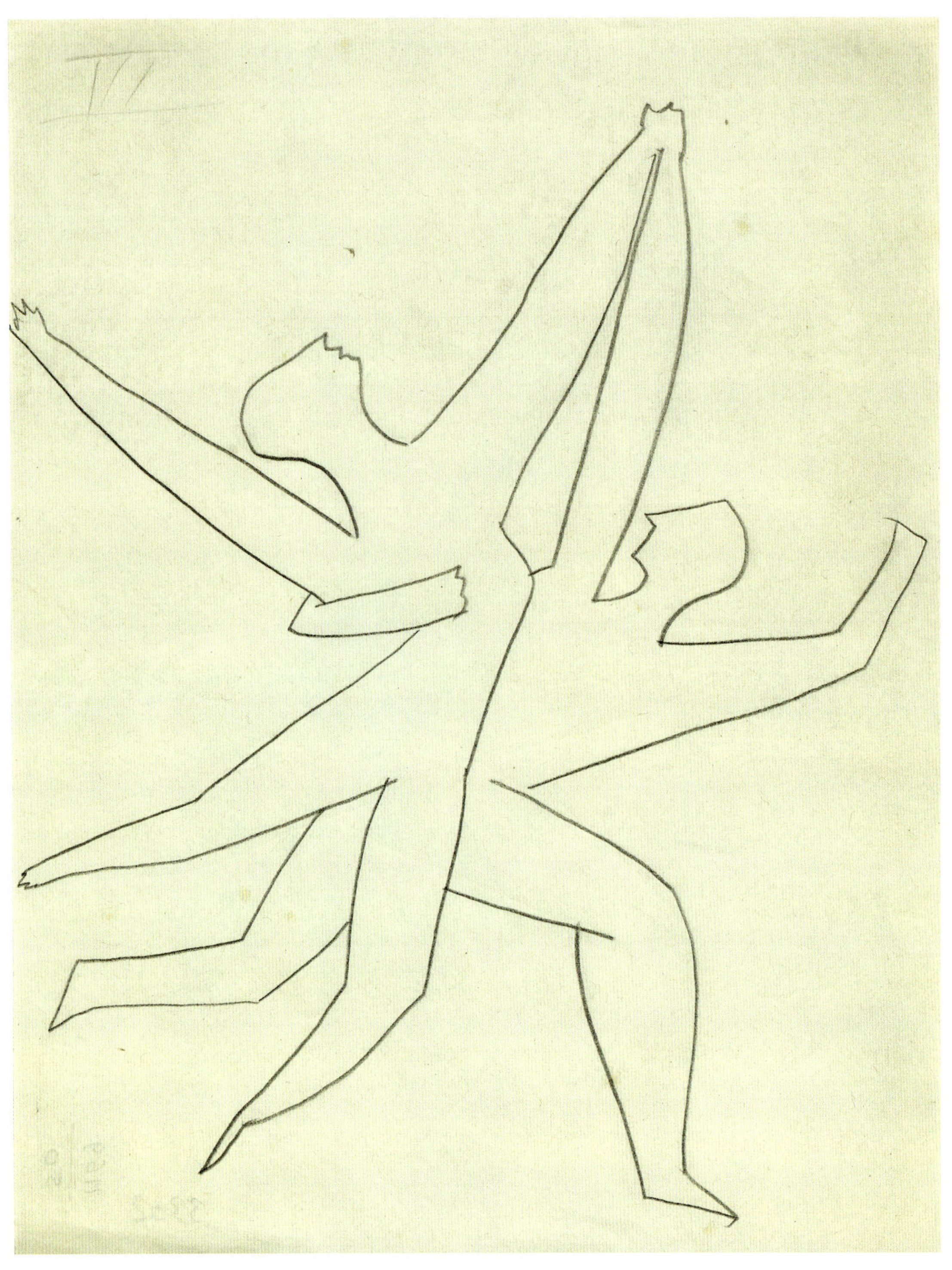

188. Pablo Picasso
Couple de danceurs III
[Two Dancers], c. 1922
Pencil on paper, 22.4 x 17.5 cm
Brussels, Fundación Almine y Bernard Ruiz-Picasso para el Arte, inv. 03302

189. Pablo Picasso
Arlequin musicien
[Harlequin Musician], 1924
Oil on canvas, 130 x 97.2 cm
Washington, National Gallery of Art, Given in loving memory of her husband, Taft Schreiber, by Rita Schreiber, inv. 1989.31.2

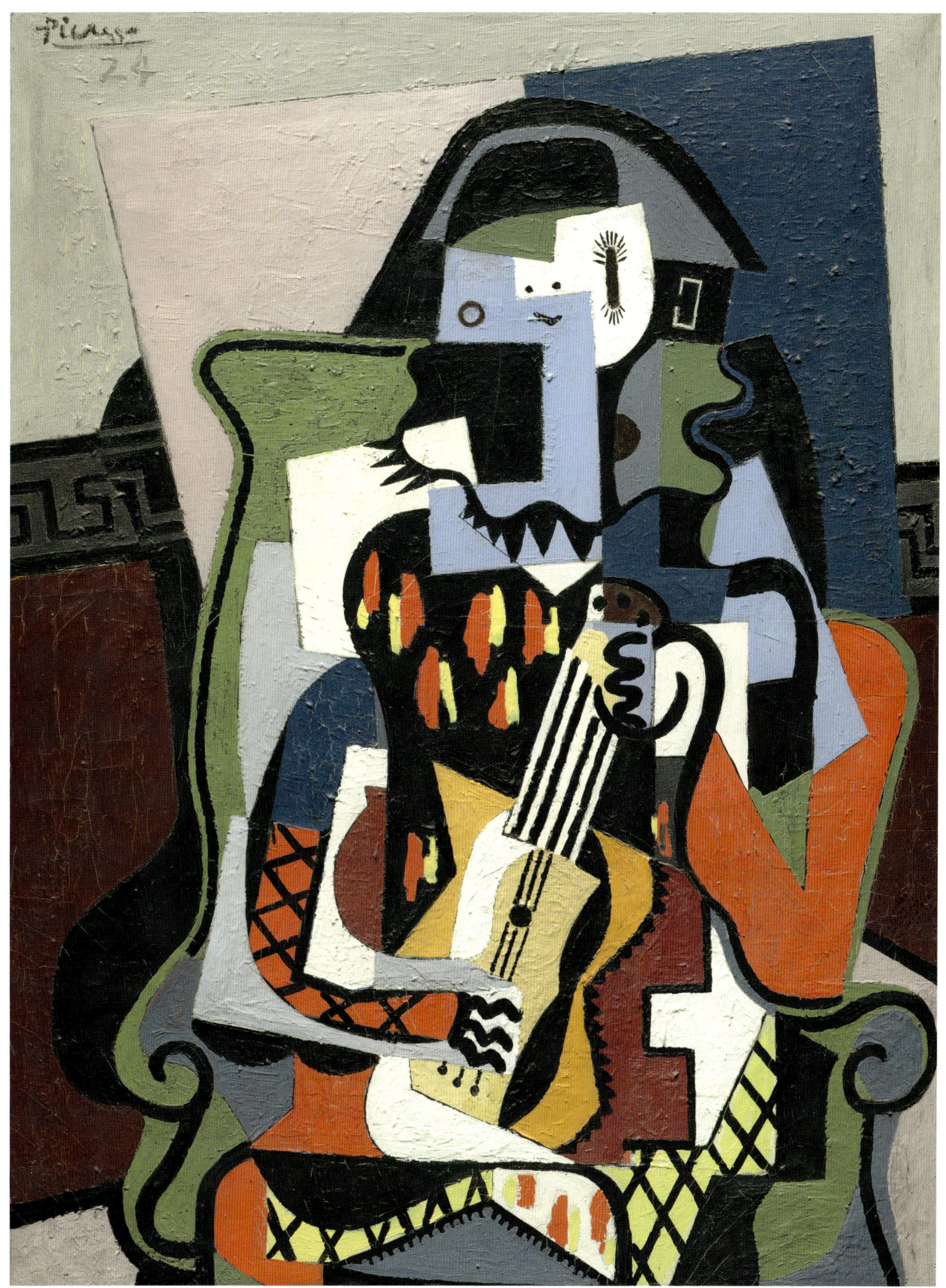
Picasso
24

190. Pablo Picasso
Trois Danseuses
[Three Dancers], 1925
Oil on canvas, 215.3 x 142.2 cm
Tate, Purchased with a special Grant-in-Aid and Florence Fox Bequest with assistance from the Friends of the Tate Gallery and the Contemporary Art Society 1965, inv. T00729

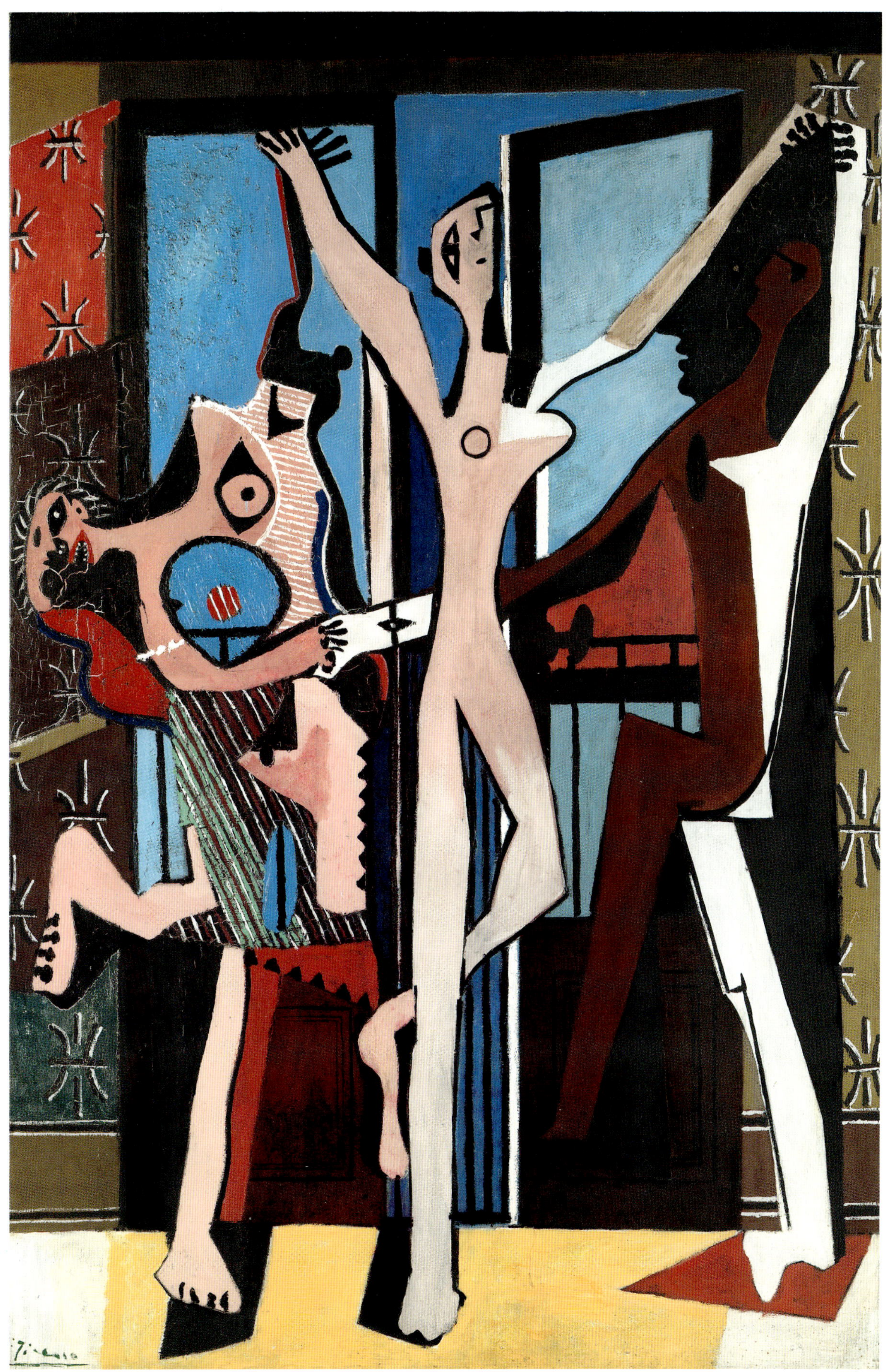

Timeline, 1915–25

1915

First meeting with Jean Cocteau, introduced by composer Edgar Varèse while visiting Picasso's atelier. During another visit, Cocteau wears a Harlequin costume in the hope that Picasso will want to paint his portrait.
His style becomes completely abstract; it is during these years that he realizes *Homme à la pipe* ([Man with a Pipe], Paris, Musée national Picasso-Paris), and *Arlequin* [Harlequin], considered a metaphorical self-portrait.
He begins working on *Homme Accoudé à une Table* ([Man Leaning on a Table], Turin, Pinacoteca Giovanni e Marella Agnelli); he creates the three-dimensional piece *Violon* [Violin]. All these works seem to be the opening chapter of what will soon unfold in the drawings for the ballet *Parade* (1917). The costumes for the American Manager and the French Manager present a dramatic and dynamic reinterpretation of Cubist vocabulary.
Max Jacob converts to Catholicism, and Picasso is the godfather at the baptism.
On 14 December, Eva Gouel, Picasso's famous "Ma jolie" (my pretty girl) since 1911, loses her long and painful battle with tuberculosis.

1916

In the spring he moves to Montrouge, on the outskirts of Paris. He comes closer to Cocteau, who often visits him in his studio. Cocteau discusses the plan for the *burlesque* ballet with him. Diaghilev, whose Ballets Russes is staging the piece, has twice rejected designs, insisting "Étonne-moi!" (Amaze me!) Cocteau's answer is to ask Picasso to realize the scenery and costumes, and for Satie to handle the music. Léonide Massine (1896–1979) is tasked with the choreography.
In return, in May Picasso offers Cocteau a portrait-sketch in uniform. Diaghilev visits Picasso to discuss the plan taking shape in *Parade*, a dance show that the Ballets Russes is preparing for in Rome, where the company is based, but Picasso agrees to work only in August.
He meets Eugenia Errázuriz and they begins to meet up regularly. She is an influential and rich patron of Diaghilev and Stravinsky, and also becomes a passionate supporter of Picasso's work, encouraging him to explore the fascinating and eclectic world of the Ballets Russes.
Picasso collaborates on the magazine and show "Cabaret Voltaire" in Zurich, which undeniably marks the birth of the Dada movement and of performance art.
Les Demoiselles d'Avignon is shown for the first time.
During these months the war continues unabated, and the ferocious battle of Verdun is fought on 25 February.

1917

January/February: Picasso works on *Parade*. He and Diaghilev agree on a contract for five thousand francs for sketches, and one thousand francs for a trip to Rome.
On 17 February he leaves Paris with Cocteau to meet Diaghilev and the company of the Ballets Russes in Rome. He takes up residence in Via Margutta, where he has a view of the Villa Medici. Picasso immerses himself in this world. He befriends Stravinsky and Massine, and begins a relationship with Russian dancer Olga Khokhlova (1891–1955). "I work all day on my scenery and on building the costumes," he writes to Gertrude Stein. "I've made many drawings and caricatures of Diaghilev, Bakst, Massine and some dancers in the ruins of Pompeii."
Futurist artist Fortunato Depero helps Picasso with the realization of some of the costumes for *Parade*.
In March he travels to Naples with Diaghilev, Stravinsky, Cocteau, and Massine.
He visits the archaeological area of Pompeii and is delighted by the *commedia dell'arte* shows that will later supply the inspiration for his *Pulcinella*.
He then proceeds to Florence and Milan.
At the end of April he returns to Paris.
In these months, he has painted not only *L'Italienne* ([The Italian Woman], Zurich, Sammlung E.G. Bührle) and *Arlequin et Femme au Collier* ([Harlequin and Woman with Necklace], Paris, Georges Pompidou, Musée National d'Art Moderne,), but has also completed several sketches of the façade of Villa Medici and the costumes for *Parade*.
The company returns to Paris, where Picasso personally supervises the execution of the costumes and scenery for *Parade* and paints the huge drop-curtain.
Parade opens on 18 May at the Théâtre du Châtelet in Paris; the show triggers diametrically opposed reactions of searing criticism and outright approval.
Picasso's relationship with Olga becomes more serious, and he follows the company to Barcelona.
On 10 November *Parade* opens in Barcelona.
Picasso's style continues the evolution that began with the drop-curtain for *Parade*. He leaves behind the rigour and abstraction of Cubism in favour of a return to the figurative and to Classicism.
When the company leaves to tour Latin America, Olga stays with Picasso, who, indebted to her, gathers a circle of increasingly sophisticated and fascinating friends around him.

Guillaume Apollinaire stages his comedy *Les Mamelles de Tirésias* [The Breasts of Tiresias], with programmes illustrated by Picasso.
The influence of *commedia dell'arte* continues in the subjects Picasso chooses, as in the work *Arlequin* ([Harlequin], Barcelona, Museu Picasso), a tribute to Léonide Massine and to their partnership for *Parade* and in the later *Arlequin au Violon* ([Harlequin with Violin], Cleveland Museum of Art). He paints *Tête de femme (Olga)* ([Head of a Woman (Olga Picasso)], Brussels, Fundación Almine y Bernard Ruiz-Picasso para el Arte), and *Arlequin et Femme au Collier* ([Harlequin and Woman with Necklace], Paris, Georges Pompidou, Musée National d'Art Moderne).
In October the Russian Revolution breaks out, and meanwhile the Italian army suffers a crushing defeat at Caporetto at the hands of the Austro-Hungarian forces.
In late November Picasso returns to Paris and sets up house with Olga at Montrouge.

1918

July 12: Picasso and Olga are married in the Russian Orthodox Church in Paris, with Jean Cocteau, Guillaume Apollinaire, and Max Jacob as witnesses.
Later, with Henri Matisse at Paul Guillaume's gallery, he exhibits works that demonstrate a clear return to realism. The Preface in the catalogue is penned by Guillaume Apollinaire.
Picasso and Olga spend the summer in Biarritz as guests of Eugenia Errázuriz. While there he paints a series of works depicting the bathers, and meets Paul Rosenberg, who becomes his new dealer. His style continues to change, approaching a more decorative sense of Cubism.
In the winter Picasso and Olga move to a two-storey apartment in the centre of Paris, at 23 Rue La Boétie, also the location of the gallery of his dealer Paul Rosenberg.
He attends the performance of *Renard* (music by Stravinsky), and meets Marcel Proust and James Joyce at dinner.
This is the year the manifesto of the Dada movement is published.
9 November: Apollinaire dies. Two days later the Armistice between the Allies and Germany is signed.

1919

May–July: Picasso joins the Ballets Russes in London to work on the set design for the ballet *Le Tricorne* [The Three-Cornered Hat], with music by Manuel de Falla. He collaborates with painter/set designer Vladimir Polunin to create the drop-curtain.
He makes numerous sketches and studies of dancers and portraits of Diaghilev, Massine, and artists such as André Derain, who is working with Diaghilev at the time.
22 July: debut of *The Three-Cornered Hat* at the Alhambra Theatre in London.
Diaghilev and Picasso begin working on a new project, a ballet inspired by *commedia dell'arte*. Stravinsky writes the music, drawing on scores by Giovanni Battista Pergolesi, while the choreography is by Massine.
The following year this collaboration will develop into the ballet *Pulcinella*, inspired by the eighteenth-century comedy *The Four Identical Pulcinellas*.
Picasso and Olga spend the summer in the South of France, in Saint-Raphaël. There, he paints a series of small works, still-lifes on tables standing before a window open to the sea, conceptually connected to the two still-life constructions held today at the Musée National Picasso in Paris, or to *Nature Morte à la Guitare Devant une Fenêtre* ([Still Life with Guitar in Front of a Window], Brussels, Fundación Almine y Bernard Ruiz-Picasso para el Arte).
He completes *The Sieste (Les Moissonneurs)* [The Harvesters], and illustrates André Salmon's *Le Manuscrit Trouvé dans un Chapeau* [Manuscript Found in a Hat].

1920

Picasso sets to work on sets and costumes for Léonide Massine's ballet, *Pulcinella*, with music by Igor Stravinsky, despite various initial difficulties due to plans repeatedly being rejected by Diaghilev.
15 May: *Pulcinella* opens at the Paris Opera.
Picasso completes studies for the opera *Trois Musiciens* [Three Musicians] for the following year. It is dedicated to the three musicians with whom he has collaborated in recent years: Stravinsky, Satie and Manuel de Falla.
He enters his neoclassical period, producing monumental nudes and, at the same time, Cubist compositions.
In the summer he returns to Saint-Raphaël. The classic *commedia dell'arte* masks – Harlequin, Pulcinella, and Pierrot – continue to be the preferred subjects for his paintings.
Picasso creates the cover for the programme for the Ballets Russes.
In 1920, Massine leaves Diaghilev's company to found one of his own. The departure of Picasso's favourite collaborator may in part explain his dwindling interest in sketches for the Ballets Russes.

1921

4 February: the birth of his first son, Paulo.
He creates sets and costumes for the ballet *Cuadro Flamenco* [Flamenco Scene], a suite of traditional Andalusian dances performed in Paris by Diaghilev's Ballets Russes. Picasso suggests that Diaghilev revive his rejected designs for *Pulcinella* rather than hand the task to Juan Gris, who had originally been considered for the project.
17 May: the only performance of *Cuadro Flamenco* at the Théâtre de la Gaîté-Lyrique in Paris.
31 May: opening of the ballet *Cuadro Flamenco* at the Princes Theatre in London.
In the summer he settles in Fontainebleau, where he paints the two versions of *Trois Musiciens* [Three Musicians] and *Trois Femmes à la Fontaine (La Source)* [Three Women at the Fountain (The Source)].
Culmination of the Cubist period and of the influences of *commedia dell'arte* imagery.
Not until 1924, at the request of Massine and Count Étienne de Beaumont, will Picasso once again design for a show, the ballet *Mercure*.
At the Leicester Galleries in London, Picasso exhibits some sixty works from 1902 to 1919.
Meanwhile, Adolf Hitler becomes the leader of the National Socialist Party and is appointed Chancellor of Germany.

1922

Picasso spends the summer in Dinard, Brittany, with his family.
He paints and draws numerous beach scenes, including the gouache *Deux Femmes Courant sur la Plage (La Course)* ([Two Women Running on the Beach (The Race)], Paris, Musée national Picasso-Paris), later used as a sketch for the drop-curtain for Diaghilev's ballet *Le Train Bleu* ([The Blue Train], 1924).
Diaghilev asks Picasso to design the backdrop for *L'Après-midi d'un faune* [The Afternoon of a Faun], with music by Claude Debussy, but,

after conferring with Douglas Cooper, rejects the subject proposed, a cool summer beach.
In December, he creates the sets for Jean Cocteau's production of Sophocles' *Antigone*, produced by Charles Dullin's Théâtre de l'Atelier in Paris, with costumes by Chanel.
He illustrates *Cravates de Chanvre* [Hemp Neckties] by Pierre Reverdy.

1923
He paints four portraits of the artist Jacinto Salvadó dressed as Harlequin.
In July he becomes friends with André Breton after being defended from an attack about the death of Cubism during a Dada performance at the Théâtre Michel involving his old friends and colleagues (film by Hans Richter and Man Ray, music by Igor Stravinsky, Erik Satie, and Darius Milhaud).
He spends the summer at Cap d'Antibes where he was invited by heiress Sara Murphy and her husband Gerald; he becomes closer friends with Count Étienne de Beaumont.
He paints *La Flûte de Pan* [The Pan Pipes] and various *Harlequins* in Neoclassical style.
Back in Paris, he paints numerous portraits of Olga and their son Paulo.

1924
Massine begins working with Count Étienne de Beaumont. He produces a short season of ballets and comedies, so-called «Soirées de Paris», held at the Théâtre de la Cigale in Paris. In hopes of recreating the artistic partnership that produced *Parade*, he invites Picasso and Satie to work on the small ballet *Mercure*, inspired by the Greek myth and produced for the benefit of Russian immigrants.
Picasso paints the drop-curtain, scenery, and costumes for the ballet, but the show, performed on 15 June at the Théâtre de la Cigale in Paris, is savaged by the critics and, like *Parade*, is not particularly successful with the public either.
The artist grants permission for his work *Deux Femmes Courant sur la Plage (La Course)* [Two Women Running on the Beach (The Race)], to be enlarged and used as a model for the drop-curtain for the ballet *Le Train Bleu* ([The Blue Train], staged by the Ballets Russes). The ballet debuts at the Théâtre des Champs-Elysées in Paris on 20 June.
Picasso spends his holidays at Juan-les-Pins with Olga and Paulo.
On 1 December, the first issue of the magazine founded by André Breton, *La Révolution surrealiste*, includes an image of a 1914 "construction" by Picasso, *Guitar* (Paris, Musée national Picasso-Paris).
Collector Jacques Doucet purchases *Les Demoiselles d'Avignon* for twenty-five thousand francs.

1925
During March and April Picasso stays in Monte Carlo, where the Ballets Russes is performing. He creates a series of drawings featuring dance as the subject, executed in a classicist style. Picasso becomes increasingly impatient with Olga and with the sophisticated world of dance. This tension and the ambivalent feeling of attraction/repulsion come out in the work *La Danse* [The Dance], currently at the Tate in London, completed at the very beginning of the summer.
In July, in Juan-les-Pins, he paints *Le Baiser* ([The Kiss], Paris, Musée national Picasso-Paros).
On 14 November he participates in the first exhibition of Surrealist painting, at Galerie Pierre.
On 15 July, in the fourth issue of *Révolution surréaliste*, Breton publishes the essay "Le Surréalisme et la Peinture" (Surrealism and Painting), illustrated with an image of *Les Demoiselles d'Avignon*.
Erik Satie dies.